GEORGE W. NORRIS

The Making of a Progressive

1861-1912

GEORGE W. NORRIS

The Making of a Progressive

1861-1912

RICHARD LOWITT

SYRACUSE UNIVERSITY PRESS   1963

This book has been published with the
assistance of a Ford Foundation grant.

LIBRARY OF CONGRESS
CATALOG CARD: 63–19724

Manufactured in the United States of America
by The Colonial Press Inc., Clinton, Massachusetts

TO SUZANNE

Contents

Preface

It is my purpose in the following pages to relate in some detail the career through 1912 of one of the more remarkable political personalities in American history. George W. Norris was an unobtrusive man. He did not attract attention because of the power of his personality, his oratory, demagoguery, control of a machine, or position as spokesman for a particular point of view or powerful vested interest. Yet he was a commanding figure in both houses of the Congress and in his home state of Nebraska.

While some individuals command attention because they rise above their backgrounds to positions of political prominence, and others, from privileged backgrounds, seek to understand the problems and viewpoints of their constituents, Norris fitted neither pattern. Like Lincoln he was an uncommon common man. He chose the simple and the unpretentious, and was more at home in the parlor than in the drawing room. He preferred small town America; Main Street was always more attractive than Connecticut or Fifth Avenue. Yet he could understand and sympathize with the common man whether he lived on a windswept Nebraska farm, in Beaver City or McCook, Nebraska, or in the slum sections of Omaha. America to him was Nebraska writ large. And when he examined the world beyond the United States, his angle of vision remained the same. He believed that people were primary, that property rights, while important, were never superior to personal liberties, and that a high sense of moral values should characterize the behavior of men in government, business, or any other area of human endeavor. His outlook could be summed up in the classic advice of a homesteader to his children: "Tell the truth, stay out of debt, don't be afraid of work, and remember when you pray that God helps those that help themselves." In the context of American thought, such views automatically classified Norris as a nineteenth-century liberal in the Jeffersonian tradition. And indeed he was, though he never read Jefferson or placed Jefferson, let alone Lincoln, among his patron saints.

But Norris was also something more. He was one of the best parliamentarians in American political history. He was fortunate in that his sparse small town education, while somewhat scanty in cultural content, stressed rhetoric and debate. From his earliest years in school he was continually exposed to parliamentary procedure, the knowledge which in later years enabled him to defeat "Uncle Joe" Cannon, win the Muscles Shoals fight, and achieve the remarkable record which made him one of the most useful legislators in American history. That he did all of these things almost singlehandedly is extraordinary in an age when party organization, machine rule, and pressure politics were expanding their influence and causing increased public and scholarly scrutiny.

As he came to political maturity the welfare state was being forged. Norris was not interested in building the power of the central government per se. But if privilege was in any way extorting undue profits from people (and people, to Norris, were the neighborly folks, not necessarily native-born Americans, he knew in Beaver City and McCook), he would not hesitate to use federal power to curb or supersede it. Moreover, his small town background helped him to understand that the Industrial Revolution, with which he never came in direct contact, had created a national economy and that only centralized authority could cope with it. The railroad, the mortgage loan business, and the land speculation of his environment made him aware that people's lives could be vitally affected by factors and forces in other parts of the state or nation, by problems not primarily local or regional in character.

As a political personality, though a stalwart Republican in his younger days, he quickly and naturally fell in step with the policies of Theodore Roosevelt, who was president when Norris reached Washington, D.C. His career in Nebraska during the Populist revolt had paved the way for his insurgency and later progressivism. He was not an intellectual. He was not given to philosophizing about political theory or the role of government. He was not one to absorb political history or the biographies of prominent Americans.

History for George Norris began with the Civil War, which claimed the life of his only brother, and continued on through the New Deal into World War II. It paralleled his life span and served as his frame of reference. Rooted in nineteenth-century values and traditions, he played a role in meeting most of the challenges of the first half of the twentieth century. And like most American liberals, he was a pragmatist. He met issues as they arose and was concerned with their effect on people everywhere. If curbing privilege meant increasing the power of the federal government, he would support such measures. If it meant government supervision, development, or control of natural resources in the interests of all the people, he would favor this as well.

In this book I have tried to present, chiefly from manuscript and other primary sources, a biography that will do justice to the man. To understand the career of a political personality who was a master of legislative process necessitates careful attention to detail—to parliamentary procedure, to bills and amendments to bills, to particular clauses in bills, to debate—in short, to the daily routine of a member of Congress. I have not tried to force any pattern upon my subject. Rather, I have tried to write concretely, to pay attention to significant details, to record observations, and to avoid excessive generalizing. Many generalizations relevant to recent American history are not based on adequate primary research and consequently are continually being revised or rejected. More valid ones, I think, will emerge after numerous studies in depth, such as that attempted in this volume, have been made.

When I began this biography I had few preconceived notions about George Norris. Working through the huge collection of his papers in the Library of Congress, processing a segment of them for the Manuscripts Division, examining other relevant collections, reading the *Congressional Record,* and doing all the other research such a study entails convinced me that I was fortunate in my continual contact with the career of an admirable person who was also one of the great men of our recent history. This volume studies Norris' career through the campaign of 1912 which witnessed his election to the United States Senate. In a concluding volume I intend to complete his biography.

RICHARD LOWITT

New London, Connecticut
March, 1963

Acknowledgments

HEARTY AND SINCERE THANKS are due to the many people whose help
was so vital to the preparation of this study—those who gave me personal insight into my subject by relating their experiences with him;
those who assisted in or made possible the research; and those who
helped ready the actual manuscript for publication.

In the course of my research I met many "old-timers" who knew
Norris and who were willing to share with me their memories and experiences. Among the few who knew Norris or the Nebraska scene
during the period covered in this volume are Mr. and Mrs. John P.
Robertson of Washington, D.C., and Mr. and Mrs. Harvey Nelson of
Glendale, California, who, besides being gracious hosts, allowed me to
jolt their memories with questions about their early years. Mrs. Robertson and Mrs. Nelson are daughters of Senator Norris; Mr. Robertson
served for many years as his secretary. To the Robertsons especially I
am indebted. Their hospitality enabled me to experience vicariously
the simple, dignified environment in which the senator lived. An interview with Mrs. Norris in McCook in 1955 served to reinforce this
earlier impression. Mrs. Norris spent a morning with my wife and me
in her home answering questions and reminiscing with us. Mr. Harold
Sutton and the late Carl Marsh, both of McCook, also shared their
memories with us. To all I am most grateful.

Fola La Follette deserves special mention among people who aided
me. Through discussions of the 1912 campaign, she helped me to a
greater understanding of its complexity and its meaning, particularly
for midwestern Progressives. She patiently answered my questions and
commented on her father's distinguished career and Norris' relations
with him. William Henry Harbaugh and the late Howard Kennedy
Beale performed a similar service by discussing Theodore Roosevelt
with me. And the late Wesley M. Gewehr, my chairman at the University of Maryland, went out of his way to arrange a schedule for
me when I was a beginning instructor so that I could take advantage
of the resources of the Library of Congress.

To name the people in the Manuscripts Division of the Library of Congress who aided me in my work would be to include virtually the entire staff from the early 1950's on. As a reader, and briefly as a member of the staff, I always felt at home in this division, more so than in any other place I have worked. Many of the staff members are now personal friends and I can almost consider the Manuscripts Division my home away from home.

In the Nebraska Historical Society Dr. James C. Olson (its director at that time), Dr. John White, and Dr. Donald Danker were most helpful. The other repositories I used will be cited in footnotes, and a collective acknowledgment to their librarians will have to suffice since it is not possible here to name all those who so generously gave of their time and energy.

The Guggenheim Foundation and the Social Science Research Council aided me at opportune times. As a Guggenheim Fellow in 1957–58 I was able to complete the research for this volume and begin writing. A grant-in-aid from the SSRC in 1960–61 permitted me to have an earlier version of the manuscript freshly typed. Connecticut College was generous in granting me annual funds from its limited resources for research and summer travel. And its library staff, particularly Miss Helen Aitner, patiently put up with my questions and special requests. For its encouragement, in this way and others, Connecticut College and Dr. Rosemary Park, its president while this manuscript was being prepared, merit a vote of thanks. So, too, do the people who efficiently typed the various versions of it: Mrs. Elsie R. Andersen, Mrs. Esther Kolb, and Mr. George Marshall. Thanks are due as well to the members of the staff at the Syracuse University Press who offered useful suggestions and rendered invaluable assistance in readying the manuscript for publication.

A host of people who discussed Norris and recent American history with me must for want of space remain unnamed. Chiefly in the academic world and scattered throughout the nation they help to make research and scholarship more meaningful, exciting, and pleasurable. In all, my indebtedness to others is heavy, although, of course, the conception and points of view expressed herein are mine. I alone am responsible for factual errors as well as for the organization of this volume.

Finally, as occurs in almost every volume of this sort, a note about the role of one's wife. My wife gave up a scholarly career of her own to further mine. Without her help this volume would not yet be ready for publication. Besides numerous other chores, at every opportunity she was there to help or prod me as the situation demanded.

GEORGE W. NORRIS
The Making of a Progressive
1861-1912

Certainly, Gentlemen, it ought to be the happiness and glory of a representative to live in the strictest union, the closest correspondence, and the most unreserved communication with his constituents. Their wishes ought to have great weight with him; their opinions high respect; their business unremitted attention. It is his duty to sacrifice his repose, his pleasure, his satisfactions, to theirs,—and above all, ever, and in all cases, to prefer their interest to his own.

But his unbiased opinion, his mature judgement, his enlightened conscience, he ought not to sacrifice to you, to any man, or to any set of men living. These he does not derive from your pleasure, —no, nor from the law and the Constitution. They are a trust from Providence, for the abuse of which he is deeply answerable. Your representative owes you, not his industry only, but his judgement; and he betrays, instead of serving you, if he sacrifices it to your opinion.

From the Speech to the Electors of Bristol
November 3, 1774
by EDMUND BURKE

Chapter 1

In the Beginning

YORK TOWNSHIP, Sandusky County, Ohio, about three and a half miles east of Clyde, which was Sherwood Anderson's prototype of small towns in the Middle West, was the birthplace of George W. Norris on July 11, 1861. On the western fringe of the Western Reserve and on the eastern border of the "Black Swamp" area, Sandusky County as part of northwestern Ohio comprised the last frontier area in the state.

Immigrants started penetrating and transforming it during the decade of the 1820's. Many were en route to lands in Illinois, Indiana, and southern Michigan; others settled, despite agues and fevers, in this level and wet region. The extreme northwestern corner of Ohio had, by the census of 1830, a population of three thousand.[1] While the original settlers had come chiefly from New York out of New England, during the 1830's others from Pennsylvania and southern Ohio were arriving along with Germans who had in the 1820's settled along the Sandusky River in Seneca County, due south of Sandusky County.

The area in which Norris was born was inhabited largely by Pennsylvania Dutch farmers. At the time of his parents' arrival in 1846, northwest Ohio was rapidly emerging from the pioneer stage but it still retained and reflected the simpler social and economic conditions associated with the frontier.

Sandusky County was primarily a wheat area; during the Civil War years it produced from two to five hundred thousand bushels of wheat.[2] It was also a vegetable and orchard district, and Clyde became a milling and later a canning center. Sherwood Anderson, who lived there some twenty years later, succinctly summed up its agricultural experience: "The soil on the farms about the town was a light sandy loam that would raise small fruits, corn, wheat, oats or potatoes, but that did particularly well when planted to cabbages." [3] Cabbages, which provided a staple for many a poor farm family and which became a major crop during Anderson's childhood, were not known to many of the earlier farmers. Stands of timber were numerous and included beech, oak, and walnut.

Into this agricultural area moved the parents of George Norris in the summer of 1846. They had been married on Christmas day, 1838, in Monroe County, New York. Chauncey Norris was thirty-one years of age at the time of his marriage and had lived most of his life in nearby Cayuga County.[4] His bride, Mary Magdalene Mook, a Pennsylvania Dutch girl of twenty, is supposed to have met Chauncey at a house-raising ceremony. The couple started their life together on a farm in Monroe County. In 1846, at the time of their departure for Ohio, they lived in Batavia, New York, with a family of four children. The youngest child, a month-old daughter, died shortly before Chauncey loaded family and furniture into a wagon and headed west to join his wife's brothers as a farmer in Sandusky County.

Chauncey succeeded on his York Township farm. He cleared the land of trees, stumps, and rocks. He planted crops of wheat, corn and vegetables, along with fruit trees, and built a modest but substantial home, still standing today.[5] And Chauncey and Mary Norris increased the size of their family in Ohio. Twelve children were born of this marriage: two died, Elizabeth just before they left New York for Ohio, and Ida, less than three years old and the last child in the family, in 1867. Eight children were born in Ohio; besides Willie—as George William was called by his parents—the only other male child was the eldest, John Henry, born in 1839. In July of 1861 when Willie was born, his father was fifty-four and his mother forty-three. His two eldest sisters were already married.

During the early years of Willie's life, the Civil War raged. The people of Ohio were bitterly divided over the issues involved. Sandusky County, in almost every major election throughout the nineteenth century, gave its votes to Democratic candidates, though not by large majorities.[6] Most of the farmers in the township—the Norris family included—were Republicans.[7] While there were antislavery and abolitionist families in the county, they did not dominate, nor was there overwhelming Unionist sentiment manifested when war was declared. The Norris family certainly were antislavery in their views, and the nearby city of Sandusky was a terminal point for the Underground Railroad.

The county, despite opposition to the Civil War, contributed its share of soldiers. Among over twenty-three hundred men who enlisted was John Henry Norris. At the outset of the struggle, he had promised his mother that he would not volunteer. However, in January, 1864, he broke his promise and joined the Fifty-fifth Ohio Volunteer Infantry. The Fifty-fifth Ohio had participated in some major engagements in Tennessee in the autumn and winter of 1863 at Missionary Ridge and in the Knoxville campaign immediately afterward. It enjoyed a brief furlough in Ohio in January and February of 1864, when John Henry enlisted. In the spring the regiment participated in the "March to the Sea." At the battle of Resaca, Georgia, in mid-May, John Henry suffered seemingly inconsequential wounds in the right hip and left thigh. Within a fortnight he was dead at the age of twenty-five.[8]

Thus the tragedy of war struck the family. Before the year 1864 was over, however, an even greater blow was inflicted upon the family circle. Chauncey Norris, on December 1, 1864, contracted pneumonia, and before the week ended, he was dead and buried in the little community cemetery, with neighbors, Mary Norris' kin, and his family as mourners. Norris later wrote this description of the family situation at that time: "Three of the girls had married and had established homes of their own. Six sisters—Henrietta, Mary Adelaide, Elizabeth, Effie Ann, Emma, and Clara—and I remained with my mother on that cold and bleak December day when my father was buried, to share the heritage of the Ohio farm." [9] Within a year Willie Norris, age three and a half, found himself the only man left in the family.

Mary Mook Norris, age forty-six, now became for her younger children the heart and soul of the family. There was an eighty-acre farm to be maintained and Mary, although pregnant with her last child, assumed this task along with her household duties. She was a loving, anxious, and above all a hard-working mother. Although she had no spare time to herself, she made some available to her children, insisting that they receive an education. The family's lot was not an easy one. Mary Norris was not only the center of the home, but she quickly became for her son home itself. She made almost every piece of clothing worn by any member of the family. At harvest time she would take her place in the field. "Her hair was unstreaked; she walked erect"; her son could never remember a song upon her lips, nor ever recall her humming a tune.[10] Her sensitive, rather melancholy temperament became a part of the little boy which he retained for the rest of his life.

Mary Norris, while providing little intellectual or cultural stimulation for her children, did much to mold their moral and social values. Her concern for the poor and their problems was later reflected in her son's concern with problems of social justice. Her interests were neither selfish nor limited to the present, and she passed on to her children a feeling for the importance of planning for the future.[11]

Though she was not a church member, she raised her children believing in the absolute goodness and righteousness of the Lord. She read the Bible aloud on Sunday afternoons to her children. It was probably at this time the only book in the home. She believed the Bible literally and frowned upon dancing and card playing for many years. Indeed, her son never attended a dance until after he left home. He was not duly impressed with the Gospel teachings he heard at home or at the church services and occasional revivals he attended. He was disturbed and confused over matters of church and religion which he later resolved, like his mother, by not joining any church and, unlike her, by reading volumes which stressed science as opposed to supernaturalism, such as John William Draper's *History of the Conflict between Religion and Science*.[12]

Even by prevailing standards the Norris family was poor. Cash on hand was always very meager and the family was a large one. But nobody was rich there or then; they lived in the simple abundance of that time and place, and did not consider themselves poor. In July, 1867, less than three years after her husband's death, Mary Mook Norris married a neighbor, Isaac Parker, whom her son later characterized as "an elderly, quiet Pennsylvanian of Dutch blood, and an expert wood-worker." Now the family circle was again complete, and part of the burden was removed from the mother's shoulders. Little is known of this marriage, except that after twenty-five years it ended in divorce.[13] Norris barely mentions the marriage itself in his autobiography, but devotes many pages to his schooling, labors, and pleasures while at home after his mother's second marriage.

Young Will Norris very quickly assumed his place in the fields, and took pride and pleasure in the work. He developed into a sturdy youngster, and though he was the "favorite" of his mother and his older sisters, there was too much work to be done for him to be coddled in any noticeable way. Every summer during his school years while living at home he worked as a farm hand either on the family farm or on neighboring ones. Long before reaching maturity he was able to do a man's work, having early acquired the strength and ability to perform the most difficult of farm chores. He also became an expert marksman in a place where squirrel hunting was considered a supreme sport.

The family farm was already well stocked with fruit trees: apple, peach, and cherry, yet his mother one warm spring afternoon called him to assist her in planting another. Will could not understand why his mother toiled to plant a tree when there were seemingly enough trees on the farm and when it probably would bear fruit only after her death. His mother's remark that somebody would see the tree blossom and enjoy the fruit impressed her son. Here was planning and concern for future generations.[14]

Will Norris attended the Mount Carmel district school, a mile and one-half from the farm house. He enjoyed school and studied almost every evening by candle light. He remembered his teachers with gratitude and corresponded with some of them in later years. And it was in the classroom that he was introduced to two subjects which would stand him in good stead later on—oratory and parliamentary procedure. From that time on, while pursuing his education, Norris was always active in the debating society, furthering his forensic ability and at the same time increasing his knowledge and understanding of parliamentary procedure.

During his years at the district school, Norris became interested in the law and in politics. He saw cases tried in the courtroom in Clyde and, enjoying this experience immensely, decided he wanted to become a lawyer. Colonel J. H. Rhodes, a local attorney, may have influenced his decision and helped to develop his interest in Republican politics. Will was an ardent supporter of President Hayes, and had followed the entire 1876 campaign through the pages of the *Cincinnati Times*. By devious means he had managed to get to Fremont, the county seat, to hear Hayes deliver his acceptance speech. The rallies, parades, bands, and oratory all aroused his intense partisanship.[15]

In the fall of 1877 Emma, Clara, and George Norris appeared in Berea, Ohio, to enroll as students at Methodist-sponsored Baldwin University. John Henry Norris had attended the University between 1858 and 1860. Baldwin advertised itself as an institution "within the reach of the poor young man and young woman." [16] This fact, plus its relatively short distance from home, must have provided an additional impetus to Mary Norris in agreeing to let her children attend. The school was in dire financial difficulties and its campus was not a particularly impressive one. Its president, Dr. Aaron Schuyler, mathematician and writer of textbooks, was an able scholar and wrote the algebra text through which Will Norris struggled. The student body for the academic year 1877–78 numbered 241. Mary Norris would have been delighted to know that the college catalogue commended Berea as a town of "moral salubrity" with "no grog shops or seductive lounging places in the village." [17]

The young students in Berea rented the second story of a house on the edge of town where they proceeded to set up housekeeping, dividing the chores among them. They lived as frugally as possible and devoted most of their time to studying. Norris and his sister Clara were enrolled in the Preparatory Department, while Emma was registered in the College Department. Norris was officially listed as a junior student in the classical course, and his record as a student at Baldwin was outstanding. At the end of the academic year, he received a perfect "10" grade for seven courses and "9.85," "9.8," and "9" for the others. Latin and mathematics were the most important subjects in the classical course of study, although Norris also studied American history, grammar, physiology, and botany.[18]

Outside of the classroom, as in Mount Carmel district school, Will participated in the debating society. However, there were now other forms of diversion available, and the sixteen-year-old scholar was quick to seize them. Singing popular songs, engaging in that most important of extracurricular activities, the "bull" session, participating in an occasional prank—these were activities that the young farm boy had rarely been able to indulge in at home. They satisfied his gregarious inclinations, especially after a period of hard academic work.

After a most satisfying year at Baldwin, Norris spent the summer working on the farm. He found this work a bit more arduous after a winter of sedentary activity. Since his funds were exhausted and his mother unable to supply him with any more, Will sought a teaching position for the fall to earn the wherewithal to continue his education. His first teaching job was in the Long School district near Whitehouse in Lucas County, Ohio, where his oldest sister, Lorinda Castle, lived with her family.

Norris enjoyed teaching school. Occasionally, especially in his first job, he had discipline problems, but in most instances his pupils were eager, attentive, and relatively tractable youngsters. Their young teacher was not always a stern, scholarly taskmaster. Living in the community with the family of one or the other of his pupils, he made friends easily. Most evenings he devoted to reading; his determination to become a lawyer was still strong. During the year at the Long School district he spent weekends with his sister in nearby Whitehouse, a gathering place for young teachers in the vicinity. Emma and Clara also spent time with the Castle family. Here the young folk would enjoy the weekend free from the socially imposed restrictions on unmarried schoolteachers in rural villages. Will Norris blossomed forth as an actor in play productions, sang in the various entertainments, and engaged in sprightly conversation, something he was usually unable to do while teaching school or working on the farm. Also, against his mother's dictates, he learned to dance.[19] Will and the other young teachers, after such pleasant weekends, would return to their students for another week of school.

Having saved as much of the $150 salary as possible from his teaching position, he declined the invitation to teach the following term. He spent the summer working at home on the farm. In the fall of 1879 he entered the Northern Indiana Normal School and Business Institute at Valparaiso, Indiana. The school, later known as Valparaiso University, was located in the southeast part of town overlooking miles of marshlands. It was administered as a nonsectarian, self-supporting, and self-governing coeducational college, even though it was endorsed by the Methodist Church and Porter County, Indiana. Its president, Henry Baker Brown, an excellent administrator and educator, developed the plant and strengthened the faculty. The institution became known as the 'poor man's Harvard' and in 1914–15 boasted a student body of six thousand, second only in size to that of the older eastern university.[20]

Two main features characterized the institution: the absence of entrance requirements and the low cost of living. There were four terms of eleven weeks each and a fifth lasting six weeks, so that a student could start or resume his studies at any one of five times during the year. The duration of a course of study leading to a degree depended on the student's previous preparation, but at least one year of residence was required. By eliminating middlemen and purchasing in quantity and by producing some of its own foodstuffs, the school had lowered the cost of living for students and staff. Board and room in Flint Hall cost $1.40 a week and tuition was $18 per term.[21] Norris completed the classical and elocution courses before turning to the law. During his years at Northern Indiana Normal School, Will was one of the more popular students, liked and respected by his peers.[22] In 1880, aged nineteen, he received a college degree and was admitted to the law course.

Norris found in Valparaiso the same spirit of social equality and democracy that he knew in Ohio. Few students came from backgrounds that were markedly different from his. Most were serious about their studies, though few were so serious that they would ignore the opportunity to engage in gregarious extracurricular activities. Will joined the debating teams and enrolled in a course devoted to debating. He developed a florid style and learned many of the tricks of oratory that were so prevalent in that period. In this way he increased his self-assurance.

Elocution courses with Professor M. E. Bogarte gave him an op-

portunity to discuss and debate politics. The election of 1880 occurred
while Norris was teaching school at Monclova, Ohio, prior to entering
law school. He participated as a member of a horse troop in a large
torch light parade for James A. Garfield. Garfield was something of a
hero to Norris and his assassination moved him deeply. While national
politics aroused Norris' intense Republican partisanship, campus
politics at Valparaiso were much more important and aroused even
more intense partisanship.[23]

In keeping with his interest in campus politics and debating, Norris
joined the Crescent Literary Society. Every Friday night there was a
public program of speeches, essays, and music in which the Crescent
and other literary societies participated. Rivalry was keen among
societies and within each society. Will Norris and Charley Hyde, representing opposing factions within the Crescent, were chosen as the
society's candidates for the oration contests against the other groups.
Bitter feeling was intensified and, when Norris won the contest with
an address, "The Traitor's Deathbed," Hyde's supporters sought revenge. This they achieved by defeating Norris by one vote in the
election for president of the society.

While the Hyde faction was celebrating its triumph, Norris and
his nine supporters met to form an organization which would have a
great influence on all their lives, the L.U.N.—the Loyal United Nine
or, as their opponents called it, the Lunatics Under Norris. The organization, to which no new members could be admitted, was officially
launched with a banquet in the Merchants' Hotel at Valparaiso on
August 6, 1883. It was agreed that every August the members would
have a reunion and a banquet. As the years went by these reunions
came to be treasured. Norris and Ermon E. Smith of Dodge City,
Kansas, who were the last survivors, attended a total of fifty-nine
banquets, the last one in 1941 at Norris' cottage overlooking Rainbow
Lake, one of a chain of sixteen lakes near Waupaca, Wisconsin. In
the early years of the organization, most of the reunions were held at
lake resort areas in Iowa and Wisconsin; in the twentieth century,
however, most were held in the L.U.N. cottage overlooking Rainbow
Lake. Here the members and their families built summer houses and
spent their vacations. Here their children and grandchildren became
acquainted and formed friendships that continued after the deaths of
the original members.[24]

The year the L.U.N. was formed was also the year in which Norris
obtained his law degree and was admitted to the Indiana bar. Thus
in the late summer of 1883, George Norris, age twenty-two, returned
to his mother's farm in York Township, Ohio, with a law degree in

his possession and his college years at an end. It must have been a very proud mother who greeted her son on his return from Indiana.

His plans were uncertain. Norris no doubt puzzled over what the future held for him and where he would practice. Colonel Rhodes in Clyde was willing to let him clerk in his law office until he made a decision. Norris accepted this offer. In Clyde he continued his studies and acted as Rhodes' office boy. He also taught a term at Mount Carmel school where he had been a pupil. It was his mother, however, who made the suggestion that brought about his departure from home. Mary Norris, learning of the booming opportunities in the Pacific Northwest from colonizing agents, conceived the idea of selling the farm and starting anew. Her son decided to go to Washington Territory, establish his law practice, and then, if all went well, he would send for her.

Using almost all his savings, Norris purchased a ticket to Walla Walla in Washington Territory and traveled across country on the recently completed Northern Pacific Railroad in an emigrant train—sleepers attached to a freight—from St. Paul. The journey lasted an entire week, and he arrived at his destination tired and dirty with his funds running low. Walla Walla, he quickly decided, was no place for a young lawyer and his aging mother to settle. The town was desolate and uninviting. Land was expensive and jobs were scarce. Norris sought a teaching position to replenish his funds and, accepting the only one available, boarded a train for Bolles Junction in a remote part of the country. Though Bolles Junction appeared on the map to be a sizable community, it was anything but that. He spent his first night there sleeping on the floor in the house of a Mr. Lee, president of the school district. The next day Norris set up housekeeping in a crude shack, formerly used by a maintenance crew on the railroad and now serving as a storeroom for railroad equipment.

The schoolroom was equally crude. Since there were but seven pupils in the district, Norris conducted school only in the mornings. The afternoons he had to himself and often went hunting or fishing with Mr. Lee. Norris found that he still was a crack shot, especially with a revolver. Occasionally on sunny afternoons, he would sit back in his chair at school and fire at woodpeckers who darted in and out of the room.[25]

Norris was not pleased either with his teaching position or with Walla Walla. He had decided to return east as soon as he could replenish his funds. At the end of the school term he went to the nearby community of Dayton to investigate the possibilities of establishing a law practice. There he managed to get involved with a logging boss in a quarrel which almost resulted in gunplay. This incident, coupled with his dissatisfaction with his job and location, convinced him once and for all that Washington Territory was not the place for him.

Thus George Norris, at the age of twenty-three, eager to put his legal talents to the test and his training to use, purchased a ticket on the Oregon Short Line and the Union Pacific to the city of Lincoln in the Cornhusker State of Nebraska.[26] He chose this state because his mother owned eighty acres of land in Johnson County, in the southeastern part of the state, and because he had a kinsman, David Mook, in the area. It also appealed to him because his late sister Effie had gone there after her marriage. Nebraska now seemed a logical place for the young lawyer to further himself in his chosen career.

Chapter 2

Nebraska, 1885–90: Prosperity

GEORGE NORRIS did not stay long in Nebraska on his first trip. His money ran out, and he returned to Ohio for a last term of teaching, this time at Warrensville in Cuyahoga County. There he boarded with a sister as an economy measure. At the end of the school term, determined to return to Nebraska, he borrowed over three hundred dollars from his sister Melissa, and received from his mother the deed to her Johnson County land.

With a college classmate and fellow L.U.N. member, H. H. Harrington, he opened a law office in March, 1885, in Beatrice, the seat of Gage County, one of the richest agricultural areas in the state. Despite the fact that Nebraska was booming, the partnership did not prosper and the partners were soon disillusioned; Norris recalled, "We had nothing to bring us business—no associations and no connections." [1] Perhaps they did not give themselves enough time to get started; perhaps they did not get along together in a small office with few clients to challenge their abilities. Whatever the reason, during the summer of 1885 the firm of Norris & Harrington was dissolved.

Harrington went back east, and Norris, in September, hoping for better opportunities, moved farther west into the thriving Republican River Valley country. He chose Beaver City, the seat of Furnas County, as his destination. Since the Burlington and Missouri Railroad had not yet reached this area, he hoped that here his practice could develop with the country. Fully aware that he would need considerable capital, Norris sold the Johnson County land for $1,500. Then, with his few belongings, he traveled by railroad to Arapahoe and thence by wagon almost due south to Beaver City.

The period during which Norris arrived in Nebraska was the most prosperous in the history of the state up to that time. With above average rainfall, agriculture prospered and, encouraged by "boomers," settlers came in ever increasing numbers. In 1880 the state's population was 452,402; ten years later it had increased to over one million people. Norris arrived in Beaver City in 1885; before the decade was over he had become secretary of the Beaver City Board of Trade and was offering agents five dollars for each person who purchased a. quarter-section of land or $1,000 worth of city property. The Board of Trade supplied these agents with advertising matter and agreed to pay the railroad fare for any settler.[2] The extension of the Burlington and Missouri Railroad throughout the western part of Nebraska was the major factor in the rapid growth of population. By 1887 a branch line of the railroad reached Beaver City, enabling it to participate more directly in the general prosperity.

Furnas County, though organized in 1873, was still in many areas raw prairie when Norris arrived in the autumn of 1885. Broken land and cultivated fields seemingly were islands surrounded by a gentle rolling sea of short grass on the slowly rising sod which was punctuated occasionally with steep slopes and rough land. The Republican River, which flowed across the northern part of the county, was the main body of water in the region. One of its tributaries, Beaver Creek, along which the county seat was located, flowed not quite parallel to it in the south central part of the county. Neither stream was navigable; the bed of each was sandy, bordered by low, sandy banks, while the Republican was not only shallow but also relatively wide.

Furnas County is located in a subhumid region, an area with a mean annual rainfall of about twenty-two inches.[3] Its rough lands and sandy areas provide excellent grazing places for cattle, while the better lands were devoted at first to corn and wheat. By the end of the nineteenth century forage crops, particularly alfalfa, were raised along the streams. Now, in the twentieth century, irrigation is used to insure more adequate crops. Along the streams are maple, ash, elm, box elder, and cottonwood trees. Cattle and produce from the county make their way into the Omaha and Denver markets.

While very different from the Ohio Norris knew and loved, the new country was not totally beyond his previous experience, and he soon came to love and later to understand it as well. Arriving as the country was being rapidly developed, he saw it originally at its very best—in a period of prosperity during a lush and languid autumn season.

Settlers in southwestern Nebraska generally did not understand the climate of the Great Plains. Many farmers and town builders moved into the region believing, from its generally luxuriant appearance, that it did not differ markedly from the known agricultural areas farther east. Others, who had heard of conditions on the plains in the previous decade, reassured themselves with the popular de-

lusion that climate somehow changed with settlement and that rainfall followed the plow. The early experience of settlers and farmers
during the 1880's was usually pleasant and profitable. They therefore
accepted these conditions as normal and regarded any marked change
from them as abnormal and temporary. It would be several years
hence before Norris and other settlers obtained a more valid understanding of the region, an understanding based on bitter experience.

On the north bank of Beaver Creek is situated Beaver City. First
settled in 1872 by J. H. McKee, it is the county seat and principal
town (the population in 1895 was over fifteen hundred[4]) of the Beaver
Valley. Here George Norris would make his home, marry, start raising
a family, and launch his career in law, in business, and in politics.
Before the prosperous decade of the 1880's was over, the community
boasted an $18,000 courthouse and a $15,000 high school.[5] Across the
square from the courthouse was an old farm building owned by
David H. Lashley, who was to become Norris' father-in-law. The
building was used as a hotel and office building. Later, in 1893, it was
torn down, and the Norris block, an office building still in use today,
was erected in its place. Beaver City, small though it was, had two
newspapers: the *Times* and the *Tribune*. The latter, a Republican
paper, was edited by Fletcher W. Merwin, who became an intimate
aide to Norris when he entered politics. The former was owned by
John T. McClure, an able lawyer, a Democrat, and later a Populist
leader in the area. Two banks, the Furnas County Bank and the First
National Bank of Beaver City, were organized soon after Norris
arrived.

At the outset, life in Beaver City was far from easy for the young
lawyer. His clothes were threadbare; he usually did most of his own
washing. In the winter he took to burning corn to keep his office
warm. Once a week he got a shave, paying at the rate of twelve shaves
for a dollar. A shoeshine was reserved only for very special occasions,
such as a trip to Lincoln or Omaha. Apparently, in his early days in
Beaver City, besides sporting the mustache already evident in his
years at Valparaiso, Norris affected a cowboy hat and possibly other
aspects of western dress.[6]

Despite his relative poverty, Norris was delighted with the region,
the town, and the people. Here he found again what he had experienced in Ohio and at college: social equality along with a feeling of
fraternity and good will among his fellow citizens. Everybody's latch-
string was out. Every man by and large was trusted and accepted
regardless of his background until he did something to convince his

associates that their trust and friendship were misplaced. Norris became so impressed with Beaver City that he tried to interest one of his sisters in buying a house and settling there.[7]

Norris easily made friends in the community and the surrounding countryside. Having joined the Odd Fellows lodge at Clyde in his twenty-first year, he now transferred his membership to Beaver City. Bob Scott, the warden of the lodge, became an early friend and introduced Norris to jackrabbit stew.[8] Scott may have been a member of the party of four who were hunting quail when Norris was accidentally shot. The members had separated, each seeking to bag as many birds as possible, when Norris was shot in the face. When the others found him, he was on the ground in extreme pain, unable to see, groping on his hands and knees, feeling for the gun, and intending to kill himself. Two of the members of the party carried him to a nearby house while the other ran for a doctor. Norris feared at first that he had been completely blinded, but found his sight returning even before the doctor examined him. Initially the doctor thought he would lose the sight of one eye, but on second examination revised this opinion and agreed that Norris' sight would be saved. Twenty-two pieces of shot were taken out of his face. At least two were permanently embedded in his flesh.[9] For several years after this accident, Norris understandably took no great interest in hunting and devoted himself almost entirely to his law practice and other business.

Norris opened a two-room office south of the courthouse square. Until his marriage in 1889 he worked in one of the rooms, lived in the other, and dined out. Despite the desire to utilize his professional training, he found it necessary to engage in other activities along with the law. Indeed, he later wrote, "The first money I made in Nebraska was in the land business, and often I made more money in the land business than in the law business." [10] Shortly after his arrival he purchased a quarter section of land which he later sold at a profit. He also started to acquire real estate in Beaver City. His activities were typical of young western lawyers who were trying to earn a living without a corporate connection as their chief source of income.

Nebraska, as a comparatively new state, desperately needed capital to maintain the prosperity of the 1880's and to attract new settlers. The inhabitants had to go outside of the state for much of their working capital. While rainfall remained adequate and crops bountiful, land values increased rapidly. Though agriculture and stock raising were the principal occupations, urban development began on a large scale, and railroad construction continued without abatement.

Enterprising farmers and town dwellers who wanted to improve their holdings found it easy to borrow money from loan companies, commercial banks, insurance companies, and even from individuals. Such mortgages seemingly offered an excellent opportunity for the small investor. They could be held in modest amounts, and the interest rates were high. Investors throughout the East and North poured their savings into companies which proceeded to loan millions of dollars in the West. By 1889 Kansas and Nebraska had 134 incorporated mortgage companies. Including companies organized in other states but operating in Kansas and Nebraska, the number reached at least two hundred. Between 1884 and 1887 the number of farm mortgages placed in Nebraska was six thousand and their value was $5,467,362.[11]

Newly arrived farmers were immediately subjected to heavy expense for buildings, farm machinery, fencing, seed, livestock, and taxes before they could show adequate returns. In the beginning, their outlay was much greater than their income. What little money they brought with them quickly disappeared. Merchants had to sell on credit, and professional men, like Norris, had to wait for their fees. The borrowing of money seemed to be a necessity for the satisfactory development of the country; without mortgages, development would have proceeded at a much slower pace.[12]

At the outset Norris engaged in the mortgage-loan business and found it profitable. With good crops and more settlers migrating to the country, land values increased and as a result, loans were given a safe margin. This led investors to seek more mortgages, and loan companies to attempt to increase their business by urging their agents, of whom Norris was one, to lend more money. Soon irresponsible agents and companies were loaning money on poor investments and encouraging farmers to borrow more than they actually needed. Some observers noted that this extensive mortgage business was draining money out of the area by the payment of interest.[13] With the failure of crops in the short-grass country beginning in 1890, worse effects would appear.

George Norris, as an ambitious young lawyer, quickly found that there were ways of making money in conjunction with legal work. He took advantage of them, and earned most of his livelihood as an agent for various companies and individuals engaged in the mortgage-loan business. If Norris was unable to collect, he could initiate legal proceedings. In the beginning all went well, but as debtors ran into difficulties, the job became a delicate and difficult one for a person with political ambitions who wished to remain on good terms with his neighbors.

For a while, Norris sold insurance as an agent of the National

Fire Insurance Company of Hartford, Connecticut. In 1889 he sought to act as agent for the Yost Typewriter Company, but was turned down on the basis that his other business and his inability to type would prevent him from showing their machine to its best advantage. In another instance, an Iowa businessman desired to obtain Norris' services to rent and care for his livery stable and other real estate in Beaver City.[14] However, these examples were extraneous to his main line of endeavor, which was that of agent for various individuals, banks, and corporations engaged in some aspect of the mortgage-loan business.

Norris' work continually took him away from Beaver City. He traveled throughout the country making collections, seeking prospective customers for loans, observing conditions, and preparing reports. In the course of this work Norris met people in all walks of life. He won the respect and confidence of most people with whom he came in contact, and formed some lasting friendships. Since many of the notes he sought to collect were small, his fees were also small.[15]

The Vigilant Wholesale Creditors' Agency of Omaha, whose motto was "The Race Is to the Swift," carefully defined the fees their agents, among whom was Norris, were to receive. If the note was paid on demand or presentation, the charges were 5 per cent on the first $200 and 2½ per cent on the excess. "In all other cases," stated their printed form, the following fees were to be charged "without respect to time or effort expended": 10 per cent on claims under $100, 5 per cent on excess to $700, and 2½ per cent on excess of $700. No charge was to be less than $1.50 and, most important, the agent making the collection would receive two-thirds of all the fees. The remaining one-third, along with the proceeds, would then be remitted to the agency in Omaha.[16]

Norris also acted as agent for some large firms which desired the services of a local attorney to make their collections. Among them R. G. Dun & Co., with headquarters in New York and branch offices in 135 cities. This company, established by famed abolitionist Louis Tappan in 1841, claimed that it was the oldest mercantile agency in the world. Other large firms such as Thurber, Wyland and Company of New York and the Credit Guarantee Company of Minneapolis acquired Norris' services. He served as agent and collector for William Deering and Company of Chicago, producers of harvesting machinery.[17] The larger firms often had a branch office or a general agent in Nebraska, and it was the office manager or agent who contacted Norris.

These companies employed Norris as an attorney when it was

necessary to bring suit against a debtor in Furnas County and vicinity. If the plaintiff lived outside of Nebraska, Norris had to make certain that the petition for foreclosure of a mortgage was in accord with Nebraska statutes before it was filed and a summons issued. There were court fees and service charges involved in these proceedings and usually a commission rather than a fee for Norris' services. In most instances, before court action was taken, Norris was consulted by the attorney in the plaintiff's home town as to the possibility of settling the case without recourse to the law. Prior to 1890, however, Norris was rarely called upon to initiate legal action. Most debtors in southwest Nebraska managed to meet their obligations, and creditors had little cause for complaint.[18]

Though Norris acted as agent or representative for many firms and individuals in the various aspects of the mortgage-loan business, he did most of his work for J. H. Miles and the First National Bank of Rulo, Nebraska, of which Miles was vice-president.[19] It is not known how, where, and when Norris met Miles, but Miles took an interest in the young lawyer, trusted him, and expressed confidence in his judgment and ability. Norris continued to work in various capacities with Miles after he left the Bank of Rulo for the one at Falls City. The association continued until shortly after the turn of the century when Miles retired. Norris discounted notes, loaned money, bought and sold land, and performed other services for Miles and the Rulo bank. At the outset, Norris was associated in this work with George Shafer of Beaver City, but by the end of 1889 they dissolved this arrangement and both men worked on their own.[20] Norris and Shafer remained on amicable terms and were associated in business again at the end of the century.

In December, 1888, Norris decided to investigate conditions in Salt Lake City with the idea of settling there and continuing his work with Miles in the Utah territory. Norris felt that he was intruding upon Shafer's business. And perhaps the incessant traveling and collecting was beginning to sap his strength. Whatever the reasons, he went to Salt Lake City for the ostensible purpose of investigating the possibility of opening a bank. After being away from Beaver City for less than two weeks, Norris returned, confirmed in the opinion that his future would be no better in Salt Lake City than in Beaver City.[21]

The connection with Miles gave Norris opportunities to participate directly in the mortgage-loan business. With his knowledge of local conditions he made good investments, securing the necessary funds from the bank in Rulo. He also invested money for members of his family, once informing his sister Melissa that he could loan $1,500 of her money "for 10% where it will be secure" and where he could make a profit on it himself.[22]

By the end of 1889 Miles decided to seek a new banking connection and close the First National Bank of Rulo. He began looking for another community in which to start a bank, finally deciding upon Falls City, the county seat. Miles' shifting of banks necessitated a rearrangement of Norris' activities so that most of his accounts could be closed when the bank in Rulo shut its doors.[23]

In the spring of 1890, shortly after the First National Bank closed, the cashier of the Bank of Rulo, a competitor of Miles' bank, wrote to Norris inquiring if he would loan money for this bank as he had done for Miles'. Norris agreed, although he indicated that he probably could not do as large a business as he had done for their former competitor because the terms on which he was to conduct this new business were now very rigidly defined. The Bank of Rulo was more cautious in its mortgage-loan business than Miles, primarily because its officers were new to the business and because economic conditions were changing.[24]

By 1890 Norris' interest in the mortgage-loan business was beginning to wane. He refused an offer from Miles to accept the position of cashier in his new bank at a salary of $1,200 for the first year and the privilege of purchasing up to one-fifth of its stock.[25] Part of the reason for refusing the offer was his desire to remain in the legal profession and to pursue the interest in politics which thus far he had been forced to relegate to a subsidiary position.

But there was another reason for refusing the offer. On June 1, 1889, when Norris was not yet twenty-eight years of age, he married a belle of Beaver City, Pluma Lashley. The Lashleys had come from Iowa to Beaver City shortly after its founding in the 1870's. David Lashley had risen rapidly as a businessman in the thriving community. He owned a considerable amount of real estate, built a substantial house, and operated a prosperous grist mill on Beaver Creek about a mile out of town. Lashley's daughter, Pluma, had been born in Iowa, in 1864, and at the time of her marriage was a tall, attractive, dark-complexioned woman three years younger than her husband. They started their life together in a rented four-room cottage which they had carefully and tastefully furnished.[26]

Before the couple had been married a year, Pluma's father died. Norris had the task of settling the estate and keeping the gristmill in operation. Shortly afterwards the newlyweds moved into the Lashley home so that Pluma would have the companionship of her mother while Norris was traveling. This relieved some of his anxiety and remorse at being away from home.

After five years in Beaver City, George Norris had established himself as a rising young man in the community. He had arrived with a minimum of cash, but through his own initiative and ability had developed a prosperous business which brought him into contact with men in all walks of life. He was becoming known, liked, and respected —a difficult feat for a person who had to collect money. He was sympathetic and fair in his business dealings, and people quickly learned to trust his word, while many business firms throughout Nebraska and some larger western and national concerns sought his services.

Within five years he had paid off most of his debts, could promptly meet his obligations, owned a few choice real estate items, and in a small way participated in the mortgage-loan business. He was happily married to the daughter of one of Beaver City's leading citizens and had a promising future. True, he was not practicing law as much as he might have desired, but he could not have secured as many agencies as he did without his law degree. Moreover, most lawyers in the region, unless they worked full time for the railroad or held public office, earned their livelihood in approximately the same way. This type of work was significant in the development of the West. In Nebraska it enabled young George Norris, during the boom period of the 1880's, to sink his roots in a region that he would henceforth consider his home. While he was able to start his adult life in Nebraska in a period of prosperity, adversity in the last decade of the nineteenth century would test his character and, incidentally, launch his political career.

Chapter 3

Nebraska, 1890–95: Adversity

THE BOOM PERIOD in southwestern Nebraska was coming to an end by the late 1880's. Since the prosperity of the country depended on satisfactory prices for agricultural produce, overproduction and overexpansion started the deflationary process which lack of rain, drought, and hot winds accelerated, thereby adding physical misery to people already overburdened with economic woes. Capital had been invested here and elsewhere in the West beyond reasonable amounts which could insure immediate returns. The debt burden, both public and private, was heavy, and some eastern investors were becoming suspicious that their funds had not been prudently invested. A day of reckoning seemed to be at hand. Drought caused widespread crop failure in 1890, and this in turn brought the situation to a head.

The farmer's woes were aggravated by the fact that the price he received for his products, despite fluctuations, went steadily downward during the last twenty years of the nineteenth century while his fixed costs, such as freight, interest, machinery, and taxes, generally remained steady or did not decline from their boom-time high level as rapidly or as far as the farmer would have liked. Seldom during these years did the market price of grain equal the cost of production. At times during the 1890's, the drought was so severe in some places that no crops were harvested and farmers were forced to turn their livestock loose to forage for themselves. A nationwide panic and depression complicated these problems, and struck the final blow to many western farmers and townspeople who pulled up stakes and moved out of the region.[1]

In this period of adversity, the companies which had been so eager to lend money only a few years before had little cash and were reluctant to lend what they had. Much money was withdrawn and potential lenders were frightened away by the court rulings which in many Nebraska counties granted stays of six to nine months or even longer, depending on the amount of money involved, before foreclosure proceedings could be made final.[2]

Unable to secure funds through real estate mortgages, many farmers were now forced to accept chattel loans—borrowing money on their livestock and agricultural implements. For the five-year period ending May 31, 1895, the number of chattel mortgages recorded by the state auditor of Nebraska was 539,323.[3] The average assessed valuation of farm land in Furnas County dropped from $3.64 per acre in 1880 to $2.09 in 1890, and by 1900 it had risen only to $2.30. In the neighboring county on the west, Red Willow, the figures ran as follows: 1880–$4.81, 1890–$1.86, 1900–$1.54.[4] Conducting business of any sort during this period was exceedingly difficult; making collections on notes as they fell due was almost impossible.

The decade of the 1890's, to the people of the short-grass country, was a time of struggle with debt, bad credit, and decreasing values. Few new debts were incurred, and old ones, owing to clamoring creditors, were reduced as much as possible. Many were foreclosed. Some people, instead of continuing the struggle, left the region; but most of them, believing that drought and bad times were the exception and that rain and better times would soon return, grimly held on. They had invested heavily in the Republican River Valley; they had raised their children and buried their dead in lonely country cemeteries; they now considered this area their home and they intended to hold on to their property.

With a better understanding of the subhumid region, drought-resistant crops, irrigation, and with a more balanced agricultural economy, the people of the future would find it less difficult to live and prosper in the midst of a challenging environment. For those who remained throughout these troubled times, a bond was forged that manifested itself in a growing regional consciousness, an awareness that their part of the West was different from other areas. The "old settlers'" picnics and reunions thus became very meaningful to these early sod-busting and sod-dwelling farmers as the last years of the nineteenth century receded into history. Norris' experiences during the 1890's enhanced his understanding of people and their problems and thereby helped to make him an outstanding public servant.

Throughout the decade his major activities in the mortgage-loan business were with the Bank of Rulo, and with Miles and the newly organized First National Bank of Falls City. Norris was pleased with the Bank of Rulo and its cashier, B. F. Cunningham, because they did not take advantage of drought-stricken farmers and avoided foreclosing whenever possible. However, while the bank was willing to grant extensions or renewals on its notes, it was reluctant to allow Norris to loan more money.[5]

In 1891 there was a record rainfall of over twenty-five inches; crops were excellent, and debtors, temporarily at least, were able to meet their obligations. Few people, however, were willing to borrow money at the prevailing rate of 10 per cent. Norris tried to convince the Bank of Rulo that he could make a few safe loans if it would accept 8 per cent interest payable in advance. A merchant in Beaver City, he wrote, was ready to borrow $2,000 on six or eight months time on these conditions. But the bank was unwilling to loan money at 8 per cent when it could loan all the money it desired at a higher rate of interest.[6] Unable to conclude satisfactory arrangements, Norris severed his connection with the Bank of Rulo in 1892.

On the other hand, Miles, who settled in Falls City in July, 1891, and went to work as cashier of the First National Bank, quickly renewed his business with Norris. Soon Norris was making almost all his loans for this bank. The Falls City bank, like the one in Rulo, had no trouble making loans at 10 per cent. Though Miles allowed Norris to place a few choice loans, he was unwilling to let him expand his activity. Because of the precarious national financial situation and the nationwide panic which began in the summer of 1893, Miles feared a run on the bank or the failure of a correspondent bank, and did not want to commit himself too deeply to any line of endeavor.[7] These events and the policies resulting from them severely limited Norris' activities.

As the panic broadened into a depression, drought and hot winds added to the plight of already desperate people. Because the rainfall was woefully inadequate in 1893 and 1894,[8] crops were almost a total failure, and Norris found it more difficult to conduct his declining business for Miles. Debtors could not sell property and creditors could not collect on their notes and accounts. By the end of 1894 Norris claimed that he had never seen money so hard to obtain.[9]

Norris' work for Miles and the First National Bank of Falls City was the most important aspect of his career as an agent in the mortgage-loan business. At the same time, however, he also acted as an agent for other individuals and concerns. He continually told creditors that it would be difficult if not impossible to collect until nature relented and abundant crops were harvested. Meanwhile, holders of notes requested extensions because they had nothing to market and no money to meet their obligations. Norris advised some creditors not to take a client to court because under Nebraska law "he would be entitled to a stay of nine months." If the debtor were conscientious and nature helpful, he might pay sooner without a court order.[10]

If the debtor were unable to pay and the company unwilling to grant an extension or a renewal (which might be secured by a chattel mortgage or increased interest), Norris would then have to institute foreclosure proceedings, an activity he seldom indulged in during the booming decade of the 1880's. By foreclosing and obtaining judgments, more than ever before, Norris now used his legal talents in connection with the mortgage-loan business.[11]

Aside from his dealings with the two banks in Richardson County, Norris now did most of his mortgage-loan business for two companies and an individual. One company, Burnham, Trevett & Mattis, was located in Beatrice and was a regional organization. The individual, Stanley E. Filkins, was a lawyer of Medina, New York, who had heavy investments in and around Beaver City. Snow, Church & Company was a national collection company with its Nebraska branch office located in Omaha.

The relationship with Burnham, Trevett & Mattis was a pleasant one for Norris. He handled their legal work, foreclosing when necessary, and found that the concern was "willing to extend every courtesy to a borrower" when he tried "to do the right thing." After foreclosing on a piece of property, Norris was requested to try to "scare up a buyer" because the land the company had acquired was of little value to it and necessitated the payment of taxes. Burnham, Trevett & Mattis, being a Nebraska concern, was fully aware of the difficult conditions people faced; the firm understood what a good soaking rain meant to a struggling farmer. Its members were also sympathetic to Norris' political aspirations, even though these aspirations would probably entail the loss of his services.[12]

When Filkins' agent in Beaver City resigned to become commissioner of the United States District Land Office in McCook, Norris hoped to succeed him. However, he was not successful until 1894, when Filkins considered enlarging his investments in the area. By that summer Norris was handling all of Filkins' Nebraska investments. He was making collections, trying to rent and sell property, obtaining chattel mortgages from customers who wanted renewals, securing judgments, and foreclosing when necessary.[13]

The relationship of George Norris with Snow, Church & Company was the most formal and least satisfactory of his mortgage-loan connections. The company, with twenty-nine offices throughout the United States, professed to be the most vigilant collection agency in the country. But Norris was not impressed with its cold efficiency. After several months he wrote the chief of the Omaha office that thus far the agency had yielded him "the magnificent sum of $1.34," a sum substantially lower than the postage fees incurred, for bringing a court action necessary to secure a judgment. The only other claim of consequence he had received was immediately taken out of his hands.[14]

Besides his difficult work in the established channels of the mortgage-loan business, Norris continued his side ventures in real estate and other activities. Several insurance companies sought his services, chiefly to aid in collections. Nebraska law required that any insurance company having an agency in a county must also appoint an attorney residing at the county seat. While real estate ventures were more time consuming than insurance work, the opportunities for making immediate profits in insurance were very limited. In 1887 he had purchased 160 acres of land in Greeley County, Kansas, for $800. Early in 1891, he purchased 220 acres of land near Beaver City for $2,400; it contained both timber and water. Since it was virtually impossible to sell land, he sometimes tried to trade lots located in Kansas and other parts of Nebraska. Occasionally property owners asked him to try to sell their property. For selling a client's land Norris received the regular commission of 5 per cent on the first thousand, and 2½ per cent on the balance.[15]

His most extensive real estate activities, however, were in and around Beaver City where he collected rent and generally attended the property of absentee owners. Norris usually took his commission out of the rent money. Collecting rent was a difficult and troublesome chore. Some tenants would depart just before their rent was due, others were forced to sell their crops at ruinous prices in order to make some payment to the landlord. A dwelling house in Beaver City could be rented for about six dollars per month. The rent on a house Norris had purchased as an investment for a sister in Ohio "from the first of May to the first of October" in 1894 amounted to $45.[16] At such rates, his commission could not have amounted to a very large sum, especially when compared to the time and energy he had to spend looking after the property.

The major problem Norris had with real estate in Beaver City involved the mill, part of which he and his wife inherited from the Lashley estate. All of the heirs agreed that Norris, the executor of the estate, should sell it. The mill was sold for $8,000 to a man named Andrew Jackson who apparently had borrowed $5,000 from the late Mrs. Lashley to make the purchase. Jackson soon failed in business and was left with no money and heavy debts. Norris decided to take over the mill and the $2,500 mortgage on it rather than allow it to be sold at a sheriff's sale. By buying the mill and renting it, he hoped to insure a steady income to pay taxes and interest on the mortgage, and eventually to make a profit for the Lashley heirs. Noris assumed responsibility for managing the mill until a buyer could be found, but, owing to the depression, found it impossible to sell the property. By the end of 1895 the mill was in a critical condition, in need of an overhauling of its machinery before it would be in satisfactory working order.[17]

While Norris was not anxious to assume the heavy responsibility of the Lashley mill, he did assume another responsibility in 1893 with greater enthusiasm. Despite the financial stringency, he had accumulated some funds and thought he could borrow even more to erect a two-story brick business building in Beaver City—the Norris Block. Early in the year he initiated the necessary real estate transactions. The local brickyard agreed to supply the necessary bricks, and contracts were awarded for the lumber and iron work. Before the winter was over all arrangements had been completed and construction was under way.[18]

Norris wanted to buy only for cash, and asked various business firms to quote him prices with this understanding. By June, however, the Panic of 1893 was well under way and banks became increasingly hesitant about making loans. Only after Miles and Norris had fully explained to the Board of Directors of the Falls City Bank their arrangements did the board members agree to take his note for $5,000.[19] Thus Norris' policy of buying only for cash was quickly jeopardized and his difficulties started. By building in a period of financial panic which quickly broadened into a national depression, Norris had overextended himself at a time when all sensible businessmen were sharply curtailing their activities.

By autumn, despite difficulties, the Norris Block was almost completed. The building faced north and east on the square, and had the name "Norris" and the year "1893" engraved on its pediment. Norris requested that the Beaver City Post Office be moved from Hopping's Drug Store to his building, suggesting among other reasons that its location would then be over five hundred feet nearer to the railroad depot. He had the building insured against fire, windstorms, and tornadoes, moved his office to the second floor, and reserved the first floor for the post office.[20] This space, however, was taken by the Furnas County Bank, which eventually caused Norris much more difficulty than the post office.

As the depression deepened, the Norris Block brought in less and less money in rent. By 1895 Norris had to borrow money on his life insurance policies to meet his mounting financial obligations. In April, 1895, the Furnas County Bank failed, depriving Norris of both the rent of his chief tenant and nearly $1,400 he had deposited in its vaults.[21]

The day after the bank failed, the next best tenant in the building, the owner of a stock of general merchandise, also failed. The other tenants, who likewise had been doing business with the bank, were unable to pay their rent. The result was that by June, 1895, Norris was receiving rents of $3 per month instead of the $74 he had originally anticipated. He had ample property but no buyers, and could not pay anything on his loans until a crop was ready for market. Norris first tried unsuccessfully to borrow from friends to whom he had previously loaned various sums, and then called upon his more affluent L.U.N. classmates, who responded most generously.[22]

The failure of the Furnas County Bank came at a most inopportune time for George Norris, interfering with the political activities in which he was engaged. Whereas previously business, to his regret, had to take precedence over politics and had to be shared with legal work, henceforth law and politics would be Norris' chief concerns. His numerous and varied business contacts helped to make his political and legal work easier. Though not a Populist (his dedication to the Republican party was too great for that), Norris well understood why the new party gained in influence and power. He knew the difficulties people faced and the grievances they harbored, having experienced some of them himself. He first began to interest himself in politics in Nebraska in 1890, just as the Populist party in the state was being organized. The People's Independent party, to give it its official name, would provide Norris with his earliest political antagonists.

Chapter 4

Populism and Politics

ON July 29, 1890, at Bohanan's Hall in Lincoln, more than eight hundred delegates and several hundred well-wishers witnessed the launching of a new political party, one that claimed to speak for discontented and economically depressed farmers and workers. This party wreaked havoc upon the traditional political structure of the state, and it swept like wildfire through the debt-ridden short-grass country of southwest Nebraska. Populists, during the decade, were elected to every major political office, though at no time were they able to dominate the state without help from the older political parties. In 1890, for the first time since Nebraska became a state, the Republican party met defeat at the polls, and numerous measures designed to alleviate the discontent that became abundantly evident with drought and depression were seriously considered by the legislature.

The Populists in Nebraska gained most of their followers from the ranks of dissatisfied Republican farmers and small businessmen. By 1894, when William Jennings Bryan wrested control of the Democratic party in the state from its conservative leaders, discontented Democrats had a leader and soon a program that articulated their needs and desires. While many Republicans would support the new party, family traditions, social pressures, and antagonisms dating back to the Civil War made it impossible for most of them to support the Democratic party. Eventually most of these people went back to their old party and tried, as Bryan had done with the Democratic party in Nebraska and on the national level, to reform it from within. Their children, growing up in a political environment that called for effective government action to promote the general welfare by curbing corporate wealth and privilege, would carry many of the ideas and policies they heard expounded in their youth into the progressive wing of the Republican party in the new century.

Many of the farmers, small businessmen, and professional men in Nebraska who remained true to the Republican party fully understood most of their opponents' complaints and recognized the validity of

27

some of their remedies. However, they felt with some justification that many Populist leaders bordered on demagoguery in their political conduct and that reform could be better obtained within the framework of the party of Lincoln. George Norris, who quickly found himself a lone Republican lawyer surrounded by a mob of Populists, was among those who took this stand.[1] He later wrote of this period, "I could see nothing unnatural about this Populist movement. It represented human misery and poverty. It came into existence as naturally as the seasons."[2] Thus at the time when Populism was sweeping across the Great Plains Norris launched his political career.

He started it in the most disastrous way possible—with a defeat. This was the only defeat he ever met at the polls until his last campaign for public office in 1942; his political life began and ended with rejection at the polls. In 1890 he sought the office of prosecuting attorney of Furnas County. His opponent, John T. McClure, was also his rival as the outstanding lawyer in Beaver City. McClure, owner of the Beaver City *Times,* was a former Democrat turned Populist, and he handily defeated Norris on election day. The Populist party gained control of both houses of the state legislature and elected two congressmen, one of whom, W. A. McKeighan, whose district included Furnas County, also received the Democratic nomination.

Norris campaigned vigorously, curtailing his other activities to devote as much time as possible to politics, and paying most of the expenses himself.[3] However, the post of prosecuting attorney did not elude him. Twice he was appointed to fill out unexpired terms and once in 1892 he was elected. His mortgage-loan business, his legal work, and his strenuous campaigning helped to make him known personally to almost every voter in Furnas County. Thus without undue effort on his part Norris became a Republican party leader. In 1891 Furnas County Republicans wanted to nominate him for district judge and rumors to this effect appeared in the press.[4]

It was politics that brought Norris into contact with W. S. Morlan of McCook, undoubtedly the most powerful figure in Republican party circles in southwestern Nebraska. As general attorney for the Burlington and Missouri he wielded considerable influence, and Norris usually requested railroad passes from him. The two men at times worked together on a case and Morlan, whenever the opportunity arose, sent legal business to Norris. Morlan was an exceptionally generous man at times; in one instance, for example, he refused to accept any money on a case in which Norris had done most of the work. Morlan was an able lawyer and was very demanding of his associates and assistants. No Republican candidate could obtain a nomination for office in Red Willow County without his approval, and he enjoyed almost as much power throughout the region.

Morlan was undoubtedly responsible for Norris' becoming the local attorney in Beaver City for the Burlington and Missouri. It is not known when Norris first assumed this job, but by 1894 he was very much a part of the company,[5] and was in its employ while he served as prosecuting attorney. But when he went on the bench—a full-time job, which his previous public office was not—he gave up this work with the Burlington and Missouri and his other business as well.

The 1892 election saw Norris again seeking the office of prosecuting attorney. Ignoring national and state candidates and issues in this election, he concerned himself almost exclusively with his particular campaign. He was optimistic about his chances. Since his opponent, a Mr. Harper, was not highly reputed as a lawyer, Norris wanted his own supporters to portray him as a capable attorney, one who would be competent to look after the business of the county. If his candidacy was presented in this light, Norris believed that despite overwhelming Populist sentiment in the county he could be elected.[6] And he was elected, even though the fusion candidate McKeighan, won handily in the newly created Fifth Congressional District which included southwest Nebraska, and a Populist, James B. Weaver, received almost a two-hundred vote majority over Benjamin Harrison in Furnas County. This was the first time in the county's history that it cast its presidential vote for other than a Republican candidate.[7]

With his election Norris found that his work as a lawyer also increased. Since the prosecuting attorney was usually about the courthouse, lawyers as well as clients throughout the county sought his services or asked his advice. Tax matters came within his purview, because with the hard times more and more people were unable to pay their taxes. And as chief law enforcement officer of the county, Norris had to prosecute criminals and take action in related matters.

With the increase in legal duties, Norris' other business, already declining because of drought and depression, was not unduly affected. However, he had to make adjustments to be on hand when the district and county courts were in session. To avoid confusion, for example, he tried to have no cases before a justice of the peace during a term of the district court. And as time went on, he resented the numerous impositions on his time and service by citizens who thought that as prosecuting attorney he should handle their legal work free of charge. As an aspirant to higher public office, as a Republican officeholder in a Populist area, he could not afford to antagonize too many people. Therefore Norris performed many petty legal services for citizens who did not distinguish between his public office and his private legal work.[8]

In 1894 he did not seek re-election and was able to devote his energies to aiding Republican candidates. As a leading politician in Furnas County he could control some convention votes, usually the Beaver City delegation, in favor of particular candidates. Consequently, party leaders contacted him to use his influence for their particular candidates. There were county, district, and state conventions in 1894 and Norris attended them all.

The state convention held in Omaha on August 22, was the most important. Norris secured passes for the Furnas County delegates from Morlan and attended to other details.[9] The delegates to the Republican state convention from southwest Nebraska must have been in a grim mood as they boarded the Burlington and Missouri cars. In May a severe frost had ruined thousands of acres of early corn. Rainfall had been far from adequate, and late in July a furnace-like wind had withered much of the corn crop. Norris and his fellow delegates looking out of their car windows saw the results of this devastation. They understood effects of panic, depression, and crop failure in terms of their own area. In Omaha they could comprehend what it meant in terms of an urban area: large numbers of unemployed, row upon row of houses with boarded windows, newspaper columns filled with notices of foreclosures and sheriffs' sales.[10]

That Norris was not unknown outside of his corner of the state was evident as the convention assembled. A candidate for attorney general wrote to him as a person "of influence in shaping the disposition of your delegation." However, Norris did not play a prominent role at the convention. Thomas J. Majors, who had the support of the Burlington Railroad, obtained the gubernatorial nomination. With the exception of the candidate for secretary of state, all the candidates came from the eastern part of the state. The entire ticket was composed of regular, standpat Republicans and the platform was fully in accord with their views. It ignored the events which Norris and his fellow delegates experienced and had to deal with in their daily lives. While it denounced the Democrats, the platform did not notice the Populist policies.[11]

Norris campaigned for the entire ticket in what turned out to be a furious as well as a confusing campaign. The results from Furnas County were most encouraging, for the county was fully redeemed from Populist control. On the state level, however, the Democrats and Populists presented a fusion ticket and their candidate, Silas A. Holcomb, defeated Majors in the race for governor. Edward Rosewater,

Republican owner of the Omaha *Bee,* had refused to endorse Majors and had thrown his paper's support behind Holcomb. This proved to be a decisive factor in Majors' defeat, as Republicans captured the other state offices, controlled the legislature, and failed to elect a congressman only in the Sixth District. In the Fifth District William E. Andrews became the first Republican congressman from this new district.

Norris was pleased with the results of the campaign. He had stumped the district in behalf of Andrews and other Republican candidates. He had renewed his acquaintance with Republican leaders in nearby counties and had met others for the first time. He now was known to a larger number of voters than ever before. The campaign in 1894 was in effect a trial run. Rather than seek another term as prosecuting attorney, Norris had decided to try for the office held by Populist D. T. Welty, judge of the Fourteenth Judicial District.

Welty was far from popular among the lawyers who appeared in his court. His ability both as judge and lawyer was questioned. Moreover, Norris was convinced that he showed favoritism to Populist defendants by continuing cases whenever possible, or by canceling, usually, the spring term of his court.[12] Whereas in the recent election Republicans had recaptured many offices from Populist incumbents, Norris now sought to redeem the judiciary from the taint of Populism.

Shortly after the 1894 election, he began to devote his energies to the judicial race. First, of course, came the task of securing the necessary delegates for nomination. By January, 1895, he had started an extensive correspondence throughout the eight counties comprising the district, sounding out sentiment and making inquiries about potential delegates who might favor his nomination.[13]

The judicial convention was to be held at McCook in mid-September, and as the summer of 1895 came to an end Norris intensified his efforts. His chief contenders for the nomination were W. R. Starr of Indianola and a Mr. Benson of McCook. But of equal, if not greater, importance to Norris was the opposition candidate. Welty was seeking renomination, but there was a possibility that McClure also would seek the nomination. McClure, who had defeated Norris for prosecuting attorney in 1890, would be a powerful opponent because he was an able lawyer and had many followers throughout the district.

When the Republican county conventions were held in August all three candiates intensified their activities to win delegates favorable to their candidacy. Norris did most of his work through letters. He relied heavily on his supporters to inform him of local developments. Once the county conventions were held, the efforts of the candidates

were focused on obtaining control of each of the eight county delegations that would gather in McCook on September 18. Since both opponents were residents of Red Willow County and a fight between
their followers could only redound to his advantage, Norris made
great efforts to win delegates from this county.

Norris and his supporters by the end of August were most optimistic. Indeed, he questioned whether he should attend the McCook convention. Supporters advised him pro and con. But in the end Norris
decided against attending, although he did put in an appearance at
several fairs in the district shortly before the judicial convention
assembled.[14]

Events were occurring just as Norris desired. The Populist convention early in September renominated Welty by a thumping majority, and the Democrats nominated a separate candidate. At the
last minute he met requests of delegates for transportation to the
Republican convention. He felt certain that he would win the
nomination.[15]

Despite the efforts of Starr and Benson, Norris was nominated on
the first ballot. Welty, though an easier opponent than McClure
would have been, still had several advantages that would prove difficult to overcome. He was the incumbent and a Populist in an area
where Populist sentiment was still powerful. His work as a judge,
which outraged Norris and other lawyers because of his flimsy knowledge of the law and his failure to hold court for a full session, pleased
the numerous defendants who had reaped the benefits of his decisions
and actions. After his nomination, Norris received the following note
from Welty:

> I feel much pleased and congratulate you on your nomination
> for the high office of District Judge, and hope you may have the
> pleasure to return the compliment after November 5th.[16]

Norris had several assets during the campaign. First he had the
help of McClure, who exerted all of his influence against Welty, using
his control of the Beaver City *Times* to this end. As a result, not a
single newspaper in Furnas County, the home county of both candidates, supported Welty. In addition there were many prominent district Democrats, such as A. C. Shallenberger, a future congressman
and governor, who helped Norris by making no effort to assist Welty.[17]

It was also to Norris' advantage that fusion between Democrats and Populists, unsuccessful in 1894, did not work during this
campaign either. The Democrats nominated a separate candidate.

Last but not least among the list of assets was Norris' own reputation for fairness and consideration in the mortgage-loan business. This insured voters that if elected Norris would not indiscriminately foreclose mortgages and agree to sheriffs' sales of property.

Early in the campaign, Norris, eager to win all possible support, may have made a visit to the German settlement, traditionally a Democratic stronghold, north of Arapahoe. The effort to win votes, however, was not always carried on scrupulously. Some of Norris' supporters actually purchased votes and later presented him with a bill for their expenses. After the campaign, one individual while explaining his expenses wrote, "I have paid all the parties I agreed to except one German, $5.00. I have not seen him since election, but he will probably be in town and I will have to pay him." [18]

C. E. Hopping, Beaver City drugstore proprietor, served as chairman of the judicial committee managing the campaign. Republican stalwarts made great efforts for Norris, because they realized that every vote he received and every victory their party won would bring the demise of the Populist party in Nebraska that much closer. Throughout the campaign, Norris was deluged with requests by Republican leaders for railroad passes to bring workers to their home precincts for election day. Railroad passes also provided an excellent method of winning disgruntled Democrats and Populists into the Republican fold. Many men, owing to the hard times, roamed about the countryside seeking odd jobs. Their votes, it was believed, would go to the candidate who provided them with transportation.[19]

By the end of October Norris' mail indicated that his chances were good; none of the letters were pessimistic. The Republicans attacked Welty as a judge. The fact that he did not discriminate between bona fide residents and nonresidents impressed some voters. Norris opposed Welty's "continual and almost endless continuancy for people who had long ago left the country with no intention of returning or redeeming their lands," and his habit of showing little leniency for resident mortgagors who were unable to meet interest payments because of crop failures and low prices. Norris argued that if elected he would grant resident farmers as much consideration as the law permitted.[20]

McClure in the Beaver City *Times* blasted Welty as a tool of the Burlington and Missouri and other partisan papers took up this theme.[21] It is doubtful that Norris, a railroad attorney who was literally trying to trade passes for votes, denounced his opponent along these lines. His campaign was geared on a more personal level;

he directed his efforts toward meeting as many voters as possible and stressing the need for judicial integrity.

W. W. Barngrover, the Democratic candidate, was not seriously considered by the electorate, most of whom regarded the campaign primarily as a race between Norris and Welty. But Barngrover's presence on the ticket prevented Norris from achieving a clearcut victory. Norris won by two votes, and only after much time was spent in debate and litigation was he granted a certificate of election.

However, shortly after the polls closed on November 5, as the first unofficial returns came in, Norris thought his election was assured without any doubt. He defeated Welty in Furnas County by over three hundred votes and by over two hundred in Red Willow, the most populous counties in the district. Indeed, he seemingly carried all but the predominantly Populist counties of Hitchcock and Frontier where Welty's majority was not as large as expected. The first unofficial results proclaimed a Norris victory,[22] a verdict verified by the eight county canvassing boards in the judicial district. The result was Norris, 4,612; Welty, 4,610; Barngrover, 431.

Judge Welty immediately raised the cry of fraud, claiming that the figures in Union precinct, Furnas County, had been changed to give Norris a two-vote lead. If the ballots had not been tampered with, Welty argued, he would have carried the precinct by four votes and with it the election. He did not say that Norris manipulated the votes, and never in the furor that arose did Welty accuse Norris personally of direct involvement in the fraud. As soon as Welty aired these charges, Norris contacted all judicial committee chairmen and requested them to examine carefully the precinct records in their respective areas for irregularities. He soon found evidence in other precincts and heard rumors to the effect that votes properly belonging to him had been rejected. One chairman wrote, "I think we can collect enough evidence of irregularities in Hayes County alone to make 15 votes in your favor." [23]

Norris and his supporters also uncovered evidence of fraud in Frontier County which went for Welty in the election. The county sheriff believed that Norris "lost more votes by irregularities than Welty," and that "a recount would increase the number" of his votes. Norris thought that A. R. Curzon, a Republican banker of Curtis, was involved in some of these irregularities, because he had not assured Curzon that if elected he would favor moving the county seat from Stockville to Curtis. Thus Norris was prepared, if necessary, to present charges to combat Welty's.[24] However, until Welty took legal

action, Norris was the newly elected judge of the Fourteenth Judicial
District of the state of Nebraska.

Since Welty's charges were public and Norris' evidence private,
the accusation of fraud would occur in many future campaigns. At the
time, however, the press throughout the state carried the story of his
election along with Welty's charges, and letters of congratulations
poured in upon Norris from delighted Republicans. What Norris expected—and this was his reason for collecting evidence of election
frauds—was that Welty would apply to the Nebraska Supreme Court
for a writ of mandamus to force a correction of the canvass. On November 15, Welty and a group of his advisers met in an Indianola law
office "behind closed doors and curtained windows," and several days
later Welty did as Norris expected. Since Norris already had evidence
of fraud and more was being unearthed by his friends, he had no
doubt he would be able to hold the office, though it might take a legal
contest to do so.[25]

Welty filed a suit charging fraudulent returns from Union precinct
in Furnas County. He claimed that his opponent's tally had been
changed from forty to forty-six after the county board certified the returns, and that it was C. S. Anderson, McClure's law partner, who
changed the votes in the pollbook on the Sunday following the
canvass. Welty alleged that the pollbook figures did not tally with
those of the county commissioners, and that the additional six votes
gave Norris a plurality of two. Both Anderson and County Clerk
McFadden were Populists who, as suporters of McClure, probably
favored Norris' election. Partisans of both men argued these charges,
while Norris' followers countered them by alleging that many Norris
votes had been thrown out by prejudiced election boards on the
grounds of irregularities in marking.

On November 26, 1895, the Furnas County canvassing board met
in Beaver City, pursuant to the mandamus of the Supreme Court, and
re-examined the judicial vote of the entire county. Their results showed
that Norris still carried the county by two votes even though the
Union precinct pollbook had been tampered with, as Welty had
charged. The converted six votes were disallowed, but four more votes
for Norris were found in the recanvass. The county tally as certified
by the board was 1,375 for Norris and 881 for Welty, making a total
for the judicial district of 4,612 votes to 4,610 in favor of Norris.[26]
In accord with these findings, on November 29, every member of the
state canvassing board signed a certificate of election which declared
Norris the legally elected judge of the fourteenth Judicial District.

The action was taken after a long session and over the initial objections of Governor Silas A. Holcomb, a Populist and a member of the board.[27]

Thus, by the end of November, Norris' election finally became official. Welty said he would file his oath of office with the secretary of state[28] and continue to serve, while he brought an ouster proceeding against Norris in the Supreme Court of the state. Norris, with McClure acting as his attorney, went to Lincoln in April, 1896, to attend a meeting of the Supreme Court at which a commissioner was to be appointed to take evidence. In Lincoln they learned that Judge Welty had dismissed his action.[29]

Norris later claimed that if the contest had been tried and his evidence presented, he would have won by between fifty and one hundred votes.[30] When a correspondent asked why he did not counter Welty's charges with evidence of his own, he replied, "We have not taken the pains to give it publicity as Judge Welty always does when he thinks he finds something wrong, but prefer to abide our time, and let the matter come up for the first time in court." [31] However, since Norris never had this opportunity, political enemies continued to charge that the election had been stolen for him.

After ten years in Nebraska, George Norris, age thirty-four, had carved a remarkable career for himself. He was about to enter upon his judicial duties after engaging in one of the hardest fought campaigns in southwestern Nebraska, and had every reason to be satisfied and even optimistic about a promising judicial career and, perhaps, higher political attainments. He was one of the youngest district court judges in the history of Nebraska.

But, despite numerous reasons for optimism, Norris was somewhat melancholy and depressed as the year ended. He was disturbed by the litigation with Welty, displeased about the behavior of some of his supporters, and burdened by the heavy expenses incurred during the campaign (over $3,500). He was afraid that a contested court case would bankrupt him, and was dismayed by the lack of aid and encouragement he received from the Republican party.[32] Norris believed that conspiracy, corporations, and corruption were united to secure his political downfall.

Norris had fought a vigorous, skilful campaign, one that few observers thought at the outset he would win. Yet a brooding sense of melancholy overwhelmed him, a sense of isolation that made him seem solemn and sad in a moment of triumph. Norris enjoyed campaigning. The melancholy that made him almost feel sorry for himself set in after the results were known. In later campaigns, too, he was aware of the fact that his party was not greatly interested in supporting his contest. This increased his sense of isolation and made him realize that in politics he was almost always on his own. These traits, evident by the end of his first important campaign, became more pronounced and were more widely observed in future years.

Chapter 5

The Family Man

DURING the campaign, the ensuing litigation, and general confusion following his contested victory, George Norris was too busy to fully enjoy his infant daughter, Hazel. Since Mrs. Norris had previously given birth to a stillborn child, the parents were especially delighted with Hazel, born in January of 1895. In February of 1897 another daughter, Marian, blessed their household. Pluma Norris proved herself a devoted wife and mother and the family circle was a very happy one.

After her mother's death in 1894 Pluma found the house too large for the needs of her family. Norris had difficulty selling the property because of the depression, but at the end of the century he was finally able to make a satisfactory arrangement. The family then moved to a house more suitable to its needs in McCook, the seat of neighboring Red Willow County.

Though he was busy with judicial and family responsibilities, Norris did not ignore his mother in Ohio. Whenever he went east, usually to attend IOOF conventions, he arranged to visit with her and his nearby sisters. He spent the entire month of August, 1896, visiting with his mother on the family farm and seeing old acquaintances in Clyde and other nearby communities. In 1897 his mother and a sister vacationed in Nebraska.[1]

In 1892 his mother had divorced Isaac Parker, charging him with gross neglect of duty on the grounds that he did not adequately provide her with clothing and other necessities.[2] In order to ease the financial burdens of his mother, who was allowed to resume the name of Norris, her son suggested that she apply for a pension as the needy mother of a gallant soldier who had died for his country.[3]

Norris was solicitous about his mother's welfare and continually inquired about her in his letters to Melissa, who lived in Clyde. Mary Norris, after her divorce, claimed that she wanted to sell the farm and spend the remainder of her days in Nebraska. But because of her failing health, the lack of a good offer for the farm, and her son's financial difficulties, she made no effort to move.[4]

By the end of the century Mary Norris was living with her daughter Melissa. She made periodic visits back to the farm, which was then operated by a tenant, and delighted in the atmosphere. She examined the fruit trees, drank in the balmy spring air, and tasted the fruit as it ripened. She discussed the prospects of the wheat crop with the tenant. Visits to the farm made her nostalgic and she talked about moving back to the old place and selling or renting the fields to nearby farmers so that she could live in the house. Her health, as she approached her eighth decade of life, was slowly deteriorating, and frequent colds depleted her strength. Her interest in her grandchildren was great, and she was full of advice on how to raise them. After a trip to Ohio in 1897, Hazel talked for months about her grandmother and was eager to visit her again whenever the opportunity arose.[5]

As a thirty-four-year-old judge, Norris found that his greying hair and recently grown beard helped to give him a more mature appearance, and made him a known figure as he traveled through the eight-county judicial district. On formal occasions he wore a wing collar, though he avoided it whenever possible in the interests of comfort. He was not yet sporting the cigar which characterized his congressional career, but was experimenting with pipes during this period. Since he preferred thinner soled shoes than he could buy in Beaver City, he bought his shoes, along with baby furniture and other items, from a mail-order catalogue.[6]

Norris enjoyed music, and after his marriage he rented and later purchased a piano. Now he could enjoy to the utmost an evening at home with friends, neighbors, and later children to harmonize with his baritone voice. Together they sang what later generations would call "the old favorites." Effervescent water and lemon sour which he ordered in Iowa added to the merriment on these occasions. It is interesting to note that shortly after he purchased a piano, Norris tried to sell his pool table, probably a relic of bachelor days.[7]

During the difficult years of the 1890's, Norris increased his library and kept abreast of current events. He purchased many law books, although shortly after his election to the bench, he was forced to sell a number of them to the West Publishing Company in order to pay his debts to that firm.[8]

Besides local newspapers, Norris subscribed to the Nebraska *State Journal*, published in Lincoln, which he relied upon for state and national news. To obtain a volume of letters by his favorite humorist, Petroleum V. Nasby, he subscribed to the Toledo *Weekly Blade*, which offered the volume. To obtain a Lincoln volume, he subscribed to the *North American Review*. He received other national periodicals, such as the *Literary Digest*, and much children's literature to encourage his youngsters as they learned to read. During the expansionist decade of the 1890's, he became so interested in Hawaii that he entered a subscription for the Honolulu *Advertiser*. Thus, in Beaver City, George Norris achieved what he had missed on the Ohio farm: the solace of music, an entrance to the world of literature, and a broader perspective on current events.[9]

During their residence in Beaver City, the growing family experienced the usual illnesses, aches, and pains. Since Norris had to be away from home for long periods of time (when court was in session he rarely managed to remain at home for more than a week), he was concerned about Pluma and the children if they were ill. In September of 1896 Norris himself was bedridden for several weeks with a lame back which mended very slowly.[10]

In March of 1897 the entire family, including the hired girl, came down with an affliction that kept Norris too busy attending sick people to open his mail. Confusion and chaos reigned in the household. In February of 1899, every member of the family, except Norris, again became sick. Pluma remained ill over a month and by mid-April she still had not fully recovered. In May, Norris used a railroad pass provided by Morlan to take her to Lincoln to seek further medical attention and to have her dental work done.[11]

When his family was in its usual good health, Norris looked forward to brief visits at home when court was in session. He relished the longer intervals when it was not in session. Norris was indeed a doting parent, watching with pleasure the development of his two daughters, Hazel and Marian. He wrote, "No sweeter nor nicer girls have the privilege of residing on this earth." Hazel looked so much like him that he claimed, "If she belonged to any other family than the one of which I am the head it would be a good cause for divorce from me." By the end of the century Hazel was taking an interest in the community and was terribly concerned about the health of a barefoot boy who went by the house, while Marian, a healthy and chubby three-year-old, talked the family almost to distraction.[12]

A few diversions also took Norris away from the family circle. Trips to IOOF conventions were an example, though Norris usually deposited his family with his mother or sister in Ohio before proceeding to the convention city. Before the children were born, Pluma and George in June of 1893 had a wonderful trip to the Chicago Fair. On the Fourth of July and other such occasions Norris indulged his oratorical talents, keeping his name before the public in a favorable way. The L.U.N. reunions, another diversionary activity, soon came to be a family affair as the members appeared with their wives and children.

It was the pressure of world events, particularly the Spanish-American War, that threatened most ominously to take Norris away from his family. He wanted to enlist and undoubtedly could have obtained a field commission, but he knew it would probably shorten his mother's life if a second son went to war. Norris was grateful that his judicial duties overwhelmed him with work at this time. He wrote to a sister, "I am afraid I will get the war fever if I am not kept busy." Though he supported the war and its results, he did not let them preoccupy his thoughts. He contributed twenty-five dollars to help pay the traveling expenses of the First Regiment Nebraska Volunteers, which had participated in crushing the forces of Aguinaldo in the Philippine Islands.[13]

Norris' major diversion, aside from his children, was the organizational life in which he participated. Occasionally this became so time-consuming that it ceased to be a diversion. But usually he delighted in it and formed many lasting friendships. In an indirect way it aided his political ambitions; lodge brothers had supported him in all of his campaigns and would continue to do so in the future. Membership in various organizations gave him a wide range of contacts throughout the state, while fraternal activities enabled him to travel and renew these acquaintances. The IOOF, the Odd Fellows, was the organization to which he devoted most of his attention while a resident of Beaver City. At the outset, Norris participated in Knights Templar conclaves in Holdrege, but by the time he became a judge his free time was almost exclusively devoted to IOOF affairs. He served as a delegate to the Sovereign Grand Lodge from Nebraska in the IOOF and attended annual sessions of that body in Boston and Detroit. In 1896–97 Norris served as Grand Master of the Odd Fellows in the jurisdiction that included Nebraska and part of South Dakota. This job, he estimated, consumed about three-fourths of his time, and he was thankful as his term drew to a close. His active interest in the IOOF declined after his service as representative to the Sovereign Grand Lodge. This was a position to which he was elected without opposition and by acclamation, an extraordinary occurrence and one which Norris deeply appreciated. His experiences, which he never explained, in the Sovereign Grand Lodge had not been what he anticipated; he became disillusioned and had no desire to be re-elected. By the end of the century Norris, though a member of several fra-

ternal and benevolent associations, was no longer an active participant
in any of them.[14]

Other than his election as a judge, most aspects of Norris' adult
life in Nebraska were not very different from those of other young
western lawyers. His interest in politics, concern with family, and
participation in various organizations were and still are typical of
lawyers in small towns throughout America. The office of county
prosecuting attorney was and still is for many lawyers the first rung
on the ladder of political advancement. Typical too, during this decade
of drought and depression, were the financial problems and accom-
panying worries. After 1896 his affairs, like other people's, began to
ease owing to the return of adequate rainfall, good crops, and, according to Republican politicians, "McKinley Prosperity."

When Norris was elected to the bench he was heavily in debt and
was preoccupied for several years with the need to pay off these
obligations. He owned property on which he had realized very little
and which he either hoped to sell or to rent profitably. His salary as
a judge was $2,500 a year, and by 1897 he was able to pay the
premiums on $9,600 worth of life insurance.[15] The struggle to get out
of debt was a long and difficult one. Throughout his life the memory
of it and the fear of its recurrence made Norris conservative about
fiscal affairs. This conservatism and his belief that no one should spend
more than his income were noted in his public life from that time on.

Meanwhile, though on the bench, Norris maintained a lively interest in his business transactions. Though he could no longer engage
in the mortgage-loan business, he continued to speculate—to buy and
sell real estate and to manage various holdings for himself and for
members of his family. When he first came to Nebraska he borrowed
money from some of his sisters. Later he invested funds for them.
When he was heavily in debt he again borrowed money from his
sisters, though he never told his mother of his financial embarrassment.[16]

Because of his financial difficulties, Norris tried to sell some of his
land. During the campaign of 1896 he found it unsalable because of
the political excitement. It was equally difficult to borrow money on
land; one company wrote, "If McKinley is elected, we think we will
be in the market but we do not care to make any investments while
there is an uncertainty as to what kind of money a person will be paid
back in." Norris was also informed by one of his creditors that unless
McKinley was elected, he would have to pay his note when due and
could expect no extension. After McKinley's election, he was able to
renew it on generous terms.[17]

When his land was occupied by a farmer, Norris usually helped decide what crops would be raised. He preferred alfalfa and sometimes gave instructions on how to plant it. When the crops were harvested, Norris received an "owner's part of the crop." At times, he would write to the Department of Agriculture making inquiries and requesting seed samples.[18]

Occasionally he had to take legal action against land purchasers who did not make payments on their notes. He did this only after giving repeated extensions and accepting numerous promises which were not fulfilled. When a case came to court Norris preferred, if possible, to reach a compromise solution. In one instance, a pair of debtors unable to meet their obligation assigned him some of their real estate in Beaver City. Other debtors made other arrangements. By 1898 conditions had improved so much that Norris told Miles, "Good level land on the bottom suitable for alfalfa cannot be bought anywhere in Furnas County for much less than $20.00 per acre and most of it is higher than that." Moreover, if the 1898 crops were good, real estate anticipated "the greatest rush" in the history of the short-grass country by the spring of 1899. Consequently Norris urged Miles to purchase land, and he tried with whatever funds he could scrape together to obtain either land or mortgages.[19]

Renting space in the Norris Block was a continuing and embarrassing problem. The empty building stood as a monument to Norris' lack of financial wisdom. After the failure of the Furnas County Bank, he assumed ownership of its safe and other fixtures; these he offered to sell to a prospective buyer if he would agree to establish a new bank and rent the space at a reduced rate. This plan, however, met with no success. Another office in the building was left vacant when its occupant, a doctor, left town without paying his rent, suggesting that Norris collect it from patients whose accounts were unpaid. However, by March of 1898 the building was fully rented and Norris' financial worries declined. He now was able to liquidate his obligations and derive some income from his real estate holdings.[20]

His most perplexing and difficult financial problem, while not fully settled at the end of the century, had turned out far better than he had expected. The death of Pluma's mother had left Norris with two items to dispose of—the Beaver City mill and the house in which the family was living.[21] The family resided in the latter until 1899 when it was finally sold, after a long search for a buyer.

The history of the mill was more complicated. In 1888 Pluma's father had given a mortgage to James H. Tallman on 240 acres of land for $2,500. This land contained Lashley's original residence, the mill, a barn, a small house for a tenant, and other improvements. At Lashley's death in 1890, his widow inherited the mill and the buildings and assumed the mortgage. Pluma's brother, Charles P. Lashley, inherited the balance of the property, which Norris later bought from him. The deed of conveyance distinctly stated that he was not to pay any part of the mortgage. The mill property, believed to be worth about ten thousand dollars, consisted of the buildings and the water power, mill race, and dam, and twenty acres of land. The mill was almost at the center of the twenty acres. At the time of her death, Sarah Lashley had not paid off the $2,500 mortgage, and it was this mortgage which caused the difficulty in settling the estate.[22]

When Mrs. Lashley and later owners sold the mill property, the conveyances all stipulated that the grantee assumed and agreed to pay the $2,500 mortgage. The owners in 1898 had improved the property and were beginning to show a profit on its operation. They were, however, unable to pay the mortgage, and the holder, after several extensions, was about to begin foreclosure proceedings in March, 1898.

At this point Norris, after borrowing funds from Miles, suggested a compromise. He proposed to pay $2,000 cash for the assignment of this mortgage, but before this offer was accepted Norris bought the mill outright from the owners. He then offered the property for sale at $4,000. Unable to locate a purchaser, he accepted the offer of George Shafer, who gave him a note for a half interest in the mill. With the help of Miles, the partners then installed modern machinery and renovated the mill. Shafer handled its management, but Norris took a lively interest in it.[23]

Drain though the will was on his time and energy, Norris was learning, almost against his will, about milling. By the summer of 1899, business was so good that the partners could not meet the demand for their flour. They installed a gasoline engine so the mill could always operate at capacity. When Norris returned to Beaver City after holding court, he immersed himself with mill business until he had to depart for another court session at another county seat. The income from the mill undoubtedly assuaged Norris for the need to work even during brief respites from judicial duties.[24]

By the end of 1899, Norris and his partner agreed to rent the mill if the right man could be found. Since the partners had spent over twenty-five hundred dollars in repairs, neither was willing to sell at a price that attracted potential buyers. The best means of getting back their investment and making a profit, they thought, was to rent the property to an experienced miller. Such a person was W. W. Tallman, who had previously worked at the mill when Norris first came to Beaver City. Norris had faith in Tallman's experience and ability and hoped eventually to sell the property to him. Thus when Norris moved from Beaver City to McCook in 1899, arrangements were being made to rent the mill,[25] and a costly, complicated, and contentious problem seemed to be on its way toward a satisfactory solution.

Though the mill consumed most of his spare time, it helped relieve Norris' financial embarrassment. In the twentieth century private business matters would not preoccupy him to the extent they did at this time. As he moved on to the national scene, Norris' financial position became more comfortable, though he rarely could afford luxuries of any kind. Fortunately his tastes were simple and moderate, and he was able to provide for the modest needs of his family without suffering the pangs of anxiety and the curse of debt he had experienced in the last decade of the nineteenth century.

By 1900 he was paying off his long-standing obligations, receiving his greatest pleasure from settling accounts with his L.U.N. friends. He returned the money formerly borrowed on his life insurance and increased the amount he held—a final measure of his improving financial status. In November, 1899, he took out an $8,000 policy with the Mutual Life Insurance Company of New York, acknowledging the fact that he was beginning to experience the prosperity that seemed to be pervading the United States. With his private life now on a financially secure basis, Norris could devote a greater portion of his time and energies to his career as judge of the Fourteenth Judicial District of the State of Nebraska.[26]

Chapter 6

Judge Norris

GEORGE NORRIS found his job as a district judge both challenging and enjoyable. In his autobiography he claimed, possibly forgetting his financial troubles at the time, that the seven years he spent on the bench were the most satisfactory years of his life. He even wondered if he had made a mistake to leave his post for a political career in Washington.[1] Certainly when he mounted the bench, he was achieving a status and a salary ($2,500) that set him well above his distressed fellow citizens.

As a judge, more so than as a prosecuting attorney or as a lawyer in the mortgage-loan business, Norris came in contact with a wide range of people and their multifarious problems, with "human nature in all of its nobility and goodness; and all of its weakness and error." All of this had its effect. During his years on the bench he wrote, "My sympathies were to be broadened, my understanding of life enriched, and my conceptions of simple justice strengthened." [2] He met a variety of situations which required either his decision or his precise instructions to a jury, and in so doing he increased his understanding, knowledge, and respect for the law and its processes.

Almost thirty years before Norris became a judge, a young Boston lawyer with a philosophical bent, reviewing a volume in the *American Law Review*, succinctly noted the significant role that busy western judges, like Norris, performed. Oliver Wendell Holmes praised them as men who were "more intent on adapting the law to modern requirements than on standing in the ancient ways." Norris, like many of his colleagues, with little opportunity in his previous preparation for the study of legal scholarship or philosophy, and almost no opportunity in his present position, would have been regarded with contempt by many of Holmes' more proper associates in the Boston bar. But as Holmes noted, with many of Norris' colleagues in mind, one could not expect of them that "businesslike common sense" which was to be found among the lawyers of the western states.[3] Holmes, with his insight and understanding of legal realities, adequately described the role that Norris fulfilled as a district judge. Norris was a realist and a pragmatist in the dispensation of justice. Conditions as they existed in rainless, poverty-stricken, debt-ridden southwestern Nebraska were basic considerations in his decision making.

To a visitor from Holmes' Boston, Norris and his colleagues on the bench and bar would have seemed rather crude at the outset. They dressed plainly; some were quite careless in their personal appearance. Few were as well educated as Norris; most had less preparation in law. Outside of the few words of barbarous Latin jargon they had extracted from law books, and usually mispronounced, they knew nothing of foreign languages unless they were brought up in an immigrant home, which they generally considered a liability. Even the English language was mingled with variations that would have grated harshly upon the ears of the Harvard-trained lawyer. If a lawyer or Norris himself said, "It looks like the plaintiff will win his case," or, of a man in jail, "He wants out," the Boston visitor would have had difficulty separating the speaker from his phrase or believing that he could really be a man of learning or ability. But if the visitor had daily contact with his western counterparts, witnessed the competitive trial in court, observed the actualities of life which concerned them, and recognized their ability "to think under fire—to think for action upon which great interests depend," he would have realized that the bench and bar of western Nebraska, though they lacked the cultural polish and intellectual tone of his own Boston, were indeed not very different in professional skill and ability. Certainly the visitor would have noted after observation and contact that Judge Norris' mind in its analytical and logical capacities was well suited to the law. He would have seen that Norris had a shrewd sense and a keen knowledge of human nature and that he was capable of clear thinking and of fluent and forcible, if not elegant, speech and writing. And if the proper Bostonian observed carefully enough he would have noted that these western Nebraska lawyers and judges, though they exhibited very few of the ornaments of learning, possibly had a better perspective of life and the things that are useful in it than many of his associates.[4]

In some respects the bar of the eight-county judicial district was comparable to a large family over which Norris presided. He soon knew lawyers in each county and met with them early in the morning in the courtroom to make up the issues and dispose of matters preliminary to the official opening of his court. He usually held two sessions in each county during the annual term of the district court, one involving equity cases and the other jury trials. The first session occurred during the winter or spring, while the second convened in the autumn or winter. There were so many cases on the docket during the first year Norris presided that he called a special session and held court during the summer months of 1896 at each county seat.

As a judge, beginning in January 1896, Norris stood in marked contrast to his predecessor, Welty. During the campaign it was charged that Welty had played politics from the bench by favoring debtors and Populists over creditors and Republicans. It was claimed that rather than foreclose, Welty would cancel a session of his court and thereby prevent debtors from losing their property. Norris too had to meet the difficult problem of ordering foreclosures and sheriffs' sales, but unlike Welty he was courteous, capable, and impartial in the administration of his judicial office.

Norris' solution to the foreclosure problem was not markedly different from Welty's. If the individual who lived on the property that was presented for foreclosure had made every effort to meet his payments but had been unable to do so because of the drought, Norris hesitated to order a sheriff's sale and thereby complete the foreclosure proceeding. Had he strictly followed the law, he would have confirmed each sale as it appeared before him, but he wrote, "It is a very hard and difficult thing to take away from a man his home when it is all he has, and where he is trying to save it and pay the debt, and has been prevented from doing so by some act of Providence, or some circumstance beyond his control."

Believing it wiser to pursue a course of mercy than to follow the strictly legal path, Norris would grant extensions whenever he thought the debtor was honest, industrious, and sincere in his desire to meet obligations. Norris admitted that some people possibly obtained extensions by "false and fraudulent representations," but he preferred "to lean to the side of mercy" and pursue the course that he thought was "mercifully and morally right."[5] This may not have been impartial justice, but given the difficult economic conditions and the desperate plight of many citizens, it represented a realistic effort to find a middle-ground between continual foreclosures and long-term extensions.

In such cases, Norris was facing an historic situation with precedents deep in the American past. Foreclosure meant that the farmer would lose his farm and much of his chattel property, and thus would be without means to plant or harvest a crop. Sheriffs' sales rarely brought in enough money to satisfy creditors, while debtors could become a public charge. Therefore whenever he was convinced that a farmer was doing everything possible to pay off his note, Norris was willing to give the person an opportunity "consistent with justice and right" to save his homestead. If after granting an extension, however, Norris had reason to believe that the individual involved was not doing everything possible to meet his obligation, he would refuse to grant a further extension, thereby bringing about the foreclosure.[6]

Norris confirmed sales only if the mortgage indebtedness was in excess of the value of the land and the owner could in no way benefit from an extension. In cases where he felt a farmer would eventually meet his obligations, he postponed confirmation until the next term. In all cases he took into account the value of the land and the means the farmer had available to meet his debt. Before Norris granted an extension, the farmer had to agree to pay on his note any cash he possessed and any income he could anticipate from his current crops, and to pay taxes on his property.[7]

Since Nebraska had no moratorium legislation until the New Deal period, each judge had to work out a solution to this problem. Norris' solution, while more moderate than his predecessor's, was at first protested with equal bitterness by the attorneys for the mortgage holders. However, after it had been applied for two or three years it met with general satisfaction. Norris believed this policy provided the best possible way for the creditor to get his money, since a sheriff's sale was no guarantee that he would be reimbursed for the full amount of his loan.[8] Thus, while Norris served as a district judge, numerous debt-ridden farmers were able to pay off their mortgages and maintain ownership of their property. At the same time Norris was able to retain the respect of both creditors and debtors and obtain the support of most citizens in the district for his fair policy. He avoided the animosities that Populist Judge Welty had aroused, and increased his chances for re-election when his term came to an end in 1899.

While foreclosure proceedings were the most important and numerous of the cases that appeared on his docket, Judge Norris had other duties to perform. Some of them had political overtones. In one instance, a bank in the district failed, and Norris had to appoint a receiver to untangle its activities and list its assets prior to final disposition. Receivers worked for a small salary; none received more than fifty dollars a month. But owing to the hard times, lawyers throughout the district sought such appointments. It was not always easy to find a competent and unbiased man. However, by the autumn of Norris' first year on the bench, economic conditions improved and these appointments virtually ceased.[9]

As a judge, Norris had to decide if injunctions should be issued upon receipt of petitions and affidavits demanding them. He also had to determine whether it was worthwhile to issue judgments against debtors who were not meeting their obligations. (In such instances he usually followed a policy similar to that of foreclosure proceedings.) Norris also felt obligated to answer requests for information addressed to him in his judicial capacity. Could he approve testimony given before a justice of the peace and on the basis thereof issue citizenship papers? Could he inform a young lawyer as to the most promising community to start a practice in his district? Of course in no instance did he offer legal advice. Legal ethics and Nebraska law prohibited this because of the possibility that he would have to adjudicate a case where his advice, if offered, played a significant role.[10]

Human interest cases provided a form of social recreation and a topic of endless discussion to citizens in small towns. When a murder case was on the docket, Norris tried to have no other jury cases pending until the case was decided. As prosecuting attorney he had appeared before a jury in cases involving murder, adultery, and other seamy aspects of the human condition. As a judge, therefore, he found no novelty in such proceedings. He looked at each case as sympathetically as possible and considered the welfare of the innocent victims of such proceedings to be of primary significance. After the jury reached its decision, he would then dispose of the case. Occasionally he disagreed with its decision and expressed his disagreement. Toward criminals Norris rarely showed clemency, sentencing them to the limit of the law.[11]

One aspect of his public life did not change from the days before he was elected to the bench: Norris, like most public officials, traveled by railroad with a pass. Now, however, he was no longer deluged with requests for free transportation. The passes were usually supplied by George W. Holdrege, general manager of the Burlington and Missouri in Nebraska or Charles F. Manderson, former United States senator and general solicitor of the road; passes for his family were usually obtained from W. S. Morlan.[12] He received passes for all railroads in the state. Fortunately for Norris, no major case involving a railroad came before him. Passes at this time were taken for granted except by a minority of disgruntled citizens and, as a former railroad attorney, Norris saw nothing objectionable—or at least nothing worthy of public criticism—in their use.

His railroad pass and the few requests he still received for free transportation served to remind Norris that, although he was a judge, he had been elected to office on the Republican party ticket. Though he did not neglect political activity, he was circumspect in his participation. He was an ardent Republican, but he was also a judge serving all the people of the Fourteenth Judicial District. For this reason he was unable to participate actively in the crucial and exciting campaign of 1896.

W. E. Andrews, incumbent congressman from the Fifth District, was one of the few Republicans Norris felt called upon to support. Indeed, he felt a heavy obligation to Andrews which he explained by referring to his recent judicial campaign:

> When all the combinations of circumstances, and underhanded politics was united against me, and when even the Republican State Committee and the leading Republican Dailies of the state were silent and gave no encouragement or support, . . . you unlike all the remainder of the leading Republicans in Nebraska, put your shoulder to the wheel, and did everything in your power to bring about my election.[13]

Both men were aware that the incumbent's chances were not very bright, since fusion between the Democrats and Populists was working once again. Norris wrote Andrews early in the campaign that "if God will send us rain, and the present Congress makes no mistakes," Andrews would have an excellent chance of returning to Washington. But rather than sit back and await these divine and fortuitous events, Norris proposed "to do a few things in the way of nominating the right man in opposition" to Andrews.

There was talk of nominating Welty as the Populist congressional candidate. Norris believed that he would be an easy candidate to defeat and proposed, if Andrews thought it desirable, to "control enough of the Populists" in Furnas and Red Willow counties to keep down any opposition at least until after Welty was nominated. Welty would make an inferior candidate, Norris explained, because his position on mortgage foreclosures, which had made him so powerful a judicial opponent, would do him little good in a congressional fight.[14] This rumor, however, was not realized and the fusion candidate, R. D. Sutherland, overwhelmed Andrews in the election.

Behind the scenes Norris played a minor role in the campaign of 1896. He informed Republican candidates of sentiment in his district and contributed to county campaign funds. He tried to commit convention delegates to particular candidates and arranged transportation to the state convention in Omaha for others. Moreover, he was besieged with requests to support various county candidates. He helped in whatever ways possible and only once did he pointedly refuse a request. This request was made by the chairman of the Republican State Committee, who notified him that the finance committee had fixed an assessment of twenty-five dollars as his share of the campaign fund. Norris refused to pay on the grounds that in his judiciary campaign the previous year he spent over thirty-five hundred dollars and received no assistance from the Republican State Committee. He believed the committee should not request contributions until the salary ($2,500 a year) from his office equaled the amount he had expended in securing it.[15]

Fusion candidates swept almost every available office in Nebraska in 1896. Bryan carried the state while Populist Silas Holcomb was reelected governor by a greater majority than Bryan obtained over McKinley. Republicans, as a result of the election, found themselves a very small minority in both houses of the state legislature. In the Fifth Congressional District, Andrews and almost all of the lesser Republican candidates went down to defeat. After the election, Republican officeholder George Norris found himself almost isolated as one of the few Republicans in public office in his district. The election, however, helped to enhance his status among Republicans as a candidate who, in a predominantly Populist area, could get elected to an important public office.

After the election Nebraska Republicans found some solace for their overwhelming defeat in McKinley's victory. Norris regretted that he was "living in Mexico" and quoted the Bible, "What doth it profit a man if he gain the whole world and lose his own soul." He remembered that others had suffered more directly than he in the past campaign. He recommended Andrews for a lucrative federal position. Fortunately his court was not in session until January, 1897, so that he had ample time to recover his perspective and consider the political future.[16]

Norris' loyalty to the Republican party remained unshaken, and he continued to participate in politics as far as his judicial duties would allow. He tried to keep abreast of state and national developments, but he did not feel qualified to comment fully upon any but district developments in his correspondence. As the 1897 campaign for state, county, and local offices got under way, Norris tried to size up the situation. It was a confusing picture.

On the first of September there occurred in Lincoln the initial convention of what Norris called "the three ring circus that is opposing us." Populists, Democrats, and Free Silver Republicans each met in separate groups at the capital city, but all agreed on a fusion ticket to oppose the Republicans in the November election. Though Norris knew that many Populists and some Democrats were disgusted with this arrangement, he was unwilling to prognosticate the outcome. If dissatisfied Populists could "be induced to come back into the ranks," then Norris thought Republican prospects would be very good. Unfortunately for Norris and his fellow Republicans, fusion was still effective in the 1897 election. Its candidates swept the available state offices and made gains in county offices as well.[17]

The results throughout the Fourteenth Judicial District were no different from those throughout the state. "Not quite a Waterloo," wrote a county judge to Norris, "and perhaps if providence permits by keeping away Bryan, drought and grasshoppers we will still be able to make a gallant fight two years from now." Another correspondent, an editor of a Republican newspaper, informed Norris of the results in his county with the quip, "We have met the enemy and we are theirs." [18]

Yet Norris was not too pessimistic about the results of this off-year election. The fusion majority in Nebraska had been reduced nearly one-half and elsewhere his party carried some states that had formerly been in the other column. Had it not been for the defalcation of two former Republican officeholders, the party, Norris believed, would possibly have carried the state. However, even in this matter, where two Republican officials were sentenced for stealing state funds, Norris could still see a bright side. By assisting in their conviction, and thus purifying their own ranks, the party "at no late date" could again win respect and confidence. Furthermore, fusion between Populists and Democrats was an ill-fitting arrangement and could not be counted on to function smoothly in the future. Thus Norris could see at this time of defeat opportunities for his rejuvenated party at coming elections.[19]

The state elections of 1898 proved that Norris was correct. Though his party lost every major state office, it retained control of the congressional seats it previously had won in the first and second districts and, most important, it won control of the state legislature. Norris ardently supported the gubernatorial candidacy of Monroe L. Hayward, who was defeated by less than three thousand votes by Populist W. A. Poynter, the fusion candidate. This time, Norris cheerfully contributed his assessment of thirty-five dollars to the state campaign fund.[20]

Norris' political pulse began to quicken after the improved showing of his party in 1898. No doubt he was flattered when friends suggested he was meant for higher office than district judge. A high ranking Nebraska Odd Fellow wanted him to enter the race for the United States Senate. Norris had previously confided to this friend that some day he would like to serve in the House of Representatives, and eventually to secure a more permanent government job, as defeated Republican incumbents from Nebraska already had done. When the state legislature met to choose a United States senator in 1899, Norris received one vote for this esteemed office.[21]

Thus as his first term as district judge came to an end, Norris, heartened by the good will manifested toward him, considered his chances for renomination and re-election. Whereas he formerly felt glum about his political future, the election of 1898, his improved financial status, and the general satisfaction with his judicial administration, made Norris' political optimism come to include his own prospects as well.

Chapter 7

Triumph and Tragedy

POPULISM was still rampant in Nebraska in 1899 when Norris' judicial term came to an end. The state was unredeemed, as far as the Republican party was concerned; it remained so after the off-year elections in 1899. Silas A. Holcomb, former governor, handily defeated his Republican opponent for judge of the Supreme Court and fusion candidates won the other state-wide contests. But in the Fourteenth Judicial District, a Populist stronghold, George Norris was re-elected by an impressive margin.

Earlier in the year, Norris was not unduly optimistic about his chances. As far as he knew there would be no opposition to his renomination. The election, however, was another question. Norris believed the Populists had a majority of between three hundred and four hundred votes in the district. If they gave their votes to his opponent, his defeat was assured. Furthermore, in February a bill was before the legislature which, had it passed, would have legislated him out of office by adding four heavily Populist counties to the judicial district.[1]

Though nothing came of this bill, Norris realized that if he were to be re-elected he would have to wean a goodly number of Populist voters back into the Republican fold. Accordingly, by July, he was requesting county leaders to send him the names of Populists who were formerly Republicans and were inclined toward the middle of the road.[2]

Norris also hoped to capitalize on the fact that fusion between Populists and Democrats rarely worked smoothly. Indeed Democrats were already threatening that unless allowed to name more candidates, they would put a separate ticket in the field. Norris knew too that John T. McClure was interested in the Populist nomination and would be a difficult opponent to defeat. Therefore Norris was most interested in news of rifts between Populists and Democrats.[3]

And there were serious rifts in the camp of the opposition. Ex-Judge Welty and his followers, recalling McClure's support of Norris in 1895, were determined to prevent McClure from obtaining the nomination. The Republicans did all they could to support these dissensions. Norris, tied down with judicial duties and not yet willing to campaign openly, conducted an extensive correspondence to keep abreast of political developments.[4]

Early in September the Populist judicial convention chose the prosecuting attorney of Gosper County, a Mr. Miller, to oppose Norris. Because Miller was not a strong candidate, and because there was dissension at the convention, Norris' chances of breaking the Populist majority in the district were considerably improved. McClure, in a speech to the delegates, indicated that he would have conducted a mudslinging campaign. Norris, therefore, had reason to be satisfied with the results of the Populist convention.[5]

The news that Republican county conventions had proceeded with a minimum of friction and a greater manifestation of party harmony than had been exhibited for many years also helped to brighten the campaign picture. So optimistic was Norris about the political situation that on September 12 he left on a vacation to visit his mother in Ohio and to attend the Sovereign Grand Lodge of the IOOF at Detroit. He planned to return in time to attend the Republican Judicial Convention at McCook on September 27. When he left on vacation there was no opposition to his nomination, and Norris boldly prognosticated, "This will be a Republican year, and . . . I ought to be reelected." [6]

As expected, he was renominated—by acclamation. Unexpected, however, was the sudden withdrawal of Miller and the substitution of McClure as his opponent. Attorney Miller withdrew because of illness; a paralyzed throat made it impossible for him to campaign. Though Norris now faced a skilful, dangerous, and difficult opponent, his optimism did not disappear. He exhorted his supporters to greater efforts. Furthermore, now that McClure was his opponent, Norris gained an unexpected ally in Welty, his previous opponent and a bitter political enemy of McClure.[7]

McClure campaigned vigorously, holding meetings and speaking individually to many voters. Norris, relying on his supporters to do this work, maintained a posture of judicious aloofness and followed the course of the campaign in correspondence and conversation. McClure undoubtedly hurt Norris personally by the type of campaign he conducted. He denounced Norris, claiming he was fraudulently elected in 1895. These denunciations had a ring of authenticity because McClure had been hired to present Norris' case in the litigation following the

1895 victory. McClure argued that while he had made use of every legal turn to sustain his client, the ethics of his profession prevented him from divulging details presented in strictest confidence. In speech after speech and in the columns of his Beaver City *Times* and other Populist papers he attacked Norris as fraudulently holding public office.[8]

These charges were effectively combated. Welty wrote letters claiming that though fraud was perpetrated in 1895, Norris was not guilty and indeed knew nothing about it. Toward the end of the campaign Welty took the stump and spoke against McClure.[9]

On November 3, 1899, the Beaver Valley *Tribune* published a series of affidavits, including a letter by Welty, a statement by Norris, and reports of two members of the 1895 Furnas County canvassing board, all refuting the charge of fraud on the part of Norris and suggesting that McClure's law partner was responsible for distorting some of the returns. Thus four days before the election, Norris with Welty's aid was able for the first time to present to the public his side of the disputed election of 1895.

Norris' notarized statement, included among the affidavits, represented the closest he came to actual campaigning. But Republican leaders left virtually no stone unturned on his behalf. Wavering Democrats and Populists were personally informed of Norris' merits by precinct leaders. Republican lawyers impressed on their clients the importance of keeping Judge Norris on the bench. One Republican stalwart spoke to most of the Populist leaders in his county and secured promises of support from others to spread the Norris gospel. He indicated the nature of his activities when he wrote, "Of course you understand these men don't neglect their own work and devote it to others without compensation, and I am advancing for you the necessary money to make the campaign."[10]

William Jennings Bryan appeared in western Nebraska in October to speak on behalf of Democratic and Populist candidates. Norris no doubt was pleased when one of his supporters claimed that Bryan's trip lost him very few votes. Biased though this observer was, he presented an unorthodox picture of Bryan as a campaigner. He wrote:

> So listless was the crowd that not even one cheer was given the party from start to finish, and although Bryan posed in old clothing to catch the rural vote it deceived no one and the farmers felt and afterwards expressed themselves that this was just a device to catch their votes. To show the apathy of the managers of the Bryan crowd, (he) spoke from an old lumber wagon. No

seats were provided and the different members of the party during the speaking sat on the sharp edges of the wagon box until
the meeting concluded.[11]

The election results showed that Norris had correctly sized up the
political situation. He won an impressive victory. Since both candidates
were residents of Beaver City, it must have been especially gratifying
to Norris to carry the community by over one hundred votes, though
he lost Furnas County, which had given him a large majority in 1895,
by a very slim margin. Ex-Judge Welty was so elated that he threw his
cap on the floor, stamped his feet, and asked his friends to burn the
cap—which they obligingly did. He also wrote Norris a congratulatory
letter claiming that the voters had "rebuked the rascality of the
would-be leaders of the Populist Party at Beaver City." [12] Welty at
last had his revenge against McClure. And McClure, who had supported Norris in 1895 against Welty, was now defeated by Norris with
the support of Welty. Factional fights among Furnas County Populists
played the major role in electing and re-electing Norris as a district
judge.

Since McClure and his followers did not charge him with official
misconduct in office, Norris believed the voters had censured and condemned the opposition for the course they pursued. The official canvass gave him a majority of 440. He ran between 1,000 and 1,500
votes ahead of his ticket and carried all but two counties, Furnas and
Gosper. While McClure won Furnas County by only twenty-seven
votes, Norris had no reason to feel disturbed about its loss, especially
since he carried Beaver City.[13]

In a letter to Welty, Norris acknowledged that Welty's efforts and
those of his Populist friends accounted for many votes. In all, the
campaign for re-election cost Norris less than fifty dollars, forty of
which at the outset he had turned over to the treasurer of the district
judicial committee. This sum is all the more remarkable when one
recalls that the 1895 campaign with its litigation and dispute almost
bankrupted him.[14]

Early in December, Norris received his certificate of election as
judge of the district court for the Fourteenth Judicial District. But he
was much too involved with the plans and preparations involved in
moving his family to McCook to take more than casual notice of it.
The house in Beaver City had been sold and by December he had
purchased a home in McCook, the seat of Red Willow County.
McCook was centrally located and was the largest, and most prosperous community in the entire judicial district. The main line of the Bur-

lington and Missouri Railroad ran through it and the Republican River flowed past it. In 1900, McCook claimed a population of 2,445. It boasted a waterworks and an electric light plant, both privately owned, along with eight churches, four schools, and a municipal park located almost directly across the street from Norris' home on Main (now Norris) Avenue in the north end of town. It had a police department, consisting of two full-time officers, and a volunteer fire department. Two public halls, a saloon, and a municipal park provided recreational facilities for the local citizenry. McCook also had a jail, though this was seldom occupied.[15]

The town had been laid out by the Lincoln Land Company in June, 1882, and was originally known as Fairview. The name was changed to honor Major General Alexander McDowell McCook, one of the famous fighting McCooks—eight brothers and a father, all of whom served as officers in the Union army during the Civil War. McCook quickly became a railroad town and a trading center for farmers who brought large quantities of corn and alfalfa for shipment to Omaha or Denver. Because the town was a division point on the Burlington and Missouri main line to Denver, the railroad employed many men in its shops and roundhouse. Other railroad employees who traveled this line made McCook their home. Until 1905 it was also the site of a United States Land Office. The community, with its pleasant homes, numerous trees, many civic improvements, and hard-working but diverse population, was a pleasant one and the family quickly felt at home. Certainly the move was a sensible one for Norris, who found the town's central location convenient for traveling throughout the district.

Before moving to McCook, Norris succeeded in settling the estate of Mrs. D. H. Lashley. He also hired two men to supervise his real estate holdings in Beaver City. Tenants in the Norris Block and elsewhere henceforth would pay their rent and present their complaints to C. H. Wilson, who superintended the building, or to J. F. Fults, who acted as rental and collection agent. Thus Norris became an absentee landlord.[16]

By the end of March Norris' family was settled in their new quarters, and Norris was able to resume his regular activities with little interference. Judicial duties were more conveniently arranged due to the more adequate transportation available at McCook. But they still kept him away from his family for extended periods. Since 1900 was a presidential election year as well as a census year, he was deluged with requests for transportation to the various Republican conventions, despite the fact that Nebraska now had a law making it a crime to give a pass to attend any political meeting, and with petitions to appoint loyal Republicans as census enumerators.

As the spring court term came to an end and the various state political conventions were held, Norris began to look forward to his summer vacation before the national political campaign was launched in the fall. He expected to visit some of his sisters and his mother in Ohio before proceeding to Richmond, Virginia, for the annual IOOF conclave.[17] There also was a gathering of the L.U.N. scheduled in August. Most of these plans went astray, however, because of unexpected misfortune in the family.

In June, Norris' mother died suddenly at the age of eighty-two in the family farmhouse at York Township. He arrived in Ohio for the funeral, emotionally upset and physically exhausted. The sight of his mother in death caused him intense anguish, though outwardly he remained calm. As her only living son, he was haunted by the knowledge "that if there was anything she most desired at the final end, it was that her boy might be there so she might give him her departing blessing." A month later Norris was still heartbroken and depressed. He claimed, "If it were not for the little ones I have here I would prefer that I might be taken back there and laid by my mother's side." The fact that Norris did not see his mother before her sudden death (she was neither bedridden nor ill) no doubt was partly responsible for this feeling of remorse. This feeling in turn helped to unleash the melancholy which now overwhelmed him.[18]

Norris gradually became reconciled to his grief during the summer of 1900, which he spent in McCook, and began to overcome his melancholy with the help of his daughters and with the news that Pluma was pregnant once again. For at least two months he did not engage in any social activities, though he did meet his financial obligations. Fortunately, his court was in recess until the fall.[19]

Among the financial matters requiring his attention was that of his mother's will. According to this document, Norris was to serve as one of the executors and as trustee for the sums bequeathed to his children. The only personal item he received was his brother's watch, a memento much prized by his mother.[20]

Norris' recovery, spurred on by his involvement with his family, was at last effected by the activities of the political campaign that was underway. Although economic conditions in Nebraska had improved considerably since 1896, a summer drought had once again caused hardship in the southwestern sections. Crops had been burned out by the blazing sun and withered by the dry heat that pervaded the region. The railroad contributed to the political uncertainty by discharging "quite a number of their employees" because of the sharp decline in traffic. For these reasons, Norris and his fellow Republicans expected the battle against the Populists and their Democratic allies to be an arduous one, despite the fact that Populism elsewhere had markedly declined or disappeared.[21]

At the end of August, Norris indulged in his first social activity since his mother's death; he attended the Sovereign Grand Lodge of the IOOF at Richmond, Virginia. He returned to McCook in September for the opening of his court and the beginning of the national campaign. There he was faced with a vexing problem: court in Hayes County was scheduled to start the same day—October 1—that Theodore Roosevelt was to speak in McCook. Though Norris "greatly admired the fighting Colonel," and hated to miss an opportunity to hear him speak, he refused to postpone the court opening to attend a partisan political meeting. Instead, he arranged for the jury panel and lawyers to go to McCook while he remained in court tending to necessary but perfunctory details.[22]

Believing it unwise for a person holding his position to make partisan speeches, Norris concluded that he probably could do more good for the Republican cause by "quietly working" with people. He thought that the campaign of 1864 was repeating itself in 1900; the attacks on the administration were similar to those made then, "and if you would take the speeches and editorials of that campaign and change the name of Lincoln to McKinley you would have them as they now appear." [23]

Thus Norris' contribution to the Republican victory in 1900 was not an obvious one. But both W. S. Morlan, the candidate for Congress, and F. M. Rathbun of the state committee were satisfied that the course he pursued was the correct one. Norris spent more than two hundred dollars of his own and engaged in many personal talks—more, he thought, than any other individual including the candidates. At the end of October he felt that he had done "a great deal of good," and the chairman of the Republican State Committee agreed. Early in November, Norris encouraged absentee Republicans with railroad passes to return to their precincts to vote on election day.[24]

The results of the election gave Republicans in southwest Nebraska cause for both elation and depression—elation because Bryan was defeated and C. H. Dietrich was elected governor, and depression because Morlan by less than five hundred votes lost to A. C. Shallenberger for congressman. While the Republican party regained control of the state, in southwestern Nebraska Norris and his fellow Republicans still had to redeem their district from the control of the Populist and Democratic parties.

In the Fifth Congressional District, where Norris voted, the Republican political picture was not promising. Since 1896 Republican candidates had been defeated in congressional elections. With the exception of Norris himself no Republican had been elected to a significant political office embracing more than a municipal or county area. Indeed, though Morlan turned in a creditable performance, the election of 1900 helped to convince many Republicans in southwestern Nebraska that George Norris was the best vote getter the party had in the short-grass country.

After the election, now that the Republican party was powerfully entrenched on the national scene, Norris believed that his next political responsibility was to help loyal Republicans obtain government jobs, particularly postmasterships. However, politics was no longer an immediate or pressing problem and he began once again to interest himself in other activities. As the year ended Norris was trying to convince J. H. Miles that money could be doubled in a very short time by taking advantage of the numerous opportunities that were developing in land speculation.[25]

Thus relaxed and somewhat elated, Norris seemed to have overcome his recent grief. His family was a constant source of satisfaction and there was anticipation of a new arrival in the spring. He was again participating in fraternal and incidental business activities. Though political ambition burned within him, there was little he could do about it at this time. Certainly he had every reason to believe that the future would offer exciting new opportunities. The political and economic upheaval of the 1890's was now receding into history and the new century seemed to offer the hope and opportunity he had envisioned when he arrived in the short-grass country fifteen years before. True, the fifteen years Norris had spent in Nebraska had not been years of complete frustration and collapse. He had risen to a position of prominence. But his hopes and ambitions led him to suspect that the coming years would be even more rewarding. However, before his expectations could be realized, an even greater loss than that of his mother would befall him.

Chapter 8

Greater Tragedy and Readjustment

THE YEAR 1901 started auspiciously enough for George Norris. While holding court for Judge H. M. Grimes in North Platte in the Thirteenth Judicial District, Norris was pleased to receive a letter from State Senator E. N. Allen informing him that if the bill recently introduced in Congress providing for another United States district judge for Nebraska was enacted, he would procure for Norris the endorsement of as many members of the state legislature as possible. Though the proposal came to naught, it revealed that other office-holding Republicans deemed him worthy of a higher office than the one he occupied.[1]

He planned to adjourn court in mid-February for two or three weeks so that he could be on hand when Pluma had her baby. Since court was held in McCook prior to adjournment, he was able to be at home for at least a month prior to the birth of the baby. Early in March Norris canceled the coming term of his court because "there was nothing of great importance" on the docket. This cancellation enabled him to spend at least two more weeks in McCook after the baby arrived.[2]

On March 21, 1901, a third daughter, Gertrude, was born to the Norrises. Five days later Pluma, age thirty-seven, was dead and Norris was left with three little girls. The suddenness of her death again threw the household into chaos and made it impossible for more than a few friends to attend the simple funeral held in the parlor of the Norris home. Once again Norris was overcome with grief, and had to rely on others to attend to the necessary details and arrangements.[3]

Overwhelmed though he was, Norris had too much to do and too many pressing and immediate matters to handle to give full vent to his sorrow. He bore his loss remarkably well, considering his reaction to his mother's death the previous year. By April he had recovered enough to tackle some of his legal correspondence.

Fortunately for the family, Norris' sister Emma came from Toledo to live with them in McCook. After the nurse left, Emma devoted most of her time and attention to the newborn infant, and Norris hired a girl to perform the remaining household chores. Emma, however, supervised, if she did not perform, all the necessary activities. The children liked her, and Norris felt no undue anxiety when he left home. He knew his family was under loving and capable surveillance.[4]

To complicate matters even more at this trying time, Hazel, age six, broke her arm. Then Pluma's sister in Arkansas, who had been unable to attend the funeral, wrote requesting various heirlooms and other items that had been borrowed from her. She stated that she was glad he had decided not to break up his home, but, if he ever changed his mind, she wanted to care for the children.[5]

By July the hired girl had left and Norris had to find someone to help his sister manage the household. Despite his difficulties, he was determined to provide a home for his daughters. Under no circumstances would he send them to live with relatives. This summer, as in the previous one, he turned down all invitations to deliver public addresses. But this summer he did make plans to attend the annual L.U.N. meeting, and in August he was again chosen as a delegate to the Sovereign Grand Lodge IOOF.

Household arrangements proved so satisfactory that shortly after Pluma's death Norris was able to pick up the threads of his disrupted life. A year later Emma went to Ohio for an operation and placed baby Gertrude with another sister in Ohio until she had recovered and was able to return to McCook. Norris took care of Hazel and Marian until her return and claimed that he and the children got along very well without any supervision, though they had the help of another hired girl.[6]

Since smallpox was rampant in parts of his judicial district, Norris canceled three sessions of his court in 1901.[7] Unable to drown his sorrows in judicial work, he turned his attention to financial affairs. He did not philosophize, as he later did, about death, nor did he seem in any outward way unduly affected by his great loss.

It was at the end of September in a letter to United States Senator Dietrich that Norris inadvertently revealed some of his anxieties and inner tensions. He commented on his recent loss, his heavy insurance burden, and other debts. He explained that he found the expenses connected with his office unduly heavy and his salary hardly adequate. It was with the hope of increasing his income that he inquired of the senator about judicial or legal positions available in the Philippine Islands. By changing his environment and by plunging into a new job, Norris hoped to solve his financial problems and begin a new existence. Dietrich, however, was unable to aid him, chiefly because Norris knew

no Spanish. The matter was never brought up again, although Dietrich
later helped him get elected to Congress.[8]

In the fall there was politics to absorb and interest him, but the
1901 campaign was not a major one. In August, Norris attended the
Republican State Convention at Lincoln where he met United States
Senator J. H. Millard and other high officials in the party. During the
campaign, he worked for the Republican ticket by conversing with
candidates and voters, but he did not participate in any formal way.
The campaign, despite the dry weather and hot winds, was unexciting,
even for an off-year election. The fusion movement was waning and
Republican candidates easily won the few state-wide posts available.
In the short-grass country the party recaptured county and local offices
from Populist or Democratic incumbents. The lone exception to this
pattern in the Fourteenth Judicial District was in Gosper County where
Populists maintained all but three of the offices at stake in the election [9]

Once the campaign was over and Norris saw how handily the
Republicans won, he rather regretted that he had not become a
candidate for Supreme Court judge. He consoled himself by reflecting
that service on the Supreme Court would have meant working much
harder for the same pay. The only object in seeking such a position,
he mused, would be to enlarge and improve his practice in the future
—since Norris presumed that he would eventually drift back into
private law practice.[10]

Thus as the year 1901 drew to a close George Norris, who had
previously envisioned better things for himself in the new century,
found himself in a rut. Trying to raise three daughters after the sudden
death of his wife, holding court and tending to numerous fraternal and
financial matters, he was active enough. But his expenses were exceeding his income and this worried him. Furthermore, though he found
satisfaction in his work, his children, and his friends, there was something missing; he was not being challenged to the full extent of his
ability. Given his ambition, a larger stage than the Fourteenth Judicial
District was necessary to make full use of his talents and compensate
for the loss of his wife. He had inquired about the possibilities of
judicial or legal work in the Philippine Islands and had regretted that
he did not seek the Supreme Court nomination; now he would have
to bide his time and make sure that he did not let the next opportunity
bypass him.

At least until early in 1902 Norris' life did not markedly differ from
the pattern that it had previously followed. Court sessions kept him
away from home. With his sister's help he was maintaining a home for

his children, although the household did not always run smoothly. Most of the hired girls neglected their chores, and Emma, whose health was not of the best, had to perform their work as well as her own.[11]

The mill at Beaver City was an old problem which he hoped to solve by selling the property. No purchaser appeared and by the summer of 1902 Norris and Shafer were willing to sell it on almost any terms, allowing payments to be made to suit the purchaser. They were anxious to get rid of what they now considered a "white elephant." To add to Norris' anxiety, in January, 1902, there was a fire in Beaver City that burned out nearly all the south side of the square except the Norris Block, which was slightly damaged.[12]

During this period, Norris became interested in the school systems of Beaver City and McCook. He met an attractive McCook teacher, Ella Leonard, and tried unsuccessfully to persuade her to accept a position in the Beaver City schools. In April, 1902, Norris was elected to the McCook School Board, and, seeing Miss Leonard more frequently, he soon began to take a more personal interest in her.[13]

Seeking a greater outlet for his talents and ambitions, Norris, early in 1902, had "practically decided" to seek the Republican congressional nomination. Fletcher Merwin, editor of the Beaver Valley *Tribune* and one of the few persons to whom Norris had confided this decision, was sure that he would win not only the nomination but the election as well.[14] Though only one Republican had been elected from the congressional district since its creation in 1892, and though he had served but a single term, Merwin's optimism was not entirely misplaced. Since 1900 the Republican party had been wresting political power throughout Nebraska from the hands of the Democrats and Populists. W. S. Morlan, who had never held public office and was considered by some to be a tool of the Burlington and Missouri, had been defeated in the congressional campaign in 1900 by less than five hundred votes. With Republicans in control of the national, state, and many county governments, and with Norris' impressive 1899 judicial victory in mind, Merwin had a basis for optimism in his realistic appraisal of the political situation.

Since Morlan had previously let it be known that he did not intend to seek the congressional seat again, Norris now had an opportunity to announce his own candidacy. Merwin agreed to make the initial announcement in the columns of the *Tribune*. Norris, however, requested that Merwin make no mention of Morlan's decision not to run. He believed that other papers would bring this out and that, if the first announcement of his candidacy noted Morlan's decision, it might appear to Morlan's enemies that he was running with Morlan's approval and backing.[15]

Before the story of his candidacy appeared, Norris was busy laying the groundwork for his nomination. He wrote numerous letters to prominent Republicans throughout the eighteen-county congressional district which embraced all of southwestern Nebraska and several southcentral counties. He claimed that he had been urged by "quite a large number of Republicans in different parts of this Congressional District" to enter the race. He said that he would take no offense should any individual oppose his candidacy, but that he preferred to know in advance how his correspondent felt about it. Norris, as in the past, did not wish to engage in a political fight unless he felt reasonably assured of attaining his goal.[16]

As he prepared for the contest, Norris thought he would be the only candidate from the western end of the district and that he would probably have the support of the delegates from the eight counties comprising his judicial district. He requested Judge H. M. Grimes in the Thirteenth Judicial District, a small portion of which was in the Fifth Congressional District, to keep him informed of political sentiment in this area. When Grimes replied that he too was about to enter the congressional race in his district, Norris wrote back, explaining what he believed to be true in his own case as well: "Your judicial district will go with you . . . and with that judicial district at your back I do not believe there will be any difficulty in getting the nomination." [17]

Along with party workers, Norris contacted lawyers and bankers who, through their daily work, usually came in contact with large numbers of people. He concentrated his efforts on his judicial district, convinced that if delegates from these counties went to the convention solidly in his favor, the nomination was assured. He continued through correspondence and courthouse conversations to let as many Republicans as possible know of his candidacy, while claiming that he had no intention of making a personal canvass for delegates. And whenever a correspondent's reply was encouraging, Norris suggested that he talk to the Republicans in his particular precinct and use his influence in securing a delegation favorable to his candidacy. In this way, while maintaining an impassive pose, Norris worked incessantly for the nomination.[18]

Late in March one development made Norris realize he would have to engage in a more vigorous campaign. Morlan came out in favor of State Senator Allen of Furnas County, and, in Frontier County, a

Dr. Andrews announced his interest in obtaining the nomination. By backing both Allen and Andrews, Morlan seemed determined to prevent Norris from receiving the nomination.

Since Morlan was the chief railroad attorney in the area, his opposition could be damaging. It meant that Norris would be unable to obtain passes while his opponents could use them freely. Neither Morlan nor Norris, however, appeared to have the support of the Burlington and Missouri. G. W. Holdrege, its general manager in Nebraska, was supporting a candidate from the eastern end of the congressional district. Despite these developments, Norris did not become unduly pessimistic. He believed in several instances that Morlan had "overdone the matter," and that Morlan's opposition could redound to his favor.[19]

Why Morlan suddenly opposed Norris is not clear. The two had never been close associates and Morlan, in their previous relations, had always been the senior figure. Perhaps Morlan thought that by opposing Norris he could deadlock the convention and, despite his official statement that he did not intend to run, obtain the nomination for a second time. Whatever the reason, Norris knew that Morlan's opposition would be most effective in Furnas and Red Willow counties, where he had considerable prestige and influence among local Republicans.

One aspect of this development was of inestimable benefit to Norris. The fact that the Burlington and Missouri Railroad officials were supporting other candidates meant that he would gain support among farmers and shippers who had grievances with the railroad and harbored increasing resentment against it. Also, the fact that he temporarily lost the ability to obtain transportation for friends and supporters made it easier for him to oppose free passes. He also gained the experience of engaging effectively in politics despite the loss of an important source of patronage, something that would stand him in good stead in later years.

Even with Morlan's help, Allen's candidacy did not make much headway. Only one newspaper, the Arapahoe *Mirror*, supported him. In a widely distributed April issue, it charged, without presenting any details, that Norris had made a "deal" for the purpose of selecting his successor. Norris quickly denied the allegation claiming it was "absolutely groundless and without any reason whatever." He added that if elected to Congress he would take no part in the selection of his successor. In this way Norris was able to keep the support of Republican attorneys who were interested in his judicial position. A statement to this effect was sent to the Beaver Valley *Tribune* and was widely distributed.[20]

By mid-May, before the county conventions met, there were more than a dozen candidates in the field. Norris, however, had a larger following than any other individual. If he received the support of all the delegates from his judicial district he would have fifty-three of the eighty-nine votes necessary for nomination. Allen, backed by Morlan, was his only opposition in the entire judicial district, and Norris did not believe that they could control many delegates.[21]

On May 20 the Furnas County convention met at Beaver City and passed without opposition a resolution instructing the delegates to the congressional convention to support Norris' candidacy. Allen appeared and withdrew his name. The activities of this convention virtually assured that all other county conventions in the judicial district would follow suit. Norris was now convinced he would have the largest number of delegates at the Hastings Convention.[22]

When the convention assembled at Hastings on June 10, every delegate from the eight counties comprising the Fourteenth Judicial District was for George Norris. The other ten counties had instructed their delegates for different candidates. Captain Adams from Superior in Nuckolls County at the extreme eastern end of the congressional district seemed to be his strongest opponent. On the first ballot Norris received seventy-one votes, while his nearest opponent, Adams, had but twenty-nine. On the fifth ballot Norris received the nomination with 122 votes, a large majority. His nomination was not obtained at the expense of party harmony; good feeling prevailed both before and after the convention which one newspaper called "one of the prettiest free-for-all political races ever run in the Fifth congressional district."[23]

Norris was largely successful in maintaining his original posture of having the office seek the man. He accomplished this with a minimum of friction and therefore could count on unified party support in the fall campaign. Further omens that augured well were abundant rainfall (over twenty-one inches, the best rainfall in over a decade), a large wheat crop, and an increasing demand for grain. Thus Norris felt confident of success in November.[24]

Before he could take a well-deserved vacation, he had to organize a congressional committee and get acquainted with party leaders in the eastern end of the congressional district. Norris chose his devoted friend Fletcher Merwin as chairman of the committee, and J. E. Kelley of McCook as secretary. Norris believed one of the officers of the

committee should live in his home town so that there would be no
difficulty in communicating. Indeed, the completed committee contained a representative of each of the eighteen counties in the district,
but only one of its officers came from outside of Norris' judicial district.[25]

With this important task disposed of, Norris, less than ten days
after the Hastings Convention, made a cautious campaign promise
designed to win him support in Hall County, the most populous county
in the Fifth Congressional District. He pledged that if elected he would
direct all of his efforts toward securing funds to erect a federal building in Grand Island, the largest city in the district. The claim of Grand
Island for a public building, Norris said, should take precedence over
that of any other community within the district.[26]

Before the Democrats and Populists held their convention, Norris
had perfected his organization for the hard campaign to come. He had
committed himself to a public building for the largest city in the district. He had contacted individuals who traveled throughout the district in the course of their business and had persuaded them to inform
him of political conditions. He had also prepared a statement and affidavits to send to Republican editors when the need arose, presenting
the facts in regard to the 1895 disputed election.[27] Thus when the
opposition nominated, as expected, the incumbent congressman, A. C.
Shallenberger, Norris was fully prepared to engage in the most difficult
campaign of his budding career, a campaign that would determine
whether he could move on to the larger stage that he sought as an
outlet for his talents and abilities and as a solution to his financial and
personal problems.

Chapter 9

The 1902 Campaign

WITH the nomination safely secured, Norris was compelled by illness to take to his bed and was not fully recovered until the third week in July. He then began setting his political house in order for the campaign.

One of his first statements was that he would assist no candidate in securing his judicial post. If he and the Republican candidate for governor, John H. Mickey, were both elected, Norris pledged to resign his judgeship after Mickey's inauguration, thereby allowing the new governor to name his successor. If the incumbent governor, Ezra P. Savage, were elected, Norris promised to resign on January 1, 1903, thereby allowing Savage to appoint a district judge.[1] By taking this stand on the matter of his successor, Norris hoped to avoid losing the support of aspirants to his post.

In an attempt to anticipate the issue of the disputed 1895 election, Republican newspapers presented their readers with affidavits, notably those written by D. T. Welty, explaining Norris' position. The 1895 election was an old issue and had not been successfully used against him in the past. Norris had no reason to believe that it could be so used at this time.

Early in the campaign, Norris made another decision that helped avoid possible pitfalls. He refused to endorse anyone for a federal position, particularly postmaster candidates. He avoided local political quarrels and disputes and notified all who sought his endorsement that he would make no effort along these lines until after the election.[2] However, Norris could not avoid requests for railroad passes. Burlington officials claimed that during the summer months so many people went off on vacation to the Colorado Rockies they thought it advisable to curtail free transportation. Despite this proscription Norris was able, when he thought it necessary to obtain transportation for individuals who might be of help in his campaign.[3]

The transportation problem became more difficult because some local Republican leaders made commitments which Norris could turn down only at the risk of losing votes. One wrote requesting transportation for a "Catholic pop" who promised to deliver at least six votes "out of his own church." Another made a similar request for a Populist who promised to work among the German farmers in Webster County. This same politician also urged Norris to provide transportation for a Populist saloonkeeper in Red Cloud who could do much good among his Bohemian countrymen. In one instance, a committee member was unable to obtain a pass for a Scandinavian leader in his county and purchased railroad tickets out of his own pocket, explaining that it "wouldn't do to lose him." These free passes represented a commitment which could pay off in votes on election day.[4]

Though Norris later had every reason to be grateful to Senator C. H. Dietrich, and possibly owed his election to the senator's efforts, at the outset he thought Dietrich was indirectly doing him harm. Dietrich desired to remove a deputy revenue collector from his post. Norris thought that such a change during the campaign would be "a very bad political move," since the collector was a Union veteran and a hard worker for the Republican party. Norris asked G. W. Holdrege of the Burlington and Missouri to persuade the senator to retain the official at least until after the election.[5]

If Norris was disturbed or annoyed with Senator Dietrich in this instance, he kept the grievance to himself. He never mentioned it again in his correspondence. And as the campaign progressed he repeatedly sought the senator's services, which were always forthcoming. Matters pertaining to irrigation and postal routes were the two areas where the senator's aid was important. Indeed in the latter area it was crucial.

On June 17, 1902, President Theodore Roosevelt signed into law a bill calling for the reclamation of arid lands in the West. Under its terms the federal government would construct dams and reservoirs for irrigation purposes. Norris was convinced that there was a natural location for a reservoir along the border of Red Willow and Hitchcock counties.[6] He desired to have a dam located there and hoped that the specific site could be agreed upon before election day. He wrote to the secretary of the interior to arouse interest in the plan.

Norris was prompted into action because his opponent, A. C. Shallenberger, claimed that he was the "sole mover and prime originator" of the law and that several projects would soon be located in the district. While Norris doubted his opponent's claims, he nevertheless requested that Senator Dietrich meet with the state engineer and any federal officials who might come to Nebraska and arrange matters so that Congressman Shallenberger would not have them in tow and thereby reap political advantage from their visit.[7]

The senator responded with a valuable suggestion of his own. He asked Norris to have Republicans in the westernmost counties write letters urging Dietrich to secure the location of artesian wells in these counties. Previously Dietrich had held a long conference with F. H. Newell, chief of the newly organized Bureau of Reclamation. Newell informed him it would be easier to recommend the digging of artesian wells if the people themselves requested it. Dietrich added that it would do Norris "a great deal of good" to let voters know that he was aware of their interests.[8] Thus with Dietrich's help Norris was able to obviate the promises of his opponent.

In this matter Norris was on the defensive, trying to neutralize Shallenberger's claims more than anything else. However, in the case of establishing rural postal routes he was able to press a telling advantage. Early in the campaign Senator Dietrich received requests from two towns in the district asking that he hasten the establishment of proposed rural routes. He relayed these requests to the post office authorities for immediate action. In the meantime, Dietrich thought, Norris might get in touch with these postmasters and have the information go out that he was consulting with Dietrich and soon expected to have the matter satisfactorily disposed of.[9] Here was a political weapon that Shallenberger, a Democrat, could not use, while Norris utilized it very effectively.

Senator Dietrich also sent Norris a letter containing two lists of rural routes in the Fifth Congressional District. One list contained routes that had been favorably recommended but were not yet in operation. Norris at his own discretion could tell interested parties that he would consult with Dietrich and insist upon having them put into operation as quickly as possible.

The other list contained routes that had been requested but were not yet inspected and approved. Here, Dietrich suggested, Norris should select those routes he deemed politically beneficial. Then he could inform people that he would urge an early inspection of the proposed rural routes. Through Dietrich's efforts the Post Office Department promised to send a special agent to investigate them. Since these routes had to be approved by officials in Washington, time was of the essence. The routes had to go into operation before election day if Norris were to benefit from the results of having brought them about so quickly.[10]

So impressed was Norris with these vote-getting opportunities that he went further and asked Dietrich if it would be possible to secure star routes for two communities which had requested them. Dietrich immediately wrote the second assistant postmaster general, who issued an advertisement endorsing one of the routes. The route was scheduled to go into operation several weeks before election day.[11]

Dietrich was also able to report by the end of September that favorable action would be taken on the reports that the special agent was filing from the district. In October he suggested that Norris inform the postmasters that official notification would soon be forthcoming. Becoming bolder as he received this news, Norris began mentioning to voters that if he were a congressman rather than merely a candidate, these routes already would have been in operation. Herein was an advantage, he argued, of having a congressman of the same political persuasion as the president.[12]

Thus through Senator Dietrich's efforts, Norris was able to take advantage of a form of federal "pork" that was unavailable to his opponent. In September he sought a more direct type of aid when he wrote the chairman of the National Republican Congressional Committee, J. W. Babcock of Wisconsin, for financial assistance. Babcock responded with a thousand-dollar contribution and several thousand copies of speeches by prominent Republicans. But throughout the campaign Norris made no effort to raise money from federal officials (including postmasters) in the district. It was the custom in Nebraska that these people pay assessments to the state committee and he had no desire to interfere with its work.[13]

Valuable though this aid was, Norris still had to campaign throughout the district in order to wrest the congressional seat from Shallenberger, a tireless and able politician. Moreover, Shallenberger brought Champ Clark of Missouri and other Democratic colleagues into the district while Norris was unable to get a prominent out-of-state Republican to speak on his behalf. Shallenberger boasted of the many bills he had introduced and of other important things he was doing in Washington. Norris noted that the bills had died in committee and argued that a Republican congressman supporting a Republican administration, ably led by President Roosevelt, could do more for the people of the Fifth Congressional District. He also explained that Shallenberger, who claimed to represent the farmers of the district, was really a banker in private life. Norris insisted that he knew more about agriculture and farmers' problems than his opponent. Toward the end of the campaign, he challenged Shallenberger to a cornhusking contest to demonstrate who the real "farmer" candidate was.[14]

Norris concentrated his efforts on the more populous eastern end of the district where he was not widely known and where the large cities, Hastings and Grand Island, were located. Most of his "non-partisan" speeches before gatherings of Odd Fellows and old soldiers in August were in this area, as were a majority of the newly established rural routes. He counted on the support of politicians in the judicial district to turn out the vote while he made himself known elsewhere. Merwin in Beaver City kept Republican newspapers supplied with news about Norris, while his own recently reorganized paper, the Beaver City *Times-Tribune,* loyally supported Norris' cause. However, Norris refused to purchase the support of at least two editors who claimed that they would endorse "the ones who furnished the dough." Fortunately he was able to arrange his judicial duties, with one brief exception, so that he would not hold court until after the election.[15]

Meanwhile, his opponent, "a man of impressive personal appearance, with piercing eyes, handsome features, a fine head set upon an athletic body, and a fine speaking voice," was conducting a relentless campaign.[16] In his speeches he stressed his support of inflationary measures and favored the regulation of trusts. He made much of his sympathy with farmers and of legislative measures designed for their benefit. On the other hand Norris, when discussing national issues, favored reciprocity as well as the protection of the American working-man and the home market. He stood with Roosevelt on the trust question and charged that "Democratic obstructionists" were primarily responsible for their existence. Any indication of his future lack of partisanship could not have been discerned in these campaign speeches. However, his former Populist opponent, Welty, manifested his loss of partisanship by issuing a statement on October 15, 1902, reviewing once again the 1895 election. He observed, "The people know him to be a man whose honesty is unquestioned and whose moral character is unassailable. They will resent as they have done before, regardless of politics, any attempt to injure his fair name or to detract from his well-earned and good reputation." Thus again Norris hoped to benefit from the gradual disintegration that was cracking the alliance between Populists and Democrats. Prosperity, good crops, abundant rainfall, and the careful weaning by politicians of former Republicans out of the fusion fold worked to the advantage of Republican candidates.[17]

After a debate between Norris and Shallenberger at the end of September in Republican City, both candidates and their advisers were so impressed with its possibilities that they agreed to hold a series of five debates commencing October 21. While Norris, unlike Shallenberger, did not have to concern himself with any serious disaffection in party ranks, he was worried lest abundant crops and prosperity, instead of being an asset, boomerang and lead to a disastrous complacency by keeping voters away from the polls. With most farmers behind in their threshing, there was a possibility that on election day, if the weather were good, they would attend to their crops and not to politics.[18]

After the second debate, Norris received an interesting evaluation from a minor Republican officeholder. He commented upon the "masterly way" in which Norris impressed the audience by citing the records of recent Republican administrations. Though the writer was biased, Norris undoubtedly agreed with the validity of his observations:

> Of one thing I am certain and that is that he (Shallenberger) was at all times on the defensive, trying to explain his record and at no time willing to tell how he would do or what he is willing to go on record as standing for.[19]

The writer concluded by observing that Shallenberger would have "to talk fast" and discuss pertinent issues, not bills that died in committee, to convince voters that he should serve another term. This letter and others show that Norris followed the administration on all points when he discussed national issues.

Another observer at this debate thought that Norris' presentation was better than Shallenberger's and that he raised enough questions on the "money matter" and "trust proposition" to cause some Populists to question their alliance with the Democrats.[20] Norris, indeed, was well prepared to meet Shallenberger in public debate. While not a flamboyant and emotional orator, as was his opponent, he impressed an audience by sound sense, logic, and familiarity with his subject. He was not an exciting speaker, but he gave the impression of an industrious and capable candidate who as a congressman would fully devote himself to the interests of his constituents. In short, the air of inherent or natural dignity which had aided him in his judicial campaigns served Norris equally well in this campaign.

However, Norris, who was downcast after the first three debates owing to the vocal support manifested for his opponent, lost his dignity and possibly his temper in the last two debates, including the one at McCook. He attacked Shallenberger in a most vindictive way, claiming he was practicing deception by masquerading as a friend of the farmer. He ridiculed Shallenberger and his family banking and business connections and pointed with pride to his own farm background and ability. It was in this connection that he challenged Shallenberger to a corn husking contest.[21]

On election day, Tuesday, November 4, 1902, the candidates, worn out by campaigning, impatiently awaited the first returns. However, the party organizations still had important jobs to perform. Helpers with wagons provided transportation to the polls; others engaged in last-minute attempts to obtain votes. Farmers busily threshing wheat had to be convinced that it was important for them to quit their fields. George Allen, an astute local politician, predicted that Norris would carry Clay County by two hundred or more votes (Norris' majority in that county was 184) and assured the candidate that though party officials in Lincoln had some doubts about Norris' ability to carry the Fifth Congressional District, he had none.[22] And Allen was correct.

Republican candidates were elected in almost every contest in the 1902 election. Mickey was elected governor by over five thousand votes, while the average Republican majority on the remainder of the state ticket was a little over thirteen thousand. All Republican candidates for Congress were elected, except in the Second District where incumbent David H. Mercer was defeated by Gilbert M. Hitchcock, publisher of the Omaha *World Herald.* In the Fifth District the vote was very close; Norris won with a precarious majority of 181 votes, receiving 14,927 to 14,746 for Shallenberger, Democrat and Populist, and 496 for John D. Stoddard, Prohibitionist.[23]

Once the results were known, pandemonium prevailed among Norris' supporters. "In 1895," wrote one, "you redeemed the Fourteenth Judicial District from Populism. Now you have restored the Fifth Congressional District." While Mickey ran ahead of Norris in most counties, Norris did much better than Morlan had done two years before. Nebraska's United States senators sent a joint congratulatory telegram proclaiming "the complete triumph for Republican principles in Districts heretofore dominated by Fusionists." Nebraska was now fully redeemed from "the Pernicious Principles of Populism and the Foolish Fraud of Fusionism," and Norris played an important role in its redemption.[24]

Norris now had to attend to many details emanating from the campaign. Merwin, who had not put in a bill for his expenses, had to be paid. He informed Norris, "There are several fellows who want something." He asked only one personal favor and that was for a railroad pass for "a tip-top good fellow" who had done some hard work among a colony of farmers.[25]

Another politician informed Norris that he had dealt with an individual who worked with him in a Bohemian settlement. He gave him the railroad pass Norris sent "and settled with him otherwise." This worker had relied on similar individuals to get out the vote; some he paid at the time and others he promised to pay after the election. His total expenses came to about two hundred dollars and included such items as hiring teams from local livery stables, advertising, hiring a band, and sending telephone messages.[26]

Thus Norris in his first campaign for national office was able to achieve a narrow but impressive victory and become the second Republican to represent the Fifth Congressional District. Improved agricultural conditions, adequate rainfall, and the generally prosperous state of the union helped to lay the groundwork for his victory,[27] as did the gradual weakening of the bonds that had held the Populist-Democratic alliance together. Above this foundation was a superstructure that included the federal aid Senator Dietrich was able to mobilize, adequate financial support from the Republican party, and the personal popularity of President Roosevelt to whose wagon Norris hitched his political star. Finally, the most significant factor was Norris himself—his personal popularity, his ability as a campaigner, his usual appearance of dignified judicial calmness in his black suit, white shirt, and black string tie, plus his devoted supporters who gave unstintingly of their time, energy, and money. Together they helped to eke out the less than two-hundred vote majority. Victory opened new horizons for forty-one-year-old George Norris. It also brought new responsibilities as well as many trivial but politically important details.

Chapter 10

Congressman-Elect

SINCE the Fifty-eighth Congress would not convene until November, 1903, Norris had a year to wait before taking a seat in the House of Representatives. The year emerged as one of the most eventful in his life, a period of endings and of new beginnings in both his private and public life. The most obvious change that occurred in the congressman-elect was in his physical appearance. When he appeared at the bar of the House in November, 1903, Norris sported a weeping-willow mustache; the beard was gone and his hair was now heavily tinged with grey. Behind the noticeable change in his appearance lay the events, some tragic and others happy, of the year of waiting by the newly elected congressman from the Fifth District of Nebraska.

After the election, Norris had the leisure to look after his personal affairs. Most nagging was the long-standing problem of the mill at Beaver City. In July, 1902, the dam to the mill was washed out by floodwaters on Beaver Creek and a new one had to be installed. In September the partners thought they had a buyer, but he had very little cash, and they did not want to sell the mill on time unless some security was given. Negotiations were also made with other potential purchasers in Pennsylvania and Iowa, but none proved satisfactory. Finally in the spring of 1903, an agreement was worked out with George E. Hotchkills of Loup City, Nebraska, whereby he paid the partners $1,000 in cash and gave them a mortgage for the balance, amounting to $4,000. Before the final details were completed, Hotchkills came to Beaver City and was operating the mill.

Both partners knew the mill property was worth more than $5,000, but neither Norris nor Shafer was a miller. Norris was no longer a resident of Beaver City and Shafer did not care to look after its over-all operation. Furthermore the partners had been unfortunate in their experience of renting the mill. They had found that as a rule the lessee, when his term was about to expire, let the property run down. This usually meant that Norris and Shafer had to devote time and energy to redeeming the good name of the mill. Therefore they decided to

79

sacrifice to make the sale. Thus, after thirteen years, Norris was finally free of this property which had caused him irritation and annoyance and which he never really wanted.[1]

Norris' real estate also needed tending. Fults and Hopping continued to look after his property in Beaver City. Occasionally Norris asked Merwin to perform a chore for him in this connection. Norris' relationship with these men was informal and friendly. Neither Fults, a lawyer, nor Hopping, a druggist, derived his livelihood from this work. They helped Norris more from friendship than for anything else. Both men continued this arrangement after he moved to Washington, D.C.[2]

During the campaign Norris was not pressed or embarrassed for want of money. He was able to give twenty-five dollars to the Odd Fellows Home Fund, though this contribution no doubt had political overtones. In October he promptly paid the premiums on two large insurance policies which totaled almost five hundred dollars. After the election Norris found, too, that he could afford to remodel his home in McCook and take his first real vacation, albeit a short one, since the death of his wife. He took a trip into Colorado and possibly New Mexico. Though his financial condition was satisfactory, he still found it necessary to request payment from people who owed him money.[3]

Norris also began to again take a more active interest in McCook affairs. In September, 1902, a public library had been opened. It was housed in the basement of the Red Willow County Courthouse where Norris held court and maintained a judicial chamber. From this vantage point he had ample opportunity to observe the large numbers of people using the library. He wrote to Andrew Carnegie the following June, requesting a donation for the erection of a separate building in the city. Eventually Carnegie did contribute and McCook today boasts a handsome public library building.[4]

Besides his personal business affairs and his emerging role as a public figure of consequence in the short-grass country, Norris was plagued all through the campaign with a health problem. Since his teeth were extraordinarily sensitive, he sought a dentist who could drill them without pain. In December, before leaving on vacation, he wrote to Dr. H. C. Miller, a dentist and also postmaster of Grand Island, inquiring whether Miller could care for teeth in a painless way and, if so, whether he could arrange an appointment. Two weeks later, Dr. Miller assured Norris that he could treat his teeth without undue pain.[5]

Norris, delighted at finding such a dentist, went to Grand Island late in April. For nine consecutive days Dr. Miller fixed his teeth, afterward claiming that it was "the largest and most severe operation" he had ever performed at one time. At the end of the eighth day Norris was taken with chills followed by fever. In spite of this he had the work completed the following day and was consumed with a fever while in the chair. Miller's fee was $125.[6]

Theodore Roosevelt arrived in Grand Island at this time and Norris appeared with him despite his illness. As soon as Norris returned to McCook, he become much more seriously ill, took to his bed, and almost died from blood poisoning and other complications. He was dangerously ill for over three weeks and did not fully recover for several months. In addition to blood poisoning, he suffered from nervous prostration and was very weak and debilitated. Fletcher Merwin came to look after him and quickly sent for Doctor C. C. Green of Beaver City. The doctors were afraid that the infection would reach the brain, in which case "the termination would have been fatal and sudden." Fortunately the blood poisoning was arrested and on May 18, 1903, Merwin wrote, "We consider Judge Norris now out of all danger." [7]

With his nervous system seemingly shattered, Norris, though he was out of immediate danger by the end of May, was still a very sick man. Microscopic examination indicated kidney trouble, though the doctors thought this to be only temporary. Norris took various tonic prescriptions to regain his strength and equilibrium, and was told by doctors and friends to get adequate rest, sunshine, and care. Dr. Green suggested that he give up smoking, and Norris did not object. At the end of May, Dr. Green announced that his patient had no need of more medicine and that, if he did not overexert himself, he would be well on the way to a complete recovery.[8]

From all over the state came letters inquiring about Norris' illness.[9] Governor Mickey requested Merwin to convey his hope for a rapid recovery and suggested that Norris, when able, call upon him in Lincoln. Merwin, who remained with Norris in McCook, handled most of the correspondence and kept the patient abreast of political developments. By June 4, Norris was again handling his own mail and informing correspondents that he expected to leave for a long Wisconsin vacation at Delavan Lake as soon as he regained a bit more strength.[10]

In his correspondence he told no one the secret which he must have divulged to those who cared for him during his illness—that he planned to be married before going to Wisconsin. After the death of Pluma in 1901, Norris, with three young children to look after and an intensive political campaign to wage, certainly had little time for romance. Yet it was obvious that he eventually would remarry, since he was desperately in need of companionship, a helpmate, and a mother for his girls. That he was considered a most eligible bachelor is evident from correspondence with a young lady in Lincoln who signed her letters "Jeanette," and of whom very little is known. She invited him to several occasions in Lincoln and, although it is not known whether he attended these particular events, it is certain that they saw each other several times. That Norris was not romantically interested in her is indicated by the fact that he did not tell her of his illness. From her letters she appears to have been much too flighty and too deeply involved in the doings of Lincoln society to suit Norris' tastes.[11]

However, Norris was becoming romantically interested in the McCook schoolteacher Ellie Leonard, who knew the first Mrs. Norris. Miss Leonard was well liked by her students in McCook, and after Pluma's death, Norris began to notice her in more than a casual way. In March, before his visit to Dr. Miller, Norris wrote A. J. Green, a watchmaker and optician, about purchasing a ring. Thus they may have considered announcing their engagement before his illness.[12] Possibly his illness and convalescence, when Miss Leonard was undoubtedly on hand often, led them to fix a wedding date.

Contemplating remarriage two years after Pluma's death must have caused Norris some trying moments. In March, at the same time he was purchasing a ring, he was also completing arrangements for the erection of a monument on his lot in the McCook cemetery. Also in March he received word that his eldest sister Lorinda, at whose home he had enjoyed such pleasant times while teaching school in Ohio, had died. He must have undergone great emotional confusion and upheaval during this period.

After the school term ended, Miss Leonard returned to her parents' home in San Jose, California, and Norris, announcing his intention of vacationing in Wisconsin, left at the end of June for the Pacific Coast. In the home of Ellie's parents, on July 8, 1903, Ellie Leonard and George Norris were married.[13]

Their Wisconsin honeymoon gave Norris a chance to recover his strength and to introduce his L.U.N. friends to his new wife when they gathered for the annual reunion. During this reunion one decision was made which pleasurably affected the L.U.N. members and their families for the rest of their lives. They decided, chiefly upon Norris' investigation and prodding, to purchase an island in Rainbow Lake where members might build cottages and where the annual meetings would henceforth be held. Only four members, including Norris, felt they were able to contribute toward the $950.00 asked for the island. The price seemed a small consideration for such a wonderful site.[14]

Rainbow Lake, a perfect vacation setting, is one of a chain of twenty-three lakes southwest of Waupaca, Wisconsin. Its clear waters still attract fishermen seeking pickerel, bass, trout, and other varieties. The entire chain, spring-fed, cold, and clear, is set in deep hollows between low rounded hills. The lakes offered opportunities for rest, relaxation, and escape from intense summer heat, and Norris came to cherish his days there as the years went by. With the purchase of the island the problem of annual meetings and vacations was forever solved for Norris and his fellow L.U.N. agitators from the old days at Valparaiso.

Meanwhile most of the friends of George and Ellie Norris read of the marriage in the McCook paper, where a brief announcement appeared. After Norris' departure for California, neither Merwin nor Norris' children, who remained in McCook with their aunt, knew his exact whereabouts. After this marriage, Norris wrote, "There came into my home . . . a real mother to my motherless children." Once again his family circle was complete and his children quickly came to love Ellie as their new mother. Indeed she soon became for these youngsters the only mother they knew, and, as Norris later wrote, "Never was there a more considerate or more tender hearted, loving mother." [15]

September found Norris and his bride back in McCook redecorating the house to suit the taste of its new mistress. Norris at this time also indulged himself and bought a fine bound set of the collected works of one of his youthful heroes, Robert W. Ingersoll, the famed Republican orator and agnostic.[16] But most important of all, the return to McCook brought with it preparations for a new life in Washington, D.C.

Not that Norris had neglected to prepare for his new role. Since the election he had been attending to political matters. One of the first things he had to consider was resigning as a district judge. He had promised not to recommend any candidate, but to allow a Republican governor to appoint whomever he desired. Norris kept this pledge in good faith. When, after the election, Governor-elect John Mickey asked him about a successor, he refused to express any choice and wrote to the governor restating his position.[17]

His first official action as a newly elected congressman was to support, along with the other Republican members of the Nebraska congressional delegation, the candidacy of Joseph G. Cannon of Illinois for the speakership of the House of Representatives. Cannon wrote him a grateful personal note, claiming that his help, along with that of the delegation, went far toward settling the contest. Norris showed no trace of independence in this matter, since Joseph W. Babcock of Wisconsin was also seeking this position, and Norris had good reason to be grateful to him. As chairman of the 1902 Congressional Campaign Committee, Babcock had helped him with funds and literature.[18]

With the defeat of Congressman Mercer in the Second District a position on the Committee on Public Grounds and Buildings became vacant. Senator Dietrich advised Norris to put in a request for this vacancy "as quickly as possible" to Speaker Cannon. Since First District Congressman Elmer Burkett was a member of the Appropriations Committee, Dietrich thought it essential that Norris secure this position to retain for the state of Nebraska membership on key committees, thereby maintaining its influence in Congress.[19] Norris made every effort to obtain it.

At this time he was unaware of any cleavages within his party. Indeed, as a freshman congressman, he was more interested in securing favorable committee assignments than in anything else, desiring above all an appointment to the Committee on Public Lands and Buildings. But as a newly elected congressman, he did not consider it wise to ask directly for the position. He therefore let Dietrich and Burkett know of his desire and requested that they discuss the matter with the new speaker before he approached Cannon.[20]

In February of 1903 Norris made a brief trip to Washington, where he talked to Cannon about service on this committee. The Speaker asked Norris to contact him again some time before the convening of Congress. When Norris later wrote to Cannon he presented his case in a way that undoubtedly appealed to the politically astute Speaker. He noted that all the other Nebraska districts that had elected Republicans to Congress had done so by large majorities, that he had been elected by a majority of only 181 votes and was the only Republican, "with one exception," who had represented the district since the advent of the Populist party. Furthermore, Norris suggested the necessity of an appropriation for a public building at Grand Island if the district were to remain in the Republican fold. This goal could best be achieved, he argued, by his serving on the Public Lands and Buildings Committee. By way of conclusion he frankly stated to the Speaker:

> There is no doubt but that the appropriation by Congress of money for the building of a public building at Grand Island would make my re-election sure, and while it is of no particular importance to the country or the Republican Party that I should be

returned any more than any other person, yet it is of considerable importance that a Republican should be elected in this district, which I think could be easily secured if this one matter were attended to. I think these matters have, perhaps, been brought to your attention by the senators from this state, and while I do not want, in any way, to embarrass you in your difficult task, still I sincerely hope you may be able to give the matter consideration which I believe it deserves, and decide it as you may think best under all the circumstances.[21]

Norris also requested information about his new duties from Charles F. Manderson, former U.S. senator (1883–95), and now chief attorney of the Burlington and Missouri Railroad in Nebraska. He confessed his ignorance of the customs, rules, and regulations of the Congress and hoped that Manderson would aid him in learning about these subjects. He told Manderson of his desire to serve on the Committee on Public Lands and Buildings and hoped that the ex-senator could be of assistance in this matter.[22] Thus Congressman-elect Norris did his best before he went to Washington to put himself in good standing with the Burlington Railroad and the Republican organization, two of the most powerful agencies in the political structure of the state.

Another important task which faced Norris at this time was that of securing the services of a competent secretary who knew the district and could keep him abreast of local developments. For this difficult job Norris wanted Merwin, who had served as chairman of his congressional committee in the recent campaign. After the election he had presented Merwin with a typewriter and a desk as a token of gratitude and soon thereafter tried to convince him to take the job. Merwin, who wanted to remain in Beaver City and edit his paper, claimed that he could not live on the salary, though he recognized that service in Washington would provide valuable experience for a newspaper editor.

Norris suggested that Merwin serve as his secretary only when Congress was in session and continue to write for his paper when in Washington. With slight modifications Merwin agreed to the plan, and Norris obtained the competent services of a seasoned political observer and a personal friend.[23]

Even though the Fifty-eighth Congress was scheduled to convene at the end of 1903, Norris' service as a member of Congress actually started the day after election when district patronage problems were literally thrust in his lap. The request for free transportation was a familiar one. But other patronage matters—primarily concerning pensions and postmasters—were new, and he set about familiarizing himself with them. Soon after his election he wrote the commissioner of pensions requesting information about the rules and regulations pertaining to the work of the bureau.[24]

In the matter of postmasters he had much more work to do. First he had to determine the politics of all the postmasters in the district, since not all were Republicans. Then there was the matter of rural routes, the granting of which had been so helpful in the campaign. By the end of 1902 Norris was explaining to irate citizens that work on rural routes had been suspended owing to a small appropriation and that nothing could be done until more money was granted by Congress. He wrote to officials in the Post Office Department requesting that the twenty-six approved rural routes in the district be put into operation and that the petitioned routes be acted upon as quickly as possible.[25]

Finally, before his departure for Washington, Norris participated in a sensational murder trial that brought him to the attention of citizens throughout Nebraska. In March, 1903, he agreed to assist the prosecuting attorney of Frontier County in stating the case for the family of the victim, a young girl named Tracy Puls, and in trying to prove that her death was caused by a bullet and bruises inflicted by one Charles Frymire.

The case came to trial in October, laden with political significance. Congressman Norris was assisting Prosecuting Attorney L. H. Cheney, while the defense was represented by J. L. White, the fusion candidate for district judge in an election that was a month away. Presiding in the courtroom was Judge R. C. Orr, appointed by Governor Mickey to fill out Norris' unexpired term, and now seeking the office in his own right. Attorney White brought these implications before the court while presenting the defense's side. He warned the jury in a harangue that lasted more than an hour that they should not be swayed "by the silent, secret influence that would be present in the prosecution of the case in the person of Congressman Norris." [26]

In presenting the case against Frymire, Norris recounted the details, including the little known fact that "Tracy Puls gave premature birth to a child of five or six months gestation, the child of Charles Frymire and that the premature birth was caused by the bullet wound in the wall of the uterus or womb." The jury returned a verdict of manslaughter, and Judge Orr sentenced Frymire to ten years at hard labor. Throughout his term he was to be placed in solitary confinement on each February 1, the anniversary of Tracy Puls' death.[27] Norris' part in this dramatic case served as a farewell before his departure for Washington to start his career as a congressman.

On November 9, 1903, George Norris, in a neatly pressed black suit, stiff white shirt and collar, and black string tie, appeared before the bar of the House of Representatives and took the oath of office. His grey hair and his neatly trimmed weeping-willow mustache added to his serious demeanor and gave increased maturity to his forty-two years. The oath was administered at the opening of a special session of the Fifty-eighth Congress. At this time he officially learned that newly elected Speaker Cannon had been most generous in his committee assignments, giving Norris the coveted place on the Committee on Public Grounds and Buildings, as well as an assignment to the Committee on Election of President, Vice-President and Representatives. Thus George Norris, the new Republican congressman from the Fifth District of Nebraska, at last had arrived on the national scene and now would have the opportunity to put his talents to the test on a broader scale than ever before.

Chapter 11

Congressman Norris

As a FRESHMAN in Congress, assigned a seat in the rear of the chamber, Norris had to worry about getting re-elected almost before he could learn the rules and procedures of the House of Representatives. Congressman Wesley L. Jones of Washington, whose seat was next to Norris, guided him whenever possible and quickly disillusioned him about the statesmanship of Joseph W. Babcock, of whom Norris had thought highly. Norris was amazed to learn that Babcock's wonderful orations had never been delivered but were merely inserted into the *Congressional Record*.[1]

Equally amazing to the new member was the knowledge that no bill could be discussed on the floor unless the Speaker, as Chairman of the Rules Committee, gave his approval. When Chairman Charles W. Gillet of Massachusetts called the Committee on Public Grounds and Buildings together, the group discussed the possibility of drafting and presenting an omnibus building bill. The senior Democratic member of the committee, John H. Bankhead of Alabama, presented a motion, which carried unanimously, that the chairman seek a conference with the Speaker and ascertain if the committee could introduce a public building bill.[2]

As a freshman member, Norris, of course, had no illusions about what he would be able to accomplish. However, with the country relatively prosperous, and with the virtual assurance of federal funds spent in the district through an omnibus building bill, Norris believed his constituents would be satisfied and contented enough to reward him with another term in Congress. He had no reason to speak, let alone to challenge his party; yet that is exactly what he did when he rose on June 13, 1904, "with no little embarrassment and some hesitancy . . . to say a word or two in favor of the Civil Service Commission and the civil-service law." [3]

President Theodore Roosevelt on November 17, 1903, had changed the removal rule giving the president and department heads greater discretion and power to remove incompetent employees. At least one member of the Civil Service Commission doubted that this change was an improvement.[4] And those members of Congress who were not in sympathy with the merit system began an attack on the civil-service system. Previously, in the Fifty-seventh Congress, the Civil Service Commission had been criticized after an effective investigation of post office scandals aroused spoilsmen in both parties. Norris, by defending the Civil Service in his maiden speech, sided with the president against the standpatters in his party. Repeal the law, Norris concluded, "and you put on the bargain counter of partisan politics the appointment of all the officers under the Government." [5]

If his first speech in Congress de-emphasized partisanship and was indicative of his later career, his only other extensive statements on the floor were intensely partisan. They were devoted to lambasting the Democrats for their continual opposition to rural free delivery. This speech is significant because it revealed an aspect of Norris that was inherent in his background and which remained with him throughout his life. It is summed up by the following sentence, delivered at the close of the address: "It is at the rural fireside that virtue, morality, and patriotism have reached their highest state." [6]

That the rural life represented the "good life" and that the city was the source of crime, disease, disloyalty, and anarchy was an attitude that prevailed throughout nineteenth-century rural America. Indeed it lingered on in the new century. Norris expressed it here in order to cast aspersions on the Democrats for their opposition to rural free delivery, but he firmly believed that he was voicing a fundamental truth when he uttered it. This partisan speech represented Norris' major oratorical effort in his first term as a congressman. But before the session ended, he was focusing on Nebraska politics and his campaign for re-election.[7]

He returned to Nebraska at the end of the session confident that the voters would approve his service in Congress. He returned as he had left, a partisan Republican and a devoted supporter of Roosevelt, seeing no incompatibility in these two positions. He also returned with as much of Speaker Cannon's approval as did any other freshman in Congress.[8]

The 1904 Republican Congressional Convention for the Fifth District was scheduled to convene at Hastings on May 12. Thus before Norris returned to Nebraska many chairmen had called county conventions and had already chosen delegates favorable to his renomination. When the Hastings convention met, Norris was renominated by acclamation, though the Hastings *Daily Republican* claimed there were two dissenting votes.[9]

With the nomination safely secured, Norris was able to observe national political developments before he launched his campaign. Because he could not afford a trip to the Republican National Convention in Chicago, he refused the invitations of Congressman James R. Mann and of an old friend of his to be their guest during the convention. He thought that the Republican convention would "prove to be a tame show, as compared with the three ringed circus at St. Louis" where Bryan had pledged a battle to keep control of the Democratic party.[10]

As Norris predicted, the Chicago convention, which on June 23 nominated Roosevelt and Senator Charles W. Fairbanks of Indiana, was a tame show. The Democratic convention witnessed the return to power of more conservative eastern leaders. Bryan lost control, and a New York judge, Alton B. Parker, who favored the gold standard, received the nomination. Parker's nomination left many devoted supporters of Bryan in the Democratic and especially in the Populist party in Nebraska and elsewhere with no choice but to vote for Roosevelt, who was closer to Bryan in his views than was Parker.[11]

The nomination of Judge Parker hastened the demise of the Populist party in Nebraska. The party had been so greatly reduced in membership that the basis of representation to the convention that chose the delegation to the Populist National Convention in Springfield, Illinois, was one delegate for each two hundred votes cast for Weaver in 1892. As one Nebraska editor remarked at this time, "The Populist party has reached the point where it is nothing with fusion and nothing without it." [12]

If the Populist party in Nebraska was in the process of deteriorating, the Democratic party, owing to Bryan's loss of control at St. Louis, was in a weakened position. Thus Populist candidates were able to dominate the fusion process. And strong Democratic campaigners, like A. C. Shallenberger in the Fifth District, decided not to participate in the election. They feared that Roosevelt would pull to victory the weaker members on the Republican ticket.

Populist ideas, after years of agitation, had gradually penetrated the Republican party hierarchy. Many of the leaders in Nebraska and on the national scene now accepted the view that government would have to play a larger role in promoting the general welfare. Certainly in 1904 the Republican party appeared as the more liberal of the major parties. And many a former Bryan supporter now made his way into the party and became a devoted follower of Roosevelt. These developments redounded to the benefit of Norris and numerous other Republican nominees.

One aspect of the campaign in Nebraska no doubt disturbed

Norris. This was the fact that Senator Dietrich, who had been so instrumental in his first campaign, did not receive party support for a second term. He had become a liability because he secured the removal of the Hastings post office into a building that he owned. Furthermore, it also became known that he had collected a salary as governor while he was already serving as United States senator.[13] Congressman Burkett of the First District received the Republican endorsement. Railroad opposition to Burkett helped to convince many voters that the Republican party was now following Roosevelt's brand of progressivism.

Norris conducted the early part of his campaign, as in 1902, by speaking before various nonpartisan groups. By midsummer local leaders were optimistic and their enthusiasm was quickly communicated to the candidate. With the lack of cooperation between Populist and Democratic state organizations, with Alton B. Parker heading the Democratic ticket and Theodore Roosevelt leading the Republicans, with abundant crops, adequate rainfall, and good prices making for a satisfied farm population, Republican leaders in Nebraska certainly had good reason for optimism.[14]

George Allen, Norris' campaign manager, worked long and hard. He arranged transportation for individuals who might be able to get votes, contacted editors throughout the district, arranged to collect funds from the postmasters, and visited disgruntled Republicans, remedying their grievances wherever possible. He also made surreptitious efforts to appeal to rank and file members of the opposition, who were ready to reject fusion. He noted, "They could fuse when Bryan was in the lead as he stood for many things that the Pops did or at least pretended to and they could follow him with very good grace, but Parker being antagonistic to everything that the Pops advocated— why it simply deadens the whole deal." In addition to these activities, Allen, a veteran, visited old soldiers and spoke in favor of Norris.[15]

The Democrats and Populists held their congressional conventions at Hastings on August 24, and soon Norris learned that his opponent would be H. H. Mauck. Shallenberger had been offered the nomination of both parties, but declined. Mauck literally had obtained the nomination through default; none of the other fusion leaders desired it. As a result, most observers believed that it would be "practically impossible" to defeat Norris.[16]

By mid-September there were four candidates seeking to represent the Fifth Congressional District in Washington, a Socialist and a Prohibitionist candidate having been chosen by their respective party conventions. The appearance of these two new candidates meant further difficulties for the fusionists as some former Populists would be attracted to both of these reform candidates. While the Republicans would gain some fusion votes, very few of their supporters would be attracted by either of the new candidates. Their appearance further improved Norris' position, and led his manager to believe, "We will catch them coming and going." [17]

Norris and his supporters were certain of ultimate victory when it became evident that Harry Mauck was a most uninspiring campaigner. He aroused little of the enthusiasm and attracted none of the crowds that Shallenberger had. Furthermore, Norris learned that Congressman Babcock, chairman of the Congressional Campaign Committee, considered Norris' race one of the closest in the nation and was determined to carry it on election day. With this end in mind, Speaker Cannon agreed to speak in the district for three days at the end of September. [18]

By mid-October Norris already had stumped throughout the district, speaking six days a week and appearing in a different community every day. Occasionally he spoke in two or more villages on the same day. In the last weeks of the campaign, Allen traveled with Norris, briefing him on local situations and introducing him to leading citizens in the eastern end of the district, which Allen knew better than Norris. Allen thought the crowds were good and that Norris spoke very well, even though the weather at the end of October was far from satisfactory for campaign purposes. Norris, in his speeches, stressed the point that those who went into the Populist movement in good faith could not conscientiously support Parker and the Democratic ticket in 1904. [19]

Despite lack of widespread editorial support and notwithstanding his colorless personality, Harry Mauck, through the efforts of his manager, waged a vigorous campaign by hurling numerous irresponsible charges at his opponent. And in the week before election Shallenberger took the stump with Mauck. As a last-ditch effort to stave off defeat, the Democratic National Committee contributed five hundred dollars to his campaign, and Bryan came to speak on Mauck's behalf. Norris heard that Bryan attracted large crowds but generated little enthusiasm. Bryan did not touch on national issues and made no mention of Parker or Roosevelt in his speeches. So confident was Allen of victory that he did not plan to spend election eve with Norris. Even Merwin, much more cautious than Allen, predicted victory. And Norris himself had no reason on election eve to doubt his chances. [20]

On election day, November 8, 1904, the Republican ticket won an overwhelming victory. Roosevelt had 336 electoral votes and a plurality of more than two and a half million votes. Republican candidates won all major offices in Nebraska. All six candidates for Congress defeated their fusion opponents and Congressman Burkett was assured of a Senate seat by polling 107,595 votes in the preferential primary. George Norris in the Fifth Congressional District received a majority of more than five thousand, polling 19,645 votes. Not a single county in Nebraska cast its vote for Parker, nor did Norris lose a single county in his district. In Perkins, one of the remote and thinly settled counties, the vote was a tie, standing 161 for each candidate. A prominent Nebraska historian commenting on the campaign wrote, "The final figures in the nation announced the death of the People's party and foreshadowed the return of Mr. Bryan as leader of the Democrats." [21]

Norris, delighted with this splendid victory, in contrast to his 181-vote plurality in 1902, claimed that aside from the president, Speaker Cannon deserved credit for the "land-slide" election results. He believed that Cannon's "able, honest and wise administration" of his position had been "one of the great elements" in the national Republican triumph. Norris wrote the Speaker, "Your position is the second one in the nation, and the confidence that all have in you has made many votes for the Republican ticket all over our country, because it has been recognized that Republican success meant the retention of yourself in that high and honorable position." Grateful to Cannon for his visit during the campaign, Norris assured the Speaker that if in his humble way he could help advance Cannon's interests he would find it an "extreme pleasure" to do so.[22]

After the election Norris had almost no time to relax before returning to Washington for the third and lame duck session of the Fifty-eighth Congress, scheduled to convene on December 5, 1904. This time Norris planned to bring his wife and three children with him. He hoped to be in Washington by the first of December, to get his family settled and the older girls, Hazel and Marian, registered in a public school before Speaker Cannon brought the House of Representatives to order.[23]

The third session of the Fifty-eighth Congress started in a most disagreeable way for the re-elected gentleman from Nebraska. Washington weather was damp and cold and soon his entire family was sick. Norris also found that his official duties involved much harder work. Merwin, who was on hand to aid him, noted at the end of January, "The Judge is mighty busy with affairs of state." Norris summarized the situation more succinctly when he remarked, "I have had my hands full." [24]

Work on the Committee on Public Lands and Buildings consumed much time. Norris was a member of the subcommittee which was considering the erection of public buildings. The subcommittee, after reviewing the Nebraska situation, recommended two buildings, at Grand Island and at York, and three sites for buildings. Within a month the House appropriated $100,000 for a public building at Grand Island. Thus Norris fulfilled a 1902 campaign pledge even though the bill ultimately was enacted into law without this item included.[25]

During this session he also showed for the first time an interest in improving the processes of government by amending the Constitution. Though House Joint Resolution 166 died in committee, his concern with it did not. The resolution provided for a national election every four years, at which time all of the members of the House of Representatives and one-half of the Senate, one member from each state, would be elected directly by the people. Every eight years there would be a presidential election. The great reform in this resolution, Norris thought, would be the election of senators by the people, though the other changes seemed equally important to him. Since his resolution lengthened the term of senators by two years, he thought it might receive favorable consideration by that body. The lower house, Norris realized, would undoubtedly agree to any resolution which doubled the term of its members, while a single eight-year term for the chief executive could readily be defended.[26]

Though he was investigating national and constitutional issues, Norris voted with his party on all major pieces of legislation and devoted most of his time to the affairs of his district. The appropriation for a federal building helped him as did his concern for Union veterans and their pensions. Since Congress was in no mood to benefit a dwindling segment of the population, many of whom were already being cared for at public expense, Norris actually could do little to aid dependent veterans. Nevertheless, he "stood ready to support any measure" which would serve to treat with more liberality and consideration these "brave and noble boys." [27]

Moreover, Norris was faced with the loss of potent patronage in his home town. In 1904 an agent of the Department of the Interior conducted an investigation of the McCook land office and shortly thereafter it was closed. The work of the McCook office, it was announced, would be included in the Lincoln land district, comprising southern and southeastern Nebraska.[28]

Sentiment in McCook was against the removal of the office. Many citizens were disposed to hold their congressman responsible. Residents having business at the land office would now have to travel to Lincoln, at the other end of the state. People were also charging that the deeds to available government lands now could be placed within easier reach of the railroads and "that crowd of grafters and swindlers," and were now beyond the reach of the people. The land office had been located in McCook since 1882, and while some citizens realized it was only a question of time before it would be closed, few were willing to admit that the time had come.[29]

Norris, realizing that the loss of the McCook land office could counteract popularity he would gain from the Grand Island federal building, set out to explain the government's policy in this matter. He claimed that its closing was legal, that other land offices were being discontinued, and that it was the intention of the Department of the Interior eventually to cancel all the Nebraska land offices except the one at Lincoln. Whether this explanation soothed aroused citizens, Norris was not able to discern. Fortunately the closing came almost immediately after the 1904 election, so that it would not be a burning issue in the next congressional campaign.[30]

Thus most of Norris' activities in the Fifty-eighth Congress were routine and pertained largely to the affairs of his district. He concentrated, as every congressman must, on serving constituents. As a freshman, however, he did speak several times on matters of more than local or sectional interest, and was becoming interested in improving the processes of government by making it more democratic and responsible. He performed his job conscientiously and may have worked harder than most members. He was in the good graces of Speaker Cannon and accepted as well the leadership and policies of Roosevelt. There was little to indicate in his first term that he would later lead the insurgency movement in the House of Representatives. It was only when the party's executive leadership broke down and senior members in Congress tried to assume it that Norris emerged as an outstanding figure.

When the lame duck session came to an end in March, 1905, Norris, his family, and his secretary were glad to return to Nebraska. They may have witnessed Roosevelt's inauguration, but, since the Norrises were not interested in participating in Washington society, it is doubtful that they attended the evening festivities. In Nebraska at the end of March, Merwin resigned as secretary because his newspaper was losing business. His resignation was unexpected and Norris would have been at a loss to replace him, had Merwin not mentioned as his successor a young lawyer in McCook, Ray McCarl, a recent graduate of the University of Nebraska Law School and an experienced stenographer.[31]

With the matter of a successor to Merwin quickly settled, Norris now had at least eight months of freedom from legislative duties and the prospect of a summer free from campaigning. In short, he could enjoy his first extended rest since his honeymoon in 1903. This vacation brought with it an opportunity to travel to Europe.

Chapter 12

The Large View: International and National

THE FAMILY, especially the children, who had talked of little else during the last month of the session, were delighted to return to Nebraska. Home in McCook, Norris sought to keep his political fences in repair. In Washington he had secured from lameduck Senator Dietrich some of the free government documents available in his office. Now he distributed them among his constituents.[1]

Thoroughly familiar with numerous departmental procedures, he was able to inform his constituents of the various rules and regulations necessary to obtain, for example, a rural free delivery route or a pension.[2] He had made sure that the Department of Agriculture knew that he represented a district where alfalfa, wheat, and corn were the principal crops and that, as a usual thing, the area did not receive as much moisture as the eastern part of Nebraska. Norris hoped the department would find it possible to conduct experiments with these crops "with a view to the introduction of varieties particularly adapted to the conditions there, which would result in a great benefit to the farmers of the district." He also had urged that seed corn, wheat, and alfalfa be sent to leading farmers for experimental purposes and that the semi-arid districts not be forgotten by government research scientists.[3]

In the Fifty-ninth Congress he had spoken in favor of an amendment providing funds for dry farming, which would make productive "a very large scope of country" that heretofore had been considered useless for agricultural purposes. In these remarks, he showed an intimate knowledge of agricultural techniques, explaining to his colleagues the "Campbell system," a method of dry farming that had been experimented with in his district.[4] Thus at the outset of his congressional career, Norris expressed an interest in improving agricultural production in the short-grass country. He knew that the soil, which basically was very rich, needed more moisture. He was intent upon

97

filling this need by increasing the farmer's knowledge of dry farming and other techniques, by putting sturdier seeds in his hands, and later by providing vast irrigation facilities that would make farmers better able to cope with the vicissitudes of nature.

In Washington Norris had supported a bill introduced by a Nebraska colleague, Moses P. Kinkaid, which, when signed into law by President Roosevelt on April 28, 1904, affected the pattern of public land distribution, particularly in Nebraska. In conjunction with the Reclamation Act of 1902 it marked a major and more realistic change in the land policy of the United States. Briefly, the law permitted anyone to acquire a homestead of 640 acres if he had lived there for five years and made at least $800 worth of improvements. Its effect was a remarkable increase of homesteading in western Nebraska, where small-scale ranching now became possible.[5]

Traveling through this area shortly after his return from Washington, Norris found that the great majority of claims had been filed by men who intended to make their permanent homes there. The settlement of this vacant land, he thought, would help remove many illegal fences that had been placed on the public domain by unscrupulous cattlemen. In conversation with a county assessor, Norris learned that in five precincts the population had increased by ninety families and that this fact was quickly registered in the rising value of taxable personal property. Such evidence helped convince him that the law was a beneficial one.[6]

However, because of the numerous violations by cattlemen in the sparsely populated sand-hills region, Norris soon modified his views. He came to favor a plan whereby the state would assume ownership of these lands and then either sell or lease them to the cattlemen. Since most of the land available under the Kinkaid Act was located in Nebraska, he believed that the state could deal with violations better than the national government, which did not have enough agents on hand to see that cattlemen did not unlawfully extend their fences and intimidate would-be settlers. Moreover, the funds derived from selling or leasing land could be used to improve the state school system.[7]

Though affairs in the district kept him busy during May and June, it was the forthcoming trip to Europe, as a delegate to the Interparliamentary Union, that excited him. To be a delegate to this conference, an individual had to be a member of the highest legislative body of his government. The union's object was to encourage a sentiment which would ultimately result in the abandonment of warfare between nations, and it had in mind, among other such calamities, the Russo-Japanese War then in progress. The organization had no official connection with any government and its work was of an advisory nature, though the calibre of its membership gave it a quasi-official status. The leader of the American delegation, Congressman Bartholdt of Missouri, had been responsible for the Interparliamentary Union meeting in St. Louis in 1904 and for Roosevelt's invitation to its members to visit the White House, where he had promised to support a second peace conference at The Hague. While Norris did not attend the 1904 meeting and had refused Bartholdt's initial request that he be a delegate to the 1905 conference, he eventually decided to attend the Brussels meeting of the union.[8]

After enjoying a brief vacation with his family in Wisconsin, Norris left New York on August 12 on the Red Star Line steamer, *Vaderland*. The vessel docked at Antwerp, and Norris arrived in Brussels about a week prior to the opening session.[9]

At the thirteenth meeting of the Interparliamentary Union the American delegation made two significant suggestions. It called for the preparation of a model arbitration treaty and recommended that steps be taken toward the establishment of an international organization with jurisdiction to enact into law such statutes as might be necessary to insure peace among nations. After much debate and discussion it was decided to refer these matters to the next meeting of the Hague Conference. Norris, as well as most of the other members of the American delegation, spoke in favor of these resolutions.[10]

At the close of the conference, the Belgian representatives invited all the delegates to a reception in the building where Napoleon's officers had assembled on the eve of Waterloo. The rooms were decorated with the colors of all nations. At the very same time the peace commissioners at Portsmouth, New Hampshire, were concluding the details of the treaty ending the Russo-Japanese War. As Norris later recalled:

> The finest band in Belgium was playing her national air. In the midst of it the music suddenly ceased. All eyes were turned to the rostrum. We saw the leader of the band seize from the decorations of the hall the American flag, and using it as a baton, he waved it over the heads of the musicians, and in answer to his action, there burst forth the rapturous strains of the Star-Spangled Banner. For a moment, and a moment only, there was silence, and then there burst forth a roar of applause which clearly indicated that everyone there understood that beneath the fathomless deep the electric spark had brought the welcome news that on the shores of America an agreement for peace had been signed. On the occasion of

nearly one hundred years before the revelry was interrupted by the booming of cannon, but on this occasion it was the joyous message that under the leadership of America the peace of the world had been established. That was an occasion . . . when it was greater to be an American citizen than to wear a crown.[11]

Norris recalled this incident and his brief trip to Germany many times during his career. Back home in McCook, after an enlightening and enjoyable European trip, Norris learned that application had been made in favor of President Roosevelt as the American candidate for the Nobel Peace Prize because of his efforts in concluding the Russo-Japanese War. Norris had mistakenly believed that the prize could not be awarded to a head of state, and would have preferred and strongly supported Congressman Bartholdt as the American candidate because of his work as head of the American delegation to various meetings of the Interparliamentary Union.[12]

Before returning to Washington, he acceded to several requests to talk about his recent trip. A friend, who attended the lecture in the Clay Center Opera House, noted that people sat still and were attentive throughout. Norris had no prepared speech, but spoke, as he always spoke in Congress or during a campaign, extemporaneously. Moreover, he insisted that, since he did not expect any pay, no admission should be charged.[13]

Though not actively participating in the 1905 state-wide campaign, Norris nevertheless urged Republican leaders to turn out the vote on election day.[14] As expected, Republican candidates won most of the available offices and Norris turned his attention to the convening of the Fifty-ninth Congress early in December. Though Speaker Cannon refused to commit himself about committee assignments, he told Norris to rest assured that the matter would receive "consideration from one who has the most friendly feeling toward yourself both from the personal and political standpoint." [15]

Norris agreed to some extent with the criticism of the rules of the House of Representatives then being voiced, but felt that the fault lay in the large and unwieldy size of the body and not, as he was later to believe, in the power of the Speaker. Limitations on debate were necessary if any work was to be accomplished. Discussion and legislation, he knew, were controlled to a great extent by the older members who enjoyed great influence in House affairs. Realizing that he would enjoy no influential role in this Congress, Norris wanted to remain on a committee where he could be instrumental in having federal funds allocated for his district. Realistic in his appraisal of the House of

Representatives and of his negligible role in its functioning, Norris, as the Fifty-ninth Congress prepared to convene, was unaware of any tyranny or undue power exercised by Speaker Cannon.[16]

Departing for Washington ahead of his family, Norris found a pleasant apartment on Mintwood Place near Rock Creek Park. In a neighboring apartment lived a freshman congressman from North Dakota, Asle J. Gronna, and the two families soon became very friendly.[17] Mrs. Norris was pregnant and the family looked forward to a new addition some time in February or March.

On February 23, 1906, very early in the morning, Mrs. Norris gave birth to twin boys, both of them dying within twenty-four hours. For a while she hovered between life and death, remaining on the critical list at Providence Hospital for several days. Her husband, unwilling to let her return to Nebraska with the bodies of the dead infants for burial, reluctantly decided to have them cremated. This experience was a painful ordeal for the entire family. It deeply affected Norris, who rarely mentioned it either in conversation or in correspondence.[18]

On Capitol Hill Norris found, when Congress convened, that Cannon had rewarded him with a place on the Committee on Labor in addition to membership on the two committees on which he had previously served. Despite his trip to Europe, he showed little interest in foreign affairs. The Alaskan boundary dispute, the Russo-Japanese War, the Panama Canal, and other aspects of American expansion were not topics of discussion in his letters or public addresses. Domestic and largely local issues occupied his attention. However, during this session his horizon continued to expand. He received a petition from the leading citizens of McCook protesting pogroms in the Russian Empire, and both he and his secretary signed it and sent it on to the president. He was also in sympathy with the idea of sending Chinese students to the United States.[19] But his primary interest in world affairs focused on the Philippine tariff measure, supported by the administration and providing for free trade with this newly acquired dependency.

On January 13, 1906, Norris delivered his longest speech of the session reviewing the Philippine question and proclaiming his opposition to the bill. He pointed with pride to the American achievement of bringing material improvements, educational facilities, and a court system to the islands. He noted that according to the tariff law in operation all revenue collected from Philippine imports was being turned back into their treasury, thereby providing funds necessary to administer this dependency. If the administration bill was passed, the

American people, Norris argued, would then have to provide these funds out of increased taxation.

He came to the core of his opposition when he noted that the beet-sugar men, who, incidentally, had established one of the first beet-sugar factories in the United States in Grand Island, Nebraska, did not favor the measure. Like them, he claimed it would benefit the "sugar trust." Since the bulk of the imports from the Philippine Islands consisted of cane sugar which had to be refined before it could be consumed, Norris noted that there was but one purchaser of raw sugar in the United States, the sugar trust. Free trade thus would further benefit the trust since it could arbitrarily fix the price for raw sugar received by producers in the Philippines. This occurrence would in turn fix the price to the American consumer. Sugar refiners would have a greater opportunity to increase their profits with no corresponding reduction in consumer prices, while the Philippine producers would not receive a better price for their sugar. Speaking of the producer who was supposed to benefit from this bill, Norris said, "We are giving him a gold brick, and while he is innocently picking at the gilt on the outside and discovering the deception on the inside the sugar trust walks away with the swag and the Filipino is holding the sack." He thought a better name for the bill would be, "An act for the purpose of deceiving the Filipino, for menacing an American industry, and for the enrichment of the sugar trust."

The menaced American industry was the beet-sugar industry, the development of which would be retarded by this measure. Since beet-sugar factories would most likely be established either in western Nebraska or eastern Colorado, Norris was concerned about any measure which could retard the future development of his district. He therefore included as part of the peroration of his argument a traditional appeal for protection.[20]

Opposition to this bill placed Norris in an embarrassing position. His views ran counter to those of the president whom he claimed to support, and his opponents in Nebraska would be sure to notice this contradiction. Furthermore, his opposition may have endangered his standing with Speaker Cannon.

Norris was criticized for his opposition but he was ready with a defense of his position. The tariff measure, he claimed, was unimportant as compared "with the great corporation question." And on this issue he was in full accord with the president. Moreover, Norris was convinced that Roosevelt advocated the measure "simply because it was recommended to him by Secretary Taft." But, Norris assured an irate constituent, his stand did not jeopardize his relations either with the president or with Speaker Cannon; "You must certainly admit that a member of Congress who would do nothing except follow the views of some other person would be nothing more or less than a cipher." [21]

Despite reassurances, Norris was concerned lest his enemies use this vote as a lever in opposing his renomination. He wrote numerous letters explaining his position and arguing that the subject had been overestimated in its importance to the president. He also was not happy about Washington rumors that he was an "insurgent" and would oppose the president on other aspects of his program. [22]

In view of his later career, it is rather ironic that Norris gained his initial reputation as an insurgent for supporting the theory of protection, while being labeled an opponent of the first trust-busting president simply because he opposed further favors to an already powerful corporation. However, criticism leveled against Norris also indicated Roosevelt's great popularity in Nebraska. The people by and large accepted his moral posture of an increased role for the federal government to curb some of the corporate privileges prevalent in American life.

Though Norris defended the theory of protection in his opposition to the Philippine tariff bill, he was not dogmatic and he recognized inequities in the prevailing Dingley Tariff. Sentiment for revision was rising, but he recognized that change for the sake of change could perpetrate greater inequities than already existed: "The very announcement that the tariff is to be revised would immediately have a very depressing influence upon the business of the entire country. Everybody would want to wait and see what the new tariff was going to be before urging any business proposition involving large sums of money." Since revision was an intricate and politically volatile subject, he said it should be undertaken immediately after an election by a special session of Congress and never during an election year when it would become an obvious political "football."

Despite sentiment for tariff modification, Norris believed that Roosevelt was eminently correct in not calling a special session of Congress for this purpose after his overwhelming election in 1904. It should only be attempted, he argued, when no other major item of legislation was to be considered. Since the administration had given priority to the question of the regulation of railroad rates, tariff revision would have to wait. This view, Norris believed, was also Roosevelt's view. No mention of tariff revision appeared in his annual message, nor did he call a special session of Congress. [23]

As Norris sagely observed, the president was more interested in railroad regulation than in the tariff. And it was to this former topic that the first session of the Fifty-ninth Congress devoted much of its attention. Norris was fully in accord with the administration's position of granting power over rates to the Interstate Commerce Commission.

For over thirty years the railroads of Nebraska had been a subject of political controversy. They were in politics, particularly Republican politics, and their influence was again noticeable now that the party had returned to power. However, Democratic and Populist hostility and suspicion, and the desire to curb their power, in the 1890's had engendered a sentiment that carried over into the new century. Many young leaders in the Republican party in Nebraska were talking very much like the Populists and Bryan Democrats a decade earlier in their hostility to railroad influence and boss rule. Such sentiment, prevalent in other states as well, encouraged Roosevelt in his desire to grant effective power to the Interstate Commerce Commision to regulate railroads and other common carriers. Norris was swept along by this rising tide in Nebraska; his attitude toward the railroads now became openly critical. The previous hostility of W. S. Morlan, the Burlington's powerful agent in McCook, toward Norris' candidacy in 1902, no doubt, helped in pushing him into the more liberal wing of his party.

Shortly before Norris left for Washington he received a letter indicative of the more critical attitude toward the railroad. The writer, a political leader, said that the stock shippers in his county were complaining of inadequate and detrimental freight service. Stock shipments to Denver, for example, were taking much more time than necessary because the Burlington lines required freight train crews to rest, while it charged the shippers from sixteen to eighteen dollars per car extra freight. The delay caused a shrinkage in the collective weight of the cattle (hence in their value), and added to their risk of injury or death.[24] Thus with businessmen, farmers, and cattlemen disturbed by the railroad's shipping policies, it required no great courage for a politician to openly attack the railroad. And many did so less from conviction than from mere opportunism.

In Washington, once the president requested Congress to enact a railroad rate bill, Norris proclaimed himself in "perfect sympathy" with these views. He intended to aid in the enactment of an adequate law that would give some legal body the power to fix a fair rate.[25]

In explaining his decision to his former political adviser, ex-Senator Manderson, chief of the Law Department of the Chicago, Burlington & Quincy Railroad Company, Western Division, Norris wrote:

> Ever since the beginning of this rate agitation, I have interested myself in the question. I had read volumes—speeches, argu-

ments, resolutions, etc., on the subject. I have devoted all the time at my disposal to this subject. I know that I have been conscientious and honest in trying to reach a just conclusion—just to the public and the railroads alike.

He claimed that hostility to the Burlington railroad in southwestern Nebraska had become noticeable only after the system had come under the control of James J. Hill in 1901. Until that time the Burlington had come as close to meeting and supplying the wants of its customers and patrons as any railroad in existence, while the people along its lines exhibited friendly feeling toward the road and its managers. Since that time, however, there had been a change for the worse; merchants and customers in the smaller towns had become prejudiced against the road and its policies. Norris illustrated what he meant by noting:

There was a time, not many years ago, when a merchant in one of these towns could order goods from Omaha, Lincoln, Kansas City or St. Joseph, knowing with an absolute certainty within an hour or two of the time when that order of goods would reach him. He could order something he had sold to a customer and be able to guarantee a prompt delivery—at least within a day or two. He could order by wire, knowing when he did so exactly when the goods so ordered would be delivered at his home station. Conditions have radically changed. At the present time it is not an uncommon thing for goods to be ordered and not delivered until from twenty to thirty days, when in the ordinary course of business it should not require more than two to three days to make such delivery, and such was the case in former days.

This lack of desire to accommodate local shippers, it seemed to Norris, had come about by the adoption of what was called "the tonnage rule," an arrangement whereby the number and frequency of trains over a particular line depended on the tonnage shipped. Some freight trains, Norris had learned from railroad men in McCook, required from twenty-five to forty hours going over one division. Such conditions, he explained, had never existed prior to the Hill management. Meanwhile, hostile sentiment, injurious to the railroad, its employees, and its customers, was spreading. Though these examples had no direct connection with rate supervision, in Norris' judgment they had much to do with prevailing sentiment on that question. He was convinced that feeling against the railroad had been brought about by changes introduced by the Hill management. Moreover, these changes explained why numerous Nebraska citizens were against the railroad and would continue to be so "without going into a very deep consideration of the merits of any particular controversy."[26]

Early in 1906 Norris returned to Manderson his pass on the Burlington system in Nebraska. Previously in the 1905 campaign all parties had included in their platforms strong statements denouncing, as particularly offensive, the granting of passes. One Nebraska historian has noted that this antipass sentiment "had its effect upon politicians who had hitherto resisted or disregarded it, and some of the principal officials assumed the halo of righteousness by ostentatiously repudiating the now disreputable tag of special privilege."[27]

Norris was certainly affected by this sentiment, though he assumed no righteous pose. He doubted if he had ever been influenced in his official conduct. "As a matter of fact," he wrote, "my constituents have been the beneficiaries of the free transportation I have had, more than myself, as it has enabled me to give personal attention to matters in distant portions of my congressional district connected with my official duties, matters that I could not have attended to personally had I been compelled to stand the entire expense of the trips." Thus he realized that the loss of a pass would add to his expenditures. By returning his pass, Norris politely severed relations with the Burlington Railroad, some of whose officials, especially Manderson, had advised and helped him in his political career and on whose payroll he had been when he was a struggling young lawyer in Beaver City.[28]

Not only did Norris support most of the railroad bills presented in this session of Congress, he also introduced one limiting the hours of service by railroad employees. Appearing before the House Committee on Interstate and Foreign Commerce he made several statements about freight train schedules, the time consumed in shipments by freight, and the long hours of service of railroad trainmen. After the witness for the Burlington Railroad denied that there were freight delays, Norris wrote several friends requesting further evidence he could use in support of his measure. Most of his examples were derived from conversation with merchants and railroad employees in McCook and elsewhere, but he now desired more specific information, such as detailed way-bills.

Nothing came of this measure because Congress was devoting most of its time to the railroad rate question. But Norris continued to collect the information he desired. Rarely, if ever, in his future congressional career would he introduce and support a bill without first having examined and mastered all the information he could find on it. Measures, such as the one he introduced, Norris believed, at least had the effect of making the railroads improve their service to prevent further government probing.[29]

He was also in accord with the administration's request for legislation calling for the careful inspection and supervision of packing houses and food and drug products used in interstate commerce. Bills to achieve these results were considered in June, 1906, and Norris was certain they would pass before the session adjourned. He was not certain, however, how effective they would be. And he was unhappy that reports filed with the president, showing that proper inspection was not taking place, had been given so much prominence. He believed that as a result the packing industry had received a damaging blow and that great harm would result for stock raisers.

Not that Norris was against the investigation and regulation of packing house methods in the interest of public health. But he felt that necessary reforms and improvements could have been made without going into so many horrible details (since the packing business was necessarily a "dirty business") which tended to affect adversely both the domestic and foreign markets for meats. Furthermore, he hoped that in the bill presented to Congress the cost of inspection would be borne by the government and not by the packers, who could take this item out of the price paid for the cattle, thereby affecting the stock raiser, the farmer, and the consumer.[30] Certainly Nebraska stockmen, concerned about provisions for the cost of inspection, found Norris' position in accord with their views. Indeed, no position that he took during this significant session was markedly out of line with the views of his constituents.

Norris reintroduced his resolution calling for a constitutional amendment affecting the terms of the president, senators, and representatives. This time the amendment received editorial notice, and a modified version of it (calling for a six-year presidential tenure) was actually discussed by Norris in the closing days of the session. His interest in improving the processes of government was receiving some recognition, primarily because it was in accord with growing public clamor for the direct election of senators.[31]

The tenor of Norris' remarks in this session of Congress, with the exception of the Philippine tariff bill, was in support of administration measures and in favor of the expansion of federal authority in instances where the public interest was threatened. Thus he spoke in support of the right of Congress to regulate life insurance companies: "Those who have charge of insurance moneys are charged with a duty not only to the State, but to all humanity." Since insurance companies, like other powerful corporate interests, were nationwide in their activities, and since most state legislation had failed to prevent their mismanagement of other people's money, he thought national supervision would be better, both for the insured and for "all honest insurance companies." The companies then would have to comply with only one set of requirements instead of many sets (contradictory state requirements) which by their very nature encouraged unethical practices.[32]

Despite his opposition to part of the president's program, he regarded himself during the first session of the Fifty-ninth Congress as an ardent supporter of Theodore Roosevelt. Indeed, during this session he had broken with the dominant corporate interest in Nebraska, the Burlington Railroad, and had championed the curbing or supervision of corporate wealth. The session revealed Norris as a Roosevelt Republican also in his support of the expanding role of government. Though he always favored economy and denounced reckless expenditures, he was willing to use the power of the central government, usually after the states had shown themselves unable to solve a problem, to promote the health and general well-being of the American people. There was no theoretical basis for this belief; his approach was essentially a pragmatic one based upon experience, knowledge, and understanding.

Since most of the opposition to the president's program came from powerful, able, conservative, and standpat titans led by Nelson W. Aldrich and concentrated in the Senate, the House of Representatives has received little attention in most discussions of Roosevelt's policies. The growing tensions between elements in the Republican party were not evident in the lower chamber because Speaker Cannon and the president worked well together. The House of Representatives usually quickly passed bills that the administration favored. Most of the fights over Roosevelt's legislative program occurred in the Senate chamber.

George Norris, a respected younger member of the House of Representatives, was gaining stature through his handling of committee assignments and his lucid and cogent remarks. He was a partisan Republican, but not an emotional or vitriolic one. He looked after the interests of his constituents so well that early in the session he was informed, "Your renomination and re-election is as good as done now." [33] Finally, though his trip to Europe the previous summer had been an enlightening and rewarding experience, his horizon was largely a national one. As Norris returned to Nebraska in 1906 he no doubt mused about the prospect of increased expenditures owing to the necessity of campaigning without the benefit of a railroad pass.

Chapter 13

The Third Campaign

As EARLY as January, 1906, Norris believed that there would be "no other candidates and possibly no opposition" to his renomination. Indeed, he had hopes that he would be given the nomination by acclamation, as was the case two years previously. And George Allen, who would again manage the campaign, reported that if, after receiving the nomination, Norris merely announced that he was for Roosevelt and a square deal, his election would be assured, so strong was the ground swell in Nebraska for the president and his policies. While some slight opposition had manifested itself in the spring, neither Allen nor Norris was unduly concerned about it.[1]

Upon his return from Washington in July, Norris examined the developing situation from his office in McCook and attended the Red Willow County convention as a visiting dignitary. Though the convention unanimously chose delegates favoring his renomination, he played a role in preventing the convention from committing delegates to any candidate for governor or United States senator. He did this because there were at least two candidates for governor in the congressional district, and considerable talk of a third; if the convention supported any of the candidates, its action could start a political fight that might affect delegates to the congressional convention.

When the delegates from Beaver precinct voted for Norris as their senatorial candidate, a spontaneous demonstration erupted in the hall and Norris feared a "stampede" in his favor. Though he never left his seat throughout these proceedings, his friends among the delegates labored hard to curb the demonstration. Norris thought the use of his name in connection with the senatorial race would have an injurious effect upon party harmony.[2]

However, when the Furnas County Convention met on the first of August, almost the same thing occurred. Merwin and other Norris supporters had to convince delegates that he did not want anything but the congressional nomination. While Norris did not deny that the nomination for United States senator was an honor he would be very

109

proud to receive, he recognized that he could not obtain the nomination. Mentioning his name, therefore, might make him a partner in controversies in which he had no desire to participate.[3]

As expected, Norris was unanimously chosen by the congressional convention which met at Hastings in mid-August. In his acceptance speech he came out strongly against the use of railroad passes and declared that a pass, in effect, was a bribe. The opposition press quickly pointed out that Norris as a judge and as a congressman had carried a pass. One paper noted, "It was a bribe then, as much as it is now, but only the Democrats and Populists said so." What the Republicans now called reform, the paper noted, was nothing but poison when it emanated from the opposition. Although Norris did not tell the delegates that he had returned his last pass, his position would have been equally vulnerable even if he had informed them.[4]

Roderick D. Sutherland, former congressman from the district (1897–1901), received the fusion nomination as the Democratic and Populist candidate. Sutherland, a Nuckolls County lawyer, was an able man, but he was not an orator like Shallenberger. Indeed, surprisingly so for a former Populist congressman, he was an unemotional and colorless personality who seemingly would have a difficult time in arousing the voters.

Before he knew who his opponent would be, Norris had written to the clerk of the House of Representatives to obtain the record of bills introduced and enacted by his predecessors. He did this to forestall criticism of his record in Congress by showing that his predecessors had done even less. Thus, when the campaign got under way, Norris was able to prevent Sutherland from attacking him along these lines.[5]

When a War Department employee from Nebraska wrote that "the Union labor crowd" would probably oppose Norris' election in the railroad towns of McCook, Grand Island, and Hastings, Norris replied that he thought the "suspicion of opposition from Union Labor" was correct. However, he had little fear it would affect the final result. But if the need arose, Norris thought that Speaker Cannon would come into the district once again on his behalf. And from an unexpected quarter, the American Protective Tariff League, Norris received an offer of help because of his opposition to the Philippine tariff bill. He politely refused this offer, realizing that it would call the voters' attention to the fact that he had opposed an administration measure.[6]

Aware that this campaign would be more expensive than previous ones because of the lack of railroad passes, George Allen and Ray

McCarl made an effort to collect campaign contributions from interested citizens. Norris, for his part, started the campaign in his usual way, appearing at reunions, picnics, and fairs, delivering supposedly nonpartisan speeches.[7]

Early in September Allen had a conference in his office in Clay Center with Sutherland prior to a fusion meeting at the courthouse where William Jennings Bryan was scheduled to speak. Allen was informed that Sutherland did not want to begin the campaign before the first of October. This suggestion, Allen claimed, would be amenable to Norris. Allen and Sutherland also agreed to conduct a "clean" campaign and not indulge in personalities. Sutherland confided that had he been at the convention he would have declined the nomination. He left Allen with the distinct impression that, barring unexpected developments, he did not think he could defeat Norris.[8]

Meanwhile, from conversations and correspondence, Norris discerned that most people were concerned about trusts and his attitude toward them. This concern gave him an admirable way of explaining his opposition to the Philippine tariff measure by stressing his hostility to the sugar trust. He also stated his general position: "Any organization of whatever kind or nature, should be governed and controlled to the end that it be prevented from stifling competition and ruining or injuring other organizations or individuals in their efforts to conduct legitimate businesses." Those who departed from this standard, he felt, should be prosecuted to the full extent of the law.[9]

Sutherland started campaigning early in October, while Norris did not begin until the week of October 8. Sutherland's audiences were not large and the only reference to Norris in his speeches was to criticize his vote on the Philippine tariff bill. His speeches were short, usually thirty minutes or less. Allen reported that Sutherland had told a gathering of Populists and Democrats at Hastings he could not afford to let his law practice suffer, that he had reluctantly accepted the nomination out of a sense of duty. Even with Bryan speaking on behalf of Sutherland, enthusiasm seemed to be lacking among the fusion groups.[10]

From Monday, October 8, until election day, Norris campaigned every day but Sundays. He traveled continually, speaking at a different rally six evenings a week. McCarl in McCook supervised the over-all arrangements, but it was up to the local leaders to hire the hall, advertise the meeting, and arrange to have local candidates and dignitaries on the platform with Norris. McCarl advised them to have all of the "boys in blue" on the platform and to see to it that Norris left the morning after the rally. Norris was expected to visit with local editors and officials, shake hands, and make himself accessible to all visitors in a hotel room.[11]

Norris, busy traveling and speaking, was fortunate in having the services of both McCarl and Allen. Both were intensely devoted and loyal to him, and both performed their arduous jobs with no prodding from him. By the end of the campaign neither McCarl, in his twenties, nor Allen, probably in his sixties, was finding enough time to do all his chores. All, including Norris, in his forties, were working long hours with little time for food and sleep. None saw his family to any great extent during this hectic period, the candidate least of all. Since Norris rarely exhibited sentiment or emotion, at times these men felt he took them for granted. But they usually knew that he gave of himself even more unstintingly than they gave of themselves. He inspired loyalty and devotion by his actions as well as by his words.

Though Norris was unable to provide transportation to bring absent voters home to vote, Allen reported that Democratic and Populist leaders, who had for years been attacking the railroads, were providing transportation. Allen was sure this news, which he wanted to release at the end of the campaign, would boomerang and cost the opposition many votes. The vagaries of party politics had thus brought "the great reform party and the old time railroad haters . . . into a combination or agreement with the corporations." In his thirty-four years in politics Allen had seen many odd combinations, but this strange alliance between the railroads and "the wreck of the great fusion party of reform" presented "the greatest mix-up of all." [12]

In the last week of the campaign Allen attended several Norris meetings. The crowds were large and the speeches good. Norris' "fine appearance on the rostrum and his fine honest look," coupled with his earnest and "straightforward way" of talking, carried conviction. His delivery was clear and distinct; his language was simple and impressive, unburdened with rotund oratorical flourishes. Allen, who mingled in the crowd trying to hear remarks about the speeches, concluded that most men in the audience agreed that Norris was "an honest and sincere candidate as well as an able one." [13]

Both McCarl and Allen expected the campaign to conclude without a hitch. Both were surprised when Norris lost his temper at the Clay Center meeting on November 2, and indulged in a tirade of personal vituperation against a local editor who had long been attacking him. The meeting started well enough, and, despite a heavy rain, the courtroom was crowded. But soon Norris lost control and bellowed forth his wrath and indignation at the hapless editor who was in the audience.[14]

Editor Palmer of the Clay Center *Sun* was a disappointed candidate for the Clay Center post office. When Norris concluded two or three years previously that the good of the service and the wishes of the party necessitated the appointment of another candidate, Palmer went into a rage and had opposed Norris ever since. In Clay County most people knew the reason for the paper's bitter opposition, and thus were not drastically swayed. However, when its editorials appeared in other newspapers, some damage did result because readers did not know the source of the opposition.

Norris, though tempted, had never attacked Palmer personally, believing it better to ignore the man than to lose dignity by a personal denunciation.[15] For this reason, his tirade was totally unexpected. He claimed the editor had said that if he did not get the appointment as postmaster he would continually criticize Norris. Palmer then interrupted and cried out that Norris' informant had lied. Norris lost his temper. Overcome with anger, he left the rostrum, walked down the aisle, shook his fist at Palmer, and thundered forth that he could prove his statement. He then proceeded to give Palmer a severe tongue-lashing. This incident, of course, created a sensation. Some people expected Norris to strike Palmer, but, after this castigation, Norris returned to the platform and went on with his speech.[16]

Allen, who considered Palmer "a drooling, drivelling, lecherous, diabolical piece of polluted humanity . . . incapable of high morality and decency," nevertheless, was sorry that Norris had given vent to his emotions. Though prominent citizens felt that he was justified in attacking Palmer, Allen, with his eye on the over-all campaign, thought Norris' energy was wasted "on so vile a creature," and was afraid that Sutherland might try to capitalize on it. A Democratic committeeman, introducing a speaker at a meeting the following night, assured the audience that no one need fear any physical damage such as occurred at Republican rallies.[17]

For Allen, Norris' speech in Clay Center was the high spot of the campaign. Allen was too busy to attend the Hastings rally on November 3 or the campaign windup at McCook on election eve. The McCook meeting, the climax of the campaign, took place in the opera house, which had a seating capacity of over a thousand. Picture posters were widely distributed and local leaders had been instructed to bring delegations. A band had been hired and invitations were sent to all the "old soldiers" to be present as guests of "the Judge" on the stage where they occupied reserved seats. Speaking before a friendly audience, Norris was in fine form, and the local candidates, some of whom were hard pressed, were grateful for the support he gave them.[18]

The 1906 campaign registered the high-water mark of the progressive movement in Nebraska. All parties had progressive platforms and several of the Republican candidates sounded like old-time Populist orators. Outside of the Second Congressional District, all major and most minor Republican office seekers were elected. In the Fifth District, Norris defeated Sutherland by more than two thousand votes which, though not as impressive as his 1904 victory, was ample and satisfactory. Since Republicans would dominate the next state legislature, a United States Senate seat for Norris Brown, who won the preferential primary, was thereby assured. George L. Sheldon defeated Shallenberger for governor by almost thirteen thousand votes. His triumph insured a progressive administration for the state during the next two years.[19]

After the results were known, the post-mortem discussions and analyses began. Norris ran well ahead of his ticket throughout the district, receiving 1,100 more votes than Governor-elect Sheldon. Though there were no basic issues involved in the congressional campaign, Sutherland probably being more liberal than Norris, the advantages were all with the incumbent. Norris had capitalized effectively on his support of the Roosevelt policies, arguing that he would be in a position to serve his constituents better as a congressman in his third consecutive term.[20]

Enjoyable as these analyses were, Norris had to interrupt them with plans relating to his return to Washington and the convening of the second session of the Fifty-ninth Congress early in December. A week after the election he wrote to Speaker Cannon expressing an interest in membership on the powerful Ways and Means Committee in the Sixtieth Congress, when several vacancies would occur. Norris made this request because he had devoted "some time to the study of the tariff question" and because he believed that the interests of the "Great West" should be given consideration. More important, he was satisfied that his ideas on the tariff question were in full accord with those of the Speaker. Cannon, gratified that Norris was re-elected, replied that he would "do the guessing on the organization of the House in the Sixtieth Congress" some time shortly before that Congress assembled, in the event that he should again be chosen Speaker.[21]

Norris was on hand when the second session of the Fifty-ninth Congress started on December 3, 1906. Though the session would last only three months, and little was expected of it in the way of legislation, he was active and busy throughout its entirety. He introduced a bill designed to provide more expeditious delivery of freight, a bill that would prevent merchants along the Burlington route in

Nebraska from having to wait unnecessarily long periods of time for delivery of their goods. Norris thought his measure had a chance of being enacted because the president had recommended such a law in his annual message. Possibly as a threat to wrest concessions from the Burlington, Norris also favored a reduction in the amount of compensation paid railroads for carrying the United States mails.[22]

Each time Norris spoke during this short session, his remarks, while relevant to the national scene, were particularly pertinent to Nebraska and conditions in the Fifth Congressional District. He spoke on one occasion in favor of improved pension legislation, particularly for an amendment which would grant widows of Civil War veterans a pension no matter what the cause of the soldier's death. He also favored a graduated pension for soldiers, increasing with advanced age. His position on this matter, of course, helped Norris to remain in the good graces of most old soldiers and their families throughout Nebraska. It also further increased Roosevelt's status with Union veterans throughout the country, since a graduated pension bill was enacted into law.[23]

With growing commercial use of the automobile, road building became a topic of absorbing interest, and Norris now gave it some attention. During the first session he had supported a measure providing for an appropriation to experiment with methods of road building. Now he offered a similar amendment providing the United States Geological Survey with $100,000 to investigate various structural materials for use in government construction of roads, dams, and buildings. Such an appropriation, he stated, would result in "cheaper and better buildings, not only for the government, but for all our people." It would save millions "in the construction of the Panama Canal and in the Reclamation Service of the Great West, and, besides, make those great undertakings more substantial and less liable to destruction and decay." It would also provide information that could materially improve broad highways and country lanes. Nevertheless, Norris insisted the actual improvement of roads must come to a great extent through state appropriations. He did not consider federal construction of highways a necessary or wise expansion of governmental jurisdiction.[24]

During this session a Senate bill, introduced in the House of Representatives by Norris, was enacted into law. It divided Nebraska into two judicial districts and called for the selection of an additional federal judge. The creation of a new district would save money for many Nebraska citizens involved in federal litigation by making the trip to the federal district court at Omaha unnecessary. In 1907, Norris' home town of McCook received the honor of being host to the first term of the newly created federal court for western Nebraska. The enactment of the law also meant that eventually funds would be appropriated for a federal building to house the sessions of the court.[25]

With the final adjournment of the Fifty-ninth Congress on March 4, 1907, Norris, weary but satisfied with his work in Washington, returned to McCook facing no immediate political worries or problems. At the end of the Fifty-ninth Congress, he had irrevocably committed himself as a supporter of Roosevelt. In defining the policies of the president, Norris stated his views about the necessity of expanding the role of the federal government. He claimed that when he spoke of Roosevelt's "leading policies," he referred "to the enforcement of the law against the rich as well as the poor, against the powerful as well as the weak." He meant, also, "that the control and regulation of railroads and other corporations, and the prosecution of all criminal offenders against the law of the United States" should be vigorously pursued. Roosevelt's policy of "insisting upon honesty on the part of all Government employees" received his enthusiastic approval.[26]

Furthermore, by the end of the Fifty-ninth Congress Norris exhibited the independence and lack of partisanship that were to be so characteristic of his later career. He had broken with the most powerful corporate interest in Nebraska, the Burlington Railroad, which was unable to reprimand him for his action, while his constituents applauded his hostility to railroad inequities. He had refused to follow the administration in supporting a tariff measure, albeit a minor one, and this opposition did not noticeably lessen his standing among the voters or with Speaker Cannon and the administration in Washington. The coming years would furnish more dramatic and courageous examples of these traits, but the first steps were taken during this Congress.

Though Norris considered himself a devoted follower of Roosevelt and most of his policies, it is to be doubted if he thought of himself as an insurgent. Certainly he was satisfied with his lot in Congress, and he realized that his improving seniority eventually would lead Speaker Cannon to promote him to more important committee assignments.[27] Possibly, too, he was aware of the fact that one of the outstanding speakers of the House of Representatives, Samuel J. Randall of Pennsylvania, had started by serving on the Committee on Public Buildings and Grounds. Certainly, as he returned to McCook in that chilly and blustery March of 1907, Norris would have agreed that, politically speaking, the best was yet to come.

Chapter 14

Seeds of Doubt

WITH almost nine months before the next Congress was to convene, Norris now had time to enjoy his family and to look after personal and political affairs in a leisurely way. He became interested in plans for a YMCA building, chiefly to provide the many unmarried railroad men in McCook with a place of residence and wholesome recreation. The local citizenry hoped to raise between eight thousand and ten thousand dollars for this project, and Norris hoped that the national headquarters of the YMCA would provide the difference, so that his home town, with a population of 4,000, could provide in this way for its young men.[1]

Norris also attended to his real estate interests in Beaver City, particularly to the renting of a new hotel building he had recently acquired. Visiting Beaver City gave him an opportunity to chat with old friends, some of whom insisted he deliver a lecture either about his work in Washington or his trip to Europe as a member of the Interparliamentary Union.[2] These activities were pleasant and leisurely. In April, Jonah K. Kalanianaole, Hawaiian delegate to the United States Congress, extended an invitation on behalf of the territory of Hawaii to become his guest as a member of a congressional party, and Norris accepted with alacrity.[3]

The group sailed from San Francisco on May Day with the ostensible purpose of investigating conditions in the territory so that Congress might have a better idea of its needs in matters of general legislation. Actually Norris had a splendid vacation. Along with other congressmen he was photographed at the summit of Mount Haleakala, while Mr. and Mrs. L. A. Thurston of Honolulu extended to him the hospitality of their home. Norris also spoke at a meeting arranged by a native prince at a public square; no other member of the party wanted to speak and he was drafted for the chore to avoid disappointing the local citizenry.[4]

He returned to McCook in June and quickly departed with his family for a long summer vacation in Wisconsin. He enjoyed his leisure and the L.U.N. reunion at Rainbow Lake, and no doubt also reflected upon the significant work of the Thirtieth Nebraska Legislature. Its achievements represented and registered the high point of the progressive movement in Nebraska. A statewide primary, a child labor act, an anti–free-pass law, and other railroad regulatory measures were among the major pieces of legislation recorded during this session. The state emerged as one of the few that had taken measures, as an editorial in the Omaha *Bee* stated, "to supplement the work of Congress under the direction of President Roosevelt to the end of relieving the people of Nebraska of railroad domination in politics." [5]

The new primary law meant that hereafter Norris would have to be nominated by direct popular vote instead of by a nominating convention. While the primary law would relieve an incumbent candidate in the good graces of his constituents of some political pressure, it also meant that most candidates would have to engage in a grueling and expensive primary before obtaining the privilege of representing their party in the fall election.

Before that time occurred for Norris, he would have served in the first session of the Sixtieth Congress, scheduled to convene early in December. Rather than start the children in school in McCook and then transfer them, the family decided to move to Washington for the opening of the fall semester. Once they were settled in the capital city, Norris planned to return to McCook to participate in the fall campaign. Early in September, McCarl sent some of the family's belongings to Washington. Norris rented suitable quarters at the Fairfax, a large apartment house on Massachusetts Avenue, near fashionable DuPont Circle, while the McCook house was rented to a local doctor. [6]

McCarl was delighted that Norris was not in Nebraska prior to the September primaries because a bitter fight occurred between Judge Orr, Norris' successor in the Fourteenth Judicial District, and Charles E. Eldred, Morlan's law partner. By his absence, Norris avoided becoming involved in the controversy.

According to the new primary law, state conventions were to be held at Lincoln on the fourth Tuesday in September of each election year for the purpose of adopting platforms and conducting the necessary business of the party organization. Though McCarl made great efforts, all unknown to Norris, to have him chosen chairman when the Republican convention met on September 24, they were not successful. Norris appeared merely as a delegate from Red Willow County. [7]

Governor Sheldon presided over the convention. Though the highest office involved in the coming state election was for Supreme Court justice, the delegates adopted resolutions pertaining to national

affairs and thereby enabled Norris to gauge public sentiment throughout the state. The convention, for example, favored legislation limiting
the use of injunctions and further controlling corporate activities.
Finally it endorsed William Howard Taft as the man most fitted to
continue the policies of President Roosevelt. Norris was wholeheartedly in accord with this position, believing that Taft came nearer
to representing these policies than any other person.[8]

Unable to obtain for Norris the chairmanship of the convention,
McCarl next suggested him as chairman of the State Central Committee. Again his efforts were unsuccessful. Both McCarl and Norris
thought it would be well for him to avoid campaigning in his own
district where he would have to support Judge Orr, thereby risking the
open enmity of Morlan and the numerous friends of Eldred, who was
defeated in the primary. Therefore Norris, in offering his services to
the state committee, stated that he preferred to speak in the northern
part of the state. The committee accepted his offer and Norris, for the
first time in his career, spoke in support of Republican candidates outside of his own political bailiwick. After the election, which resulted
in another impressive Republican victory, the secretary of the state
committee thanked Norris for his efforts and informed him that the
committee proposed to maintain its headquarters and begin preparatory work for the national campaign of 1908. Thus in 1907, prior to
his departure for the opening of the new Congress, Norris found himself working in close harmony with the Republican organization in
Nebraska. He had served it well in the 1907 campaign; his services and
advice were sought by party leaders. Such a harmonious arrangement,
previously unknown to the representative from the Fifth Congressional
District, boded well for the coming national campaign when it was
generally assumed Bryan would make a third attempt to win the
presidency.[9]

However, before Norris could concern himself with the 1908
campaign, his presence was required in Washington where the first
session of the Sixtieth Congress convened at noon on December 2,
1907. McCarl, to Norris' great regret, remained in McCook practicing
law and working as best he could by answering routine letters, sending out various government documents and copies of Norris' speeches,
and handling pension claims and other matters.

For matters that required personal attention Norris utilized the
services of an able young attorney with an historic name. James K.
Polk looked after correspondence requiring information from various
government departments. A part-time stenographer handled correspondence requiring a personal reply. It was not an entirely satis-

factory arrangement but it was a workable one, chiefly because Polk was very competent. At best it was thought to be a temporary arrangement until McCarl's financial position improved. As possible compensation, Norris was delighted to learn that an office would be available to him in the House Office Building which was to be officially opened in January, 1908.[10]

Once the session got under way, Norris learned that Speaker Cannon had not seriously considered his request for membership on the Ways and Means Committee. His committee assignments were the same as those he had held in the previous Congress—Public Buildings and Grounds, Labor, and The Election of President, Vice President, and Representatives in Congress. If he was disappointed, his papers reveal no record of it. But he was beginning to give much attention to the rules and procedures through which the Speaker exercised authority, and, before the session was concluded, Norris presented a resolution designed to deprive the Speaker of some of his power. In doing this he allied himself with a small but vigorous band of insurgents in the House of Representatives.

At the beginning of the session, however, Norris was not concerned with challenging the authority of the Speaker. The country was in the midst of a financial panic and many citizens feared that repercussions would be felt throughout the economy. Carefully following the course of the panic, Norris concluded that remedial legislation was required to prevent banks from speculating. He noticed in the press that Governor Edward Hoch intended to ask the Kansas legislature to levy an assessment on banks for the purpose of guaranteeing deposits. His thoughts had been developing along similar lines, namely, levying an assessment on deposits in national banks for the purpose of creating a fund to pay off depositors in case of failure. In the previous Congress he had talked to several members of the Banking and Currency Committee and had concluded that such a measure stood little chance of being favorably received. The Panic of 1907, however, convinced him that he should again try to introduce a measure to protect depositors. It was more pertinent at this time and, if the Banking and Currency Committee would not consider it, at least Norris could air his views on the floor of the House.[11]

He gave careful study to the proposition, obtained information from many sources, and discussed it with banker friends in Nebraska. His idea was to have the secretary of the treasury levy an assessment upon all national banks, basing the assessment upon the average deposits of each bank. The fund thereby obtained was to be used solely for the purpose of paying off depositors of any national bank that failed. The bill also provided that when any bank had paid into the fund an amount equal to a certain percentage of its average balances, it should be relieved from any further assessment until the amount paid in was less than the percentage of its balances. Thus each bank in time would virtually have a paid-up insurance policy against possible losses.[12]

Since his object in preparing the bill was to create confidence in national banks and to prevent runs on banks similar to those which had occurred in New York and elsewhere, Norris readily accepted the advice of bankers. He also suggested that Governor Sheldon of Nebraska introduce a similar bill applying to state banks. He realized if Congress enacted his bill and the states did not respond with similar measures most state banks would probably become national banks, since depositors would prefer to leave their money in an obviously more secure banking institution. However, Norris thought most states would follow the federal example as they had already done in the case of pure food laws and railroad regulation.[13]

He was quick to point out that his proposition was not a government guarantee of deposits, such as Bryan advocated and the New Deal later enacted. He was opposed to such a scheme for reasons of both practice and principle, but some legislation was necessary lest the public be further cheated by dishonest men in the banking business. He noted that bank examiners and other officials were reluctant to correct the practices of errant bankers by closing their banks because of the injurious effect it would have upon money matters in general and the panic it might induce among depositors who would seek to remove funds from legitimate and honestly conducted banks as well.

His bill, if enacted, would have prevented honest bankers from being injured by the failure of another bank. And it could have led bank examiners to insist on a stricter observance of the law without fear of accelerating a panic by penalizing mismanaged banks operating to the detriment of both the banking community and the public. Finally, Norris concluded that if such a law had been on the statute books, the Panic of 1907 would never have occurred. True, there might have been a disturbance in New York, but, he asserted, banks throughout the country would have gone on the same as ever. Thus the legislation he formally proposed to Congress in a long speech on January 7, 1908, would give depositors confidence and would bring relief not only to them and to the men who borrowed but also to the banker himself. In short, it would be a blessing to all concerned.[14]

Norris, like individuals in and out of Congress, gave serious attention to other aspects of the banking and currency situation beside the matter of protecting depositors. He favored a more "elastic" currency if it could be achieved without injuring its stability. However, most of the measures he had examined on this subject appeared to be injurious because of the fear engendered in depositors by currency being issued not on the basis of bonds but on the basis of a bank's total assets. Such a currency, Norris felt, while undoubtedly putting more money into circulation, would cause a greater disturbance than prevailed in 1907 when in a future crisis banks reduced their assets. Thus he believed an asset-based currency could not achieve a more flexible monetary system.[15]

Another change Norris thought beneficial was to require banks to keep a larger amount of their reserve fund in their own vaults, thereby lessening the amount of funds they could lawfully deposit in other banks. Such an enactment would avoid bank failure due to excessive speculation. He also thought a law preventing national banks from loaning money on call at exorbitant interest rates would probably do some good. But Norris believed that his bill, which would take away from the depositor all fear that the bank would squander his money, was the one that would not only relieve the prevailing panic situation but would also make its recurrence practically impossible. At the same time it would bring out of hiding a large amount of money that fearful citizens were afraid to deposit, or, as Norris stated it: "Old stockings and old tin cans would be emptied, and yield up their golden treasure, and the money of the country would assume its legitimate and proper sphere in the channels of business and trade throughout the land."[16]

This session of Congress, as expected, witnessed a large number of banking and currency measures. Norris, who was not a member of the committee that would report such bills, did not expect his measure to be seriously considered. But by presenting it early he at least hoped other members might agree with some of his ideas and later incorporate or add them to a bill that Congress would seriously consider. This strategy failed and he was far from satisfied with the measure that Congress finally agreed upon. The Aldrich-Vreeland Act provided for emergency currency based on commercial paper, rather than currency reform. Norris would have to wait until the Wilson administration before Congress would enact a measure that provided for reform rather than relief.[17]

Related to the problem of banking and currency reform was the proposal to establish a postal savings bank system which, though discussed, was not acted upon during this session. The objections Norris

raised to this proposition related to the question of how the government should use the money. He wanted the deposits to be utilized in
the localities where they were made; otherwise they might drain one
portion of the country to supply another. To avoid this situation, Norris
hoped some plan could be devised so that these funds would be
deposited in and made available to local banks. Furthermore, the government, by depositing these funds in local banks, would in effect be
guaranteeing the deposits and would help bring hoarded money into
circulation. Since the clamor for a postal savings bank arose because
bank deposits were not secured, Norris pointed out that the bill he
had introduced to protect depositors provided the same thing in a more
direct and effective way. Indeed, he argued, if Congress passed "proper
currency regulation," the demand for postal savings banks would
cease. If not, the agitation would increase and postal savings banks
of some kind would have to be established.[18]

Though the bill to protect bank deposits consumed most of his
energy and attention at the outset of this session, Norris received much
correspondence criticizing the pension allotments in the McCumber
Act passed by the previous Congress. He therefore devoted some time
to this subject. He thought that the pensions granted should be more
liberal, but most of all he was concerned with the injustice of pensions
provided for the widows of old soldiers. Under the existing laws, a
widow, to obtain a pension of twelve dollars a month, had to show
that her husband died as the result of a disease or disability originating
in the service. This provision, he argued, was inconsistent, unreason-
able, and unjust, because unless a widow could do this she only would
receive a pension of eight dollars a month or possibly nothing at all,
owing to a "peculiar wording" of pension laws enacted during the
Civil War period. Believing that widows of old soldiers should all get
twelve dollars a month, Norris unsuccessfully in the Fifty-ninth Congress had offered an amendment to the McCumber Bill. Now in the
Sixtieth Congress he again presented a bill to remedy this situation.
And in April, 1908, the president signed a measure including more
liberal pensions for widows. Thus Nebraska veterans, already receiving
pensions or adjusted benefits through his efforts, knew that they had
in Norris a congressman who was ever alert to their interests.[19]

Aside from speeches on banking and pensions, Norris did not
present any lengthy remarks for the consideration of colleagues or
constituents. Nevertheless, he was acutely interested in legislative
developments. In accord with his previous judicial experience was his
concern about unduly severe punishment. The opportunity to express
his views arose because the House of Representatives in January, 1908,

considered a bill which codified all the criminal laws of the United States. The code had last been revised in 1873. The new codification to be accepted had to be presented as a bill and voted upon. At one point in the reading, Norris commented that too severe a penalty sometimes defeated conviction, as juries would be inclined, if the offense were not very grave and the penalty too severe, to find the defendant not guilty. He believed that greater discretion should be left to the court deciding a case and that specific punishments should be made more flexible.[20]

Many Democrats who did not take this work as seriously as Norris began to offer amendments for the purpose of making political speeches. Amendments were presented, speeches were made, and then the amendments were usually voted down, since the Republican party controlled the Congress. The object of the Democrats was to put the Republicans in the position of voting against amendments which appeared to be just and fair. And indeed most of them were just and fair, but they were in most instances already covered by law or contained in different portions of the bill being considered. Since the codification was being presented more as a matter of form than anything else, Norris became disturbed at the clever tactics of the opposition. These tactics, beside being dilatory, gave the Democrats an opportunity to develop a possible campaign issue.[21]

On the morning of January 21, 1908, the discussion disclosed that apparently most of the Democrats were opposed to lawyers and bankers serving in Congress. Considerable talk was also devoted to the use of free passes and the possibility of amending the Hepburn Act to provide for them. These developments, which consumed most of the morning without any discussion of the codification bill, seemed utterly ridiculous to Norris, and he proceeded to make them appear so to his fellow congressmen. When he obtained the floor to speak, he said he was impressed with the remarks of Champ Clark, the Democratic leader in the House of Representatives, who had presented an example of a man who sold his bank stock before coming to Congress. Clark commended this as conduct worthy of emulation. Norris agreed. He then went Clark one better by claiming a member ought not to be a farmer, because Congress might consider agricultural subjects, or a merchant, because he might have to legislate on the tariff or other matters affecting his business. The final result would be that Congress would be comprised of individuals "who have no occupation whatever, who have no means of gaining a livelihood." To achieve this logical conclusion from Clark's premise, Norris introduced the following amendment:

And any member of Congress who shall engage in the practice
of law, or who shall deliver Chautauqua lectures for pay, or who
shall engage in farming or manufacturing, or who shall have any
occupation whatever, or who shall patronize any national bank by
depositing any money therein, or who shall patronize any railroad
company by riding thereon, or who shall purchase any material of
or sell any material to any corporation shall be hanged by the neck
until dead and thereafter be prohibited from holding any office of
profit or trust under the Government of the United States.[22]

Another topic which generated much discussion was curbing the
use of injunctions. The administration, favoring moderate legislation,
did not endorse or present a particular measure. Norris was in favor of
a law that would prevent the abuse of injunctions, but he would not
support any measure to abolish their use. While he was willing to
admit that federal judges often had been reckless and careless in granting injunctions, he believed courts should retain authority to issue them
in certain cases without notice; namely, where irreparable damage
would result if time was taken to give notice. Norris' position would
not appeal to those leaders of organized labor who wanted to abolish
the writ, nor would it suit those businessmen who saw much good in
government by injunction.[23] His interest in the topic lasted throughout
his career, and in later years he would achieve one of his most notable
legislative victories in curbing the misuse of injunctions.

Norris supported the president in his desire to continue the Inland
Waterways Commission. Norris favored the idea of developing the
waterways of the nation, particularly those in the Mississippi Valley.
An overall plan to develop these waterways, of course, would benefit
Nebraska, but the entire country would benefit from the reduction
in freight rates that would follow such development. Thus Norris and
other proponents of inland waterways were aware that such a program,
beside aiding conservation, would tend to reduce railroad power and
influence in mid-America by providing the railroad with water competition.[24]

Though he was interested in more liberal legislation and championed the president's suggestions whenever possible, like Roosevelt,
Norris knew prior to a presidential election there would be no significant changes tending to engender controversy.[25] Moreover, Norris,
who had no plans of voluntarily retiring from Congress, had to consider measures with an eye toward the coming election. In regard to
his position on legislative matters, all but the most partisan Democrats
would have found much to approve in his record. Too many voters,

however, required more tangible notice of his service before they would pass favorable judgment on his work. Thus McCarl was kept busy distributing government documents and seeds, and Norris answered numerous requests for all kinds of relevant and irrelevant information about government services.

To aid and impress constituents even more, Norris made arrangements with the Department of Agriculture to have an expert lecture before farm organizations and other groups. He also sought through his work on the Committee of Public Buildings and Grounds to secure larger local appropriations. Though his membership on the committee insured the fact that the district would be included in every bill reported to Congress, he still could not satisfy all communities. Furthermore, he had to meet charges of favoritism toward McCook which, through his efforts, eventually obtained a courthouse as well as a post office.[26]

While Norris continued as a consistent supporter of the retiring president, the most important development of this session as far as he was concerned was his announced hostility to the rules by which Speaker Cannon exercised his authority. Prior to the Sixtieth Congress, when a band of insurgents for the first time in a sustained and open way criticized both the Speaker and his power, Norris never revealed himself as a critic of the rules by which Cannon administered the House of Representatives. Indeed he had prided himself on his friendship with Cannon and, throughout the long struggle, retained respect for the Speaker as a person of knowledge and ability. When Congressman E. A. Hayes of California wrote prior to the convening of Congress in September, 1907, he was not sure where Norris stood on this topic. In reply, Norris openly and definitely committed himself to insurgency for the first time. He favored a change whereby the Committee on Rules would be expanded and elected by the House instead of appointed by the Speaker.

Though many members were in favor of such a change, Norris doubted whether it would receive strong support because the caucus at which such a change could be made took place just before the beginning of a new Congress, and the many new members would probably follow the leadership of those in positions of power and seniority. Thus any change not favored by these new men was usually doomed to failure, and Norris, though he promised to vote for a rules change, did not think it would occur in the immediate future. It was the caucus system that was the basis of the Speaker's power. Though Norris later was instrumental in depriving the Speaker of his authority to choose the Rules Committee, he realized that this reform to be meaningful would have to be followed by the destruction of the party caucus.[27]

Norris and the insurgents conducted no prolonged battle during the first session of the Sixtieth Congress. The Panic of 1907 and the coming national election precluded any open party strife. However, Norris courageously let it be known precisely what he intended to do, if the opportunity ever arose. On May 16, 1908, he introduced a resolution providing that all standing committees be appointed by the Committee on Rules. According to this resolution (H.R. 417), a new rules committee consisting of fifteen members would be selected by the membership from candidates representing different geographical groups. The Norris resolution was sent to the Committee on Rules to be disposed of by its chairman, Joseph Cannon.[28] (Norris later produced this same resolution from his pocket and sent it to the desk to be read, thus precipitating the historic struggle which deprived the Speaker of his membership on the Committee on Rules.) Norris, in effect, on May 16, 1908, warned Cannon to be on guard.

Thus when the first session of the Sixtieth Congress came to an end on May 30, 1908, his position was widely known. Norris knew that to a great extent public opinion in Nebraska and other western states was opposed to Speaker Cannon. He received widespread support for his resolution, and soon claimed, "It is on account of such friends more than on account of any personal wish that I feel like staying in the fight."

Of course, he had no other alternative, since his resolution heaped upon him the displeasure of the Speaker and most of the party leaders in the House of Representatives. It put him "out of the shadow of approval" and in many ways it promised to make his work and life in Congress most disagreeable. It meant that almost all the "favors and courtesies" extended to other congressmen would be denied to him. The die was cast when he presented this resolution. Norris now would have to place principles above party as long as he remained in political life. It was this resolution of May 16, 1908, more than any other single event that made Norris into an insurgent Republican, one who would challenge a fundamental pillar of party control, and eventually the outstanding independent in American political history. However, his immediate job was a difficult one; namely, to educate the people who applauded him for the position he took to an understanding that he no longer could perform all the services he once did for them. He had to see that his constituents, who generally thought in terms of personalities and not of principles, did not forget the principle involved and condemn him for being unable to obtain patronage and favors. Indeed, his continuance in public life depended upon the ability of his constituents to understand this situation.[29]

Though Norris was well aware of the implications of his position, his constituents seemingly were satisfied with it. Instead of defending his action, Norris, in the coming campaign, would have to explain why he had not opposed Cannon earlier, and why he had been so friendly to him.[30] But, before the campaign got under way, Norris hoped to rest and regain his energy by traveling to Europe as a delegate to the Berlin meeting of the Interparliamentary Union.

Returning to Nebraska from Washington in July, he was soon engulfed in the rising tide of party politics. Before he became completely involved, he lectured before Chautauquas and other assemblies. In most instances he talked about the work of the Interparliamentary Union and used an address he hoped to deliver before pacifist conferences at Lake Mohonk, New York, and Greensboro, North Carolina, later in the summer. Though he was interested in the work of the Interparliamentary Union and pacifist groups, and though he was strongly urged to attend the conference in Berlin on September 10, Norris did not go because the expensive trip would have consumed at least four weeks of valuable campaign time.[31] His reasoning was wise because the 1908 campaign for re-election to a fourth term in the House of Representatives was to be one of the most difficult of his entire career.

Chapter 15

Victor by Twenty-Two Votes

THE 1908 campaign was not only one of the most difficult in the career of George Norris, but also one of the most significant in terms of his growing insurgency and political independence. It made dramatically evident to him the fact that while it was important to oppose the Democrats, it was equally important to maintain only a minimum of coordination with the Republican organization. In effect he was fought on two fronts in this campaign—by the Democrats and by his own party. At the outset only the first enemy was apparent.

Nebraska Republicans in September, 1907, endorsed William Howard Taft to carry on the policies of President Roosevelt. At the state convention at Omaha on March 12, 1908, Nebraska became the first state to declare for Taft. And as early as November, 1907, Norris agreed with his fellow Republicans in this choice. He did this first in an interview published in the Lincoln *Journal*, then in correspondence, then in his participation on the executive committee of the Nebraska Taft League.[1]

In the Fifth Congressional District by January, 1908, there was a movement to elect Norris a delegate to the Republican National Convention. But he refused to allow his name to be considered, claiming he did not believe the honors should all go to one man as long as other worthy, able, and competent individuals were available. "Members of Congress," he believed, "should not undertake to dictate in these matters and should under no circumstances use the power of their position to control conventions."[2] Moreover, he had his own campaign to consider.

George Allen, whom Norris, before his break with Cannon, had successfully recommended for the postmastership of Clay Center, could not serve as campaign manager. The heavy responsibilities of campaign manager fell on the capable but inexperienced shoulders of J. R. McCarl, who reported early in 1908 that few individuals openly sought Norris' place on the Republican ticket. On the other hand, there were persistent rumors that the Democrats would nominate Fred

Ashton, a state senator from Grand Island, as his opponent. Ashton had the reputation of being an unscrupulous campaigner. And scuttle-butt indicated that Norris, who preferred to conduct a campaign in which issues and principles predominated, might be in for an espe-cially tough fight, as would all the Republican candidates, since it was an open secret that Bryan would be the Democratic standard-bearer.[3]

However, politics did not really generate much excitement until Congress adjourned and the major national conventions met, the Republicans in Chicago on June 17 and the Democrats at Denver on July 7. Norris remained in Washington while Republican delegates chose Taft and James S. Sherman of New York as their standard-bearers. He returned to McCook early in July and shortly thereafter filed an application to have his name placed on the official primary ballot as a Republican candidate for the office of representative in Congress from the Fifth Nebraska Congressional District.

To help candidates, the Republican State Central Committee worked out a plan by which it hoped, more than ever before, to coordinate the campaign and simplify financial arrangements. Con-tributions to the state committee would be utilized equally by con-gressional committees. Republican postmasters would not have to make separate contributions to each of these committees as had been the case in the past. But they now were requested to contribute 3 per cent of one year's salary instead of the usual 2 per cent. This arrange-ment had been worked out before Norris returned to Nebraska. Find-ing that other Republican congressmen already had agreed to it, he had little alternative but to accept it as well.[4]

Though Norris was on the best of terms with the Republican State Central Committee, he nevertheless refused to participate in its affairs. He preferred the role of the lone political operator, even though he had recently cooperated more than ever before with the Republican organization in Nebraska. Since his days on the bench, Norris refused to participate in party squabbles or selection of officials. He held himself aloof but was always prepared to support the ticket once nominations had been made. He never tried to build a political ma-chine, and this fact applied to his entire political career. No postmaster or any other officeholder he had recommended was ever called upon for any kind of support.[5]

After the September primaries the party slates were completed and Norris learned that Ashton would be his opponent. Beside Bryan's popularity in Nebraska, Norris had an additional handicap. The Democratic candidate for governor, A. C. Shallenberger, resided in the Fifth Congressional District, where the popularity of both Bryan and

Shallenberger undoubtedly would help Ashton. Furthermore, both congressional candidates realized that many former Populist voters who had supported Theodore Roosevelt would probably vote for Bryan. Since the platforms of the major parties contained many progressive planks, both candidates undoubtedly knew that while Roosevelt could outshine Bryan as a personality if not as a liberal, Taft could not on either score. Thus even though Ashton was a poor public speaker, he had a chance to unseat Norris on election day.

Norris had further reason to be concerned. Friends said Ashton was tricky and unscrupulous, and these warnings convinced him it might be impolitic to leave the country at this time to attend the Berlin meeting of the Interparliamentary Union. Finally there were many political squabbles, including one pertaining to prohibition, that threatened to upset the harmony that previously prevailed within the Republican organization. Thus before the campaign got under way Norris knew that he would have a hard fight, though nobody realized just how hard it would be.[6]

Early in September Norris was in touch with the National Republican Congressional Committee in New York to get prominent speakers to appear in the district. He was convinced that the Democrats would make every effort to carry it, since it was not as strongly Republican as most of the other Nebraska districts. Yet knowing all of this, he still did not see any particularly distressing obstacles in his path. Since he believed that despite promised support from Bryan and Shallenberger, Ashton could be defeated, Norris arranged to spend almost half his campaign time outside of his district. Complacency was supplemented by a desire to play a role in the national campaign, indicative of his rising status as a member of Congress.[7]

Both United States senators from Nebraska were intending to speak on his behalf, and Governor Charles Evans Hughes of New York, touring the country for Taft, would speak at Hastings and possibly at McCook before the end of September. Norris himself refused all opportunities to speak in his own district prior to October in hopes of receiving—and on the false grounds that he had received—speaking assignments from the state committee. No such assignments were given him, however, and as September came to a close, Norris had done no campaigning and much explaining to those whose requests he had turned down.[8]

In response to inquiries at this time he felt called upon to explain his views on the House rules and the Speaker. Moreover, he learned that his opponents were criticizing him as a "Cannon man." Therefore he came out in opposition to the re-election of Cannon as Speaker, claiming that Cannon had used "the power of his high position to prevent the consideration of legislation asked for by the people and desired by a large body of the membership of the House of Representatives." His most serious objection, Norris explained in a published statement, was to the Speaker's opposition to any change in the rules which would modify or lessen his arbitrary power. In other words, he believed the Speaker "ought to be the servant of the House, doing its will, rather than the master controlling its action." Preventing discussion and throttling legislation should not be within his power. However, Norris realized that Cannon was not unique in the exertion of arbitrary power. He made it clear that his conflict was not so much with the Speaker as with the rules, not so much with Cannon as with the system.[9]

Certainly, Norris agreed, stringent rules were necessary in a body as large as the House of Representatives, and the Speaker ought to be the presiding officer. But in his power to appoint chairmen of standing committees and in his dominance of the powerful Committee on Rules, which determined the order of business and procedure, the Speaker exercised arbitrary authority. Norris explained that his resolution would make the Speaker merely "the dignified presiding officer of the greatest representative parliamentary body on earth." [10]

This statement represented the extent of Norris' campaign thus far. The state committee, handling all financial arrangements, had not sent him any funds while his opponent seemed to have unlimited means at his disposal. This discrepancy was soon noticed in the enthusiasm of some newspapers whose support had been purchased by the Democrats. While Ashton was attacking him in the press and in his speeches, Norris, without funds, was bound by an arrangement which was supposed to allow him to speak in Nebraska outside of his district but which actually kept him at home in McCook. And he had promised to campaign in Kansas early in October. Therefore it would not be until the second week in October that he could begin campaigning in the Fifth Congressional District.[11]

Norris was so discouraged that he contemplated withdrawing from the contest. He actually drafted a withdrawal letter but was prevented from mailing it by some devoted friends. While he would have enjoyed nothing more than campaigning and attacking the opposition, he believed that he could not fight the Democratic party, the Republican organization in Nebraska, and the lethargy of many local Republicans. If he were to be re-elected, he would need assistance and cooperation, and if neither was forthcoming, he intended to withdraw from the campaign.[12]

In early October he revealed that the treasurer of his campaign committee had not received any funds, nor had he been notified of contributions collected in the district. Thus no posters, leaflets, or advertisements for Norris had yet appeared. Finally, he was dismayed to learn, after his arrival in Kansas, where he was to speak on behalf of Republican candidates, that he had been chosen for the signal honor of traveling with Taft during his campaign trip through Nebraska. Norris learned of this decision from newspapers in Kansas. It seemed to him that the announcement had been given to the press even though the state committee knew that such an arrangement could not be carried out since he was speaking in Kansas at the time Taft toured Nebraska.[13]

While Norris was campaigning in Kansas, McCarl was desperately trying to raise funds from people who had not contributed to the Republican campaign chest. He spent part of a day at party headquarters in Lincoln where he heard the depressing news that the state committee had already used all of the money collected from the Fifth Congressional District. Indeed, the only good news McCarl learned in Lincoln was that Congressman Willis C. Hawley of Oregon and possibly Governor Sheldon would speak in the district.

Though McCarl was disheartened with this situation, he was equally determined to see it through and go into debt, if necessary, to get Norris re-elected. He wisely decided not to make the matter public knowledge, lest he jeopardize all chances of a reconciliation with the state committee and further damage Republican prospects in the campaign.[14]

McCarl kept loyal Republicans supplied with information about Norris' record in Congress to aid in refuting Democratic charges that he was not a loyal supporter of Roosevelt and was friendly with Speaker Cannon. But rather than devote his energies to refuting misrepresentations about Norris, McCarl began to investigate Ashton's record as a member of the Nebraska legislature. Among other items, he found that Ashton opposed all antiliquor legislation and this fact, he knew, would prove helpful in an area where prohibition had many supporters. Ashton's opposition to the primary law might also be of interest to many voters.[15]

On October 12, 1908, Norris at long last opened his campaign with a well attended evening meeting at Orleans in Harlan County. Thereafter he spoke once or twice on all days but Sundays. Once he was speaking, meeting the people, defending his record, and attacking that of his opponent, his discouragement disappeared. There was little time to lean back in an office chair, plant his feet on the top of the desk, and between puffs of the inevitable cigar discuss the political situation. The cigars were always with him, but the leisure moments were few and were usually confined to an editor's or lawyer's office or a hotel lobby.[16]

With Norris continually speaking, with Senator Albert J. Beveridge of Indiana and both United States senators from Nebraska as well as Governor Sheldon all appearing in the district and endorsing Norris, McCarl soon felt better about the course of the campaign. Since the campaign treasury was almost empty, he used his own money to have posters and handbills prepared for distribution. He drafted for publication in all Republican papers a statement entitled "Ashton Legislative Record," pinpointing Ashton's opposition to many of the recently enacted progressive reforms of the Nebraska legislature. It also provided documentation of the charge that Ashton was an agent and lobbyist for brewers.[17]

McCarl was working seventeen and eighteen hours a day directing the campaign; he also was overdrawing his account at the First National Bank of McCook which fortunately continued to honor his checks. He was discouraged about the early course of the campaign and doubted if Norris, owing to his long absence from the district, could cover it adequately. Though in mid-October he felt he was fighting a losing battle, his friendship for Norris was "the saving clause in this measure." On his account McCarl could not think of quitting and was determined, despite handicaps, to battle right down to election day.[18]

As the campaign moved toward its climax, the congressional candidates became briefly involved with the national effort. Because Nebraska was Bryan's home state, he was relentless in his attempt to carry it on election day. Both parties made determined efforts to appeal to the voters, but the Democrats made the greater effort, and Bryan devoted more time to the state than Taft. Without Roosevelt to appeal to Nebraska voters, many of them decided to leave the Republican fold and return to the candidate whom they had supported in 1896 if not in 1900. Rising Bryan sentiment made the role of Republican candidates exceedingly difficult because their opponents had the opportunity of being pushed to victory on the strength of Bryan's vote-getting appeal. This was particularly true in the Fifth Congressional District where Bryan personally endorsed Ashton. The effect of Bryan's appeal for a straight party vote would be of the utmost importance because it affected Norris' chances.[19]

But Norris continually made a good impression, and Ashton a correspondingly poor impression. Optimism began to return to the Norris headquarters. Everyone involved exerted himself to the utmost; prominent Republicans appeared in the district; and the Republican press gave increased support. McCarl faced the outcome with greater confidence. Victory, however, was not yet assured, and Norris' worries grew to include personal anxiety when he learned that his middle daughter, Marian, was ill with diphtheria, and that the family was quarantined.[20]

Reports confirmed what McCarl and Norris both already knew—that the race would be very close and would probably be decided only after all the ballots had been counted. One further bit of perplexing news was the appearance of a third party in Hall County where Ashton resided, called the County Option League. While this group would take votes from both parties, it was hard to tell which candidate would suffer most.[21]

To the very end of the campaign Norris stressed his record as a follower of Roosevelt in Congress. His speeches carried conviction, and his honest, forthright presentation created a favorable impression even among Democrats. The impression was more marked when contrasted with his opponent's campaign. Ashton delivered few speeches and personally canvassed for votes on the streets, in the saloons, and elsewhere. He cast aspersions on Norris' honesty and character and misrepresented his record as a congressman. At the same time, the liquor interests supporting Ashton were exerting great efforts to defeat both Norris and Governor Sheldon. Their agents circulated among temperance people the report that both men were "whiskey men"; in the saloons the agents reversed themselves and argued that Norris and Sheldon were temperance men.[22]

In the last week of the campaign the Democrats made a tremendous effort for Bryan. McCarl meanwhile planned to make the Hastings rally scheduled for Tuesday, October 27, the great event of the campaign. The businessmen of McCook, who put up the four-hundred-dollar guarantee required by the Burlington officials, sold enough tickets to cover their investment in a special train. At least one hundred and fifty voters from McCook expected to make the trip. At each town along the line, a band and a speaker would greet the train, though the engineer agreed to stop whenever anyone wanted to get aboard. The "Norris Special" was scheduled to arrive in Hastings between three and four o'clock in the afternoon and would depart at ten-thirty in the evening.[23]

While these plans were being made, the State Central Committee unexpectedly sent a check for over four hundred dollars to McCarl and smaller amounts to all but one of the county chairmen in the district. These funds helped them to provide transportation and meet other expenses to insure a full Republican turnout on election day. McCarl claimed the check "saved our lives out in the Fifth [District]." He now predicted victory by a majority of over three thousand votes. Favorable reports of the impact of Norris' speeches and of the rise in Norris sentiment aided by the success of the "Norris Special," helped him arrive at this conclusion.[24]

By the end of October the work of McCarl and Norris was virtually concluded. There remained only the election eve rally at McCook for Norris. Shortly after midnight on election night, McCarl was expected to inform the Republican National Committee of the results. He planned to be at work tabulating the votes all night or at least until Norris' victory was assured. As it turned out, both the candidate and his manager waited much longer than election night before the official result was known.[25]

Though the election of 1908 represented another Republican victory on the national scene, Taft did not do as well as Roosevelt in 1904, while Bryan did much better than Alton B. Parker. Though Bryan had only 162 electoral votes to 321 for Taft, one historian has noted, "There was a national vote cast for Bryan, and it was urban as well as rural; it was Eastern, Western, Southern and Northern." [26] Nebraska gave its electoral vote to its adopted son who carried the state by over four thousand votes. In the Fifth Congressional District Bryan carried ten of eighteen counties, including Red Willow, Norris' home county. He lost populous Hall County, where Ashton resided, by eleven votes. The Democrats also managed to defeat Sheldon, whom Norris claimed "was as good a Governor as Nebraska ever had." Three Democratic congressmen were elected, while Republican incumbents E. H. Hinshaw in the Fourth District and M. P. Kinkaid in the Sixth, both of whom, incidentally, were opposed to Speaker Cannon, were clearly re-elected. The results in the Fifth Congressional District were so close and the returns so confusing that no one knew who was elected until the last ballot was officially counted.[27]

Since the vote was so close, McCarl insisted that each committeeman be on hand for the official count to see that no "honest mistakes" occurred. The results revealed that Norris had defeated Ashton by twenty-two votes, 20,649 to 20,627. While Ashton carried his home county by fifty-three votes, Norris ran ahead of his ticket in this county. The committeeman from Hall County complained, "The Railroads simply overwhelmed us"; not a single Republican was elected in Hall County in 1908. In view of the outstanding Democratic triumph in the counties comprising the Fifth Congressional District, Norris' scant victory stood out as a signal achievement against a very dark background.[28]

On November 8, five days after the election, Norris obtained a set of official figures that assured his return to Congress. With a slim margin between defeat and victory there was a distinct possibility that Ashton would contest it. Norris requested that the Nebraska secretary of state notify him immediately of any suspicious returns so that he might commence proper action against the canvassing board of the county where these returns originated. He made this request because of rumors that his opponent, aided by "an unlimited checkbook," might try to bribe a county clerk to make an intentional error when filing the vote.[29]

Norris viewed his election as a triumph over "a checkbook" and over malice. Though his majority was small and he had to meet a large portion of the expenses himself, Norris was nonetheless gratified by his victory. He was disappointed by the defeat of J. F. Boyd in the Third Congressional District and of Governor Sheldon. Above all Norris regretted the defeat of William P. Hepburn in Iowa, the leader of the small band of Republicans in the House of Representatives who were challenging the rules by which Speaker Cannon exercised his power.[30]

On the evening of November 12, a victory celebration was held in McCook. And on November 13, 1908, the secretary of state notified Norris that he very much doubted if Ashton would undertake to contest the election. But all through November Norris and McCarl anticipated a contest and prepared themselves accordingly. It was only when he received a certificate of election in January, 1909, that Norris finally was convinced that Ashton would not initiate a contest.[31]

That the 1908 campaign was one of the most difficult in the career of George Norris there is no doubt. That it played an important role in the development of his insurgency and political independence is equally certain. He was in the process of showing his independence of party machinery in the House of Representatives when his campaign experience convinced him of the wisdom of running campaigns with a minimum of coordination with the Republican organization. Hereafter he would tend more and more to pursue his own course and, if anything, he would complain about party interference. With the burden of a mismanaged Republican organization in Nebraska, with the hostility of Speaker Cannon in Congress, with little money to conduct his campaign while the opposition seemingly had unlimited funds, with few friendly newspapers supporting him, and with the liability of a late start in speaking, Norris was able to eke out a twenty-two vote plurality, while the Democrats with Bryan as their standard-bearer won a singular victory in Nebraska if not on the national scene.

Norris' growing independence of party organization was a major element in his insurgency. It developed gradually and logically out of his experience and was molded by no single incident. The fact that he represented a political "burnt-over" district which, since his arrival in the late 1880's, had strongly supported all shades of political opinion from respectable Republicanism to belligerent Bryanism may have made his position somewhat easier. But basic to the success of the role he was to enact was the personality, courage, and integrity of the man himself. Unassuming, modest but straightforward, presenting facts and issues sometimes for hours on end, avoiding personalities, diatribes, and emotionalism, relying on the friendship of a small band of friends, and without a political machine to aid him, Norris was able to gain and hold the respect of voters. Whereas many Populists and Democrats added emotional fervor to the issues they raised, Norris presented reason and logic with the probity of a country judge turned politician. That he succeeded in his insurgency throughout a long career attests not only to his ability but also to the highmindedness of the constituents whose interests he represented. The second session of the Sixtieth and the entire Sixty-first Congress witnessed the eruption of insurgency in a way that brought Norris and his cohorts to the attention of a nationwide audience and, despite his narrow victory, made his constituents proud of his performance.

Chapter 16

Insurgency

PREPARING to return to Washington for the second session of the Sixtieth Congress, Norris expected to participate in a fight against the rules of the House of Representatives. He, of course, was eager to do battle, but he was saddened by the fact that William P. Hepburn of Iowa, a long-time opponent of the rules, would be ending his distinguished career with this short or lameduck session. Hepburn was one of four Republican incumbents, generally inimical to the House rules, who were defeated for re-election in 1908.[1] Though the ranks of the insurgents would be increased as a result of the election, none had Hepburn's prestige and seniority and few had his general over-all ability.

As usual during a short session, Mrs. Norris and the children remained at home when Norris left for Washington on December 2. McCarl also remained in McCook to practice law and to manage affairs in the district. Norris again sought the services of Attorney Polk and hoped to hire a stenographer to handle his correspondence and possibly to serve as a receptionist in his office in the new House Office Building. During the Christmas holiday recess he intended to vacation on the Isle of Pines off the southern coast of Cuba. Norris expected to be busy during this short session, and the vacation would provide an opportunity to recover from the rigors of an arduous campaign.[2]

However, no sooner had he arrived in Washington and unpacked his bags than he hurriedly made arrangements to return to McCook. His youngest child, Gertrude, had fallen ill and the doctor had diagnosed her illness as diphtheria. She was given antitoxin and put to bed. The family feared her heart might be affected. By returning to McCook and spending the period of quarantine with his family, he could help with the task of amusing two healthy girls while Mrs. Norris attended a convalescing one. On December 9, 1908, two days after the session started, he was granted an indefinite leave of absence.[3]

Arriving home and entering quarantine, he found Gertrude well on the road to recovery. On December 21 the quarantine was lifted. For the second time in less than two months the house was fumigated and almost everything had to be moved out and back. Though Gertrude's case was a mild one, two periods of quarantine with less than a month's interval between them must have been a trying experience for Mrs. Norris and the children. Norris decided to remain at home until after the Christmas holidays, canceling his plans for a trip to the Isle of Pines.[4]

Thus Norris was not on hand when, on the evening of December 11, 1908, a small band of insurgent Republicans gathered in the Interstate and Foreign Commerce Committee room for the purpose of planning a fight for more democratic procedure in the House of Representatives. Hepburn presided over the meeting and was authorized to choose a committee of five, with himself as chairman, to propose possible changes. It was suggested that the rule of recognition be revised, that the committees on Elections and Rules be made elective, and that membership on the latter committee be increased.[5]

Four days later, a resolution was proposed that a special committee report not later than February 1, 1909, any changes in the existing rules that might seem desirable. Though the resolution was not considered, the vote on the point of order not to consider it was 149 to 136, indicating the possibility that the insurgents and the Democrats by voting together might eventually control the House.[6] However, until that day arrived, the insurgents would have to be satisfied with bringing their fight to the attention of the public by harassing the Speaker and condemning his arbitrary power.

In January when Congress reconvened Norris was present to lend aid and support to his fellow insurgents, banded together for the first time in their battle against the House rules. As a solution to the problem of making the House truly representative, the insurgent group accepted Norris' plan for the Committee on Rules to be selected by the members on the basis of geographical groups and for the committee in turn to choose members of all the standing committees. Norris, Hepburn, John M. Nelson of Wisconsin, and others in the group agreed that a change of speakers or a change of political parties would not lessen the power of the Speaker. Only a change in the rules would remove the source of his power and solve the problem. Norris succinctly stated this position when he argued, "The rule that gives the Speaker power to appoint all the Standing committees of the House, which practically control all of the legislation of the House," was the rule that was most obnoxious to those who thought that the Speaker had too much power.[7]

He conceded, of course, that rules were necessary and that most of them served a useful purpose. He was opposed to unlimited debate in a body of almost four hundred members and he accepted without qualification the "Reed rules." [8] However, notwithstanding the fact that most of the rules were the result of wisdom and experience, in "one or two particulars" they were not only wrong but vicious and ought to be changed. He mentioned the power of the Speaker to appoint all standing committees and noted his "most serious objection to the rules of the House." The most objectionable and vicious of all was the fact that there was "practically no provision within the rules themselves" for amendment or change except by the consent of the Speaker.

Here, as Norris and his fellow insurgents knew, was the core of their dilemma. Any resolution to change the rules would be referred to the Committee on Rules, of which the Speaker was chairman and dominant figure and chose or approved its membership. Once the members adopted at the beginning of a Congress the previous rules, Norris claimed, they "tied the hands of the House absolutely as far as any change" was concerned. They made it virtually impossible during the course of that particular Congress to amend the rules without the consent of the Speaker.

Knowing that a rules change would not be reported out of committee, Norris nevertheless proceeded to discuss his resolution[9] which offered a solution that the insurgents believed would equitably solve the problem without undermining the political balance of the House by forcing insurgent Republicans into an uneasy alliance with the Democratic minority. His resolution called for a new committee on rules that would not only be representative of the entire membership but would also be subject to the will of the majority.

Representative James Mann of Illinois immediately perceived the weakest point in Norris' resolution when he noted that it gave the fifteen members of the committee the authority to delegate to a subcommittee of its members, not less than three in number, "the power to report special rules to the House of Representatives for the transaction of business." This subcommittee within limits would have all the authority of the full committee. Mann wanted to know why the power of the House, which Norris thought was being absorbed through the rules by the Speaker, would not likewise be absorbed by this subcommittee.

Norris replied that this would not occur because the committee provided for in the resolution derived its authority from and was responsible to the entire House rather than the Speaker. It was more likely, he believed, that fifteen members, elected by the geographical division prescribed in his resolution, would better represent the ideas and purposes of the House than would the members of the Rules Committee chosen by the Speaker. But Mann did not see it that way. In one case fifteen members would confer power on a subcommittee of three, while under the prevailing rules, a majority of the dominant party, assembled in caucus, conferred power on the Speaker. Though Norris suggested the only possible answer to Mann's question, his antagonist was not convinced of its validity. In his response Norris also made clear that he was not implying that Speaker Cannon usurped any authority or power. Indeed, throughout this long and sometimes bitter struggle, Norris always insisted, as did some of the other Republican insurgents, that he was opposed to the system and did not intend to cast aspersions on Cannon or anyone else. Finally Norris, apparently impressed by Mann's criticism, stated that he held no brief for his plan. If another plan could achieve the same results he was willing to accept it, provided it was offered in good faith and not simply for the purpose of causing delay and confusion.[10]

However, Norris' remarks did not comprise the major assault upon the rules during this session. This honor was reserved for Hepburn as his farewell address after twenty-two years of distinguished service in Congress. But before Hepburn delivered his speech the insurgents made some important decisions. On January 27, 1909, Hepburn announced their acceptance of Norris' resolution and of another expedient designed to secure greater freedom in the consideration of measures.

This expedient proposed to set aside each Tuesday, except during the last six days of a session, when no business except that on the House Calendar and the Calendar of the Committee of the Whole House on the State of the Union would be in order.[11] On "Calendar Tuesday" all committees would be called in regular order and each committee could call up any bill on either calendar. Motions to adjourn, recess, or rise were not in order before 4:45 P.M. Furthermore, on Calendar Tuesday general debate on a measure in the Committee of the Whole could be closed at any time after the expiration of forty minutes. And, finally, proceedings under this rule, which if enacted would have markedly curtailed the power of the Speaker only one day a week, could be suspended for the day by a two-thirds vote.[12]

On February 9, 1909, a resolution to amend the rules embodying these proposals was introduced by twenty-nine Republican members, including all of Nebraska's Republican congressmen. The resolution (H.R. 551) was sent to the Committee on Rules for Cannon, its chairman, to consider.[13] While none of the insurgents seriously expected anything except publicity to come from the resolution, few realized the opportunity it presented the Speaker. By accepting the idea of Calendar Tuesday he could make a concession to his critics and, undoubtedly, split the ranks of the insurgents. Calendar Tuesday, of course, would not seriously damage the Speaker's power and would not in the least alter the rules of the House, the source of his power. Indeed some moderate insurgents, like Augustus P. Garner of Massachusetts, probably would have been amenable to fighting for only Calendar Tuesday.[14]

On February 18, 1909, Hepburn delivered the major speech of the session against the rules. It was entirely fitting that he should have done this. Though he was the leader of the Republican caucus and chairman of a powerful committee, Hepburn had been attacking the rules longer than any other person in Congress, long before the other insurgents were elected to the House of Representatives. A polished orator and a dangerous opponent in debate, Hepburn used his talents of biting satire, keen wit, and scathing ridicule to challenge the arbitrary power of the Speaker. In his speech Hepburn gave voice to the basic dilemma of the insurgents and predicted the fate of their resolution: "Oh, it is easy to get into the Committee on Rules, but by what hoist and by what petard would we get out of the Committee on Rules?" [15]

Speaker Cannon must have been thankful and the insurgents sad that this speech was Hepburn's last as a member of Congress. Though the February resolution of the twenty-nine insurgents was never reported to the House, on March 1, 1909, within four days of the end of the Sixtieth Congress an amendment was presented and adopted calling for a "Calendar Wednesday" when no business but the calling of the committees would be in order. Cannon thus made the most of his opportunity to split the ranks of the insurgents by offering a mild concession as an amendment to the rules.

Norris was furious at Cannon's use of the resolution to harm the insurgent cause, and gave vent to his wrath:

> Mr. Speaker, I believe that this proposed rule is the most useless, perhaps harmless, and worse than worthless proposition that has ever emanated, especially coming at this particular late day, from the Committee on Rules. It is, in my judgment, the most comical parliamentary joke that ever came down the legislative pike. In its application it is a homeopathic dose of nothingness.[16]

He argued that since the rule provided it should not be in effect during the last two weeks of Congress, the members of the House were at this late date placed in "the foolish and ridiculous position" of ac-

cepting a rule that would not have any effect in the Congress in which
it was adopted. He called it "a sop to the people of the country to
deceive them in their demand that this House shall modify its rules
so that it shall be really a representative body instead of a one-man
machine." [17]

Periodically in the last years of the nineteenth century, isolated members of the House of Representatives had spoken against the rules but
never in the past had the opposition assumed the proportions of an
organized movement. Now, however, in the last months of Theodore
Roosevelt's administration it was rapidly increasing and assuming national proportions. Speaker Cannon, colorful and gruff, quickly became
in many newspapers and magazines and in the public mind an over-
bearing, bearded, cigar-smoking ruler who tyrannized the House of
Representatives. While Republican insurgents in Congress and a plank
in the Democratic platform of 1908 criticized the rules, many of the
journalistic articles attacked the man. Thus the House rules and the
Speaker by the end of 1908 became a subject of national attention, and
"Cannonism" a system that insurgents sought to eradicate. Though
Norris, as a result of his service in Congress, came to favor changes in
the rules, he nevertheless maintained respect for Cannon and the position he held. Most citizens, however, were more concerned with the
man than with the source of his power.[18] Meanwhile, pressed and
harassed on all sides by members of his own party and by the Democratic opposition, by the press and by increasing public clamor, "Uncle
Joe" began to utilize the tremendous power the rules gave him to fight
and perhaps punish his antagonists. Indeed, he had not spoken to
Norris since he introduced his resolution in May, 1908.[19]

It should be noted at this point that during the Roosevelt administration, Speaker Cannon and the rules were never a major obstacle to
the president in advancing his legislative program. Most of Roosevelt's
difficulties were with the Senate, and, in most instances, the House
quickly passed the bills the administration desired. Roosevelt, though
he might not have liked or admired Cannon, worked well with him,
consulted with him frequently, wrote him often, and listened to his
advice about the tenor of opinion in the House of Representatives. In
short, harmonious relations prevailed between the president and the
Speaker throughout most of the Roosevelt administration. As a result,
Norris saw nothing incongruous about supporting Roosevelt and ad-
miring Cannon. But the ill will evident in the Sixtieth Congress carried over into the Taft administration, when the president, who did
not like the Speaker, found it difficult to cooperate and work with him,
partly because Taft exerted much less effort than his predecessor, and

partly because Cannon, now thoroughly aroused and angered, was much less inclined to cooperate.[20]

Thus as the Sixtieth Congress came to an end, the fight against Cannonism had come out into the open and, of course, would be continued in the next Congress. Though this struggle was the most significant aspect of Norris' service in the short session, he concerned himself with other matters as well. The most important of these was the tariff issue, since the incoming president had announced his intention of calling Congress into special session to revise it. Important, too, was the growing sentiment for a postal savings system, while many merchants were concerned lest a parcel post system be established. They claimed the establishment of such a system would enable the large mail-order firms to drive retail merchants in small towns out of business.[21]

Norris pointed out that a parcel post system was already in existence and that those who favored it really desired the Post Office Department to carry larger packages at lower rates than the law provided. Believing that express company charges were exorbitant and unjust, he was inclined to favor a reduction in the postal laws so that rates would take into consideration not only size and weight, but distance as well. If this were done, retail merchants in small towns would not suffer unduly from mail-order competition, and both merchant and farmer would benefit from the competition thus forced upon the express companies.[22]

Like many of his constituents, Norris was interested in the concept of a postal savings bank. A plank in the Republican platform of 1908 favored the enactment of such legislation. However, he did not intend to support any measure that would siphon funds from the area of deposit to a large city. He believed that deposits in a postal savings bank should not be granted special tax exemptions. In this respect, his views differed from the bill introduced by Senator Thomas H. Carter of Montana, a bill which granted postal savings bank deposits exemption from taxation and levy on execution.[23]

While both a parcel post and a postal savings measure would be enacted during the Taft administration, it was the tariff that received immediate attention once the new administration got under way. Norris believed that the tariff ought to be removed from wood and all of its products, and that the rates on grain ought to be retained at their prevailing high level to protect farmers and millers from foreign, particularly Canadian, competition. He realized, however, that a new tariff law would have to be the result of compromise and would contain many items he would not favor.[24]

But discussions of these issues were merely skirmishes for battles to come. The attack against the Speaker dominated the short session as far as the House of Representatives was concerned. Meanwhile most Republicans looked forward to Taft's inauguration on March 4, 1909. While feelings were mixed, few if any were indifferent about the departure of Roosevelt from the White House. Most congressmen, whether Democratic or Republican, were unhappy about the prospect of foregoing their deserved vacations for the dubious privilege of remaining in Washington, possibly throughout the summer, to prepare a tariff which under any circumstance was bound to create acrimony and discord. Norris, in February, wrote to the president-elect requesting the special session at least a week later than the tentatively scheduled date of March 10, thereby allowing the western members of Congress to return home for a few days and still be back in time for the beginning of the session. Ordinarily, Norris knew, it did not make much difference if some members were not present at the start of a session, but the desire of the insurgents to challenge the rules made it necessary for all to be present at the outset when the fight would take place.[25] Taft, though he did not acknowledge Norris' letter, complied by calling the special session to convene on March 15.

Norris left Washington on March 4, before the new president took the oath of office. He was not sufficiently impressed with the grandeur of inauguration ceremonies to go out of his way to witness one. He was back in Washington shortly before Congress convened ready to participate in the rules fight.[26]

Norris, of course, knew that a large majority of the Republican caucus favored Cannon's re-election as Speaker. It would be impossible to defeat him, but the insurgents believed there was "a fair chance" of amending the rules at this time. And Norris intended to battle for reform "until the last ditch shall have been reached." If beaten, he knew there would be no hope for favors and consideration during this Congress.[27]

On March 15, as soon as the session started, parliamentary maneuvering began over adopting the rules of the previous session. Once these rules were adopted, virtually all hope of modifying them would be ended. Norris dramatically pointed up the issue, and incidentally noted that the new administration would be a far cry from the previous one:

> Mr. Speaker, there will be no change in the rules that will be satisfactory or produce satisfactory results either to the House or to the country that does not take away from the Speaker the

right to serve on the Committee on Rules and the right to appoint all the standing committees of this House. . . . It is to be
regretted, Mr. Speaker, that we were not left to settle this question without any outside influences. During the vacation Members of this House have been worked upon by the various departments of this Government, especially what are known as the
"insurgent" part of the House; Senators, Cabinet members, and,
I regret to say, the President, have all been working in behalf of
the Speaker and his machine; so that we have had a combination
of the Senate, the Cabinet, the Executive, and the "knights of the
Iron Duke," all combined in an assault upon that little band of
insurgents.[28]

Unfurling their banner, the insurgents were risking their political
lives. Newspapers claimed that if defeated they would be punished by
loss of important places on committees and by loss of executive patronage. Norris' response to this challenge was as follows:

If we are to be punished for standing for a principle which we
believe to be right, then let the lash be unfurled. Do your worst.
We will not be intimidated. We will not surrender. I would rather
go down to my political grave with a clear conscience than ride
in the chariot of victory, a congressional stool pigeon, the slave,
the servant, and the vassal of any man, whether he be the owner
and manager of a legislative menagerie or the ruler of a great
nation.[29]

Lest he be pushed too far in opposition to the chief executive,
Norris clarified his position by proclaiming his confidence in Taft. The
real power in government, he said, was being exerted not by the president but by the "Iron Duke" who, "sitting upon his throne, crowned
with the power given him by the rules, reaches out his mighty hand
and forces even the Chief Executive to do his bidding." For Norris, at
last, the struggle had degenerated to the level of personalities. He also
predicted, "We insurgents may have the life crushed out of us by the
machine, but the cause is right, and in the end it must prevail." [30]

Despite insurgent opposition, the previous rules were modified to
improve the functioning of the House while not hampering the Speaker's control of the Committee on Rules or his power to appoint standing committees. This modification, which received some Democratic
support, was the result of an arrangement made by the Speaker with
Democratic Representative John J. Fitzgerald and other Democratic
members, whereby the Speaker promised to support a higher duty on

petroleum products in the impending tariff bill in return for enough Democratic votes to prevent the insurgents in alliance with Champ Clark from further amending the rules. The rules that were adopted, under this compact, provided for a unanimous consent calendar which eliminated the daily procession to the Speaker's office to obtain permission to consider bills meeting with general approval. Calendar Wednesday was strengthened by changing the requirement for setting it aside from a majority to a two-thirds vote, and finally a recommittal motion was permitted after the previous question had been moved on any bill. Such a motion was not in order before this.[31]

Thus defeated, the lonely insurgents knew that before the special session was concluded they could expect the wrath of the Speaker to manifest itself in lowly committee assignments. They had supported amendments offered by Champ Clark to amend the rules, amendments that would have deprived the Speaker of most of his authority. But because of the defection of Democratic members these amendments were defeated. The only positive achievement they could discern was in the form of national press coverage which publicized their struggle to a large audience. Norris, for the first time, came to the attention of a national audience and many citizens, no doubt, admired his perspicacity in analyzing the issues and his courage in antagonizing the Speaker and possibly the president.[32]

Incidentally, despite his attack on the Speaker's power and his campaign promise to vote against Cannon, Norris voted for him and received, at the same time, two votes for Speaker.[33] By voting for Cannon, Norris could remain within the Republican organization and retain a vote and a voice to change the rules. If he disregarded the party caucus and voted against Cannon, Norris was aware that Cannon still would be re-elected and his own standing would become even more precarious. He had argued that if there was no possibility of defeating the Speaker the insurgents should vote for his re-election.[34] Norris remained throughout this fight one of the more moderate insurgents who managed to separate growing hostility to Cannon from a primary desire to modify the rules.

Once the fight to amend the rules was lost the House settled down to the urgent business of the special session—preparing a new tariff law, though an undercurrent of hostility prevailed.[35] A measure was introduced in the House by Sereno Payne on March 17, 1909. The bill, providing for generally lower rates, met with more approval than most observers had expected. The insurgents presented no organized opposition to it. Norris, believing that an unduly high tariff encouraged trusts and monopolies, favored some reduction, though the loss of tariff revenue would have to be balanced either by increased taxation or curtailment of expenditures. He preferred eliminating extravagant appropriations, especially for the navy. He had voted against such appropriations since he had been in Congress, but "the country seemed to demand the upbuilding of a big navy, and the President was very enthusiastic in his demands for the same." Therefore he realized that any reduction of rates would have to be balanced by increased taxation.[36]

Norris succeeded in adding a significant amendment to the tariff bill. The subcommittee which prepared the measure unanimously placed petroleum and petroleum products on the free list. At the insistence of Speaker Cannon, the chairman called a meeting of the subcommittee to reconsider this decision. After bitter debate, in which the Speaker insisted that Republican members abide by party principles and promises, the committee by a partisan vote agreed to put a tariff of 25 per cent on petroleum and petroleum products.[37]

Before Norris was elected to Congress, the tariff on petroleum and its products had figured in a congressional campaign in the Fifth District. Consequently, he was very much interested in this particular portion of the tariff. The bill was considered under a special rule which made it impossible to place an item, by means of amendment, on the free list. Therefore, on April 7, 1909, Norris presented a motion to reduce the 25 per cent duty on petroleum and its products to a nominal 1 per cent. After some debate in which Speaker Cannon took the floor to speak against it, Norris' motion prevailed, whereupon Payne, sponsor of the measure in the House of Representatives, informed the members that the duty as amended would not pay the cost of collection. He requested unanimous consent that petroleum and its products be placed on the free list.[38]

Norris' action in reducing this important schedule of the tariff won immediate approval from his constituents. McCarl wrote from McCook that he had not been able to find a man, "Democrat or Republican or indifferent," who was not pleased with his "victory on the oil proposition." Most newspapers were generous in their praise of Norris, whose popularity was on the rise after the low point of the 1908 election.[39]

One of the things that pleased Norris most with the tariff bill that passed the House on April 9, 1909, was the fact that it followed a suggestion in Taft's inaugural message and provided for an inheritance tax as a means of balancing the loss of income from the generally lowered rates of the Payne bill. He had always favored an inheritance tax. While in theory an income tax was generally conceded to be the most equitable tax, as a matter of practice Norris thought it the most diffi-

cult to collect because it offered too many opportunities for evasion
by dishonest citizens. On the other hand a graduated inheritance tax
posed no such difficulty. Ideally it could be collected from the bequests
received by the beneficiaries so that the larger the amount received,
the larger the rate of taxation; however, the plank in the tariff measure
merely taxed the sum left by the deceased. Despite this mild objection
to the inheritance feature of the bill, Norris was delighted and was
certain it would bring in considerable revenue.[40]

The debate on the tariff in the Senate was one of the notable events
in the history of that distinguished body, lasting well on into the summer. The House, having passed the measure on April 9, had little important business to conduct until the Senate reached some agreement.
Thus many House members, having little to do in the capital city, requested leaves of absence because of important business. Norris obtained such a leave on April 12, 1909,[41] and chose to conduct his important business in the Panama Canal Zone. He returned to Washington on May 2 to find Senate debate raging, as a handful of Republican
members subjected the tariff to what some of its supporters, no doubt,
considered an agonizing reappraisal.[42]

On May 14, Norris decided to go home until the Senate debate was
concluded. In McCook he relaxed with his family, kept abreast with
his correspondence, and avoided all public commitments, including
Fourth of July addresses, because of the need to return to Washington
as soon as the Senate passed the tariff bill. By July 7 he was back in
Washington and glad to be where the heat was less intense than it had
been in Nebraska.[43]

By a vote of forty-five to thirty-four on July 8, the Senate passed its
version of the tariff bill with ten Republican members, including both
Nebraska senators, voting against it. The next day on the floor of the
House, Norris followed the lead of La Follette by characterizing the
bill as a revision upward. Norris argued that unless the upward revision of rates in many schedules was rejected, specifying particularly
gloves and hosiery, the Republican party would not be true to its
pledges. He quoted speeches by Taft to illustrate the party's pledge to
reduce tariff schedules and suggested a resolution whereby the House
would concur in those Senate amendments which reduced the tariff
and would go into conference on the balance. Unless the members
voted for this resolution, Norris warned they would not have another
chance to discuss the bill. When it returned from conference committee, it would probably contain several hundred items. Members would
not get a separate vote but would be required "to accept all or reject
all." [44]

By adopting his proposition, the House could dispose of all Senate amendments where rates were reduced. In doing this, the members would have an opportunity to express themselves on every one of them. Whereas if the measure was sent immediately to conference committee the members would lose control over the bill, because the Speaker would choose conferees sympathetic to his high tariff views.[45] However, as Norris no doubt expected, his proposal failed. It received insurgent support on the Republican side of the House.

The conference committee remained in session until early August trying to adjust all items where Senate and House measures provided for different rates. The president attempted to convince it of the necessity of reduced rates on gloves and hosiery, while also demanding free iron ore, coal, hides, oil, and a lower duty on lumber.[46] Norris, remaining in Washington during these deliberations, feared the conferees would eliminate the inheritance tax provided in the House bill and substitute the Senate provision for a corporation tax. Since the president now advocated this latter proposal which, Norris thought, was prepared by the attorney general, he knew that a corporation rather than an inheritance tax would be included in the law ultimately enacted by Congress. He also knew that House members would vote for or against the bill with no chance to consider particular items.[47]

At the end of July, by the narrow margin of 191–186, the House defeated a recommittal motion, with Norris and most insurgent members voting with the minority. On the final vote to accept the conference committee report, Norris and some of the moderate insurgents were included among the 195 members who voted in the affirmative. Prior to these votes six progressive Republican senators appeared on the House floor in an effort to convince members that the measure should be sent back to conference committee.[48] Failing in their efforts, the senators continued their battle in the Senate chamber, but when the roll was called on August 5, 1909, the conference report carried by a vote of 47–31 with only six Republican senators voting against it. This time both Nebraska senators voted with the majority. Thus after bitter debate in both houses, but especially in the Senate, the Payne-Aldrich tariff bill was sent to President Taft for approval, which was quickly given on August 5, 1909, before the special session of the Sixty-first Congress formally adjourned.

In summing up his attitude toward the Payne-Aldrich tariff Norris said he fought the bill from start to finish in most of its essential features. However, he admitted the law had much in its favor. Though he had voted against many schedules and for every parliamentary proposition that would have kept the conference report in committee, he still voted for the bill. He did this because the Payne-Aldrich tariff was "infinitely better than the Dingley law," since it was molded "on the right principle." It raised the tariff on luxuries and lowered it on necessities; 'not enough," he admitted, "but it was a step in the right direction." According to Norris, the true principle of a tariff was that it should represent the differences between the cost of production at home and abroad. The Payne-Aldrich tariff did not do this, but, Norris believed, it approached this goal much better than did the Dingley tariff.[49]

On the day before the special session came to an end when the House was considering an "urgent deficiency bill," Norris spoke against an item which granted an automobile for the vice-president and the Speaker. It presented him with an opportunity for indirect and facetiously amusing criticism of the Speaker: "If we should buy this automobile for the Speaker and he should become adept and an expert in the management of it, as he undoubtedly would in a short time, his natural inclination to run over people when assisted by an automobile would make it dangerous for everybody in the community." However, it was the Speaker who had the final word at this time. On the last day of the session committee assignments for the regular session of the Sixty-first Congress were announced. Norris now fully felt Cannon's power when he found himself downgraded to membership on the insignificant committees on Coinage, Weights, and Measures, and on Private Land Claims, committees which he claimed were "dead and committees in name only." [50]

Returning to Nebraska, Norris believed that many of his constituents sympathized with his position and resented the actions of the Speaker. He knew, too, that his ability to be of service to his constituents had been and would remain severely curtailed as long as Cannon was Speaker. However, his position and that of his fellow insurgents was not yet clarified because no one knew for certain whether Taft intended to continue the policies of his predecessor or whether he would move into the more conservative camp dominated by the able and powerful senator from Rhode Island, Nelson Aldrich. Norris therefore resolved to bring his case before his constituents, lest opponents take advantage of his weakened position. Thus, instead of a vacation for what remained of the summer, he sought a way to present his position to the public and, if possible, to increase his income.

Chapter 17

The Eve of Conflict

WHEN Norris returned to Nebraska in August, 1909, the prevailing sentiment in that state had become more progressive in response to national developments such as the insurgency revolt, to reform movements in other states such as Wisconsin, and to clamoring for further measures to protect citizens against banks and bosses. The legislature, controlled by the Democrats for the first time since statehood, enacted under Governor A. C. Shallenberger more liberal legislation than under Republican Governor George L. Sheldon. A bank guarantee law designed to protect depositors, an idea Norris had suggested in Congress, was the most important piece of new legislation. Other measures changed the primary from a closed to an open election,[1] provided for the election of educational officers and judges on a nonpartisan ticket, and established the "Oregon Pledge Law," requiring legislative candidates to state that if elected they would vote for the candidate for United States senator receiving the highest preferential vote. But the most important sign of increased progressivism to Norris was the widespread approval by Nebraskans of his course of action in Congress. Indeed, rumor had it that he would seek the senatorial nomination in 1910 in place of Senator E. J. Burkett, who was regarded as too conservative.[2]

Norris was noncommittal regarding this nomination. He preferred to wait until party opposition to Burkett clearly crystallized and other candidates came forward. He claimed too that he was not particularly anxious to be a candidate for the Senate. Life in Washington presented "too many disappointments and too much opposition of a disagreeable and often of a dishonorable kind."[3]

The Norrises had planned to spend their summer traveling to the Pacific coast to visit relatives of Mrs. Norris. The special session of Congress, however, had forced them to abandon this idea. Instead, Norris made arrangements for several Chautauqua lectures beginning in September. Most of the talks were to be presented under the auspices of the University of Nebraska's extension lecture program for very modest fees.[4]

Norris spoke on three topics: peace, the Panama Canal, and Cannonism, with the last subject proving to be the most popular. His lecture, "The Dream of Peace," was an able presentation favoring the settlement of international disputes by a court of arbitration. Though most of the talks were delivered in churches, Norris' pacifism did not have a religious base or orientation. It emanated primarily from his experience as an American delegate to the Interparliamentary Union conference at Brussels in 1905. "Ever since then," he wrote in 1908, "I have been greatly interested in the subject." And the more he examined it, the more convinced he became that "the greatest disgrace of the present civilized age is that war is in any case and under any condition a possibility."[5]

He suggested that if the United States and England took the lead and settled all disputes by arbitration, "All the world would doubtless follow in their footsteps." He favored a vast network of separate treaties rather than a single treaty to which all nations would agree. And he thought the men appointed as arbitrators should be granted a long term so that they could make a careful study of international law and the administration of international justice. Then, too, with long terms jurors could rise above national prejudice and decide questions purely on their merits. Thus when a controversy arose the machinery to cope with it would be immediately available.[6]

Norris also coupled these lectures with a plea for a smaller navy, claiming the reason the peace forces in America were divided was that they could not agree on naval policy. While he favored curtailing naval expenditures,[7] other peace advocates held that the best way to obtain peace was to be prepared for war. Accepting the necessity of maintaining an army and a navy and claiming that from 60 to 70 per cent of the nation's revenues were spent for war or the preparation for war, Norris, nevertheless, hoped that these expenditures could be curtailed as the civilized world began "to shake off the shackles of barbarism." Since war was a frightful reminder of the "barbarous ages" he considered it a disgrace "to the present civilized age" that any nation think of waging war with any other civilized nation, "when the difficulty could so easily be settled by arbitration."[8]

In his lecture on the Panama Canal, Norris hoped to communicate some knowledge of what the government was doing there so that his constituents could comprehend, for example, some of the difficulties encountered by the engineers in charge of the project. Though audiences listened attentively to the address, none received it enthusiastically.

At the end of the second lecture when the audience was about to be dismissed, somebody called out: "Before you go, Mr. Norris, tell us about the Cannon fight; that's what we want to know about." Whereupon Norris, unprepared for another lecture the same evening, talked for an hour and aroused the first real enthusiasm of the evening. Thus it quickly developed that the lecture "Cannonism and the Remedy" was the most popular of the three.[9]

In these talks, during the question period when the audience reverted to politics, Norris replied that it was too early to say anything definite about his senatorial candidacy, though he did claim that he could not afford to make the race. In doing this he presented a basic criticism of the direct primary system.[10] In the formal lecture he discussed the rules, the tariff fight, and the injustice of Speaker Cannon in depriving insurgents of their standing on committees, in refusing to recognize them in the House chamber or to speak to them in the corridors. Obviously, there was no need to prepare this lecture; it was delivered extemporaneously. Its structure varied with each delivery but its contents remained the same. When the series ended, Norris, evaluating his experience on the platform, said his audiences were of but one opinion on the matter; namely, "They are all insurgents." [11]

With lecturing concluded, he made plans to return to Washington for the second session of the Sixty-first Congress, which was to open on December 6. Mrs. Norris and the children had left McCook in mid-September so that the girls might enter Washington schools at the beginning of the school year. The family rented quarters in the North East section of the city. McCarl again remained in McCook, devoting whatever time he could to acting as Norris' secretary. And Norris, on his part, renewed arrangements with Polk, the Washington attorney who had proven so helpful, and hired a stenographer for his office, Room 214 of the House Office Building.[12]

Since rules for this Congress were already in effect, there was no open fight when the second session got under way. The situation continued as in the previous session: the House of Representatives conducted its business in its usual way, while an undercurrent of insurgent discontent revealed members who sought an opportunity to force the issue of the rules to a vote. Rumors were rampant and Norris learned that Cannon thought a fight should be made against every insurgent seeking re-election. While many Republicans hoped for an insurgent victory, Norris knew that few would dare to vote with them. On the other hand, he realized that there were many Democrats who would have liked to see the insurgents defeated but who would not dare to vote against them.[13]

Thus it was in an atmosphere of anxiety and tension that he prepared to examine and execute the nation's business. His removal to what were for all intents and purposes nonexistent committees meant that he would have more time to investigate issues. While prohibition was not a significant issue before the Congress, the people of Nebraska considered it of great political importance. Norris was very cautious and refused to consider it from any but a legal point of view: He said that while prohibition was a state and local issue, the federal government had done much to regulate and curtail abuses in the interstate shipment of liquor.[14]

On the equally explosive issue of woman suffrage, Norris took a somewhat stronger position. He claimed that suffrage was a state function, and that Nebraska, or any other state, could provide for universal suffrage. He admitted that he was not opposed to woman suffrage if the state desired it. But he would not champion the cause until he became convinced that women desired the franchise.[15]

Of more immediate importance were the issues of taxes and postal rates. Businessmen, particularly in Lincoln and Omaha, were concerned about the corporation tax, while those in the Fifth Congressional District, along with many of Norris' rural constituents, were concerned about postal rates. Norris, seeing no possibility of repealing the controversial tax, focused his attention on the postal situation. He believed that the administration had not considered both sides of the proposition. For example, the president claimed that it cost the government nine cents per pound to transport second class mail, especially magazines. To Norris such information indicated not that rates should be increased but that the government was paying too much for carrying the mail. He noted that express companies, competing for business, were still profitably carrying second, third, and fourth class mail for less than a penny a pound, primarily on short hauls. In most instances they left the unprofitable long hauls to the government. Therefore, he argued, "If the express companies can carry mail for less than a cent a pound, we ought not to pay the railroads nine cents per pound for carrying it." [16]

The Post Office Department, he suggested, could profitably carry most mail under a zone system charging more for long than for short hauls. The express companies operated on such a basis and the government would do well to follow their example. Thus the solution necessitated no increase in postage on newspapers and magazines but required reduction of the amount paid to railroads for carrying this mail. Furthermore, as Norris understood it, the government had a monopoly on mail matters. If its power were enforced, express companies could be prohibited from carrying second class mail, thereby securing to the government the benefit of profitable short hauls. Unless he could be convinced of the error of his reasoning, Norris announced that he intended to vote against any postal rate increase.[17]

Along with postal matters, Norris also gave careful consideration to legislation pertaining to land and internal improvements. Homesteaders called attention to financial difficulties in the North Platte irrigation project. The project, which incidentally was not in Norris' district, benefited from the Pathfinder Dam in Wyoming, constructed under the terms of the Reclamation Act. The settlers had originally been told that water rights would cost them no more than thirty-five dollars per acre. The price had since been raised to forty-five dollars per acre plus maintenance, and the inhabitants now found it impossible to meet their payments, support their families, and maintain adequate school facilities. Having traveled over this country, Norris was convinced that the law needed amendment. The financial burden would defeat the government's purpose, making it difficult if not impossible for the farmers to get their lands into full production and meet their payments too.[18]

Norris believed that the settlers should be relieved of their payment obligations for the first two years, allowing them to direct all their efforts toward cultivating the land. Once the land was workable, payments would begin. Norris wanted to amend the Reclamation Act to improve its usefulness, since he regarded it "as one of the most wholesome laws that was ever passed, for the West and, in fact, for the entire country." [19]

Despite this praise, Norris criticized section nine, which provided that money allocated for reclamation be equalized every ten years among the public land states in proportion to the funds different states had furnished by the sale of public lands. This section "was the worst feature of the act" and accounted for projects that had been commenced without due consideration. He did not believe that public lands belonged to any particular state or that money from their sale should go back to the particular localities from which it originated. Such beliefs, he thought, could "make a failure of the reclamation business." Officials ought to be permitted to use the money where it would yield the best returns, thus benefiting all who desired to settle in the West and removing almost all political considerations.[20]

Along with irrigation, dry farming represented another technique for developing portions of the West. Both methods offered opportunities for the ultilization of millions of acres that heretofore had been considered useless for agricultural purposes. Hardy W. Campbell first developed the technique of dry farming and had demonstrated it throughout the West. Campbell's work, however, was done outside of government service, and Norris wanted to increase the Department of Agriculture's appropriation bill so that it could encourage his method.[21]

Norris also offered an amendment granting twenty-five thousand dollars to encourage experimentation with artesian wells for irrigation purposes in localities where farmers could not obtain sufficient water from streams. He did not expect the government to irrigate the land, but once artesian wells were shown to be feasible, people could then bore their own. He considered such an expenditure a valid use of public funds, one that would eventually enable large areas to raise crops and support prosperous farming communities.[22] Norris' concern with agriculture was not limited to Nebraska. His remarks evinced his knowledge of the arid regions which, if intelligently worked along lines suggested during the Roosevelt administration, could fruitfully develop the vast inland empire of the United States.

When Norris showed his interest in the conservation of natural resources, he moved from issues of local and regional interest to a burning national question which was before the public in the form of a controversy between Chief Forester Gifford Pinchot and Secretary of the Interior Richard Ballinger. In the House of Representatives the controversy appeared as another phase of the struggle of the insurgents against the power of the Speaker.

Louis R. Glavis, a special agent in the land office in Seattle, dramatically charged that the secretary had connived with the Cunningham coal group, portrayed as a front for a Morgan-Guggenheim syndicate, to validate withdrawals from the public domain of choice Alaska coal lands. Pinchot backed Glavis in these assertions while Ballinger denied that he had been dishonest. Taft, in September, 1909, exonerated Ballinger and fired Glavis. And when Senator Jonathan P. Dolliver of Iowa, in January, 1910, read a letter on the Senate floor by Pinchot in defense of Glavis, Taft followed suit by removing Pinchot as chief forester. This row already had prompted Gilbert M. Hitchcock, a Nebraska Democrat, to introduce a resolution in the House of Representatives on December 6, 1909, providing for a committee to investigate the conduct of the General Land Office in the Department of the Interior. On December 21, Senator Frank P. Flint of California requested that the president transmit to Congress the information upon which he had acted in exonerating Ballinger of the Glavis charges.

On the same day Wesley L. Jones of Washington read on the Senate floor a letter from the secretary of the interior, in which Ballinger "courted the widest and fullest inquiry by Congress." He requested that the investigation include not only the General Land Office but the Department of the Interior and the Bureau of Forestry as well. Norris agreed with Ballinger on this point and said that he would do all in his power to bring about a fair, honest, and searching investigation of the matter. But he was not certain that such an inquiry was possible, chiefly because the Speaker was not anxious to see too probing an investigation.[23]

After the Christmas recess Senator Jones offered a resolution providing for an investigation of the Department of the Interior by a joint committee of twelve members, half of whom were to be chosen by the vice president and half by the Speaker. On January 7, 1910, when the House of Representatives considered this proposition, Norris called for a broad, inclusive investigation which would have "the confidence and the faith of the American people." To bring this about, he suggested that the committee "ought to be elected by the House of Representatives and not appointed by the Speaker." He then offered an amendment "that the committee will be elected by the House of Representatives from the members of that body." The combined votes of the Democratic members and the Republican insurgents carried the resolution and thereby insured a fuller and fairer hearing than otherwise would have been possible. At the same time Cannon was administered a stinging and severe rebuff, his first in the battle against the insurgents.[24]

Cannon suffered defeat because one of his staunchest lieutenants, John Dalzell of Pennsylvania, made the mistake of yielding two minutes of his allotted time to Norris, who had been unable to gain recognition from the chair. The Rules Committee had previously agreed that the Senate resolution should be debated for six hours, three hours on each side. Any member who spoke would have a right to make a motion to amend, but all such motions would be voted on at the close of the debate. At that time, Norris and twenty-five other insurgents joined forces with the Democrats to carry the amendment with three votes to spare. More than thirty of Cannon's reliable Republicans were absent.[25] Thus Cannon suffered his first defeat and undoubtedly realized that in Norris he had a foe whose understanding of parliamentary procedure and maneuvering rivaled his own. From this incident it should have become evident to Cannon that he would have to maintain eternal vigilance to prevent the insurgents from receiving another opportunity to gain the upper hand.

Norris' motion evoked a great consternation. Since the amendment provided no method by which the House could vote, it was decided to delay the choice of members on the investigating committee. The Republican machine and the Democrats each held caucuses, while the insurgents, who were now well organized, met at the spacious residence of Congressman William C. Lovering of Massachusetts. Here they decided to insist on naming at least one member of the committee. The Democrats would name two and the regular Republicans the remaining three members. They also decided that neither Payne nor Dalzell, Cannon's chief aides, should be allowed to sit on this committee. They were able to insist upon this arrangement only because the Democrats in their caucus accepted it, while Speaker Cannon undoubtedly did not want to force the issue and risk another rebuff.[26]

Norris, though unanimously tendered the insurgent position on the committee, refused on the ground that critics would say he introduced the amendment to promote his own advantage. He suggested that Edmond H. Madison of Kansas be selected, and to this the group agreed. With Madison's appointment the twelve-man committee was not evenly divided; administration supporters chosen by the vice president and the Republican caucus in the House of Representatives still dominated it. But Madison's presence assured Glavis and Pinchot of at least one sympathetic member who would insist that their side be given a full hearing. Therefore, as a result of his amendment, Norris claimed, "A real investigation was had."

During the investigation, the attorneys for Pinchot and Glavis, though unable to prove their clients' assertions, were at least able to demonstrate that Ballinger had no enthusiasm for and little sympathy with the cause of conservation. Louis D. Brandeis impeached the integrity of the administration by showing that crucial documents offered as evidence against Glavis' charges had been predated. As a result of these and other findings, the investigation, launched as a gesture to political expediency, proved to be a considerable burden to the Republican party in the next presidential election.[27]

Since Taft thought the charges leveled against his secretary of the interior were unjust, and since he regarded Pinchot "as a good deal of a radical and a good deal of a crank," [28] he was none too happy about Norris' amendment. To Taft, Norris and the insurgents were committed to the cause of Pinchot and would be incapable of coming to a just verdict based on evidence if that evidence in any way threatened the policies and the friends of the previous administration.

On the other hand, Norris and his fellow insurgents believed that Taft had allied himself with the Republican old guard and was undermining the Roosevelt policies. Even worse, the president had sided with the Speaker in this controversy and with the cause against which the insurgents had been fighting. As a long-time, bitter foe of conservation, Cannon, in the eyes of the insurgents, had now won the administration to his point of view. The president, the insurgents were now convinced, would have to be regarded as a traitor to the Roosevelt policies and another bulwark in the system of privilege they were attacking. Taft's treatment of the insurgents, too, reassured them that they were correct in their evaluation.

On January 6, 1910, the day Dolliver read the Senate Pinchot's letter endorsing the Glavis position, Norris wrote the president:

> There was published in the newpapers of January 5 an Associated Press dispatch to the effect that you had decided to deprive the "Insurgents" in Congress of all executive patronage. The article referred to purported to come direct from the White House and inasmuch as it had remained unchallenged and undisputed I feel warranted in assuming that it is true and has your approval. I am likewise led to this conclusion because the recent recommendations from "insurgent" Republican Congressmen have not received the favorable consideration by the heads of Departments formerly accorded.[29]

He explained to the chief executive what the insurgent members of the House were striving to do. He insisted that they had never made any attempt to influence votes "upon any proposition other than the rules of the House," and that they were loyal Republicans who believed in carrying out in good faith the pledges of the party. Moreover, he claimed the insurgents had taken "no stand against the present administration" even though the president at the outset of his term of office took a stand against them in their effort to change the rules.[30] The president, of course, had the legal right to deprive any member of patronage if he so desired, but Norris thought that if a reason was given for this action, "common fairness and justice" demanded that the correct one be presented; namely, that the insurgents opposed the rules, and not, as had been suggested, that they were unworthy members of the Republican party.[31]

Previously, in December, 1909, as the Ballinger-Pinchot controversy moved toward a climax with the convening of Congress, Taft decided to use the patronage weapon against insurgent Republicans on the grounds that they were doing everything to bring the Democratic party into power. The president apparently took this position at the insistence of Cannon and other party leaders.[32]

When Taft responded to Norris on January 10, 1910, the day he dropped Pinchot from government service, he convinced Norris that he was being punished for his fight against the rules. Taft claimed Norris' letter contained "such misstatements that I must answer it." He denied Norris' charge that he had made any statement to the press and averred that he had taken no part in the fight over the House rules. Then he presented a forthright statement of his position:

> What I declined to do was to join those who differed from a majority of the Republican Party and stayed out of the caucus, when as leader of the party I am dependent upon party actions to secure the legislation that has been promised. It did not then seem to me, as it does not now seem to me, that as titular leader of the party I should take sides with fifteen or twenty who refused to abide by the majority votes of the party, but that I should stand by whatever the party decides under the majority rule, whatever my views as to the wisdom of the rules, which are peculiarly a matter for settlement in the House itself. It has been a custom for a Republican administration to honor the recommendations of Republican Congressmen and Senators with respect to local appointments, subject, however, to the condition that the candidates recommended should be fit for the place. This custom has grown up with a view to securing a party solidarity in acting upon party questions. The only indication that I have given has been that with respect to legislation which I have recommended, there should be party action to discharge the promise of the party platform, and that those who feel no obligation in respect to it can not complain if their recommendations are not given customary weight.[33]

The president, by refusing to accept Norris' thesis that the insurgents were loyal Republicans who were only challenging the rules, placed them in the position of opposing the Republican party. This created a dilemma for the insurgents, but they were too far committed to turn back or stop in their fight against Cannonism. The Ballinger-Pinchot controversy seemingly offered them a way out. They were loyal Republicans, loyal to the policies and principles of Theodore Roosevelt, while Taft, Cannon, and the old guard were destroying the very things that had made Roosevelt and the party so popular with the American people. Thus by 1910 the insurgency movement in the House of Representatives had become part of the conflict between progressive and standpat Republicans that was to tear the party asunder.

Norris, however, refused to accept Taft's statement as final. He felt that the president, by stating in effect that he had taken no part in the fight over the rules of the House, had impeached his integrity. Norris thought it only fair, since he first made the statement, that he should present the evidence upon which it was based; namely, claims by insurgents that Taft labored to convince them to support the Speaker in his effort to adopt the old rules. "If you were taking no part in the fight," Norris wrote, "then you were most woefully misrepresented by some of your closest advisors." [34]

Norris then listed all the measures wherein he had supported the president, while noting that the Speaker and his followers were opposed to practically all of them. He claimed that Cannon had made committee assignments so as to "prevent the enactment of many, if not all, of these measures." Thus Norris attempted to answer the charge that the insurgents were not good Republicans and, by presenting evidence that they supported many more planks than did the followers of Cannon, he implied that the insurgents had reason to complain that their patronage recommendations were being ignored. He wisely concluded that he was in no way "piqued or grieved" that executive patronage had been taken away from him. Whether it was returned or not he intended to do all in his power to help his party redeem in good faith the pledges it had made to the country.[35]

Taft, unwilling to accept Norris' premise that he was a loyal Republican while administration men were violating party pledges, immediately responded. He claimed that his only interference in the rules fight in March, 1909, was to try to effect a compromise by suggesting to all congressmen who came to see him that majority rule must prevail if the legislative burdens assumed by the party in its platform were to be enacted. To Norris and the other insurgents, this statement was a validation of the charge that the president had used his power against them. Taft implied that he was withholding patronage from the insurgents because they chose to ignore the obligations of the Republican platform. He wanted only to prevent them from placing opponents of the administration in federal offices, thereby making it easier for the Democratic party to reassert itself. However, as of the date of this letter, January 11, 1910, Taft had withdrawn patronage from only four insurgents: William Cary and Irvine Lenroot, both of Wisconsin, Clarence B. Miller of Minnesota, and Norris. Soon others found that their recommendations were ignored.[36]

The insurgents, of course, had reason to be bitter and to complain about their shabby treatment by the president. During the tariff fight, when old guard Republicans saddled Taft with what in many respects he considered an unsatisfactory arrangement, he never once threatened to use the patronage weapon against them.[37] By exerting it against the insurgents, Taft neither strengthened the Republican party nor gained support of his legislative program since, as Norris pointed out, the insurgents were already giving him more support than the regular Republicans on most issues.

Once news of Taft's action reached the home districts of the affected members, public sentiment, already critical of the administration, became even more hostile. The president's action, based on the premise that the insurgents with their patronage were aiding the Democratic party, helped only to widen the growing breach in the Republican party and to convince the insurgents of Taft's betrayal of his predecessor's policies. It was a singular example of inept leadership which, against his own inclinations, forced Taft into a firm alliance with the old guard in the Republican party.

Thus, by January, 1910, the stage was set for the notable, dramatic, and historic battle that culminated the insurgency revolt against the power of the Speaker. Norris and his cohorts, deprived of their patronage and committee standing, ignored by their colleagues in the House of Representatives, branded as disloyal Republicans and avowed enemies of the administration, had everything to gain and nothing to lose by finding a legislative lever to open a wedge in the House rules.

Norris, as a result of his resolution calling for the election of members to the Ballinger-Pinchot investigating committee, had emerged as the insurgent leader.[38] He had revealed himself as a skilful parliamentarian, equal or almost equal in knowledge and ability to Cannon himself. Though his position in Congress and his life in Washington were now unpleasant, he did not intend to deviate from his course under any circumstances. Letters from constituents approved his stand and helped convince him that popular support would continue even if patronage would not. A friend, sounding public sentiment, wrote:

> Yesterday I was on the Street, and I sidled up to a group of men, who were talking about the Administration, and they agreed among themselves that they expected Taft would quit the office, as much a hated and despised man as ever Grover Cleveland was. I don't know how all this is going to end. Something will have to be done. People are not sticking by Party so closely as they were a few years ago, there is not nearly so much politics as in former years, people are wondering now, where they are at, and how they are going to remedy the wrong—that has its grip on the country today. Unless the insurgent movement wins out, there will be a Democratic President next time. Probably people are not always

going to stand for half a dozen men to rule. My business takes me in Missouri, Oklahoma, Texas, and Kansas, and as a matter of fact there don't seem to be any parties any more among the common class, it is any thing now to clean up the machine.[39]

Another more succinctly stated, "The West is warm over the fight you are having and satisfaction is expressed everywhere with the stand you have taken." Both the Omaha *Bee* and the *Nebraska State Journal* were giving space and attention to Norris, claiming along with other papers that Taft was rapidly losing whatever popularity he had in the West. McCarl was convinced that loss of patronage would make Norris more popular than ever with the voters in the Fifth Congressional District and would improve his chances for the senatorial nomination. McCarl felt that no "standpatter" would have a chance against Norris in the 1910 primary, either congressional or senatorial, and that no Democrat, not even Fred Ashton, would be eager to oppose him in the election.[40]

Thus Norris, heartened by public approval of his position, was convinced that the fight the insurgents were making was just and was based on sound principle. He was more than ever determined to continue it, regardless of the outcome. With patience and fortitude he awaited an opportunity to drive a wedge into the procedural block that Cannon and his chief lieutenants were utilizing to prevent the insurgent Republicans and the Democrats from administering him another defeat similar to the one already experienced in the Ballinger-Pinchot controversy. Norris hoped that it might come soon. If not, he would still be satisfied that he had helped to sow the seeds that would allow others to "reap an effective harvest for free and untrammelled representation in the House." [41] As it turned out, an opportunity was not long in forthcoming.

Chapter 18

Insurgency Revolt: Part I

ON THE EVE of the conflict, the House of Representatives had 391 members. Each of these gentlemen was usually assigned a place on any two of the fifty-six standing committees of the House by the Speaker, who, at the same time, chose the chairman of each of these committees. The Speaker also had the power to refer bills to committees where he knew they would be reported as he desired. As chairman of the all-powerful, five-man Rules Committee, he could make anything in or out of order at any time. In the Speaker's chair, Joseph G. Cannon usually refused to recognize anyone unless the member first stated his purpose. Consequently most members visited the Speaker's room beforehand and requested recognition rather than undergo the embarrassment of having their requests to speak denied and noted in the *Congressional Record*.

Committee assignments, as Norris and the other insurgents well knew, could make or break a member's reputation by placing him in the foreground on important issues or by relegating him to an insignificant position in the congressional hierarchy. The Speaker thus could curb the ambition as well as the ability and usefulness of any member. The insurgents, besides being demoted in their committee assignments, knew that no bill they filed would be seriously considered and that recognition from the Speaker would not be easily forthcoming. This knowledge, of course, did not silence them. When the House resolved itself into the Committee of the Whole for purposes of debate and amendment, all members were granted some time for speechmaking or questioning if they so desired.[1]

The insurgents, as has already been noted, had no desire to repeal the strictly parliamentary rules of the House. They realized that rules were necessary in a large legislative body and were in accord with most of them. Their desire was to make the Speaker a presiding officer with no extraneous powers. Under the prevailing rules the Speaker was all-powerful and was responsible, once duly chosen and installed, to no one for the remainder of the Congress, while he had it within his power

166

to promote or destroy the careers of members who met with his favor or displeasure. As a journalist, referring to the insurgents' goal, put it:

> They would take the Speaker's purely political power: to obstruct, impair or control legislation: to thwart the will of the majority: to limit genuine debate: to pack important committees with the representatives of Big Business: to control the ambition, ability, and usefulness of members of Congress: to make him the sole political judge of what laws may be enacted and what measures shall be defeated.[2]

Until the opportunity to bring about this change presented itself, the insurgents by themselves could do little in terms of introducing or even improving bills. However, aided by the Democrats, they were able to take advantage of any slips Cannon and his lieutenants made. And, on their own, since they first organized in December, 1908, they exerted tremendous efforts to educate the public in the righteousness of their cause. Their nuisance value was a growing source of embarrassment to both Cannon and the Taft administration and a boon to the coalescing progressive cause.

Sentiment against the Speaker and his power was growing throughout the country, especially in the Middle West. In February, 1909, *Success Magazine* asked its subscribers, "Do you believe that the rules of the House should place in the hands of the Speaker the power of determining the membership of the Committees?" Within three weeks, 11,134 readers voted "No" and 364, "Yes." To the question, "Do you believe that Joseph G. Cannon should be elected Speaker of the House of Representatives?" 10,825 voted "No" and 539 voted "Yes." [3] On a state-wide basis, T. A. McNeal, a columnist for the Topeka *Daily Capital*, published in January, 1910, the results of a poll he had conducted among Kansas Republicans. To the question, "Are you opposed to the rule of Cannon in the House and Aldrich in the Senate?" 1,579 answered "Yes" and 81, "No." [4]

By organizing, the insurgents were able to make themselves an effective group, though their membership fluctuated between twenty-five and thirty and complete unanimity was rare among them. After Hepburn's retirement at the end of the Sixtieth Congress, Augustus Gardner of Massachusetts served as chairman of the group. John M. Nelson of Wisconsin acted as secretary and his office was utilized as a meeting place. With Edmond H. Madison of Kansas they functioned as a committee on strategy[5] which ably directed the insurgent forces in the first major conflict over the rules. However, by 1910, Norris had emerged as the outstanding figure among the insurgents.

As an indication of his rising prominence, Norris in 1910 published several articles in *La Follette's Magazine* explaining the insurgents' position, accomplishments, and desires for the future.[6] His interviews and correspondence with members of the press increased substantially. In his letters, he explained the insurgent position and occasionally attempted to correct misconceptions that appeared in articles. Letters in the latter category were usually not for publication, while those in the former were. In his correspondence with journalists, Norris revealed more fully the workings of the House. He explained that there was not as much "log rolling" in Congress as there was subservience to the Speaker's will. Deals were made, Norris knew, but as a rule they had the approval of the Speaker, if, in fact, they did not originate with him. Furthermore, he understood that reform usually came slowly and in the way of compromise, and that many who had been most active in a fight might not be on the scene when victory was won.[7] Actually, in the case of the insurgents, most of them were on hand when victory was achieved, and all of them must have known that it was, at best, a partial triumph.

Since the term "progressive" was coming into widespread use, Norris made some effort early in 1910 to distinguish between an insurgent and a progressive as they affected politics. The insurgency movement, he claimed, arose in the House when some Republicans demanded a change in the rules; its primary aim was to change these rules and to curb the Speaker's power. Progressives, on the other hand, sought more widespread reform; they wanted to curb not only machine rule in the political arena, but corporation control in the social and economic realm as well. While many of the insurgents were progressives as far as other reforms were concerned, some were standpatters on all but the rules issue. There was no attempt to organize Republican dissidents "along any line except that of taking away from the Speaker some of his extraordinary power." Norris summarized the insurgent position as follows:

> We want the House to have an opportunity for itself to pass on the questions and we therefore desire to take away from the Speaker the power given to him by the Rules of the House which prevent the House from participating in legislative action. We want the House to be representative of the people and each individual member to have his ideas presented and passed on, and at the same time to be required to assume his share of the responsibility.[8]

To his constituents, Norris explained that he was not discouraged, though he was convinced that Taft would be unable to carry out the

Roosevelt policies. Indeed, Norris believed that the president had allied himself with Speaker Cannon and Senator Aldrich against these policies. Yet despite overwhelming opposition, he knew that the insurgents had been making "some impression on the machine." Referring to the power of the Speaker, Norris, in mid-January, 1910, said, "It is going to pieces, there is no doubt about that." But he envisioned its collapse in the next Congress as a result of the 1910 elections.[9]

Throughout February Norris and the insurgents busied themselves with legislative matters. Then in March the insurgents, allied with the Democratic members, found an opportunity to inflict a petty personal humiliation on the Speaker; they amended an appropriation bill to deprive both the Speaker and the vice president of a fifteen-thousand-dollar allowance for automobiles.[10] However, appropriations had nothing to do with the matter that soon thereafter provided an entering wedge and precipitated a revolution in the House. It started innocently enough with a discussion of the census.

Democratic Congressman Adolph J. Sabath of Illinois, a member of the Committee on the Census, introduced a resolution, not fifty words in length, providing that in the approaching census enumerators ascertain the mother tongue of all persons born abroad, thereby providing more adequate information about the languages and the national origins of the American people. On the next day, Wednesday, March 16, Speaker Cannon recognized Edgar D. Crumpacker of Indiana, chairman of the Committee on the Census, for the purpose of presenting this minor resolution as an amendment to the census bill. While there was no opposition to the amendment, Crumpacker's proposal brought forth a storm of criticism because it violated the sanctity of Calendar Wednesday which Cannon had conceded to the insurgents a year before in the first major battle over the rules. Many members felt that the introduction of the Sabath resolution at this time created a dangerous precedent and impaired the value of the one day when members did not have to seek the Speaker's permission to gain recognition.

Democratic Representative John J. Fitzgerald of New York, who had suggested Calendar Wednesday to Cannon as a compromise measure in the 1909 fracas, was vigorous in his protest and raised a point of order. Cannon, after listening to the debate in which, incidentally, the insurgents rarely participated, ruled that the census amendment was in order "under a higher law than the rule of the House, or, for that matter, higher than a statutory law under the Constitution." It was a privileged question under the Constitution (Article I, Section 2) and as such claimed precedence over all House procedures. The Speaker's decision, however, was reversed by the members —a rare occurrence in the House—by a vote of 163 to 112.[11]

Crumpacker, like Cannon, thought the resolution was privileged. Somewhat piqued [12] over the refusal of the House to consider it on Calendar Wednesday, he reintroduced it the next day, St. Patrick's Day, March 17, 1910. When a point of order was again made, Speaker Cannon, rather than suffer another humiliation, shrewdly referred the question to the members for decision. The House, by a vote of 201 to 72, overwhelmingly decided that the resolution was privileged and in order, indicating that it was less concerned with the constitutional question than with the desire to preserve the integrity of Calendar Wednesday. Incidentally, Norris and other insurgents voted against the proposition that the census amendment presented a question of high constitutional privilege.[13]

Before the vote was taken, Norris engaged in a discussion with Marlin E. Olmsted of Pennsylvania in which Norris inquired if a committee report was necessary for a constitutionally privileged motion. He asked asked whether any member could come in with a bill that had not even been printed and take up the time of the House on the ground that it was a matter privileged by the Constitution. Olmsted, a Cannon supporter, adroitly parried Norris' probing by implying that the Speaker, and not a mere member, could answer such questions.[14] Here then was the opportunity the insurgents had been awaiting, though it is doubtful if any but Norris realized it at the time.

Once the vote was taken which declared the amendment privileged, the House proceeded to adopt the amendment. Norris thereupon sought the floor, stating, "Mr. Speaker, I have a privileged resolution." At about three o'clock in the afternoon on his third effort to gain the Speaker's attention, he was recognized. The revolution was under way:

MR. NORRIS: Mr. Speaker, I present a resolution made privileged by the Constitution.

THE SPEAKER: If it is a resolution made privileged by the Constitution, the gentleman will present it.[15]

Amid general laughter, Norris pulled from his pocket a creased and crumbled piece of paper which he sent to the desk for the clerk to read. The smiling, deferential grin on the Speaker's face quickly gave way to a look of grim determination as the clerk read the resolution, similar to the one Norris had presented in the Sixtieth Congress (May 16, 1908). It called for a Committee on Rules consisting of fifteen members, geographically distributed, nine of whom should be members of the majority party. The Speaker could not be eligible for membership on the committee which would choose its own chairman.

Cannon's chief lieutenant, John Dalzell, immediately made the point that this resolution was not in order, that it was not privileged. Norris, citing the census amendment, insisted his resolution was privileged under the Constitution and thereby entitled to consideration. Article I, Section 5 of the Constitution wherein it is stated that "each House may determine the rules of its proceedings" provided the basis for the claim that the resolution was privileged. He said the Constitution granted him a right to introduce this resolution, that under the recent decision of the House on the census amendment it must be in order.[16]

Norris crystallized his position when he said:

> When the House went on record that the census proposition was in order, it was not in accordance with my individual view. I did not believe it was privileged. But this must follow, as a logical result, it seems to me, in that case that the privileged nature of the resolution did not depend on its being reported by a committee or considered by a committee, but it was privileged, if privileged at all, because the Constitution made it so.
>
> No committee consideration, no committee report, would add or take away from its privileged nature. I am not responsible for the position in which the House has placed itself; but to be consistent, it seems to me this resolution would have to be held privileged the same as the others.[17]

Cannon, having been overruled the previous day by insurgent and Democratic votes, fully understood his precarious position. Ninety-nine members had not answered when the roll was recorded shortly after noon, and the Speaker realized that the absent regular Republican members would have to be present to vote on any ruling if he were not to suffer further defeat. Yet, if the entire membership of the House were on hand, Cannon knew that the insurgent Republicans and their Democratic allies could probably defeat him. The only chance he had —and it was a long one—was to delay making a decision until absent Republican members could be urged to return and he could seek ample precedents for deciding, despite the census decision, that Norris' resolution was not in order.

Thus the House settled down to a long period of discussion and debate. In one of the very rare instances in the history of the House, every member said what he wanted to say and took as long as he wanted in saying it. The debate on the merits of the question before the House was presumably for the benefit of the Speaker, to provide him with information necessary for his ruling. But Cannon was rarely in the Speaker's chair. Since the Democrats and the insurgents refused to countenance any adjournment until the Speaker made a ruling, and since there was no power to compel him to rule, the group supporting the Norris resolution prepared to spend the night in session and to maintain their forces on the floor to prevent any sudden recess for lack of a quorum. Norris personally had no objection to an adjournment, though he went along with the members who wanted the Speaker to make a ruling beforehand.[18]

Partners to both sides of this controversy stated their positions in speeches of varying ability and eloquence. Norris, having had his say at the outset, said little. Frequently the House chamber reverberated with applause and cheers or cries of "Rule, Rule," as the members, realizing it would be many hours before a ruling was forthcoming, gave vent to their partisanship while the Speaker, the central figure in the debate, could in effect do little to exercise authority and curb the more boisterous members. One of the more dramatic incidents occurred when Henry Allen Cooper of Wisconsin called upon a number of insurgent Republicans to testify to the punishment they had received in the way of unfavorable committee appointments. Speaker Cannon had been out of the chamber at the outset of Cooper's speech. Upon his return he stood on the lower steps of the Speaker's platform, resting his arm upon the clerk's desk. From this vantage point, raised slightly above the crowd of members who were milling in front of him, he glared down into the face of the "insurging" Cooper.[19]

Cooper had just mentioned the case of Augustus Gardner of Massachusetts. He shouted that Gardner had voted for the present Speaker, but because Gardner had voted against the rules he was deposed from his place as chairman of the Committee on Industrial Arts and Expositions. Suddenly the Speaker sprang into action and interrupted Cooper. He asked Gardner to come forth and explain why he did not retain his chairmanship. Gardner, called to the floor from an adjoining lobby, came forth and explained, while Cannon smiled, that he had retired voluntarily because he wanted to be free to speak and act as he pleased on insurgent matters.

However, Cannon did not have much time to enjoy this victory because Cooper then called upon Charles W. Fowler of New Jersey, Victor Murdock of Kansas, and Norris, each of whom related to the House how they were punished for opposing the autocratic rule of the Speaker and his organization. As Cooper called each of these gentlemen, they were pushed through the crowd up to the open space before the dais to speak, while Cannon, leaning against the clerk's desk, "rigid in every line of his body," turned occasionally to Vice-President Sherman who, along with many senators, had appeared on the floor of the House.[20]

Once Cooper had concluded his remarks, Cannon resumed the Speaker's chair and explained he would rule on the point of order only after due consideration of precedents. After the House again refused to adjourn or recess, the Democrats amid great excitement continually shouted, "Rule, Rule." But Cannon, once the shouting started, merely smiled, kissed the tips of his fingers towards the Democrats, bowed politely, and then recognized J. Warren Keifer of Ohio who spoke at length in support of the Speaker, despite much disorder and many interruptions which now characterized these proceedings more and more.[21]

As evening turned to night and night to dawn, Cannon still refused to make a ruling on the Norris resolution. The wordy battle raged on, but fewer members appeared on the floor to participate. The Speaker sought a few hours' sleep in his office, while other members did the same at their desks, in their offices, or in the adjoining lobbies. There were so few members on the floor during the exhausting night session that the sergeant-at-arms and several deputies were ordered to seek members absent without leave and bring them before the bar of the House.

Continually the Democrats and the small insurgent group voted against any recess or adjournment despite efforts by Republican members to achieve one or the other.[22] Indeed, at times in the early morning hours of March 18, the House of Representatives did not appear to be in session, as the following entry in the *Record* indicates:

THE SPEAKER PRO TEMPORE: The House will be in order. Gentlemen will understand the impropriety of singing on the floor, even though the House is not at this moment transacting any business. The House is not in recess.

CHORUS: "There'll be a hot time in the old town tonight."

THE SPEAKER PRO TEMPORE: That was last night, not tonight. (laughter). The House will be in order.[23]

In a more serious vein, Norris at 5:20 A.M. proposed an adjournment until noon. He felt that the group, having exemplified its principle, was now wearing itself out needlessly. Ollie M. James, a Kentucky Democrat, replied that "for the people's rule of the Congress of the United States" he was willing to lose a night's sleep. He protested against any concession to personal comfort which would tend to detract from the impressiveness of the object lesson they were giving the American people of devotion to the public business.[24]

At 6 A.M. Speaker Cannon returned to the House chamber. He appeared slightly worried. His voice was not the least bit husky, and the early morning hours were spent discussing whether less than a quorum had the power to issue warrants empowering the sergeant-at-arms and his deputies to bring in absent members. During this discussion some members snoozed in their seats; some read the morning papers; others gathered in small groups. Though nothing of consequence occurred during the morning hours on the floor, the official reporters who had been at their posts since noon the previous day noted that thus far they had taken down 146,000 words, more than three times the daily average.[25]

Throughout the proceedings on March 17, the galleries were filled with an appreciative audience that overflowed into the corridors. During the evening the entrance to the House was flanked by automobiles. While the audience had thinned out in the early morning hours of March 18, galleries once again reached capacity long before mid-morning. Men and women prominent in the life of the nation's capital as well as members of the families of the participants below were on hand.[26]

Meanwhile, behind the scenes, three distinct compromise efforts were made by the regular Republicans, and all were humiliatingly rejected by the insurgent Republicans and Democrats. The first conference was held in Gardner's office. The proposition submitted by the Cannon delegates called for a ten-man Rules Committee, consisting of six Republicans and four Democrats. Nothing was said about keeping the Speaker off the committee, though the regulars said they were willing to make a gentleman's agreement that the Speaker would not seek membership. The conference came to nought. The radical insurgents insisted that the Speaker specifically be excluded from the committee, though their more moderate colleagues were willing to accept a compromise which would have postponed the operation of the elimination provision until after Cannon's tenure as Speaker had expired. The only point to which all factions agreed at this first conference was that the committee should consist of ten men.[27]

No sooner had the delegates filed into the House chamber than the regulars requested another conference. This time they suggested a fifteen-man Rules Committee, but again said nothing about the Speaker's membership. This conference, like the first, failed to reach any understanding and for the same reason. The insurgents and the Democrats were in accord that the Speaker must be removed from the Committee on Rules.[28]

It now appeared that further negotiation was futile. Norris asserted that a majority of between ten and fifteen votes would carry his ruling. "We will beat them. There is no doubt of the result unless there is some legerdemain." This prediction was endorsed by Champ Clark, the Democratic leader. Both men felt, indeed all participants and observers knew, that Cannon would soon be compelled to face the issue he had been dodging for almost twenty-four hours in the vain hope that enough votes could be mustered to save him from humiliating defeat.[29]

When the Speaker ascended to his desk just before noon he was greeted with jeering cries of "Rule, Rule, Rule." Cannon smiled grimly at his Democratic tormentors and announced that he would be prepared to rule in the near future. The delay in ruling was due to a desperate effort by Cannon's lieutenants to secure some sort of compromise. The Speaker's position was becoming even more precarious, not only because the Democrats and insurgent Republicans were holding their ground, but because many Republicans representing close districts, particularly in the West, were flooded with telegrams demanding that they vote against Cannon for a liberalization of the rules. This knowledge and the realization that several of his supporters would be compelled to break ranks undoubtedly forced Cannon to seek a compromise.[30]

Thus, sometime before noon, the regulars sought another conference, their final effort at compromise. This time they announced their willingness to accept the Norris resolution, provided the sentence excluding the Speaker from membership on the committee be removed. This of course was not acceptable to Norris, Gardner, Irvine Lenroot of Wisconsin, and E. A. Hayes of California, the insurgent delegates. While this conference was in session, on the floor of the House of Representatives, W. E. Martin of South Dakota moved for a recess until 4 P.M. Champ Clark demanded a roll call and the conference came to an abrupt end as the participants returned to the floor to vote. On this vote the regulars defeated the insurgent and Democratic coalition by a vote of 160 to 152, and the House recessed for two hours, at the end of which time it was hoped the Speaker would make his ruling.[31]

As soon as the recess was announced, the Democrats went into caucus and reiterated their decision to oust the Speaker from the Committee on Rules, though they decided to modify the structure of the committee from that proposed in the Norris resolution. They consulted with Congressmen Dalzell, Walter I. Smith of Iowa, and John W. Dwight of New York, all prominent Cannon aides, as to possible concessions to which the Speaker might agree. The aides, however, refused to give any information as to the Speaker's intentions.[32]

Norris, interviewed at the start of the two-hour recess, said the delay in proceeding had no significance. He appeared worn and haggard, his unshaven face was lined and pale. Yet his voice was clear and calm and exuded confidence as he said, "If the regulars will consent to take the Speaker off the Committee on Rules we will settle this matter in short order after the recess." Both sides, he added, were already in agreement upon an enlarged committee. However, during the recess as during the earlier efforts at compromise, no side was willing to yield on its position on the Speaker's place in relation to the committee; compromise was impossible on this point. The insurgents at a caucus during the recess reaffirmed their position. All groups realized that the outcome would be decided on the floor.[33]

When the House reconvened at 4 P.M., the Speaker said he was ready to rule. James A. Tawney of Minnesota offered a motion to postpone the business before the House until the next day, March 19. After brief discussion the motion was carried 163–151 with the insurgent-Democratic coalition again in the minority.[34] After twenty-six hours in continuous session, everyone concerned looked forward to the opportunity for a night's sleep and a chance to freshen up before the final ordeal on the morrow.

On Saturday, March 19, the House of Representatives met at noon with more than 350 of its 391 members on hand and the galleries filled to capacity. As Speaker Cannon entered the chamber and ascended to the dais, a great burst of applause and cheers arose from the Republican side of the aisle and from the galleries. Cannon, with an air of deep concern, gazed about the chamber and brought down his gavel with a loud bang that reverberated throughout the room. Reverend Henry N. Conden offered a brief prayer. Upon its conclusion, conversation began again, though most members remained in their seats as the clerk read the Journal of the previous day's proceedings. As the session started, people lined the corridors and stairways, in hope of witnessing the conclusion of this historic struggle.[35]

Cannon announced his readiness to rule on the point of order, after the clerk again read the Norris resolution. The Speaker read his ruling in a deliberate voice that could be heard distinctly by everyone. When Cannon proclaimed the point of order against the Norris resolution, there was tremendous applause which soon gave way to table-pounding on the Republican side. Insurgent Republicans and

Democrats remained silent. Every seat in the press gallery was occupied, while on the floor below senators were sitting or standing in
the rear.[36]

Before order was fully restored, Norris was on his feet shouting,
"Mr. Speaker, I appeal from the decision; and on that I move the
previous question." Dalzell immediately followed with a move to lay
the appeal on the table. This was rejected by a vote of 182 to 164,
whereupon Norris again moved the previous question on the appeal.
His motion prevailed by a vote of 183 to 160. The House was now
ready to decide on the Speaker's ruling. The decision on this crucial
question was another defeat for Cannon by a 182–162 vote. The Norris
resolution (H.R. 502) was now pending before the House.

During these roll calls confusion reigned. A motion to adjourn was
shouted down so vigorously that no roll call was taken. When the
results of each vote were made known the opponents of the rules
shouted and pounded. As the shouts over the defeat of Dalzell's attempt to table Norris' appeal pervaded the chamber, Cannon stood
motionless in his place. His set features were silhouetted against the
American flag behind his chair. With his opponents before him shouting, stamping, pounding, and applauding, Cannon presented a picture
of a doughty old warrior, magnificent in defeat.[37]

During these roll calls Clark was busily preparing an amendment
incorporating the suggestions of the Democratic caucus of the previous
day. At the same time Gardner and Norris consulted with each other.
It soon became known that the insurgents and Democrats had agreed
to an amendment to the Norris resolution. It would provide for a ten-
man Rules Committee consisting of six Republicans and four Democrats, with representatives of each party selected by caucuses and
elected by the House. In addition, the insurgents agreed to participate
in the Republican caucus and abide by its results as to the choice of
members.[38] Though many insurgents were unhappy about this amendment, they had no alternative but to accept it if their fight were to
accomplish anything at this time.

With his resolution pending before the House, Norris sought an
agreement dividing the time for debate. Suggestions and counter-
suggestions relating to the course that should be followed and the
parliamentary status that would apply to the consideration of the
resolution added to the confusion. Unable to reach any agreement and
with the Speaker requesting "regular order," Norris announced that
while he preferred his original resolution many of his associates favored a substitute measure. Therefore he sent to the clerk's desk the
following amendment as a substitute for his original resolution:

There shall be a Committee on Rules, elected by the House, consisting of 10 Members, 6 of whom shall be Members of the majority party and 4 of whom shall be Members of the minority party. The Speaker shall not be a member of the committee, and the committee shall elect its own chairman from its own members.

Resolved further, That within ten days after the adoption of this resolution there shall be an election of this committee and immediately upon its election the present Committee on Rules shall be dissolved.[39]

Representative James Mann of Illinois attempted to get Norris off the floor on the ground that his right to that privilege had expired, but the Speaker affirmed Norris' right to hold the floor and suggested that his resolution was in order. Norris held the floor for about an hour, yielding to such members, including a few regulars, as desired to be placed on record.

Champ Clark requested the floor and amid a storm of applause proclaimed that this was not "a fight against the Honorable Joseph G. Cannon personally," but against a system. Clark was followed by several other speakers including Lenroot, Gronna, and Victor Murdock. In concluding the debate Norris forcefully disavowed any personal feeling in his efforts for the revision of the rules, stating that "those of us who favor this rule represent a principle here far beyond the personality of any man or any set of men." He denied the charge that the insurgents were anti-Republican, concluding, amidst derisive laughter and applause, that "from every hamlet, from every fireside, and from every farm of Republican constituents today there are going up prayers and hopes that this resolution to change the rules of the House will be successful here today." [40]

The amendment was approved by a vote of 193 to 153, and the insurgent revolution was then doubly consummated by the passage of the Norris resolution as amended by a vote of 191 to 156. During these roll calls the Speaker stood in his place, gavel in hand, presenting a countenance that gave no indication of his feelings. He was under the constant scrutiny of two thousand visitors as well as of all the people on the floor below. Earlier he chatted with a clerk and was seen laughing heartily. After the results were announced, Norris moved to reconsider the vote by which his resolution was adopted and to lay that motion on the table. Without objection, it was so ordered; the substitute amendment now prevailed as the adopted resolution.[41]

Here, as far as Norris was concerned, the insurgency revolt should have ended. The Speaker had been removed from the Committee on Rules. While this was not all Norris desired, a break in the Speaker's power had been made and further reforms at the convening of the next session of Congress would certainly be easier to obtain. Therefore Norris, upon the acceptance of his amendment, moved to adjourn. But this revolution in the procedures of the House, like all revolutions, would not proceed merely as far as its original movers desired. It soon got out of hand. From a fight for principle it degenerated to a squabble over personalities, presenting dramatic scenes which made those of the previous days pale by comparison. Norris, the more moderate insurgents and Democrats, would be swept aside as the extreme radicals among them gave vent to their passions, with some encouragement from the Speaker.

Chapter 19

Insurgency Revolt: Part II

IN THE CONFUSION that followed Norris' motion to adjourn, Cannon spoke in a calm voice. "The Speaker," he said, as if asking a favor, "asks the indulgence of the House for not exceeding three minutes to make a statement." Norris announced his willingness to withhold the motion and the chamber became silent. Cannon then began a speech that was one of the most remarkable and dramatic, if not the most impetuous, ever delivered before the House. He reiterated his belief in party rule and announced that his party, despite the fact that the country believed it had a majority of forty-four members in the House, was no longer in control. The Democratic minority, aided by "the efforts of the so-called insurgents," was now in the majority. The fact that he was not in harmony with the actual majority was evidenced by the vote to create a new Committee on Rules.

Two courses were open for Cannon. One was to resign and permit the new majority to choose a Speaker in accord with its aims and purposes. The other was to allow "the combination" to declare the office vacant and elect a new Speaker. Cannon did not choose to follow the first course because he did not want to endanger the passage of legislation necessary "to redeem Republican pledges and fulfill Republican promises." More important, however, was the fact that he regarded a resignation as "a confession of weakness or mistake or an apology for past actions." Since he believed he had construed the rules as he found them and as they had been construed "by previous Speakers from Thomas B. Reed's incumbency down to the present time," he therefore saw no need or reason to resign.

Then Cannon threw down the gauntlet to the opposition and announced that since there was "no coherent Republican majority in the House of Representatives, therefore, the real majority ought to have the courage of its convictions and logically meet the situation that confronts it." Reaffirming his belief in party rule, he announced his willingness, as a matter of the highest privilege under the Constitution, to entertain a motion to vacate his office and elect a new Speaker in accord with the wishes of the "Democratic and insurgent Members who, by the last vote, evidently constitute a majority of this House." What occurred next was described in the *Congressional Record* as "loud and long-continued" applause on the Republican side; great confusion in the Hall." [1]

Amid the demonstration, J. Swager Sherley of Kentucky hurried to converse with Oscar W. Underwood of Alabama, while Albert S. Burleson of Texas arose waving a piece of paper and demanding recognition. Rushing to the Speaker's desk, Sherley shouted for adjournment. Burleson shouted that his resolution should be read and immediately voted upon. Other members shouted and the Speaker called for order. He said there were matters that could take precedence over a motion to adjourn and requested that the Burleson resolution be read. This resolution, accepting Cannon's challenge, provided simply "that the office of Speaker of the House of Representatives is hereby declared to be vacant, and the House of Representatives shall at once proceed to the election of a Speaker." [2]

Up to this point Norris had remained quietly in his place at the rear of the chamber. Now he rose, proceeded to the open space before the Speaker's chair, and doggedly refused to give way to the Democrats and insurgent Republicans who came forth to offer advice. He insisted it was only out of courtesy to the Speaker that he had withheld his motion to adjourn which should now be the business of the House. Cannon acknowledged the validity of Norris' remarks and called for a voice vote on the motion to adjourn. The "ayes" and "noes" of the members all registered at the same time and only increased the tumult, but Cannon decided the "noes" had it and that the House had refused to adjourn.[3]

However, Norris refused to be downed so easily. Claiming that he had never heard the announcement on the vote owing to the confusion, he demanded a roll call vote, whereupon Cannon requested that all in favor of such a vote rise and be counted. Only fourteen members, including Norris, stood. Thus the House declined to adjourn.

The insurgent Republicans were now caught between rapidly solidifying party lines. The Republicans were determined to vindicate Cannon, while the Democrats, with misgivings on the part of some, rallied behind the Burleson resolution to remove the Speaker. Under these circumstances, the insurgent ranks split asunder. The more moderate among them, following Norris, continued to insist their battle was against the rules per se and not against Cannon, the Repub-

lican party, or its legislative program. On the other hand, nine insurgents, including four from Wisconsin and two from Minnesota,
joined with the Democrats in the effort to depose Cannon.[4]

Before the crucial vote, Cannon surrendered the chair to Sereno
Payne amid loud applause on the Republican side. He nodded and
smiled to his colleagues as he went to his office to await the result.
During this interlude Norris was busily conferring with insurgent
members, requesting and even begging some to vote against the
Burleson resolution. All but nine of the insurgents cast their votes
against the resolution. For the first time throughout the conflict most
of the insurgents voted in unison with their Republican colleagues.
When the 192–155 vote against the Burleson resolution was announced, almost all the Republicans arose and yelled themselves
hoarse. Some wept. Payne, after surrendering the chair to Speaker
Cannon amid a scene of wild enthusiasm, moved to adjourn and at
5:30 P.M., March 19, the House officially adjourned. Most Republicans,
however, remained in the chamber to serenade the Speaker with the
strains of "For he's a jolly good fellow." As they sang, Speaker Cannon
stepped down from the dais. Nodding and smiling, he held a reception, shaking hands and receiving the good wishes of his loyal supporters.[5]

As a result of the revolution of March 19, 1910, Norris became a
figure of national prominence. His name was intimately connected
with the proceedings in the House, his picture appeared in newspapers throughout the country, and his views were sought by reporters.
In the public mind he was the personification of the insurgency movement. The press, which had been instrumental in supporting the
insurgent cause, now presented Norris as the insurgent David who
slew the tyrannical Goliath known as Cannon. As one editorial put
it:

> Mr. Norris has been the real parliamentary leader at almost
> every crisis when the insurgents have won a point or gained a
> real victory. He has proved himself able, from the outside of the
> citadel, to discover weaknesses in the entrenchments of the or-
> ganization, which the organization itself did not suspect. In the
> present fight—a fight, by the way, which was opened exactly one
> year from the date when Cannon and Tammanyism won their
> disastrous victory of March, 1909—he has again proved his title of
> the Rupert of insurgency.[6]

Interviewed after Congress adjourned, Norris claimed "a great
victory for the insurgents and the people." It would now be possible

for the majority of the House to "work its will" on matters affecting the nation's business. He still thought, however, that his original resolution "was far superior to the one which was adopted by the House." [7] He realized that while the overthrow of Cannon represented a great victory for democratic control of the House, "it did not place the power where it would be exercised in the most practical and democratic way." Chairmen and members of standing committees, instead of being chosen by the Speaker, would be chosen in party caucus where the Speaker still exercised a powerful voice and the insurgents little or none. But Norris was aware then and later that compromise was necessary to achieve partial reform which would make further progress easier.[8]

Speaking for the insurgents, Norris said they did not expect consideration when the Republican caucus met within the prescribed ten-day period to select members of the new Rules Committee. The insurgents did not intend to ask for representation on the committee nor would they take action to modify the rules any further at this session. He claimed, however, that at the beginning of the next Congress they would make a fight to deprive the Speaker of the power to appoint standing committees.[9]

When the new Committee on Rules was presented on March 25, it was accepted unanimously. Not an insurgent Republican or an independent Democrat appeared on the roster of its members; all were appointed in party caucus, and with the exception of Cannon all former members of the five-man committee were on the new ten-man committee.[10] On the surface it appeared as if a committee controlled by the Speaker were merely doubled in size and controlled by the Speaker's closest political friends with John Dalzell acting as chairman. However, a revolution had occurred; a spirit of independence had been manifested in the House and a minority of members had dealt a severe blow at the source of the Speaker's tremendous power. This new spirit was displayed throughout the remainder of the Sixty-first Congress though no further radical departures from established procedure were made. While most of the insurgents quickly entered the progressive camp, others, like Hamilton Fish of New York, Butler Ames and A. P. Gardner of Massachusetts, and Andrew J. Volstead of Minnesota, returned to the regular Republican ranks. With the revolution against the rules thus consummated, the members returned to consider more mundane matters.

Six weeks after the event, Norris tried to evaluate its meaning: "There is a freedom of action that has never existed before since I have been a Member of Congress." While the upheaval was far from a complete victory over the machine, it allowed for more independence of action than anything that had occurred for many years. Norris admitted that the personnel of the new committee was not satisfactory, but, he explained, a small handful of insurgents in a party caucus could not control committee membership.

To the charge that the reorganized Committee on Rules was still in effect controlled by Cannon, Norris replied that it was not a matter of much consequence to practical legislation. He insisted the committee would not dare to present any rule that curtailed individual action or gave the machine control over particular legislation. "The day of such domination," he claimed, "is absolutely over, and the Speaker with all of his power, is not able to push such a rule through the House." Ideally, he observed, his function should be similar to that of the policeman on the corner: "There is no danger of the store being robbed, so long as he is there." [11]

The rules fight added to Norris' strain and tension. He was worn out, but could not rest because he had to be on hand while the House considered important railroad legislation. By May he was so exhausted that he contemplated going to a sanitarium to recuperate.[12] He became depressed, regarding himself as something of a failure, at least financially, and feeling that he had been unable to provide adequately for his family. He found his existence lonely, and because of his precarious party position, unpleasant. He disliked life in Washington and would have welcomed a chance to leave. But he had no intention of quitting under pressure, of "showing the white feather." If the Nebraska voters chose to retire him, he would not regret their decision; nevertheless, he intended to seek their approval in the coming election.[13]

Though the rest of the session was anticlimactic, Norris soon took a keen interest in legislative matters and claimed that the new situation resulted in improved legislation. As an illustration of the more relaxed atmosphere, less than a week after the revolution Norris obtained the floor and humorously twitted colleagues who refused to follow a committee's recommendation on a bill before the House. The members enjoyed his bantering remarks and when his time expired, it was extended by unanimous consent for five minutes. He reproached the regular Republicans who refused to follow the committee for their insurgency. He appealed "to these young men," saying amid laughter and applause, "For God's sake, boys, get back on the reservation before it is everlastingly and eternally too late." [14]

Given this new spirit, Norris hoped a bill providing for publicity of campaign expenses might merit serious consideration. This matter had long interested him and had become urgent during the 1908 campaign when his opponents unscrupulously spent large amounts of money. In the previous Congress in April, 1908, Norris had prepared a report to accompany the first bill ever reported on this subject. The bill, proposed by Samuel W. McCall, a conservative Republican from Massachusetts, was referred to the Committee on Elections of President, Vice President, and Members of Congress which held extensive hearings. Roosevelt, Taft, Bryan, and many members of both houses had urged Congress to take action. After long debate the committee unanimously supported the bill and Norris was selected to prepare the report. All these efforts came to nought because of the Speaker's opposition. Later in the session, because of public pressure, a somewhat modified version of the same bill was again introduced. With the help of the Speaker, who suspended the rules to prevent amendments, it was passed, but it died in the Senate because of Democratic opposition.[15]

Early in the Sixty-first Congress McCall reintroduced the bill. It was sent to the same committee, which again reported favorably on it. Norris, no longer a committee member, inserted a copy of his original report in the *Record*. The bill, he remarked, would go a long way toward purifying elections. Political machines, operating under cover of secrecy and dominated by bosses, interfered with freedom of action by public officials and made exceedingly difficult, if not impossible, legislation demanded by the people. These machines could not exist, "at least to any harmful extent," if they were not supported by secret contributions from individuals desiring to profit from the conduct of the public servants they influenced. The "searchlight of publicity," he thought, would soon put these machines out of business and drive the political boss into oblivion.

Norris' opinions on this matter revealed traits characteristic of many progressives. He had a simple solution to a complicated problem which he saw in moralistic terms. He was optimistic but did not think the bill would solve the problem completely. It was merely "a step in the right direction" which deserved the hearty support of those who desired "to give the people themselves the greatest possible amount of participation in governmental affairs." [16]

The bill was passed by the House and soon thereafter, with slight modifications, by the Senate. On the last day of the session Norris urged his colleagues to reject the conference report because the provision calling for the publication of expenses prior to an election had been removed from the House bill. By rejecting the report, he argued, the bill itself would not be lost, as there would still be another session of the Congress. The bill would not lose its place on the calendar, and might well become a better law. Congressmen, however, were in no mood to accept this reasoning; the report was accepted and before the day was out the emasculated bill was signed into law by President Taft.[17]

While Norris was not entirely in accord with this measure, he knew that it received consideration only because of changed conditions in the House. The new environment was also responsible for railroad legislation with which he was in hearty agreement. In January, 1910, at the request of the administration, Congressman James Mann introduced a bill enlarging the rate-making power of the Interstate Commerce Commission and creating a commerce court to handle appeals from commission rulings. Included in the measure was a clause allowing railroads to acquire competing lines.

The House, when it considered the bill in April and May, modified it along progressive lines, favoring competition by removing the provision allowing mergers of competing roads and by accepting amendments for physical valuation and equitable charges to obviate long and short haul discrimination. The House also approved a provision bringing telephone and telegraph companies under the jurisdiction of the ICC. These amendments were carried by the Democrats and the progressive Republicans who were recruited from the ranks of the former insurgents. Norris, while not playing a major role in the passage of this bill, nevertheless favored these and other strengthening amendments. He believed the Mann-Elkins Act to be the most progressive railroad measure enacted during the decade, though it attracted less discussion and publicity than the Hepburn Act of 1906.[18]

Norris was pleased with the way the House amended the bill. Before the curtailment of the Speaker's power, the bill would have passed in its original form. Now, according to Norris, it was "the longest step in the right direction that has ever been taken at one time." This step had been achieved because interested members, including many insurgents, had devoted at least three weeks, working day and night, to the bill. After the House version of the bill went to the Senate, Norris revealed how effective their efforts had been. He wrote:

> Some of these most valuable amendments to this bill were offered by the so-called Regulars, but as a matter of fact were prepared by some of the Insurgents at secret sessions. Wherever we could find any record in favor of a particular amendment that we believed ought to be adopted, we secured its introduction by such member, if possible, and some of these members have of-

fered these amendments without the knowledge that the amendment itself was prepared and worked out by a meeting of some of the so-called insurgents.[19]

The fight for improved railroad legislation further convinced Norris that the real friends of progressive legislation in the House were the insurgent Republicans. They were able to achieve this success only by cooperating with Democratic members. Though the Republican party took credit for the Mann-Elkins Act and other legislative achievements, none of the progressive measures, said Norris, would have been enacted in their final form "had it not been for the victory which we obtained over the machine in the House, by which the atmosphere was entirely changed and the secret, unexplainable, but yet positive control of the Speaker and his machine was partially destroyed."[20]

On June 17, at the unanimous suggestion of the Committee on Rules, a motion was adopted, providing a calendar on which members might register motions to discharge committees from further consideration of bills which had not been reported. Known as the "Discharge Calendar," it provided means by which a bill could be forced out of committee. Up to this time the only way to discharge a committee was to move to suspend the rules; such a motion could be made only on the first and third Mondays in every month. Norris supported this resolution, believing it another step in the direction of curtailing the Speaker's power. He added what may be considered a peroration on the insurgency revolt and its significance:

> But for that victory we would not have this opportunity of another advance presented us to-day. We all know there is a change of atmosphere in this House. There is more individual freedom and less coercion. There is more individual liberty and less machine control. The result is better legislation, better laws, better government. This result has been brought about, this freedom has been obtained by the unequal, desperate, and sometimes discouraging fight made upon the rules by the hated and despised insurgents. With malice toward none, without ill will or feeling against any man, without patronage or political favor, opposed, abused and misrepresented by members of their own party, they have steadfastly stood for a fundamental principle of representative government that was being violated in this House, and by virtue of such violation the rights of the people were being neglected and sacrificed.

> The good results of their bitter struggle have been apparent for some time. Machine control in the House of Representatives is

disappearing. There is still room for improvement, but the action of the Committee on Rules to-day indicates that the House will yet be its own master; and when that time comes about, the insurgent will receive his reward. He gets considerable consolation out of this condition here to-day, and it affords me no small degree of satisfaction on this occasion to welcome to the insurgent ranks practically the unanimous membership of the House. We give you the glad hand of fellowship, and although your coming is rather late, and it may be your action is moved in some degree by fear of what might happen if you did not come, yet we receive you with open arms and promise to kill the fattened calf in your behalf.[21]

Thus Norris considered himself a spokesman for the insurgents and was so regarded by friend and foe in and out of Congress. His sudden fame must have been a bit overwhelming; it taxed his physical stamina and burdened him with further responsibilities. Though the possibilities for self-aggrandizement did not impress him, he soon began to meet a wider range of people and to emerge as a prominent progressive on the national scene. His battle against the House rules soon expanded into a concern for issues affecting progressive politics.

In May, 1910, he spoke at a dinner of New Jersey progressives in Newark. During the same month a California progressive requested literature and information that could be used to help the movement in that state. Samuel Gompers invited him to a conference early in June, while Pinchot asked Norris to visit him. In short, before he returned to Nebraska to campaign for re-election, Norris was entering the progressive fold. During the campaign he moved into their camp and thereafter emerged in the upper echelons of the progressive ranks.[22]

Chapter 20

Entering the Progressive Fold

EMERGING as a national figure in 1910, Norris presented a picture of a stockily built man of medium stature with a mass of black hair flecked with grey and a closely clipped reddish brown mustache. His appearance literally bespoke action. He walked briskly, talked tersely and to the point. His chin projected aggressively and his mouth shut in a thin fine line. His left eyebrow drooped deceptively, a result of the old hunting accident, but the sharpness of his eyes belied any implication of listlessness. He dressed simply, if not carelessly, usually in brown or black, and his coat generally fitted badly over a pair of muscular shoulders.

Norris gave the impression of energy personified. He had a queer trick of pursing up his mouth to emphasize points he wished to make. However, in personal appearance he still looked like a country lawyer. Simple in tastes, quiet in dress, he had little to distinguish him outwardly from other small-town business and professional men. His favorite exercise was mowing the lawn and his favorite diversion was reading Dickens' novels.

Whatever fame he had achieved was primarily the result of playing the parliamentary game against almost impossible odds. As a master strategist, he had helped to undermine boss rule in the House. Since believers in good government were engaged in similar struggles throughout the country, Norris and the insurgents conveniently served as a symbol of what a small intrepid group could accomplish. To a generation of Americans most of whom believed that the problems and evils in American life were not of a fundamental nature, Norris and his fellow insurgents showed that the cure lay in the readjustment of the mechanisms. While the reformers in the Senate stressed tariff changes, railroad regulation, and similar social and economic issues, the House insurgents, as previously noted, were split as soon as the question arose of removing Cannon from the Speaker's chair. Norris realized that the relaxation of the House rules provided freer debate. A change in the rules was not a panacea but merely an initial step, necessary to the full and free confrontation of important social and economic problems.

Despite his sudden prominence Norris remained noticeably unaffected. He did not speak frequently, but when he arose from his seat in the southeast section of the House chamber in the "Cherokee Strip," a Republican pocket amid the abandoned society of Democrats, members listened attentively. Though he appeared to be an average man, and though his actions were not as enthusiastic and emotional as Victor Murdock's, no one doubted that he was a legislator of superior ability.

When not on the floor, Norris spent most of his time in his office, a cigar in his mouth and his heels on the desk. It was there that he pondered the question whether to be a candidate for a fifth term or to seek the Republican senatorial nomination from incumbent E. J. Burkett. From his arrival in Washington in December, 1909, to his departure at the end of June, 1910, Norris was besieged with requests to become a candidate in the senatorial primary. In the beginning he was noncommittal, though he did ask friends to sound out sentiment and keep him abreast of it. He soon learned that Burkett was regarded by progressive Republicans as a mere opportunist, "slippery and slimy Elmer," and that unless the party nominated a progressive candidate, almost any prominent Democrat, such as Bryan or Congressman Hitchcock, "could wipe the earth with Elmer." [1]

The appearance of Burkett clubs which passed resolutions criticizing the insurgent movement angered Norris in February almost to the point of committing himself as a senatorial candidate. "If my insurgency is to be a test of my Republicanism," he was quoted as saying, "then I think the sooner we know where we stand the better." Since the primary law permitted voters to express their preference for United States senator, Norris thought seriously of entering the race, though personally, he confessed, he preferred to stay out of the fight. [2]

While he continued to express distaste for life in Washington, he also insisted that he could not retire or pursue a course that would show any indication of backing down or of cowardice. If he decided for a Senate seat, he intended to delay announcing his decision to keep the primary campaign as short and as inexpensive as possible. This indecision kept the political picture in Nebraska in a state of constant confusion, while Norris, exhausted, depressed, lonely, and ill, mulled the matter over in his mind. [3]

By June, Norris still had not announced his decision, but he had been talking the matter over with his "insurgent brethren." Almost without exception they urged him to be a candidate for the House and not the Senate. He also discussed the problem with people outside of Congress, among them Gifford Pinchot. Their advice was practically the same. While all of his confidants invariably said they would have liked to see him in the Senate, they also claimed that because of his role in the rules fight he should remain in the House at least one more term. His district, they said, would be watched by the entire country. When the issue was presented as a challenge to ascertain whether people approved of the insurgents' course, Norris decided it was his duty to seek a fifth term as a representative.[4]

He arrived at this decision in Washington in mid-June, less than two weeks before Congress adjourned. Once it was made, he decided to speak for progressive candidates in some western states before returning to Nebraska and his own campaign. Leaving Washington, Norris felt certain that he would be re-elected in November. The promise of the coming campaign restored his mental outlook and alleviated his mood of depression. Though physically exhausted and desperately in need of a vacation, Norris nevertheless felt that he could thrive on campaigning, especially since he had an important issue to present.[5]

Believing that the welfare and success of the Republican party depended upon progressive members, he was determined to do his part by campaigning for such candidates. He also believed that an organization should be established with this purpose in mind. Thus, after speaking in New York State and elsewhere in the East, early in July Norris departed on a speaking trip through Kansas, Colorado, and Wyoming, and his secretary thought he might also campaign in Oklahoma, Washington, and North Dakota.[6]

On July 12, 1910, Norris' youngest daughter, Gertrude, was quarantined for scarlet fever. Her serious illness cut short his speaking trip. He returned to McCook to be with his family and to get a brief rest before launching his own campaign. McCarl was anxious to get him home, and wanted Norris to visit with friends, editors, and politicians throughout the district before campaigning began early in the fall. Since Norris was the only Republican candidate to enter the congressional primary, no campaign would be necessary until September.[7]

As Republican county conventions chose delegates for the state convention, many also passed resolutions endorsing Norris and his role in attacking Cannonism. Because of the quarantine period, Norris did not expect to attend the state convention at Lincoln at the end of July, though he was anxious for it to adopt a resolution condemning Cannonism.[8]

Progressive Republicans feared that there would be an effort to make the state convention "stand pat" and that Burkett and his followers would try to prevent an endorsement of Norris' work in Congress. Thus progressive hopes soared when on the afternoon of July 25 it was announced that the danger period was just about over and that Norris would be temporarily released from quarantine. Monday evening he boarded the train with the Red Willow County delegation for the convention which would convene the next morning in Lincoln.[9]

At the convention he was defeated by Senator Norris Brown for the position of permanent chairman. The conservative Republican press claimed this setback as a great victory for their cause. Since Norris arrived only a short time before the convention convened and made no serious effort to obtain the post, his defeat was no indication that the delegates were conservative. When John L. Webster, the attorney for the Omaha Street Railway Company and a standpatter, was placed at the head of the Platform Committee, progressive delegates thought that machine control would prevent any endorsement of Norris' work. But Norris himself prevented this from happening. Bypassing the Platform Committee, he secured recognition from the unsuspecting chairman, Norris Brown, and introduced from the floor a resolution condemning Cannonism and at the same time pledging Nebraska Republicans to the support of the insurgent cause. This resolution, which caught Burkett, Rosewater (editor of the Omaha Bee), and other standpat leaders offguard, was passed by an overwhelming majority and clearly indicated the temper of most Nebraska Republicans.[10]

As soon as he returned from Lincoln, Norris went back into quarantine for more than two weeks. McCarl returned to his campaign preparations and noted with some dismay the increased out-of-state mail. He knew that the National Republican Congressional Committee would not aid Norris with funds and that the state committee would supply little or no aid. Therefore he requested officeholders in the district to send contributions direct to the congressional committee.[11]

Norris had been too busy with his own affairs to follow Theodore Roosevelt's activities as he prepared for his western trip. On August 23, the day Roosevelt started his trip, Samuel Merwin, the editor of *Success Magazine* in New York, wrote to Norris:

I suppose you know by this time about what is coming from T. R. in his western speeches. Have you seen a copy of his

Osawatomie speech? Confidentially, I read it through last week. While it is sometimes hard to tell from a manuscript just how it is going to sound when it is uttered and started around in the papers, it read to me like one of the most terrific progressive insurgent broadsides we have had so far. Apparently T. R. forced by circumstances as well as by his own temperament into the ranks of the progressives is going about it with his characteristic vigor to try and take the lead on the right side.[12]

Norris, however, did not take notice of Roosevelt's famous speech. Nor did he attend the Roosevelt speech in Omaha several days later; Norris, who had been invited to attend, was speaking in Wisconsin on behalf of La Follette and other progressive candidates whom he had promised to help "in the event the battle became too strong." [13]

Almost all of Norris' speeches during the campaign were on Cannonism, a subject of great interest to his audience. It was an ideal topic because it could be presented as a nonpartisan discussion or explanation or, with very little effort, as a partisan campaign speech. Though John M. Nelson, an insurgent colleague, later criticized Norris on the grounds that he "placed himself decidedly in the front seat" and did not mention Nelson's own role in the fight, Norris' speeches and those of other prominent progressives were eminently successful in achieving their main goal—that of assisting La Follette. He was renominated in the September primary by a majority of over 102,000 votes.[14]

Norris left Wisconsin on September 3 to speak at a rally in Minneapolis on September 5. From there he went on to Nebraska. En route he was injured slightly in a railroad accident. Though he was hardly up to it, he left McCook on September 14, to begin his own intensive campaign. Norris now refused all out-of-state speaking requests, including one from Hiram W. Johnson, the progressive Republican candidate for governor of California. He remained in Nebraska busily campaigning until election day.[15]

Following his usual pattern, Norris generally traveled alone to meetings, stayed at the local hotel, and conferred with local leaders and citizens. McCarl remained in McCook, directing and coordinating the over-all campaign. Toward the end of September he wrote, "Conditions are splendid all over the district." He felt certain that disgruntled and disappointed Republicans would still vote for party candidates and that some Democrats would be likely to cross party lines and vote for Norris. In this campaign there was none of the anxiety and distress so prevalent in 1908.[16]

The 1910 campaign in Nebraska was complicated by the liquor issue which disturbed many voters and which Norris avoided in his speeches. When Governor Shallenberger in 1909 signed a law requiring all saloons to close at 8 P.M., he lost all chance of renomination. James C. Dahlman, the colorful ex-cowboy mayor of Omaha and a strong opponent of liquor legislation, obtained the Democratic nomination and campaigned by promising the voters free beer on the Capitol grounds at the time of inauguration. His opponent Chester H. Aldrich supported the Republican plank calling for county option. The Anti-Saloon League gave its support to Aldrich, while Bryan refused to support Dahlman because of his "wet" position. Bryan, a temperance man, favored county option and campaigned for the entire Democratic ticket, except the nominee for governor. The fact that many voters planned to split their tickets because of the liquor question probably benefited Norris by giving him many Democratic votes.[17]

Norris' meetings were well attended and his speeches well received. As McCarl noted, "When given an opportunity to get the facts before the people, he usually leaves with more friends than he had prior to his talk." Norris worked hard at campaigning, speaking twice a day for several weeks towards the end of October. But this time he had significant help. While Senator A. B. Cummins of Iowa spoke on three consecutive days at Hastings, Holdrege, and McCook, Congressmen Madison and Murdock from Kansas each devoted two full days to speaking at various points throughout the district.[18]

The major criticism hurled against Norris by R. D. Sutherland, also his opponent in 1906, and other Democratic speakers was the fact that he did not vote for the Burleson resolution to unseat Speaker Cannon. Norris, of course, always discussed this matter and explained his position. According to McCarl, once this had been done, the voters invariably approved his course. The Omaha *Daily News* aided considerably by publishing an editorial explaining his position on the Burleson resolution.[19]

On the other hand, James A. Tawney, who was in Nebraska in October, saw an account of one of Norris' speeches and was shocked to read that Norris had said Burleson presented a motion to depose the Speaker "after a conference with Representative Tawney, one of Cannon's chief supporters." Tawney claimed that this statement was "absolutely and unqualifiedly false" and hoped that he would correct the impression created by this misstatement of fact. Tawney's letter indicates that Norris may have been embellishing speeches to dramatize his position.[20]

To prevent Irish-American citizens from voting the straight Democratic ticket merely to support Dahlman's "wet" position, McCarl asked former Congressman J. J. McCarthy to speak in the district at the close of the campaign. McCarthy gladly accepted.[21]

Norris maintained his stamina and voice throughout the entire campaign. A week before its ending he spoke for almost two hours at a small town in Nuckolls County, and those who attended, Democrats and Republicans alike, said it was the best talk they had ever heard. Then on November 3, five days before election, the Nebraska newspapers printed a strong endorsement of Norris from Senator La Follette, thus undermining Sutherland's charges that Norris was not a true progressive like La Follette. And Congressman Murdock informed Norris that his name had been mentioned in at least eighty-six of the ninety-one speeches he had delivered since leaving Washington. By continuing to fight to change "the vicious system of personal control" in the House, the insurgency revolt, said Murdock, would become "not a passing incident in politics, but epochal in the history of American legislation." [22]

Norris returned to McCook on November 7, election eve, and closed his campaign in the Masonic Temple Theater that evening. Norris received a great ovation from the capacity crowd and was visibly affected by the tribute paid him. A visitor claimed that Norris' speech was equal, if not superior, to any given by Senator Beveridge. Norris had now done his part of the job; it remained for the voters to do theirs.[23]

The results of the 1910 election in Nebraska gave neither party a decisive victory. Aldrich was elected governor and Republican candidates won all available executive offices. Hitchcock, however, defeated Burkett by almost twenty thousand votes in the preference vote for United States senator, and the Democrats also won a majority in both houses of the state legislature and elected their congressional candidates from three districts. Republican candidates were successful in the fourth, fifth, and sixth congressional districts. Norris rolled up a substantial majority in the Fifth District, defeating Sutherland by slightly more than four thousand votes. He carried all but three of the eighteen counties in the district.[24]

In McCook, where almost one thousand votes were cast, less than two hundred were registered against Norris. He was elated with his victory since it showed that his constituents approved his course in Congress, but was cautioned against any celebration because there were "too many Republican funerals in the country to make any demonstration." [25] In the House the Democrats won a majority of sixty-three seats, while reducing the Republican majority in the Senate from twenty-eight to eight. The Democrats also elected governors in many traditionally Republican states including New York, Connecticut, Massachusetts, Maine, and New Jersey, where Woodrow Wilson embarked on his political career. Only in the West, where the progressive movement was rampant, did the Republican party hold its own. Despite the one outstanding progressive defeat—that of Albert J. Beveridge—Miles Poindexter of Washington, John D. Works of California, and Norris' former Washington neighbor and colleague, Asle J. Gronna of North Dakota all entered the Senate and enabled the progressive membership of that body to hold the balance of power. Though Republican leaders expected to suffer reverses in 1910, no one was prepared for the magnitude of the defeat. Only two of the numerous candidates endorsed by Roosevelt were elected to office. Indeed, only the Democratic party could obtain solace from the results of the 1910 elections.

After the election Norris admitted to intimates that he regretted his decision not to enter the senatorial race. He did not comment upon his future course, but was pleased with suggestions that he enter the next senatorial race.[26]

Since the lame duck session of the Sixty-first Congress was scheduled to convene early in December, Norris was able to spend little time in Nebraska before returning to Washington. His congressional career, which at the outset of 1910 seemed doomed to frustration and oblivion, now seemed to have vast potential as a result of the insurgency revolt and his re-election. Members in the coming session would greet a new, optimistic Norris—a national figure, interested in a wide range of reforms, whose advice and services were sought by progressives throughout the country. The election of 1910 had demonstrated the progressive temper of the citizens of Nebraska and other western states. Victory assured Norris that the voters approved his course and would support him in demanding further reforms. Victory convinced him that with the assistance of a few devoted, hard-working men he could handily defeat a Democratic opponent and surmount opposition in his own party despite his inadequate funds. It also assured him more than ever of his ability to win the senatorial seat. Thus when he left McCook, Norris was much more than the representative of Nebraska's Fifth Congressional District. He was a symbol, soon to become a spokesman as well, for progressive-minded citizens throughout the United States.

Chapter 21

The Insurgent as Progressive

LESS THAN a month after the election, Norris was in Washington for the short session of the Sixty-first Congress. Any hopes he may have had for a leisurely session were quickly shattered. The breach in the Republican party was already too large to permit any easy reconciliation of the opposing factions, and during this session further issues and events would widen the gap. Believing that he would return to Mc-Cook in March, Norris did not bring his family and took a room at the Y.M.C.A. His secretary again remained in McCook tending to his law practice and intending to keep Norris informed of political developments, real estate matters, and investment possibilities. When the House was in session, Norris usually spent the forenoon in his office, the afternoon in the House, and the evenings working in his office or relaxing in the Y.M.C.A. swimming pool.[1]

The House convened at noon on December 5, 1910. A week later Norris spoke on a measure providing for an inheritance tax in the District of Columbia. He proclaimed an inheritance tax the fairest way to raise revenue and stated that it could prevent the amassing of large fortunes which most progressives "admitted to be detrimental to good government if kept up for several generations." [2] Throughout his long career Norris took advantage of every opportunity to speak in favor of an inheritance tax, gaining acceptance of his views only once, during the Wilson administration.

Though deprived of his patronage by the president, Norris thought he foresaw a reconciliation when early in the session he suggested that Taft appoint a Nebraska jurist to fill a vacancy on the Supreme Court. Norris sent information about several Nebraska candidates, but all attempts at harmony between the two men ended when Taft appointed a conservative, Willis Van Devanter of Wyoming, to fill the post.[3]

Norris continued to expound his views on judicial matters. On January 25, 1911, the House was considering an amendment that sought to raise the salary of federal circuit judges from $7,000 to

$8,500. Norris opposed the measure, arguing that the increase would elevate judges to a higher station in society, encouraging them "to forget human rights and human liberties." He believed that the present salary was sufficient to enable a judge to be independent of any interest or financial consideration. Norris summarized his views, derived from his own experience as a judge, as follows:

> Our judges should be absolutely independent of every outside influence and of everything which might have a tendency to in any way interfere with their official duties. They are the most important public officials of our Government. They should be absolutely free and unbiased, so that they can weigh the evidence and decide litigation alike between the rich and the poor, the high and the low. They should never be so far removed from the people—from the common, struggling citizens—that they will forget the just and fair rights of any litigant. The judges' salaries should be sufficient to keep them from want, from privation, from hardship, and to give them all the necessities and all of the reasonable luxuries of life. The salary should never be so high as to attract any man on account of its money consideration alone. The best judge, as well as the best citizen, is the man who realizes that money alone can not bring satisfaction or happiness; that the rights of property, while the same should be protected according to the spirit of the law, should never be permitted to outweigh or to cover up the rights of the individual. Men whose life work and whose life study have been in the direction of an understanding of the law and the principles of equity and justice, and who follow such lines because they love it and not for the money there is in it, are the men in whose hands the scales of justice should be placed.[4]

So persuasive was Norris and so economy-minded was the House that the amendment was defeated. But his interest in the federal judiciary did not end with these remarks. When the president considered Walter I. Smith, one of the staunchest regulars in the House, to succeed Van Devanter on the Circuit Court of Appeals, E. H. Madison of Kansas suggested Norris as a suitable candidate.[5] Madison talked with Taft and asked McCarl to send recommendations showing that Norris had been fair and fearless on the Nebraska bench, meting out justice to litigants regardless of their financial or social condition. Madison received a large number of recommendations, including one from the entire Supreme Court of Nebraska, but, as was expected, the president nonetheless named Smith to the post.[6]

Throughout these hurried negotiations, Norris did nothing to encourage his candidacy. His friends suggested his name because they did not wish to have another conservative on the federal bench, and because they did not want the administration to have the excuse once again that no progressive candidates were available. Norris' candidacy was an effort on the part of the progressives to dramatize an issue, succinctly stated by Senator Cummins, who wrote: "Why send progressive men to Congress to enact progressive measures, when the Interests may rely upon the Federal Bench to give them relief when those progressive measures come before the courts for judicial construction?" [7]

Reactions to the judgeship issue varied. Some were sorry Norris was not appointed, while others rejoiced because he could now run for senator. Many felt that the progressives' purpose in suggesting his name was to counter the president's nominee with a better one from their wing of the party, thus challenging Taft's announced intention of treating equally all groups within the Republican party.[8]

Norris was a passive and silent judicial candidate in part because he was involved in another skirmish with the standpat element in the House. On January 5, he introduced two resolutions amending the House rules. One proposed a revolutionary reform by making the proceedings and votes of every committee of the House available to the public, thereby preventing committees from evading responsibility by throttling bills. The other was designed to remedy a defect in the "motion to discharge" rule, thereby preventing the clogging of the calendar. Both bills were sent to the Committee on Rules, though neither was presented on the floor.[9]

Several days later, on January 9, the insurgent position seemingly received a setback, when Charles E. Fuller, a regular Republican from Illinois, presented an amendment to one of the rules. When challenged that the resolution was not in order, he claimed for it the constitutional privilege that had been previously accorded the Norris resolution. Speaker Cannon in effect repeated his ruling of March 19, 1910, that the resolution was not in order. In this instance he was sustained by a rousing 235–53 vote, with all of the insurgents, none of whom participated in the discussion, voting with the minority and most of the Democrats not voting, though Oscar Underwood, who played a prominent role in the insurgency revolt, voted with the majority to sustain the Speaker.[10]

While Cannon and his supporters claimed that this vote was a vindication of their position, Norris prepared a statement which claimed that none of the rules enacted in 1910 had been abrogated.

Though the 235-53 vote was indeed a setback, he vowed that the fight "for progressive American principles in legislation" would continue. The attacks on the rules during this short session, he thought, were inspired by a small group of the "old guard" with a view to discrediting the accomplishments of 1910. He claimed that the Democrats, who supported Cannon in this ruling, were playing politics.[11]

If Cannon experienced vindication early in January, by mid-January he experienced further defeat. The fight developed from an attempt to utilize a rule that gave the House the power at specific times to discharge a committee from further consideration of a bill. The insurgents and Democrats believed that this ruling, which had been enacted in the second session of the sitting Congress, was iron-clad—that, as soon as the consideration of bills by unanimous consent had been concluded on every first and third Monday of the month, the House was then bound to consider motions to discharge committees from the custody of specific bills. Cannon declared that the rule did not make it mandatory for the House to take up such motions, but simply made them in order if the House wanted to consider them. When the vote was taken on January 16 on the appeal from Cannon's decision, twenty-two insurgents and all but one of the Democrats present voted against the Speaker. The attempt to sidetrack discharge motions was rejected by a vote of 145-126.[12]

Since the rules received much attention during this short session, Norris took the opportunity on the first anniversary of the start of the insurgency revolt, Saint Patrick's Day, to prepare a strong statement. Claiming that the victory did more to make the House a truly representative body than any other incident in the history of Congress, he asserted that it was "a fight between representative government and machine control, a conflict between the people and the Special Interests." He noted that now there was growing sentiment "for more publicity in governmental affairs and for a higher standard of efficiency in public officials." The growing acceptance of the initiative and referendum, the widespread demand for direct election of delegates to national conventions and of United States senators, were indications that the "great progressive movement" was surging forward and would continue until the reins of government were restored to the people. He also decried partisanship by asserting that "patriotic public service" was more to be desired than "party solidarity." This anniversary statement was one of the earliest public pronouncements of his growing awareness that he was more a progressive than a Republican.[13]

Along with other prominent progressive Republicans, Norris helped to form the National Progressive Republican League, in January, 1911, with the avowed object of promoting popular government and progressive legislation. As an indication of his new status, Norris was chosen first vice president of the organization, which was headed by Senator Jonathan Bourne of Oregon and had among its members Senator Brown and Governor Aldrich of Nebraska. At the outset the league unofficially served as a rallying point for opposition to President Taft and his standpat supporters in Congress.[14]

Nebraskans reacted favorably to the creation of this organization and to Norris' official position in it. His prominence continued to grow in progressive Republican circles. He was chosen to deliver a eulogy in Congress honoring the memory of the later Senator Dolliver. Thus in the last session of the Sixty-first Congress, he continued to be the outstanding progressive leader in the House.[15]

Norris devoted much time and energy to legislative problems. Since the session would be the last during Taft's term in which the Republicans would control Congress, the administration made greater efforts than usual to enact its legislative program.

Important to Nebraskans was proposed legislation to establish a parcel post system. Many opposed the plan because they thought "it would foster the development of an enormous trust, create an oppressive monopoly, destroy the properity of all country towns, seriously injure tens of thousands of jobbers and country merchants, drain the rural communities of their capital and population, aggravate the evils of centralized wealth and congested cities, and benefit no one but the great retail mail order houses in the big cities, and the express companies." The farmer's local market, they argued, would be destroyed, and with it would go his educational, social, and religious benefits as well. Realty values would decline and further taxation would be thrown upon already overburdened shoulders. Retail mail-order houses would benefit enormously, but country merchants and farmers would face financial ruin as well as loss of their way of life.[16]

Agitation against parcel post mounted rapidly during the short session and reached a climax in the following Congress when a parcel post measure was enacted into law. Norris kept the criticisms in mind, but argued that if the system took distance into account most of the difficulties could be obviated. If the charge were in proportion to cost and took into account the weight of the parcel and the distance it traveled, he thought the doom of the farmers and rural merchants would not materialize. Furthermore, a fair parcel post system would lower exorbitant rates charged by express companies which, according to a report of the ICC made an average profit of 50 per cent of all invested capital in 1909.[17]

In this session, as in the past, Norris voted against the annual addition of two battleships for the navy. The custom of adding two ships per year was inaugurated by Roosevelt to keep the navy at fighting strength and to provide for the scrapping of obsolete vessels. While Norris believed in a moderate naval increase, he thought it more urgent that the government devote its attention and funds to agreements for arbitration treaties. He thought the time was ripe for the United States to propose to other civilized nations an agreement to arbitrate all future difficulties. Both progressives and standpatters were divided on these issues and there had never been any concrete attempt to unite them.[18]

Concerning military affairs, Norris favored the national guard rather than a large standing army, though he never gave the matter very careful scrutiny.[19] He became more involved with military matters and took stronger stands on them as conditions in Mexico deteriorated during the last months of the Diaz regime. Norris insisted on strict neutrality, denying that the president had any legal right to use the army or his official position to influence Mexican affairs. "The fact that the armies in the field are destroying property such as railroads, mines, etc., in which citizens of our country have a financial interest," Norris explained, "ought to have no effect whatever upon the course our Government should take." He maintained that since the destruction of property was a legitimate method of warfare, citizens investing in foreign countries always took the risk of war and must abide by its results. The private citizen, not the government, was involved.[20]

The major piece of business before this session was the reciprocity agreement with Canada which was sent to Congress on January 26, 1911. In negotiating it was agreed that reciprocity would be effected by concurrent legislation in both countries instead of by a treaty. The proposed legislation would admit nearly all agricultural products except wool without duty. A few minerals, as well as iron and steel plates and wire, were also on the free list, while innumerable manufactured items would move across the border at reduced rates which would be identical in either direction. Generally speaking, the free list included raw materials imported by the United States. The schedule provided American publishers with cheaper newsprint by calling for free paper and wood pulp, and thereby assured a base of popular support for the arrangement.[21]

Norris opposed this measure because he considered it unfair to the farmer's interests. It removed agricultural tariff protection without reducing the farmer's costs. Free trade for the farmer and not for the manufacturer seemed to Norris to be another example of discrimination against the rural regions. He could not see why America should not be protected from Canada as well as from any other country. A rate that assured the difference in the production cost of the article imported, with perhaps a small profit to the American producer, ought to be applied to all articles subject to tariff legislation, regardless of country of origin.[22]

At the outset Norris was alone in his opposition to Canadian reciprocity. The Nebraska newspapers, and all of Nebraska's congressional delegates except Norris, were in favor of it. It was pushed through the House on February 14, by gag-rule tactics, with no opportunity to offer amendments, little chance to comment, and, unlike the Payne-Aldrich Tariff, with Democratic support. Norris protested, wishing to send the measure back to committee with instructions to put on the free list some of the farmer's necessities. His protest was to no avail; the bill easily passed the House by a vote of 221–93. Among the former insurgent members, eighteen favored it and nine, including Norris, opposed it. The measure carried because of Democratic support. The majority of Republicans voting on the measure opposed it.[23]

Unable to express his opposition on the floor, Norris had his lengthy remarks inserted in the Appendix to the *Congressional Record*. Since the House had already agreed to a bill providing for a permanent nonpartisan tariff commission which would determine the difference in cost of similar articles produced at home and abroad, he thought the commission could aid in determining rates that would be applicable to all nations alike.

As an agrarian, he insisted that danger to American institutions would surely come if legislation helped to decrease rural population and drive more people into already overcrowded cities. Indicating his connection with nineteenth-century rural America, a bond he had in common with many progressives, Norris added:

> But it is also in the city that we have the slum and the breeding places of anarchy, ignorance, and crime. It is there we have the mob. It is in the city that we have the machine politician and the political boss, where, by organization and machine control, the elective franchise is seriously interfered with. On the other hand, upon the farms are located the conservative, patriotic, and thinking voters of our country. Uninfluenced by the machine control or

the political boss, they are the balance wheel in our form of government. In time of danger and in time of war we lean with confidence and pride upon the strong arm and the willing and patriotic heart of the American farmer.[24]

He could not comprehend why the United States should surrender markets for the advantage and development of the Canadian economy at the expense of the American farmer. He suggested that "the instigators of this plan" might have framed it as a punishment to that portion of the country whose Republican representatives had the courage to protest the high schedules in the prevailing Payne-Aldrich Tariff.[25]

He ordered 25,000 copies of this speech from the Government Printing Office and had them sent to McCook for distribution. The job of informing Nebraska's farmers would be difficult, since all the large daily papers, sympathetic to either free trade or free newsprint, favored the measure. Yet the fact that Norris stood alone would make it easier for him to expound his position because voters would want to know what prompted his opposition.[26]

Nebraska farmers, however, would have ample time to obtain an understanding of the reciprocity agreement. While the measure quickly passed the House, it immediately ran into trouble in the upper chamber where standpat qualms and progressive opposition grew rapidly, provoking a swell of senatorial oratory that did not abate in time for a vote to be taken before the session ended on March 4. Taft, to save reciprocity, was forced to call a special session and to hope that the Democrats would continue their support of the measure. The president's inability to obtain its passage during the third session of the Sixty-first Congress assured opponents of the measure an opportunity to educate their rural constituents to its inequities.

Because the short session presented a major legislative issue that had not been resolved, members of Congress looked forward to a summer of fervid debate in hot, humid Washington. The debate on reciprocity pushed Norris further into the progressive camp, led him to despise intense partisanship, and convinced him that reconciliation with the Taft administration was impossible.

Comic relief to the serious doings of Congress was provided for Norris by the condemnation and censure he received from the Society for the Protection of Poodle Dogs in the District of Columbia. On February 5 he delivered an impromptu address before an audience of young men in the Washington Y.M.C.A. He reflected on his blissful domestic condition and advised his audience in favor of marriage. He claimed "To be a husband and a father is the noblest ambition of every male human being." Following Theodore Roosevelt, he believed that young men who wanted to do good for their country and humanity must marry and raise children. "Of all the joys that life can give," he said, "the baby is the best." [27] He observed, however, that many wealthy people were raising more poodle dogs than children, and related the following incident with irony and humor.

Walking along Connecticut Avenue one day he saw a well-dressed woman come out of a luxurious mansion and enter a carriage. In her arms she carried a beautiful poodle, "all decked out in ribbons, trinkets and flowers." Norris pitied this wealthy woman who, he supposed, was childless and therefore wasted her affection on a poodle. But soon the door of the mansion opened again and a maid emerged wheeling a baby carriage. Norris assumed from the baby's clothes that it was the child of the woman who had just departed. First he felt sorry for the child, but upon reflection he shifted his sympathy to the poodle because under the circumstances the baby seemed to be in the best company. Poodles, he believed, should never replace children. "Too often in America today rich women care nothing for their offspring, but would rather bestow their foolish affection on pets that amount to nothing." Few wealthy mothers, Norris concluded, gave their first and best thought to their children.[28]

This address aroused an immediate and violent response from wealthy women and poodle-lovers all over the country. Washington's leading matrons unanimously condemned Norris and defended their pets. The male president of the Washington Kennel Club stepped into the breach and praised socially prominent women and their lap dogs, declaring, "If more men would attend to their children as they should, we would not hear so much of this talk of the American home being ruined." To protect himself Norris contemplated moving out of Washington and taking other precautions to escape the crowd of women and dogs pursuing him.[29]

As humorous as this incident may seem, it shows that Norris' remarks were seldom without purpose. In this case he was condemning conspicuous wealth, a social phenomenon at odds with his progressive views and rural values. Later efforts along these lines would usually be more political and pertinent in their application. However, whether the tenor of Norris' statements was serious or humorous, he seldom failed to inform his listeners.

When Congress adjourned on March 4, 1911, he quickly returned to McCook and his family. All plans for an extended vacation had to be shelved when Taft announced his intention of calling the new Congress into special session to consider the unresolved Canadian reciprocity agreement. Hopes for a brief vacation, as well, were dissipated shortly after his return to Nebraska.

Chapter 22

Widening the Breach

THE Sixty-second Congress, Norris' last as a member of the House, was called into a special session on April 4, 1911, by President Taft. The new Congress would convene exactly one month after the old one had expired, giving Norris about three weeks in McCook. Instead of resting, he worked ten and twelve hours a day on a matter he planned to introduce in the coming session. McCarl thought he looked "like thunder, worse if anything than he did at the close of the [1910] campaign." Home cooking and the pleasure of his family's company brought some improvement, but Norris was not well. Friends were worried that the special session would "get him" if he did not pay more attention to his health.[1]

Though he would not openly admit it, Norris too was concerned. After his return to Washington, he confided to a doctor that he had begun to realize he was on the verge of a nervous breakdown as a result of four years of overwork without an extended vacation and under intense political pressure.[2]

His worries about his health and his eagerness to participate in the burgeoning progressive movement created mixed feelings about spending the entire summer in Washington. He thought the Democrats, rather than accept reciprocity, would attempt a revision of the tariff to embarrass the administration still further. Moreover, he was not sure whether the Democrats expected to appoint all the House committees and proceed with general legislation or whether the work of the special session would be confined exclusively to the reciprocity measure. He planned for the former but hoped for the latter. Prior to his return to Washington he had a severe attack of lumbago which forced him to relinquish the few engagements he had made while in Nebraska.[3]

Fortunately Norris recovered rapidly and was able to leave McCook at the end of March in time to attend a meeting of progressive Republicans called by John M. Nelson for the afternoon of April 3. The term "insurgent" had been replaced by "progressive" in Nelson's invitation, and soon fell into disuse as the latter term was felt to be more inclusive. The purpose of the meeting was to discuss and, if possible, agree upon some plan of action with reference to the caucus, the choice of a minority leader, committee assignments, and other matters.[4]

When the first session of the Sixty-second Congress convened on Tuesday, April 4, the small band of progressive Republican members were determined to continue the fight for improved parliamentary procedures and better legislation. During this Congress the Democrats had a majority in the House, and Champ Clark replaced Cannon as Speaker. At their initial meeting the progessive Republicans decided not to oppose the candidacy of James R. Mann for minority leader. Norris had the highest regard for Mann even though he had been a devoted Cannon supporter in the rules fight. One of the hardest workers and best parliamentarians in the House, Mann was always scrupulously fair, though he rarely displayed any inclination to be lenient during partisan controversy.[5]

The Senate, however, was still controlled by the Republicans. Though its progressive ranks were seriously depleted by the defeat of Beveridge and the death of Dolliver, a new group included Asle J. Gronna and Miles Poindexter, former insurgent members of the House, and John D. Works. William S. Kenyon of Iowa, replacing Dolliver, joined their ranks several weeks later. With each chamber of Congress controlled by a different party, the last two years of the Taft administration would be characterized more than the first two by jockeying for political effect, to create and define issues for the 1912 campaign. Throughout the turmoil, the struggle between progressive and conservative Republicanism continued. Given these conditions, it is surprising that this Congress enacted as much nonpartisan but progressive legislation as it did.[6]

Norris noted with satisfaction some marked changes in the organization of the House. For the first time the rules provided that the Committee on Ways and Means be elected and endowed with the power to appoint other committees. Representatives were assigned to only one important committee, thereby obviating the fear that members of the Ways and Means Committee would appoint themselves chairmen of powerful committees. As in the past the minority leader was to assign places to minority members. The committees, when finally determined, were "elected" by receiving the formal approval of a caucus and then of the House. These new rules, though they still left something to be desired, represented a long step toward the greater freedom the former insurgents desired.[7]

One morning shortly after Congress convened, Norris was invited to the minority leader's office, where Mann frankly asked him what committee assignments he wanted. The question and the change in procedure greatly surprised Norris and, before he could answer, he was offered a place on the Judiciary Committee. Norris readily assented. From his recent oblivion as far as committee assignments were concerned, Norris now found himself on a prominent committee at the suggestion of a Cannon lieutenant.[8]

At the start of the session, during consideration of the rules, Norris suggested several further changes. He stated that the members should be free to offer amendments and vote on them rather than being subject to caucus control and the need to vote accordingly. While he still favored a fifteen-member Committee on Rules, he realized that caucus control was a more limiting evil and had to be eliminated before any further significant rules changes could be made. Control by caucus, though better than control by the Speaker, still prevented the free selection of all committee members by the Ways and Means Committee as the rules now provided. Norris felt that the time was not far distant "when the progressive, patriotic sentiment of the American people will drive the caucus and the political boss and the political machine out of business." [9]

Norris also favored an amendment making committee business and records public. Such publication would prevent suspicion and rumor from being reported as fact. When secrecy was necessary, he believed committee members should say their work was of such a nature as ought to remain private.[10]

Norris read with considerable interest the reports of Governor Woodrow Wilson's speech before the National League of Democratic Clubs at Indianapolis criticizing the secrecy that surrounded the work of the standing committees. Committee secrecy, Norris wrote Wilson, was one of the best ways for the machine politician to kill legislation demanded by the people. The blame, he suggested, was formerly with his party, but now that the Democrats controlled the House, it was equally divided between both parties.[11]

The purpose of the changes that Norris suggested was to increase the power and freedom of individual members at the expense of both the Speaker and the party organization. Curbing caucus control and committee secrecy, limiting the Speaker's power, and abolishing gag rules prohibiting members from offering amendments would help to achieve this purpose without destroying the ability of the House to function. Norris was aware, however, that partisanship would prevent these changes from being realized. Though the Democrats had criticized the previous rules, they now accepted and imposed most of them, seemingly forgetting their earlier statements about arbitrary rules and procedures. As long as men blindly followed leadership they did not believe to be honest or pursued purposes they did not think would accomplish good, individual freedom would be unobtainable in the House. Norris hoped that political parties, an integral part of American political life, would improve in caliber by attracting progressive and honest men who could unite in favor of good legislation.[12]

Another suggestion Norris put forth in his attempt to encourage greater individual responsibility, was a limit or decrease in House membership. Certainly an increase in membership would necessitate the surrender of rights and prerogatives to some smaller governing body. Indeed, it was the present size of the body which enabled the caucus, secret committee hearings, and arbitrary rulings by the Speaker to flourish without serious opposition. Reducing the size of the House, Norris argued, would not affect the basis of representation because the influence of each state would remain proportionally the same; but the gain in improved procedures would be immeasurable.[13]

Early in the session Norris turned his attention to the proposed amendment to the Constitution calling for direct election of United States senators. He favored it. While further rules changes would grant individual representatives greater freedom and responsibility, direct election of senators would insure broader democracy by placing greater control of government in the hands of the people. It would allow state legislatures to devote more time to lawmaking and would enable the voter to cast his ballot for candidates who represented his ideas on state-wide issues without considering the candidates' choice for senator. Furthermore, direct election would make it more difficult for organized wealth or political bosses to dictate the selection of particular candidates. The fact that the Senate had recently considered the fraudulent election of William Lorimer of Illinois and had welcomed him nonetheless, gave added weight to arguments for the amendment.[14]

In the hope of bringing about the rejection of the amendment, opponents combined it with one that took from Congress the right to control congressional elections. Norris favored separating the proposition, but so effective were the dilatory tactics that it took another year and the approaching presidential campaign before Congress in May, 1912, approved the Seventeenth Amendment.[15]

A further procedural matter that Congress considered during this special session was the admission to the union of the last contiguous territories of the United States, Arizona, and New Mexico. This issue was fraught with political significance, reflecting the breach between progressives and conservatives in both parties. Norris favored the admission of both territories, though he had some qualms because the Arizona constitution included the provision that recall apply to the judiciary. He believed this to be dangerous, but since the proposed constitution had been made by representatives of the people in accordance with their wishes, he considered it his duty to approve it.

In defending the initiative and referendum clauses in these constitutions, he used arguments similar to those he had presented in supporting the direct election of senators. These provisions, while not insuring good government, would promote political understanding and responsibility. If properly used, he predicted, initiative, referendum, and recall would be tools to promote better legislation, help restore government to the people, and insure its resting upon the consent of the governed.[16]

Once procedural matters were disposed of, the House turned its attention to a reconsideration of the major piece of business before it, the Canadian Reciprocity Agreement. Norris' position, clearly defined in the previous Congress, remained unchanged. On April 21, 1911, before the House adopted the measure by a vote of 268–89, he tried to send the bill back to committee with instructions to amend it.[17] Reciprocity was debated for seven weeks on the floor of the Senate beginning in mid-June until its final passage on July 22.

Meanwhile the Democrats in the House, anxious to appeal to midwestern farmers in the 1912 election, had Oscar Underwood, chairman of the Ways and Means Committee, introduce the farmer's free list bill which passed the chamber a month later. Norris supported the bill because it offered some relief to the farmer, providing for free lumber, free boots and shoes, and many other items which the farmer bought. He hoped it would rectify some of the inequities of the reciprocity agreement.[18]

Norris also tried to get Underwood to consider revising the sugar schedule. Failing in this, he called for an inquiry into the operations of the sugar trust. When these efforts came to nought, he supported another measure proposing a drastic downward revision of the tariff on wool. World production of wool had not been equal to the demand for several years, and Norris felt that there was no good reason for a high wool tariff. However, as was the case with the farmer's free list bill, these Underwood tariff measures were promptly vetoed by Taft.[19]

In the last days of the special session, Norris regaled his colleagues with a pointed but humorous narrative of the recently approved reciprocity measure:

> In my judgment, when true history is written and this much-abused and much beloved child called "Reciprocity" is properly labeled, it will be found that she is a sort of a cross, having both Republican and Democratic blood circulating in her veins. It will be found that she had a Republican father and a Democratic mother, and this brings us at once to the consideration of the question of her legitimacy. I have heard of no marriage ceremony concerning her parents, and if this unfortunate child is able to establish the legitimacy of her birth it will be necessary for her to prove a common-law marriage.
>
> At the ceremony of her birth, the doctor having charge of affairs was furnished by the interested railroads, the nurse was provided by the Beef Trust, and her swaddling clothes were purchased by the brewers. To compensate the infant for the uncertainty of her parentage, and also to deceive farmers of the country, who were robbed of the honest and just protection which is rightfully theirs, the high-sounding and beautiful name of "Reciprocity" was given to the child. A name usually indicates the nature of the thing named, but in this instance the beauty of the name was intended to conceal the real nature of the child and to cover up the sin of its parents.[20]

In this vein he criticized everyone who supported the agreement. In Washington, both parties vied for the credit, but in Nebraska and throughout the Mississippi Valley the measure was truly an orphan child, disowned and ignored. In the 1911 conventions in Nebraska, reciprocity was not mentioned by the Republicans or endorsed by the Democrats.[21] But Norris had no intention of ignoring the issue when he returned to Nebraska and considered his political future.

Shortly after the House passed the measure, Norris delivered the most ambitious speech he had ever made. It concerned an issue which affected not only his constituents but citizens throughout the country, and represented a congressman's venture in muckraking at a time when journalists were tiring of such probes. Norris' sources, though not all verifiable, were extensive, and included information from the Library of Congress and the Bureau of Statistics. He attacked a greedy and unscrupulous trust, a monopoly on an international scale that included a foreign government among its directors and extorted its levies from victims throughout the world. In a carefully prepared speech on April 26, Norris attacked the coffee trust.[22]

The immediate purpose of his speech was to expose this powerful trust with the ultimate hope of securing remedial legislation to curb its activities in the United States. He introduced his subject by commenting on the worldwide tendency toward combination. Competition when throttled inevitably led to monopoly which "if unrestrained and uncontrolled" always resulted in "an unfair and an unequal distribution of the products of labor and of wealth." Whereas most combinations that attracted public attention affected comparatively few people, this particular combination levied its tribute in pennies but counted its contributions by the millions and was a "daily uninvited guest" in homes, whether mansions or hovels, throughout the world.[23]

The coffee trust began with the 1906 attempt by São Paulo, one of the states of the Brazilian government, to assume control of the world's supply of coffee. The state bought all the coffee produced within its border and held it from sale until the price rose. After two years, however, it became evident that the undertaking was too great for the state, and a new and more gigantic plan was undertaken. São Paulo issued bonds amounting to $75,000,000, guaranteed by the government of Brazil. With the proceeds the state purchased Brazilian coffee and held it off the market. The bonds were handled by English, French, German, Dutch, and American bankers; J. P. Morgan and Company, the National City Bank, and the First National Bank together took $10,000,000 worth.[24]

A committee of seven men, one chosen by the Brazilian government and six by the bankers, supervised and controlled the disposal of the coffee purchased. The coffee was shipped to representatives of these financial concerns and stored to be sold in such quantities and at such prices as agreed upon by the supervising group. As a guarantee for the payment of the bonds and interest, the Brazilian government agreed to levy an export tax on coffee and to remit the proceeds weekly to the financial backers. The government also agreed to enact a law prohibiting the planting of additional coffee trees and to prevent as far as possible an increase in the supply. Thus ample provision was made for the control of the coffee market until 1919, the year the bonds were to mature. Since it takes six or seven years for a coffee tree to reach its full bearing capacity, no great increase in the coffee supply from other countries was expected to threaten the arrangement.[25]

Norris next noted that coffee had already more than doubled in price. World consumption had averaged for the previous four years about 17,900,000 bags, while world production for the same period had averaged over 18,600,000 bags. Thus in the face of continual over-production, prices had steadily and regularly advanced. During this same period Brazil annually produced more than 14,000,000 bags of coffee. It exported to the United States about 23,000,000 bags during the period from 1907 to 1911, while American coffee imports from all other countries during these years were a little over 5,000,000 bags.[26]

The basic question Norris raised with his description of the coffee trust was what could be done about this international plan for the valorization of coffee. American law was not applicable to Brazil, nor could European bankers be brought into American courts. The American participants could be punished only if they violated American laws. However, Norris was convinced that by a change in tariff laws, indirect action at least could be taken against the government of Brazil and its states.

Norris' remedy was twofold. He suggested first that American corporations involved in the agreement be prosecuted for violations of the Sherman Act. He suggested, second, that Section 2 of the Payne-Aldrich Tariff Act, providing for raising rates against nations which discriminated against the United States, be amended to include in-stances where a government became a party to an arrangement de-signed to increase prices to American consumers. However, if this suggested amendment did not bring relief, Norris then was willing to consider another scheme whereby all coffee entered free of duty until the amount slightly exceeded our domestic consumption. If at that point a high duty were imposed only on Brazilian coffee, Norris was certain that Brazil would be compelled to come to terms. Thus the amount of coffee consumed by the American people and not the manipulation of a special committee would more nearly determine the domestic price.[27]

Unless some such action were taken Norris thought similar steps to control the supply and price of rubber soon would be undertaken. He concluded with a brief statement of the role of the United States, as he envisioned it, in its dealing with other nations:

> As a Nation and as a people we are in possession and control of the natural resources and are occupying a situation that, by de-manding and asserting only what is right and fair, we will be able to secure justice to our people without doing any injury to the people of any other nation. To this we are entitled, and we should be content with nothing less. With a spirit of entire friendliness

toward the balance of the world we should demand and exact common justice to our own people. We should apply the doctrine of the Golden Rule to all the people of the earth and at the same time should insist that the rule work both ways. We should give justice to all others and should demand that the recipients of our favor repay us in kind.[28]

Unfortunately this speech, the most ambitious thus far in his congressional career, attracted relatively little attention. There was no congressional investigation and the Department of Justice took no steps to invoke the Sherman Act against the American banking firms. The department assigned a special attorney to investigate the matter, but nothing came of it. No sensational exposure appeared in the public press, and only the coffee merchants commended the speech and gave it some publicity. The results were unimpressive and the speech did not appear to be worth the effort.[29]

The study and the speech, however, were important in increasing Norris' knowledge and in helping him formulate his views. He was more than ever convinced that competition was the best way of conducting business and that government action would be necessary to preserve competition and obtain fair play for American consumers. He envisioned the international scene as an extension of the domestic. The problems and their remedies, he believed, were basically similar; only the scale was larger. In either case—that of domestic corporation or international monopoly—the American government had the responsibility of protecting its citizens.

By the end of the first session of the Sixty-second Congress Norris was regarded as the progressive leader in the House. While concerned with the interests of his constituents and battling for more democratic procedure in the House, he devoted his attention to issues of broader interest as well. His remarks in Congress now commanded the attention of most of his colleagues. But politics, with the Democrats controlling the House and seeking to define issues for the 1912 campaign, prevented his suggestions from receiving serious consideration during this special session. While the Democrats were attempting to consolidate 1910 election gains in preparation for the coming presidential campaign, progressive Republicans were also weighing chances of capturing the Republican party and nominating one of their leaders for the presidency. Norris was an active participant in these deliberations, but his most important concern was his own political future and the senatorial election of 1912.

Chapter 23

La Follette for President

WHEN not devoting time to congressional matters during the spring months in Washington, Norris turned his attention to Nebraska and his political future. He brought mailing lists up to date and sought suitable lists in other congressional districts. He sent the people on these lists copies of one of several of his speeches—"The Caucus and the Rules," "The Valorization of Coffee," or his views on Canadian reciprocity. The tariff speech was the most popular, but Norris thought it advisable to circulate as well copies of his speech calling for the direct election of senators.[1]

By this time Norris was certain that Taft could not win Nebraska in 1912; only a progressive candidate stood a chance to hold the state in the Republican electoral vote column. Though he had doubts as to the possibility of preventing Taft's renomination, he was encouraged by reports indicating rising sentiment against the president. Like other former Taft supporters, he had lost faith in the president's claim of following the Roosevelt policies. His sympathies and associations, Norris argued, had been with wealthy people despite the fact that the president was a comparatively poor man: "He has never yet known what it is to work or to be dependent upon the sweat of his own face for support." Though Taft had lost the support of "the Cannon and Aldrich machine" on the Canadian Reciprocity Agreement, Norris believed he would make no effort at reconciliation with the progressive members of his party. Norris thought, too, that the president had "a personal dislike, if not a personal hatred" of him, because Taft thought, with some justification, that Norris was one of the individuals responsible for much of his discomfort.[2]

On Sunday, April 30, 1911, Norris and other prominent progressive Republicans in and out of Congress attended a conference in Senator Bourne's office in the Capitol. At this lengthy meeting all agreed that Taft could not be re-elected in 1912, though they conceded that the president probably had, through his control of the federal patronage, sufficient strength to bring about his renomination. As to the question whether to try to nominate anyone else, all agreed it would be better to make the effort and fail than to make no attempt at all. They agreed, too, that the fight should be made in the name of Theodore Roosevelt, but were promptly informed by Gilson Gardner, a friend of Roosevelt and Washington correspondent of the Scripps papers, that under no circumstances would the former president consent to the use of his name. Senator Cummins then said, "There is but one man who should be considered as the Progressive candidate, and that is Senator La Follette." Once again everyone agreed. Norris promised to do all in his power to further the Wisconsin senator's cause in Nebraska. La Follette, after further discussion, consented to make the attempt, provided funds could be found to support his efforts.[3]

When the Progressive Republican League of Nebraska invited Norris to attend a meeting at Omaha at the end of May, he suggested that if Nebraska emphatically endorsed the candidacy of a progressive Republican her voice would have great influence in the selection of delegates from other states. But he quickly learned that all was not well among Nebraska Republican leaders and that the friction between them involved him. Victor Rosewater, editor of the Omaha Bee, whom Norris had never regarded as a political friend, claimed he favored Norris for the Senate in 1912. Rosewater had engaged in a bitter patronage quarrel with Senator Norris Brown and now supported Norris as a means of evening the score. Norris was thus pressed to announce his intentions.[4]

Until this time he had been noncommittal, but by mid-June he was more specific about his plans. He expected "in due time" to announce his candidacy, even though 1912 looked like a Democratic year. Norris thought that he could get the nomination but would be defeated by a Democratic landslide in the election. Meanwhile, until an opportune time arose to announce his candidacy, he championed the cause of La Follette and, in this way, kept his name before the voters as the outstanding progressive Republican in the state.[5]

In the midst of these political developments Norris celebrated his fiftieth birthday, an event which caused him to do some serious reflecting on his past, present, and future. He felt that he was now "going down the other side of the hill." In one respect, the financial one, he considered himself a failure. Though he had no desire for wealth and did not believe money to be "the chief object in life," he was disturbed about his inability to provide for his old age. On the positive side, outweighing his financial worries, were his accomplishments and the knowledge that they were appreciated. "The greatest happiness that can come to a man," he said, "is a consciousness of having done his duty fully and fearlessly." [6]

During the special session he had supplemented his income by occasionally delivering speeches. Unwilling to be away from Washington for any length of time, he limited his engagements to nearby areas. He delivered the commencement address at the Rockville High School in Maryland, spoke for the National Progressive League in Pennsylvania and Maryland, and addressed the Winter Chautauqua at Binghamton, New York, and the Boston City Club. His topic at most of these lectures was Cannonism, and audiences were disappointed when he spoke on anything else. [7]

Despite his unwillingness to leave Washington, progressive Republican politicians in Nebraska urged him to return for the state convention in July, announce his candidacy for the Senate, and assume a prominent position in the Nebraska progressive movement. But Norris, using the pressure of legislative duties and lack of funds as an excuse, preferred to watch the fluid political situation from his vantage point on the Potomac. There he could benefit from any feuding that might occur among Nebraska Republicans and at the same time maintain a statesman-like posture that would impress the average voter. [8]

As county conventions chose delegates for the state convention, efforts were made to place Norris supporters on prominent committees. While sentiment for Taft or Norris Brown was not particularly strong, McCarl was worried lest the organization choose a "standpatter" or a "crazy" progressive as temporary chairman. The Republican press was trying to portray all progressives as this latter type—as radicals. Norris was concerned lest the convention endorse reciprocity and the Taft administration. If it began to take this direction, he intended to go to Lincoln and asked to be placed on the Red Willow County delegation so that he could gain admission on the convention floor if necessary. [9]

Norris' request, however, arrived too late for McCarl to get him on the delegation. The Red Willow County convention on July 19, following the lead of several other conventions, had endorsed La Follette for president and Norris for the Senate. [10] Delegates at the state convention, fearful of an open split in the party, refused to pass any resolution endorsing Taft and his policies. While Norris sentiment was evident, many delegates thought he had done enough for La Follette and too little for himself. All expected an announcement of his senatorial candidacy at any moment. Summing up the convention for his chief, McCarl wrote:

No one seemed to think you had been injured. Everybody seemed to think that you got through fine, considering the fact that you had endorsed La Follette. However, this came from the Taft men. Many of them like you and will do you some good next April. All in all, I am satisfied with conditions at this time. If we can only improve them and not let them get worse.[11]

The sentiment shown at the convention helped Norris resolve his decision. He first informed friends he would announce his candidacy after Congress adjourned, but then changed his plans and made the announcement late in July. His evaluation of the forthcoming presidential race was substantially correct:

It looks as though it is going to be a Democratic year, and unless Taft can be defeated for the nomination and assuming also, that Woodrow Wilson, or some other progressive Democrat is nominated, Nebraska will surely go Democratic by an overwhelming majority, and will very likely carry everything with it on the ticket. I hardly expect La Follette to be nominated. The chances are all in favor of the renomination of Taft, but I think it will pay to make the fight anyway.[12]

Thus when the special session of the Sixty-second Congress ended on August 22, Norris was committed to the cause of La Follette and to a long and arduous campaign for the senatorial nomination. In a sense he had been campaigning since March, 1910, when he forcefully came to the attention of all Nebraska voters. From what he had been able to discern, he believed that sentiment in the state was more united behind his candidacy than behind that of any other candidate for major political office in 1912. On leaving Washington he asserted that he would win the primary by a great majority, but added that the party could avoid disaster only by preventing Taft's renomination.[13]

His first talk was scheduled for Sioux City, Iowa, on September 4. Next he was to speak at the State Fair in Lincoln, following Secretary of Agriculture James Wilson. The secretary, it was announced, would defend the Canadian Reciprocity Agreement and show that duty-free farm products and protected manufactured goods were designed to benefit Nebraska farmers. Norris had hoped the issue would remain in the background until after the 1911 election since it had no place in a campaign for justices of the Supreme Court and members of the Board of Regents. But once Wilson had said he would speak, Norris agreed to present the other side.[14]

Thus on September 6, before several thousand people, he scathingly denounced reciprocity. The speech was similar to others he had delivered on the subject, but familiarity with the topic made it all the more effective. His remarks were frequently interrupted by loud bursts of applause. From this time on until the end of October he spoke throughout Nebraska chiefly on the subject of Canadian reciprocity.[15]

On September 21, Canadian voters turned out of office the government of Sir Wilfred Laurier, responsible for negotiating the reciprocity agreement. The victorious Conservative party abrogated the measure, and President Taft found that his efforts were in vain, his prestige at low ebb, and his party irreparably divided. Norris thought that, despite the defeat of the measure in Canada, voters would still remember with displeasure those who had favored it, Senator Norris Brown among them.

Norris tried to show that free trade in agricultural products was detrimental to the American farmer and that tariffs on such items raised their value. He used wheat as an example and compared its price in different parts of the United States, Canada, and in Liverpool. Farmers, he claimed, were selling wheat on the domestic market and not on the world market; the price outside of the United States was not the American price plus the cost of transportation, but was lower than this total and sometimes lower than the American price itself. As conclusive evidence of the relationship between the presence of tariffs and higher market value, he cited the fact that the day after Canada rejected reciprocity, the price of wheat rose from three to seven cents in every market in the United States. It went down a little in Winnipeg and remained stationary in Liverpool. Through these speeches Norris introduced many a Nebraska farmer to the complexities of tariff legislation and nurtured seeds of hostility toward the Taft administration and the reciprocity measure.[16]

Early in October, Taft appeared in Nebraska on a western tour to arouse sentiment in favor of arbitration of international disputes. On October 1, he spoke in Omaha and Norris was among the guests seated on the stage. The next day a reception was held for Taft in Lincoln, but Norris was not invited to attend this meeting or to travel on the president's train. In order not to seem piqued, Norris sent a note claiming he had other business requiring his attention. The note did not prevent the circulation of reports that he purposely snubbed the president but, having attended the Omaha meeting, Norris felt he had done all that political etiquette required.[17]

Norris' absence at the reception in Lincoln merely heightened the chilly welcome Taft received. Three bands, two hundred Civil War veterans, and six automobiles took part in the procession, and crowds lined the streets. But, an ardent La Follette supporter noted, there was a minimum of applause during the parade and after Taft's speech. The only burst of applause came when the president mentioned Bryan and his support of arbitration treaties. Gilson Gardner reported that 75 per cent of the Nebraska Republicans were for La Follette.[18]

Striving to arouse progressive sentiment, Norris worked under a heavy handicap. He lived in the less populous western part of the state, and had never campaigned in Omaha or in other prominent eastern towns. Another drawback was the fact that progressive sentiment in Nebraska was not yet as vigorous as in Kansas and Iowa, and Nebraska Republicans were more opposed to Taft than they were in favor of La Follette. Norris claimed that "the great common people of Nebraska" were not as progressive as the rank and file he had met in the East. "In all my travels," he explained, "through Pennsylvania and other eastern states, I found that when Republicans were opposed to Taft, they were invariably for La Follette." [19]

On October 16, the Conference of Progressive Republicans convened in Chicago with delegates from thirty states. The resolutions adopted declared that the progressive movement was a struggle on behalf of the people to wrest control of government from representatives of special privilege. To achieve this end they aimed to nominate and elect men who would truly represent popular will and carry out the progressive policies pledged by the Republican party. Favoring a presidential primary law or any other scheme by which the people would gain the right to express their choice, the conference enthusiastically endorsed La Follette's candidacy. The meeting, according to Senator Moses Clapp of Minnesota, "was a most unqualified success." [20]

Although speaking engagements prevented Norris from attending the conference, he did offer some suggestions. He put forth a plan asking supporters for one-dollar subscriptions; this method would improve finances, show voters that funds for the "people's campaign" were coming from the people themselves, and encourage supporters to work for the success of the cause. Norris also suggested the writing and circulating of a pamphlet that would explain La Follette's views and combat the lack of publicity for him in the press. Norris was confident that La Follette could win the Nebraska primary by a large majority and was gaining admiration and affection for "the little fighting Senator" to whom, he felt, "the progress and advancement of liberty and justice" already owed so much.[21]

Between speeches, he participated in the state campaign, advocating the election of candidates without regard to partisan politics. He argued that no man's vote in 1911 should be controlled by his views on the presidential nominee. Most of these so-called non-partisan campaign speeches, delivered in the southern part of the state, were in answer to those made by Bryan requesting support for all Democratic candidates. Bryan had argued that progressive Republicans could help La Follette's cause by voting the Democratic ticket in 1911. A few voters challenged Bryan to commit himself to La Follette if the Democratic convention in 1912 nominated a conservative candidate. Bryan refused to make such a commitment, though some people claimed his remarks tended in that direction. While Norris was relaxing his political partisanship with every passing year, Bryan was unrelenting in his.[22]

At the end of October, Norris returned to McCook for a brief rest. He spent part of November speaking in Idaho, Oregon, Washington, and Montana. Though he would have preferred to speak about other subjects, he was resigned to spending the month discussing Cannonism. He knew from previous experience it would be futile to discuss anything else. Whenever possible, he tried to deliver speeches on behalf of La Follette.[23]

With little respite since Congress had adjourned, Norris was busy speaking and making himself known to large numbers of people who knew him only through reputation. He had done little campaigning on his own behalf, preferring to criticize the Taft administration and support the progressive program and principles of the Wisconsin senator. As Congress gathered in December, 1911, Norris seemed willing to have his destiny determined by La Follette's success or failure in Nebraska.

In this campaign as in later ones, Norris made no great effort to appeal personally to Omaha voters, though he did not ignore the population center of the state. He preferred to campaign actively in the farm areas and smaller towns, seeking the rural vote and leaving Omaha to the machine politicians. In this way he was able to maintain freedom from compromises and commitments and to pursue his campaign with a minimum of political interference. But as Congress convened, Norris, though not forgetting politics completely, became absorbed with pressing congressional business and left McCarl in McCook to manage the primary campaign.

Chapter 24

Business as Usual

THE SECOND SESSION of the Sixty-second Congress, in an atmosphere of mounting political intensity, convened at noon on Monday, December 4, 1911. George Norris, though involved in a fight for the Nebraska senatorial nomination, nevertheless managed to participate fully in the ordinary business of the session. He fought old fights and initiated new issues. Throughout this long session, he continued to reveal himself as one of the ablest men in the House, a devoted public servant fighting for improved legislation and a chance to further the cause of popular government.

At the outset of the session Norris indirectly lent his name to the cause of prohibition by attending a banquet sponsored by the National Anti-Saloon League. He was the only Nebraska legislator present, among more than fifty representatives and senators. As a teetotaler, he had occasionally given money and legal advice to the cause, but was never active in the league and had tried to avoid prohibition as a political issue.[1]

The fight against the coffee trust, initiated in the previous session, was continued at this time. Correspondence with coffee importers further convinced Norris that it was necessary to introduce a bill providing for the free admission of coffee from all countries whose output was not controlled or manipulated by the valorization scheme. The bill would also call for the free admission of Brazilian coffee to a point a little beyond the limit of domestic consumption. Such a plan, in his judgment, would force Brazil to reject the valorization scheme. On June 17, 1912, the House accepted Norris' views, passed this measure, and sent it to the Senate. Though Norris called Senator Cummins' attention to the bill, no action was taken by the upper chamber.[2]

Soon after the House settled down to business, Norris, as in the previous session, engaged in sharp skirmishes over the rules. The Democrats, now in control, appeared to be as arbitrary and partisan in interpreting them as the Republicans under Speaker Cannon. On January 11, the insurgents, led by Norris, attempted to upset the power of Republican leader James R. Mann to name all Republican candidates for places on House committees. They attempted to set aside the nomination of Philip B. Campbell of Kansas, a regular, to succeed the late E. H. Madison on the Committee on Rules, and to substitute another progressive Kansan, Victor Murdock.

Opposed by both Democratic and Republican leaders, the insurgents were beaten on the floor by a vote of 167 to 107. Of the 107 votes cast in favor of Murdock, 26 were Republican and 81 Democratic. All the votes against the proposed substitution were cast by Republicans. Norris had nominated Murdock, but Oscar W. Underwood, the Democratic leader, exhorted the members of his party to uphold Mann, whom the Republican caucus had authorized to select committee members.[3]

Norris' statements attacked both the caucus method of selecting committees and the right of either party to prevent nominations from the floor. Since the pertinent rule (Rule X) provided that committee members be elected by the House, Norris claimed the right to substitute another name for the one proposed by the minority leader. While not criticizing Mann's appointments, he claimed that caucus approval was not the proper way of selecting committee members.[4] Minority sentiment, he felt, should be registered by nominations from the floor, and a Republican with views similar to Madison's should be chosen to replace him. Though defeated, Norris at least had the opportunity to state his case. Progressive membership on the Committee on Rules was reduced to one, Irvine Lenroot of Wisconsin.[5]

In an introduction to a pamphlet published in 1912, Norris argued that the chief evil of Democratic management in the House was caucus control. By this means the freedom of individual action, partially gained in 1910, had been nullified and the political machine firmly re-established. The caucus, an unofficial instrument by which a majority was controlled by a minority, perpetuated machine rule in the House even though Cannonism, the term that the insurgents had found so convenient as a symbol, was no longer in vogue.

To Norris, the primary difference between progressive Republicans and progressive Democrats was their attitude toward the caucus. Republican progressives, as a fundamental tenet, opposed caucus rule and machine control; they paid allegiance to no political boss and accepted individual rather than caucus responsibility. Democratic progressives were not yet ready to declare their independence of caucus rule, a species of "parliamentary slavery" inconsistent with free representative government. Norris concluded, as he had in March,

1910, that the defeat of Cannon did not overthrow the system of machine rule. He wrote:

> The members of the House of Representatives, coming directly
> from the people, should be absolutely free to follow the dictates
> of conscience in every official action. There should be no caucus
> on matters of legislation. There can be no real freedom as long as
> the people's representatives, with gagged lips and shackled hands,
> continue to worship at the shrine of King Caucus.[6]

On February 3, Norris led a fight against a rules change which he
thought would restore power to the Speaker. Representative Robert
Lee Henry of Texas introduced a motion amending the discharge
rule. It was claimed that the operation of this rule, instead of preventing the "killing" of bills in committees, "had resulted in a congestion
of business on discharge days," the first and third Mondays in each
month. Henry's amendment, which was adopted after long debate by
a vote of 150 to 130, virtually repealed Rule XXVII which the Democrats led by Champ Clark had fought so hard to pass in June, 1910.[7]

Norris considered the motion a step backward, "a surrender of the
rights of the individual member and a wonderful increase of the
Speaker's power." The prevailing rule provided that the motion to
discharge committees would have precedence over a motion to suspend the rules. The Henry amendment reversed the procedure. Since
the Speaker had supreme power of recognition in motions to suspend
the rules, he could if he desired recognize friends who would move
to suspend the rules on the days discharge motions were to be considered. Norris complained that if the proposed motion carried, it
would have the same effect as writing the following sentence in place
of the existing rule: "This rule shall have no effect and be of no
validity except in cases where the Speaker wants it to be." [8]

Two years after Norris' famous rules fight of 1910, he issued no
statements and was interviewed by no reporters. Indeed, his experiences under Democratic control of the House revealed that the fundamental fight to make every member a free individual, uncoerced
and uncontrolled by political machinery, was still being fought. Open
votes, uncontrolled by a caucus or a powerful member, were still impossible to obtain. Recognizing that much remained to be done, he
nevertheless would have admitted that much beneficial legislation had
been accomplished since March, 1910.[9]

Though these two incidents, that of the caucus in January and the
Henry amendment in February, gave Norris his chief opportunity to

challenge the House rules under Democratic control, he criticized them at other times as well. On February 24, while the House was considering a report calling for an investigation of the "Money Trust," he found another chance to challenge caucus control. The Democratic majority acting through a party caucus seemed determined that the Banking and Currency Committee should be instructed by a harmless resolution, granting it no additional power or authority, to conduct an investigation. Norris demanded a strong resolution. He appealed to Democratic members who favored a comprehensive investigation to reject the dictum of their caucus and help strengthen the resolution. Norris used humor and verse to convince members of the need for a thorough study, and eventually was successful. The investigation was completed in 1913 by a subcommittee led by Representative Arsene Pujo of Louisiana.[10]

In July Norris spoke out against a ruling which made it impossible to offer and vote upon amendments to the bill the House was considering. Such a rule destroyed the legislative process. "What is the use of debating a bill," he queried, "if you have decided in advance by a rule that it shall not be amended?" He claimed that the ruling resulted in poorer legislation and deprived members of a legitimate function of their legislative prerogatives. The operation of the House under Speaker Champ Clark still left much to be desired by Norris and his progressive colleagues. But with a presidential campaign getting under way and with Norris seeking a senate seat, no concerted effort was made to challenge Speaker Clark's domination.[11]

Though critical of their rulings, Norris agreed with the Democrats when they considered revising the sugar schedule. While Nebraska was not yet a major sugar-producing area, its farmers, in an effort to diversify production, were raising considerable quantities of sugar beets, especially in western irrigated areas, and a large sugar beet factory was in operation at Grand Island. Since the sugar schedule was one of the most complex in the Payne-Aldrich Tariff, Norris first sought detailed information as to conditions in the industry. He discussed the matter with Republican members who favored lower rates and proposed to introduce several amendments if the Democrats did not present a satisfactory measure.[12]

Though favoring a reduction in the sugar schedule, he still considered himself a firm believer in the protection principle. He believed that a tariff should measure the difference between the cost of an article at home and abroad. "The true protectionists," he affirmed, "are just as anxious that the tariff should not be too high as they are that it should not be too low." If it were too low, it would flood the American market with products of other countries where the standard of living was lower. These products in turn would either lower American standards or drive out of business the American producers of such articles. If, on the other hand, the tariff were placed much above the cost of production, as was the case with most items in the Payne-Aldrich Act, it would enable American producers to combine and raise their prices to exorbitant levels. The tariff in such cases would keep out the foreign product and encourage domestic monopoly as well. Such combinations could not exist if a tariff were prepared in accord with the suggestion that once domestic prices were raised beyond the difference in the cost of production, the foreign article would reduce the price. Thus Norris, a believer in a protective tariff, could argue in favor of lower rates.[13]

He was also a firm believer in a nonpartisan tariff board. However, he considered the board provided in the Payne-Aldrich Tariff a temporary and makeshift affair. He found no fault with the personnel of the board, but rather with the limitations of its powers. Moreover he believed that a nonpartisan tariff board should report to Congress rather than to the president; it should report particularly to the House, which was charged by the Constitution with the initiative in all tariff legislation. Norris also favored House approval of presidential appointees to this board. While he was not sure exactly how these appointments should be made and how long appointees should serve, he was certain that no American tariff had ever been properly considered.[14]

Thus, in March, 1912, when he voted for a free sugar bill, Norris had to explain this departure from his protectionist views. Free sugar virtually would have eliminated the American beet sugar industry which was serving as something of a brake on the practices of the "Sugar Trust." This monopoly controlled the nations' sugar supply, except that made from beets, and at the time was making large purchases of stock in various sugar beet companies. Since the American Sugar Refining Company (the trust) was the sole refiner, it favored free sugar as a means of lowering the cost of its raw material—a reduction that would not be fully passed on to the consumer.[15]

Yet, despite inroads by the trust into the sugar beet industry, Norris believed that sugar beet factories (there were seventy-one in the nation at that time) were preventing a complete monopoly of the sugar trade. Therefore he favored a small duty on beet sugar or a small bounty to the producers to keep them in existence "and to save the American people from the evils that will come from an arbitrary and tyrannical control of the price of sugar by this great monopoly." This protection would save the nation from complete dependence upon foreign sugar in time of crisis. Norris incorporated these views into an amendment providing for a small bounty extending over a ten-year period.[16]

He also protested the Dutch Standard Color Test in the sugar schedule. He called it iniquitous, infamous, indefensible, and wicked. This provision kept out of the American market a cheaper grade of sugar which was of as good quality as refined sugar but lacked only the color. Since the invention of the polariscope, which provided a scientific method of testing sugar, Norris claimed there was no possible excuse for retaining in the law the Dutch Standard Color Test. Its removal would provide another way of lowering the price to the consumer.[17]

After presenting his views on the sugar schedule, he then charged that the free sugar bill was proposed by men who did not expect to see it enacted into law. It was a politicians' maneuver in a great political game. Since all tariff measures had to originate in the House, he intended to vote for free sugar even if his amendment were not accepted. In that event the Senate might properly amend the bill and the conference committee could further relieve the consumer. Thus on March 17, he voted for free sugar. However, no action was taken by the Senate during this session of Congress.[18]

Important as this matter was, Norris nevertheless devoted most of his energies to legislation reorganizing the Post Office Department. Since 1910 he had been given no voice in the naming of postmasters nor was he consulted in the distribution of other patronage plums in Nebraska. With personal experience to guide him, he now engaged in a concerted effort to take the post office out of politics. As an individual who had received campaign funds from postmasters, he knew that these men were expected to make political contributions and that the public saw little or nothing wrong with it. By prohibiting employee contributions, the ordinary voter might be encouraged to participate more directly in politics. Thus, early in January, 1912, Norris introduced a bill which proposed to put almost everybody connected with the Post Office Department, except the postmaster general, under the classified civil service. The measure was sent to the Committee on Reform in the Civil Service where the Democrats had to decide its fate.[19]

Soon after introducing the bill, he explained, "The machine politicians in both parties are opposed to it bitterly, and some men who

claim to be for it in the open will be secretly trying to knife it."
Though confident that this type of legislation was bound to come, he
was under no illusion that it would be enacted at this time. Public
sentiment had yet to be fully aroused. When Norris claimed many
congressmen secretly favored such a law, he knew that few would
support it until their constituents demanded it. Furthermore, because
the Democrats had high hopes of winning the presidency, many
would oppose the measure in that they wanted to reward loyal party
workers.[20]

After considerable discussion and investigation, Norris decided to
introduce another bill to avoid the constitutional objections which
might be raised against his original one. If the Post Office Department
were to be removed entirely from the influence of partisan politics,
the postmaster general should also be selected without regard to partisanship. Norris contemplated providing a ten-year term for the postmaster general.[21]

To arouse public sentiment, Norris prepared several articles, the
most important of which appeared in the March, 1912, issue of the
Editorial Review under the title, "Why Not Take the Post Office
Department Out of Politics?" While he did not mention the bill, he included many of its points in the article, wherein he argued that the
Post Office Department ought to be a great business corporation instead of a great political machine. After the article appeared he wrote
to Roosevelt suggesting that the former president write a signed
editorial for the *Outlook* upon the question of the Post Office Department in politics. Roosevelt readily agreed and promised to use as his
text the bill Norris had introduced. Thus while Taft was using the
department to build political strength for his renomination, Norris
and Roosevelt were trying to arouse sentiment to place it under civil
service.[22]

Believing in progress, Norris was optimistic that eventually effective reform could be achieved. But idealist and optimist that he was,
he had been too long in politics not to be a realist as well. He explained the inevitable march of progress as follows:

> The world is progressing and the combined efforts of special
> interests, political bosses, and political machines cannot stop the
> march of progress. It will take the crystallization of a public senti-
> ment to bring this about, but public sentiment is stronger, as his-
> tory shows, than the political bosses and political machines, and
> eventually they must give way. They usually give way one step
> at a time. They have done this in the Post Office Department.

The last step however, will be taken just as soon as there is such a demand from the people that the political boss is unable to resist it longer, then he will get onto the band wagon and try to claim some of the credit. . . . The people are more powerful than the politician. He controls for a while, but if the people make the right kind of an effort they can always win. They will win this fight. It is only a question of whether it will come soon or whether it will come a year from now. That will depend more upon the people themselves than upon anything else.[23]

Though the House actually considered Norris' bill, he knew it would not be enacted by the Sixty-second Congress. But he also knew that much profitable discussion had been engendered and that some favorable sentiment had been aroused. In July he spoke extensively in favor of making the postmaster general a nonpolitical appointee. Capitalizing on the extraconstitutional aspect of the cabinet, he noted that there was no law requiring a cabinet member to be a political adviser. He called for a ten-year term for the postmaster general, divorced from partisan political considerations, who could devote his attention and ability to the business management of the department.[24]

Indirectly related to Norris' bill was the measure providing for a parcel post system which reorganized the delivery of packages on the basis of size, weight, and distance under the auspices of the Post Office Department. Legislation calling for a parcel post system had been enacted by the first session of the Sixty-second Congress in 1911, but before service could begin, appropriations and decisions regarding rates and zones had to be made. In consultation with David J. Lewis, a Maryland Democrat and an expert on the subject, Norris concluded that it would be proper for the government to condemn the property of express companies and take over their business, rather than merely compete with them. Whatever profits honestly existed in the express business, he claimed, ought to go to the railroad and its stockholders. Whatever extravagance existed in express rates ought to go to the shippers in the form of reasonable rates. In any event, proper reduction of rates, whether the merchandise were carried by express companies or by the post office, would redound to the public's benefit. However, when the time came to vote on the proposition to have government take over the express companies, all the Democrats, including Lewis, who had previously favored such a measure, voted against it. Norris explained their defection on the ground that Democratic leaders had quietly given them to understand that it would be to the best interests of their party to postpone action until after the election.[25]

While matters relating to postal affairs were his chief legislative concern, Norris did not ignore other issues. He was not greatly concerned, for example, with the issue of immigration, but admitted that he favored restrictive legislation. Because of his agrarian bias, he was concerned that the majority of recent immigrants were settling in cities and avoiding rural areas. He singled out the Italians, who generally made their way to urban areas despite efforts to scatter them. For the same reason, he felt that a great many immigrants from southern Europe were not desirable and that educational restrictions did not provide a proper method for excluding them. On the other hand, "Germans, English and Norwegians" made excellent citizens because many of them were willing to till the soil. Thus Norris viewed immigration as he viewed many items of legislation—as a factor tending to further the imbalance between urban and rural America.[26]

In this session Norris was responsible for one item which was regional in nature, but which helped immensely in his senatorial campaign. He introduced a bill limiting the right of way of the Union Pacific Railroad to one hundred feet on each side of its tracks, two hundred feet wide in all, except in such places where the railroad had actually used the entire four hundred feet it claimed under a recent interpretation of its charter. The railroad, contending for the four-hundred-foot right of way, had threatened proceedings against landowners whose property fell within this limit on the grounds that the owners had either usurped or not properly purchased railroad land. Thousands of farmers and businessmen in Nebraska, Colorado, and other western states were threatened with loss of part of their property if the railroad's interpretation prevailed. In cities such as Grand Island the railroad would be entitled to take in the street running parallel to its tracks. In some instances, streets on each side of the railroad could be included in the four-hundred-foot right of way.[27]

Norris' bill was sent to the Judiciary Committee, and hearings began early in April. N. H. Loomis of Omaha, chief attorney of the Union Pacific Railroad, testified against the bill, while representatives of citizens in Greeley, Colorado, spoke in favor of it. Loomis had sought a compromise with Norris but, failing in this attempt, concentrated his efforts on Brown and Hitchcock, Nebraska's senators, neither of whom testified in favor of Norris' bill.

Early in June the measure passed the House and was soon pending before the Senate Committee on the Judiciary. Norris consulted with

members of the subcommittee assigned to examine the bill and testified at a hearing. During most of this period, Loomis remained in
Washington, trying to prevent favorable reports on the measure first
by the House and then by the Senate Judiciary committees. Norris
and Loomis both knew that opposition would fade if the bill reached a
stage where a record vote could be obtained. But the Union Pacific,
Norris claimed, was pulling every string to prevent such a vote from
being taken. Norris sought as much publicity as possible, claiming
that the support of Nebraska's newspapers would assure passage of
the measure.[28]

Late in June the bill was passed by the Senate and signed into law
by the president. To contest the measure, the Union Pacific would
now have to go to court and prove the bill a violation of its charter
rights. Towns along the railroad's route applauded Norris' role in
championing this legislation, while railroad officials bitterly condemned it. Soon the bill became a controversial issue in Norris' campaign for a Senate seat.[29]

While the right-of-way measure affected only a limited number
of voters in Nebraska and other western states, it sought to provide, as
did all the bills he introduced, a "square and honest deal" in
political and governmental affairs. Affecting a broader popular base
and capitalizing on the interest aroused in an exciting election year,
Norris introduced two measures calling for a presidential primary.
Neither of them was enacted, but they did serve to arouse further
interest in this more direct way of choosing candidates.[30]

Though many citizens were outraged by the trampling under foot
of the rank and file desires by the "well regulated and well oiled"
machine at the Republican convention in Chicago in mid-June, the
Democrats, anxious to capitalize on these proceedings, did not allow
the primary bills to get before the House. Norris, equally anxious,
sought support of his bills among the leading progressive contenders
for the presidency. Roosevelt, victim of the Republican machine at
Chicago, announced he was heartily in favor of such legislation and
promised to do all in his power to help the movement. Woodrow Wilson, who previously had expressed an interest in such legislation, did
not respond. Norris claimed that a word from Wilson to the Democratic leaders in the House would have done much to insure the passage of some legislation on this subject.[31]

While the legislative achievements of this session of Congress were
sparse because of party deadlock (each chamber was controlled by a
different party) and the unfolding presidential campaign, important

issues concerning large segments of the population were discussed. A few such measures were enacted during the last year of the Taft administration; others, under a Democratic Congress during the first Wilson administration. Agricultural legislation, of great concern to Norris, came in this latter category, but was easier to achieve because the path had been cleared for it during the Sixty-second Congress. On March 29, 1912, Norris introduced a joint resolution to provide for the appointment of a Farmers' National Cooperative Credit Commission, and two months later, on May 29, he appeared at a hearing before the House Committee on Agriculture. In the interim, two similar resolutions had been introduced, one by Representative A. F. Lever of South Carolina, the other by Norris' friend and former colleague, Senator Gronna.

Norris said before the committee that as an agrarian he believed that land was the best security available and the foundation of all prosperity. He sought ways of making life on the farm and in the country more attractive while preventing the further decline of rural population. He desired information about ways and means of extending credit to farmers, enabling them to use their land as security.

The need for easier credit was evident to all who examined agricultural conditions. Farmers could not borrow from national banks using land as security. At other banks they usually could not borrow at as low a rate as the merchant because their security was not liquid. Thus the farmer was compelled to sell his crop almost immediately after harvesting it, when the market price was at its lowest. In many instances the crops were bought by speculators who held them until the price went up. Norris and others hoped to provide the farmer with ample credit facilities so that he would not be forced to sell his crop at such an inopportune moment. The report of the Country Life Commission in 1908 and the resolutions of 1912 emphasized the need for farm credit and the growing sentiment in its favor.

Though critical of many investigatory commissions, Norris noted that Congress had sent a group of bankers to Europe to investigate the monetary situation, and called for a similar investigation dealing with agricultural matters. Such a study would secure much important information about existing credit institutions, enabling legislators to write satisfactory bills applying the knowledge of European credit systems to the American scene.[32]

Some of the members of the Committee on Agriculture were convinced that farm credit was a state issue and that Congress should not provide for such a commission. Norris countered by saying that since the matter was of interest to all the states, the federal government ought to bear the expense of getting the basic general information. Furthermore, he concluded:

> We have spent thousands of dollars for the investigations of the Monetary Commission, why not spend a few dollars to make an investigation for the benefit of the farmer, who is the real source of all prosperity? Make him prosperous and happy and the whole country will prosper and the whole world will be happy. I ask for the farmer nothing but what has been granted to the banker—nothing unfair, nothing in the world but a square deal.[33]

Congress took no action during this session, but shortly thereafter sent not one but two special commissions to Europe to investigate rural credit conditions. The result was the enactment of the Federal Farm Loan Act in 1916.

Busy as he was with both legislative and political developments during this long and wearing second session of Congress, Norris delivered eulogies in memory of two recently deceased colleagues, both of whom had been staunch allies in the fight against Cannonism. James P. Latta, a Democrat, had been a member of the Nebraska congressional delegation, while Edmond Madison had been "the nearest and the dearest" friend Norris had in Congress. His eloquent tribute to Madison's memory was his most painful undertaking since his arrival in Washington. As Norris said of Madison, so one could say of Norris as he concluded his service in the House:

> His country was his idol, his conscience was his master, and humanity was his God. He never hesitated to defend what he believed to be right, and he always denounced evil wherever he found it.[34]

Several days after Norris delivered this eulogy, the Nebraska primary election was held. The primary and the complex and difficult campaign which was to follow hovered over him and influenced many of his congressional decisions during the long period from December, 1911, to the end of the following August.

Chapter 25

La Follette vs. Roosevelt

NORRIS remained in Washington while McCarl, finding it impossible to live in Washington on the $1,500 salary provided for congressmen's secretaries, stayed in McCook to organize and conduct the primary campaign. This arrangement cost Norris several hundred dollars each year for extra clerical help during especially busy periods.[1] At first it was complicated and cumbersome, but eventually it worked fairly well. In 1912 it proved a boon to Norris because it kept him out of the state and out of the bitter factional strife which ruined the chances of many hopeful candidates.

McCarl was well suited for his position. As a member of the executive committee of the Progressive League of Nebraska, he had a voice in policy determination. He knew the Nebraska political scene well and had directed two of Norris' previous campaigns. Able, hard-working, and pleasant, McCarl was liked and trusted by most political leaders. Norris had complete faith in McCarl's honesty, thoroughness, and efficiency.

This primary campaign, it was quickly decided, would be conducted apart from other campaigns. Norris refused, as always, to buy the support of any newspaper. He kept out of all statewide primary contests, claiming he would endorse the Republican nominees. He was committed, however, to the candidacy of La Follette, and intended to further his cause in Nebraska.[2]

At the end of 1911, the progressive Republicans in Nebraska were beginning to expand their activities. They supported La Follette and quickly endorsed Norris. While there was very little Taft sentiment in the state, La Follette leaders were worried lest the politicians supporting the administration promote a boom for Roosevelt to split the progressive forces. If this occurred, Taft might capture the Nebraska delegation. The situation was complicated by the fact that while the voters would express their presidential preference in the April primary, the law specifically did not commit the convention delegates to vote for the winning presidential candidate. La Follette leaders were anxious to get their campaign underway and hoped that Norris could persuade the Wisconsin senator to visit Nebraska early in 1912.[3]

During this period Norris was sure that Roosevelt was not a candidate and that he was in sympathy with the La Follette movement. Norris was afraid, however, that some Taft people, realizing that the president's cause was hopeless in Nebraska, might organize under a Roosevelt banner "simply for the purpose of getting into the convention," where they would then support Taft. Thus Norris suggested that in every congressional district La Follette supporters seek to wrest control of the party organization from the standpatters.[4]

Unfortunately for La Follette supporters, the complications Norris and others feared actually occurred. On the morning of December 22, 1911, a petition was filed in the office of the secretary of state placing Roosevelt's name on the ticket, thereby causing a further split in Republican forces. The petition was filed by John O. Yeiser of Omaha, a member of the Advisory State Board of Pardons and an associate of Victor Rosewater, standpat National Committeeman from Nebraska. Under Nebraska law, no one could decline such a nomination, although the petition could be withdrawn. Roosevelt could have avoided the issue by requesting that his name not be placed on the petition.[5]

Norris still believing that the former president was not a candidate, wrote him explaining the situation. He asked Roosevelt either to avow his candidacy or to demand that his name not be printed on the official primary ballot. He concluded that if conditions arose making it necessary and expedient for the convention to nominate Roosevelt, "and if in such an emergency you could be prevailed upon to permit the use of your name as a candidate, all La Follette delegates would be then, as they are now, your enthusiastic supporters." [6]

On January 2, 1912, Roosevelt answered, saying, "No man has been authorized by me to put my name on any ballot, or to get up any petition in my interest, or to take any action on my behalf." Previously he had written to Yeiser that he did not wish to be a candidate and would not speak on his own behalf. However, Roosevelt made it clear that while he was not a candidate, he had said nothing about what he would do if tendered the nomination. He also refused to request the withdrawal of his name from the primary ballot on the grounds that such a withdrawal would probably hurt La Follette's candidacy far more than it would Taft's. Thus Roosevelt would neither authorize the use of his name nor request its withdrawal.[7]

Answering Roosevelt's letter, Norris noted, "If nothing is done to meet the predicament with which we are confronted in Nebraska, the result, I fear, will be that the state and others similarly situated, will be carried by the Taft delegates, on account of the division in our ranks." To prevent this, he thought Roosevelt should either ask his friends to support La Follette delegates or request that his name not go on the ballot. If the nomination were then offered to Roosevelt because La Follette could not obtain it, all La Follette delegates would enthusiastically support the former president. In this way, Norris explained, progressive Republicans could campaign with united ranks and insure progressive delegations from states where primary laws were operative.[8]

Despite these developments, progressive Republican leaders were still optimistic. F. P. Corrick, secretary of the La Follette League (formerly the Progressive League), made an arrangement whereby both factions united on a common slate of delegates and agreed to endorse R. B. Howell over Rosewater for national committeeman. Thus anti-Taft men could support a set of progressive delegates who, if elected in the primary, would vote at the convention for the presidential candidate receiving a plurality of the Nebraska primary votes. This arrangement, while not satisfactory to the La Follette leaders who did most of the arduous organizational work, at least prevented chaos from dominating the progressive camp. It also assured Republican voters who were progressive in their sentiments that Taft men would not represent Nebraska at the national convention.[9]

Since Roosevelt did not issue a statement taking himself out of the Nebraska primary, Norris concluded that he wanted the nomination. Men who had spoken with the former president said he was "very emphatic and pronounced" against the renomination of Taft and did not want to eliminate himself for fear that he might be the only man who could beat Taft. Norris did not think it "square" for Roosevelt to allow the use of his name in Nebraska, and he hoped no quarreling would develop between Roosevelt and La Follette followers. He intended to continue supporting La Follette, and hoped to avoid controversy by stressing opposition to Taft rather than differences between the progressive factions.[10]

Meanwhile, Norris' application as a candidate for the Senate reached the secretary of state on January 19. At the time McCarl was spending three days in Lincoln "with good results." Visitors were on hand for a meeting of Taft men and a gathering of farmers. The Taft men chose a full set of convention delegates, presidential electors, and a candidate, Rosewater, for national committeeman. According to McCarl, most farmers favorably recalled Norris' position on reciprocity and Cannonism. Local politicians reported Norris sentiment. Everywhere Norris and Governor Aldrich were recognized as the progressive leaders.

McCarl also reported overwhelming Roosevelt sentiment; "It's my judgment that if he is a candidate he will secure the delegation from Nebraska, hands down." A La Follette manager reported Roosevelt sentiment in the towns, but the farmers were for La Follette. If Roosevelt were not a candidate, almost everyone agreed, La Follette would have most of his votes. The uncertainty as to the former president's intentions was making it difficult to organize a following for La Follette.[11]

Aldrich's position, too, was uncertain. Ostensibly he was for La Follette, but, according to rumors, he had been "coquetting with the Taft fellows" to win their endorsement and thereby avoid a primary fight. Norris was concerned that the governor did nothing to silence Yeiser in his attempts to get a Roosevelt slate of delegates on the ticket instead of an accepted slate of progressive Republican delegates.[12]

Norris did very little on his own behalf during the primary campaign. Most of his correspondence concerned the over-all political situation and his support of La Follette. However, he assured friends that he was in the senatorial primary in good faith and wanted to be nominated and elected. Though rumor had it otherwise, Norris insisted he had not agreed with Senator Brown to remain in Washington throughout the primary campaign. The senator, like Norris, preferred to tend to his congressional duties. Brown relied on the Republican organization to push his candidacy. His bitter feud with Rosewater, however, indicated that harmony among the regular Republicans did not prevail when offices other than the presidency were at stake.[13]

At the end of January, in an effort to thwart the Roosevelt movement in Nebraska and restore harmony among progressive Republicans, Norris wrote a long letter to Yeiser calling on him to support La Follette. He insisted that he would be for Roosevelt only if and when La Follette were unable to obtain the nomination at the Chicago convention. If the delegates pledged themselves in this way, followers of both men could work in harmony for the progressive cause. Norris, in effect, told Yeiser that the proper thing for Roosevelt men to do was to support La Follette, lest they insure a Taft delegation to the Republican convention.[14]

Yeiser's reply indicated that harmony would not be easily restored. He informed Norris that he ought to get aboard the Roosevelt bandwagon, lest the Roosevelt followers find it necessary to choose a senatorial candidate committed to their man. Norris was led to believe that Yeiser was motivated by the desire to attend the Chicago convention as a delegate at large and was using Roosevelt's candidacy as a way of doing so.[15]

The letters of Norris and Yeiser were published and stimulated much discussion throughout the state. Norris supporters began to feel that while fidelity and constancy to La Follette were noble qualities, caution and recognition of rising Roosevelt sentiment also had their value. In spite of Yeiser rather than because of him, Nebraska sentiment was crystallizing around Roosevelt, who was predicted to win the preference vote. La Follette did not appeal to large numbers of rank and file voters because it was believed that his progressivism was too radical. While most Americans favored reform and progress, few wanted it in "trainload lots." Therefore they found Roosevelt a more acceptable candidate, more respectable and moderate than La Follette. Such views were prevalent among a growing number of Nebraska Republicans, but Norris learned that in his congressional district voters were more in accord with his views. A Republican conference in Hastings on January 27 strongly endorsed both La Follette and Norris.[16]

Despite growing Roosevelt support, Norris had no intention of leaving La Follette and he so informed Yeiser early in February. He reiterated the view that the fight for La Follette was in no sense a fight against Roosevelt. Although Norris knew that Yeiser could make good his threat to enter another candidate in the senatorial primary against him, he refused to allow such tactics to affect his actions; "I can afford to be defeated, but I can not afford to be driven by a threat." [17]

Thus stood the situation between the two progressive Republican factions early in February when Louis Brandeis gave the La Follette League a boost by stumping the state. Launching his tour in Fremont, Brandeis spoke once or twice a day in favor of La Follette's candidacy. He also praised Norris for his work in Congress. A La Follette supporter reported that he made a "great impression." His speeches received wide press coverage. Shortly thereafter, Republican meetings at York and Fremont, where the Boston lawyer had spoken, adopted resolutions endorsing Norris for the Senate.[18]

Meanwhile, in Washington, Norris was calling for harmony between the Roosevelt and La Follette factions. R. B. Howell of Omaha, a candidate for national committeeman in the primary election, called on Norris after conferring with Roosevelt and likewise spoke for harmony among Nebraska progressives. Norris, thinking it useless to write any more letters to Yeiser, now wrote to Governor Aldrich requesting him to provide leadership and prevent any split in the progessive ranks. On February 7, after a conference between Yeiser and Frank Harrison, a representative of the La Follette League, it was announced that there would be one primary ticket for La Follette and Roosevelt forces. While Norris was not directly instrumental in establishing party harmony, his numerous letters paved the way for it.[19]

Though Yeiser now was eliminated as a candidate for delegate-at-large, the Roosevelt forces won much by this announcement. At the time it was made Republicans in five of the state's six congressional districts had already named La Follette men as their delegates. The La Follette League, which had done the basic political spadework, agreed to give Roosevelt the chance of capitalizing on their efforts. The reported collapse of La Follette at the annual banquet of the Periodical Publishers' Association at Philadelphia on February 2 and the subsequent loss of many of his prominent supporters undoubtedly prompted the conference between Yeiser and Harrison. Uneasy Nebraska supporters of the Wisconsin senator welcomed its result since it gave them a chance to support Roosevelt without appearing disloyal to La Follette and the progressive cause. An uneasy harmony was restored to the ranks of Nebraska progressive Republicans, though Roosevelt officially was still not a candidate.[20]

Norris reported that La Follette's breakdown had resulted in the cancellation of his meetings. He also reported that many La Follette men had now decided to come out openly for Roosevelt. Representative Lenroot had told Norris that La Follette's collapse would probably make it necessary for the senator to withdraw from the contest. While Norris understood that La Follette was in "a serious physical condition," he did not endorse Roosevelt. In his correspondence he still supported the Wisconsin senator, though he often repeated that he was not opposed to Roosevelt, who, according to Norris, was anxious for him to win the senatorial nomination.[21]

On February 12, progressive Republicans met in Lincoln to perfect their primary ticket. Norris received "a very cordial endorsement for Senator." Nevertheless, this was a tense and exciting meeting because Governor Aldrich, representing the Roosevelt forces, took a strong position against endorsing La Follette, while C. O. Whedon, a vice president of the La Follette League, was equally insistent upon an outright endorsement. After a strenuous session a set of resolutions satisfactory to both camps and a slate of progressive delegates were presented and unanimously accepted.

This meeting was significant because it put an end to controversy among progressives on all levels but that of presidential preference.

Both Roosevelt and La Follette would appear on the ballot, but the rest of the ticket would include only one name for each office. The sixteen delegates sent to the Chicago convention would vote for the candidate who won the preference vote. Controversy and animosity, however, continued over the matter of plurality versus majority. It had yet to be decided whether a clear plurality would have to be achieved by one of the three presidential candidates or whether the combined Roosevelt-La Follette vote would be sufficient to send the common slate of progressive delegates (fourteen of whom were devoted La Follette men) to the nominating convention.[22]

In McCook, McCarl reported the situation to be "up in the air," as it was in other areas as well. Everybody seemed to be awaiting Roosevelt's speech in Columbus, Ohio, where it was believed he would accept the invitation of eight Republican governors, Aldrich among them, and announce his candidacy. McCarl thought that if Roosevelt accepted, he would probably defeat both La Follette and Taft in Nebraska. La Follette alone could defeat Taft in Nebraska, but Roosevelt alone could score a much more impressive primary victory—one which would aid other progressive candidates as well—because he could command not only La Follette supporters but many Taft men as well. Norris' candidacy would benefit more with Roosevelt on the ticket as the lone progressive Republican presidential aspirant.[23]

Norris, however, was certain that both Roosevelt and La Follette would run in the Nebraska primary, and that further efforts to get either candidate to withdraw were worthless. There was no statute specifically requiring elected delegates to support the victorious primary candidate, but popular opinion on this matter was so strong that all delegate candidates quickly pledged themselves to abide by the popular vote. Thus, if one of the progressive candidates did not get more primary votes than Taft the president would receive the Nebraska votes at the convention.[24]

Since Norris' name was endorsed by both progressive factions, his candidacy would not unduly suffer because of factional discord. If both Roosevelt and La Follette remained on the ticket, however, McCarl assured Norris, "Things will be in a bad shape." There was growing sentiment because no arrangement could be made whereby one candidate would withdraw, that both must be selfish and consider themselves more important than the progressive movement. If no withdrawal arrangement were forthcoming, observers felt that Nebraska progressive leaders should endorse one of the candidates, probably Roosevelt since he was more popular, in a final effort to stave off a Taft victory.[25]

Bowing to the mounting pressure of public opinion and the example of prominent progressives, Norris began to shift his position on La Follette shortly before the former president officially announced his candidacy on February 21. Norris still favored La Follette, but recognized the practical necessity of backing Roosevelt to narrow the issue to a fight between "the Taft men and the progressive men." If La Follette would do likewise, Norris believed he would prove himself "the greatest man in the country," and "invincible four years from now." [26]

Meanwhile the La Follette League in Nebraska, rent asunder by the same forces that impelled Norris to endorse Roosevelt, was deluged with letters urging it to boost Roosevelt. R. B. Howell, who never had shown any open preference for Roosevelt over La Follette, announced his shift and thought the league ought to do likewise. By the end of February, Nebraska progressives were stampeding to Roosevelt, and J. J. McCarthy, the president of the La Follette League, thought it impossible to check them. F. P. Corrick, the secretary of the organization, shifted to Roosevelt believing that the former president's candidacy would insure a progressive victory in Nebraska. But Frank A. Harrison, a diehard La Follette leader, remained loyal to the Wisconsin senator though he was not optimistic.[27]

By the end of February the first phase of the Nebraska primary had come to an end. Though there were two progressive Republican presidential candidates, it was evident that Roosevelt was the more popular. The thorny problem of progressive delegates and the way they would vote at Chicago had been solved. As a senatorial candidate, Norris was scheduled to appear on both the La Follette and Roosevelt ballots, with hopes of getting votes from Taft men as well. Though animosity and bitterness remained, the issue had become more clearly defined. Much of the confusion was dispelled when Roosevelt announced, in Columbus, Ohio, "My hat is in the ring."

Now with less than two months before the April 19 primary, Norris, who was busy in Washington with legislative chores, had to perfect an organization and get his record before the voters. At the same time he had to avoid further involvement in the Roosevelt-La Follette controversy, lest diehard supporters of either candidate discharge their anger against him by voting for his opponent.

Chapter 26

Primary Victory

WITH the perplexing questions of Republican presidential candidates and convention delegates clarified by the end of February, Norris could now pay more attention to the senatorial primary campaign. Remaining in Washington, he watched unfolding events with great interest because of the embittered feelings aroused by the La Follette-Roosevelt controversy.

McCarl reported conditions in Nebraska to be considerably improved. He had returned to McCook early in March from a trip throughout northern Nebraska, where he found men in all walks of life favoring Norris' candidacy. Particularly encouraging was the support businessmen were giving Norris. McCarl had contacted men in the southern and western counties, but had done very little as yet in the populous northeastern part of the state.[1]

Norris' chances were also improved by the support of Joseph Polcar, editor of the Omaha *Daily News*. Norris suggested that Polcar alert readers to possible confusion that might arise between the names Norris Brown and George Norris, differentiating between the two men. He wanted Polcar to stress the fact that while Brown stood for machine control, Norris believed in "absolute independence." Norris thought that such stress would create a better impression of the work he was doing in Congress and the odds against which he fought. But unless Brown indulged in a personal attack, Norris had no desire to make an all-out fight against his opponent.[2]

By early March, F. P. Corrick of the La Follette League had decided that the movement was more important than the man. He tried to maintain a neutral posture and to devote his energies to obtaining funds from all interested groups. His enemies, however, thought he was convinced that Roosevelt would be nominated and therefore did not want to fight lest he lose his chance for patronage.[3]

Norris agreed with Corrick. In North Dakota, where the first primary of the presidential campaign was scheduled for March 19, supporters of Roosevelt and La Follette were rumored to be very bitter toward one another. In Washington, leaders on both sides deprecated this feeling but seemed unwilling to compromise to any degree. To avoid a similar occurrence in Nebraska, Norris argued that progressive leaders ought "to take the bull by its horns" and do what was best for the cause, regardless of the wishes of either faction. Since both factions were supposedly striving for the same thing, he thought it foolish that their ranks should be split by a conflict over personalities. Frank A. Harrison disagreed with Norris' position, claiming that there were "a whole lot of La Follette men who would not vote for the Colonel under any circumstances." La Follette's name, he argued, should remain on the ticket until the outcome of the North Dakota primary presented a means of further evaluating his strength.[4]

Further confusion occurred on March 12, when Corrick received a telegram from La Follette announcing that he could not consent to any combination on the delegate slate or to the printing of the name of any other candidate upon petitions or ballots in connection with his own. Corrick burned this telegram, intending to go through with "the compromise ticket business." He explained the Nebraska situation to the Wisconsin senator, noting the steps already taken toward the goal of electing a delegation that would assist in writing a progressive platform at the Republican National Convention, and concluding with a statement that he thought it unwise for any presidential candidate to interfere or attempt to defeat that purpose. Norris agreed that no candidate had the right to dictate what course progressives should take in any given locality.[5]

While he admired La Follette, Norris was grieved at the course he was pursuing. Norris believed that the principal object was to prevent the renomination of Taft by placing a progressive Republican at the head of the ticket, and he had no further intention of supporting a person who was no longer the most available or the most popular candidate. Convinced that he was battling for a principle, Norris wanted to do everything possible to insure its triumph without destroying a candidate's chances by factional strife.[6]

Meanwhile, Norris' campaign was proceeding satisfactorily. There was strong Norris sentiment throughout the state, though McCarl was worried that the newspapers were not paying him sufficient attention. The difficulty, of course, was that extensive interest in the presidential controversy overshadowed the senatorial race. McCarl suggested that Norris improve his newspaper coverage by returning to Nebraska for five or six days before the primary election on April 19. By campaigning in Nebraska, he would compel the newspapers to present his record. By appearing in Omaha, preferably with Roosevelt, Norris could solve the difficult and as yet untackled problem of appealing to voters in the most populous community in the state. His candidacy thus would be well publicized shortly before the voters made their decision in the primary election.[7]

Despite McCarl's pleading, Norris thought it unwise to return to Nebraska, where he would be in the middle of the La Follette-Roosevelt controversy, and thought he could better serve his cause by remaining in Washington. At this time North Dakota voters went to the polls in the first primary election of the campaign. Out of 49,264 votes cast in the Republican primary, La Follette received 28,620, Roosevelt 19,101, and Taft, 1,543. The results created a sensation in Nebraska. Harrison was beseiged by well-wishers assuring him that if La Follette spoke in Nebraska the Roosevelt boom would be "busted." Many observers now believed that La Follette had a good chance of winning the Nebraska primary election.[8]

By the end of March the bitterness that Norris feared became evident in the Nebraska campaign. W. L. Houser, La Follette's campaign manager, delivered a vitriolic speech against Roosevelt. Houser attacked Governor Aldrich in an attempt to force him to request Roosevelt's withdrawal in Nebraska. Norris feared that the La Follette men, who seemed desperate and more anxious to fight Roosevelt than Taft, might attack him. To Norris, some of La Follette's supporters now seemed "insanely mad" and determined to undermine the progressive cause.[9]

In the Wisconsin primary on April 2, the La Follette ticket carried the state by almost three to one over Taft. With no Roosevelt slate in the field, the former president received only 628 votes. Fresh from this victory, La Follette made plans for a vigorous campaign in Nebraska, starting with an evening rally in Lincoln on April 5. McCarl wanted Norris to announce that he would return to Nebraska to help elect progressive Republican delegates. But Norris, convinced that his views on this matter were correct, and convinced that his nomination was fairly sure, did not respond to this suggestion, but remained in Washington continuing his campaign through correspondence.[10]

Norris believed his nomination to be assured because he thought the great majority of Republicans to be either for Roosevelt or La Follette. He was convinced that the support for Taft and Brown came from the "old wheel-horses of the party," prominent men in many communities. A stranger observing the political situation in many Nebraska towns might readily conclude that everybody was for the administration ticket, but closer observation, Norris believed, would reveal deep and bitter resentment toward the Taft administration. In his own case, Norris surmised that while the voters did not actively dislike his opponent, they wholeheartedly approved Norris' own aggressive stand on important issues. The fact that some postmasters— appointed by the regular Republican organization—offered to contribute to his campaign convinced Norris he could capture the votes of Taft supporters as well. Because he was against reciprocity while Brown favored it, Norris was virtually assured of the farm vote.[11]

La Follette conducted an arduous four-day campaign in the state beginning on April 5. To the relief of Norris and other worried observers, he did not stoop to personalities but discussed issues. Indeed, he endorsed Norris in all of his speeches except that in Omaha, where he erroneously supported Brown until he was told of his mistake. La Follette canvassed the state with six other speakers, including his daughter, Fola. No one launched a personal attack on Roosevelt.[12]

As reports of La Follette's tour reached Norris, his anxiety about bitter factionalism in the progressive camp eased considerably. La Follette was well received in Nebraska. Traveling by automobile over dusty country roads, he spoke in the open air and had to contend with wind and dust. But he spoke well and, though somewhat hoarse, made a good impression. In Sutton, in the Fifth Congressional District, he gave Norris a strong recommendation, whereupon the audience cheered and threw hats in the air. If similar sentiment existed throughout the state, a friend assured him, "you would go in a whooping." [13]

As the primary campaign moved toward its climax, McCarl stepped up his activities by taking frequent trips. While most of the reports he received claimed that Norris' prospects were good even in Omaha, he did not know whether to believe them completely. He explained his dilemma:

> Well, I have been having a hell of a time. Possibly you have an idea it isn't a job to try to perfect a sort of a working organization in about seventy-five counties in which you don't know a total of fifty people. Well, that's been my job and I have been working at it for many long, weary days, but I believe I am getting things in rather good shape, hope so anyway.[14]

Norris had begun to worry about the effects upon his candidacy of the Roosevelt-La Follette controversy. La Follette had repeatedly endorsed him, but Norris knew he would lose a great deal if Roosevelt ignored him when he spoke in the state. If, on the other hand, Roosevelt also endorsed Norris, his senatorial nomination would be assured. With Roosevelt scheduled to speak on April 17 and 18, just before the primary, tension mounted. The day before the former president was to appear, Norris received an urgent telegram from Aldrich requesting him to issue a statement calling upon La Follette men to support Roosevelt in order to prevent a division of the progressive forces and a Taft victory. Norris wired back, "Such advice should be given by state Progressive League not by me." [15]

Governor Aldrich was concerned about a story in the Sunday *State Journal* of April 14, reporting that Norris had advised Nebraska Republicans to vote for La Follette "first, last and all the time." Norris issued a flat denial and so informed R. B. Howell, who was traveling with Roosevelt. Whether Roosevelt learned of this denial is not known, but the former president did not endorse Norris when he spoke in Nebraska.[16]

Norris did not expect Roosevelt to speak in his behalf. He did not think it right to ask him to take any part in local elections. If Roosevelt chose to endorse him, he would be more than pleased, but under no circumstances would he request such support. Norris would not publicly endorse either of the progressive presidential candidates for fear of losing some of his own supporters. He believed that a vote for La Follette in Nebraska might be construed as half a vote for Taft, but thought that most progressives would vote for Roosevelt.[17]

Friday, April 19, saw 133,603 voters go to the polls in Nebraska to cast their primary ballots. The total number of males of voting age in 1912 was 364,132. The percentage of those voting at this primary was 36.69 which compared with 28.38 per cent at the first primary in 1907. Though the returns came in slowly, it was soon evident that Roosevelt would win by an overwhelming majority. He received 46,795 votes to 16,786 for La Follette and 13,341 for Taft. Thus all sixteen of the state's Republican delegates would support his candidacy at the Chicago convention. Norris' majority was not as impressive as the former president's. He defeated Brown by more than five thousand votes, 38,893 to 33,156, while Aldrich and Howell, progressive Republicans, defeated their more conservative opponents for governor and national committeeman by more substantial majorities. In the Democratic primary Champ Clark won the Nebraska delegation, while Norris' first congressional opponent, former Governor Shallenberger, was designated to be his opponent in the senatorial campaign.[18]

Messages of congratulation poured in upon McCarl in McCook and Norris in Washington. Norris was delighted to learn that he had acquired a substantial lead long before returns from distant western counties, which he was almost certain to carry, began to arrive at party headquarters in Lincoln. He carried Douglas County, in which Omaha is located, by a small majority, though it had been predicted that Brown would carry it by a 2-to-1 majority.[19]

While others were happy or sad depending on the fate of their favorite candidates, McCarl and Norris had little time for emotion. McCarl immediately started preparations for the coming campaign, while Norris was still involved with congressional duties. But he too was looking ahead, particularly to the Republican convention in Chicago, where he predicted a fierce fight to nominate Roosevelt. Now that the former president had won so impressive a primary victory, Norris openly endorsed his candidacy as representing the desire of the overwhelming majority of Nebraska voters.[20]

The La Follette supporters in Nebraska, more than any other group, had reason for bitterness and recrimination. They had started a movement which others would now direct and control. Frank Harrison offered no excuses; they were overwhelmed by the Roosevelt bandwagon. He did point out, however, that La Follette had done very well in communities where he had spoken, and that railroad workers had stood by his candidacy. He also claimed that "Aldrich men knifed Norris all over the state," and that consequently the senatorial race had been much closer than originally anticipated. But Harrison observed the result was "good enough for Norris" who had straddled the presidential issue.[21]

Thus Norris, though his majority was the smallest among candidates seeking state-wide Republican nomination, successfully crossed the first hurdle in his race for a seat in the Senate. While Senator Brown had been generally consistent as a progressive, his friendship for President Taft was the weak spot in his armor. At various times he had resolved doubts by standing with the president. He had not been slavish about it, and more often than not he had voted with the progressives. But on the Payne-Aldrich Tariff and the Canadian Reciprocity Agreement, issues which aroused much antipathy in Nebraska, Brown had supported the president on the final vote.

On the other hand, Norris, as a congressman, was regarded as one of the staunchest fighters for the progressive cause. He was one of the prominent victims of the administration's attempt to ruin the progressives politically by withdrawing patronage. He had been the leader of the fight against Cannon and machine rule in the House, a firm friend of the farmer, and a leading figure in the fight against reciprocity with Canada.[22] Voters in Nebraska knew and understood this. In the primary they chose Norris despite the fact that he was personally unknown in the larger communities of the state. Undoubtedly the deciding factor was Brown's friendship with Taft and Norris' opposition to the administration; Nebraska Republicans in 1912 wanted nobody suspected of friendship toward the Taft administration.

Chapter 27

Preliminaries

PROGRESSIVE REPUBLICANS emerged from the Nebraska primary in a most advantageous position. Nearly all of their candidates had been elected, and their leaders now assumed a more dominant position in the party hierarchy. Much depended upon the outcome of the Republican National Convention in June. If Taft were nominated, F. P. Corrick, who had directed the over-all progressive primary campaign, assured Norris that they would have to "hustle good and plenty to elect anything on the Republican State Ticket." Governor Aldrich would have a difficult campaign no matter who was nominated for the presidency because he had antagonized citizens representing all shades of political opinion through inept moves and hasty decisions. Norris, still busy in Washington with legislative duties, had made no serious blunder during the primary campaign, and was the strongest candidate on the entire Republican ticket, though his plurality was not as large as the governor's.[1]

A week after his primary victory Norris, by way of a diversion from politics, spoke at a large meeting in Washington celebrating the anniversary of Odd Fellowship in America. He had been working under strain and pressure and now rheumatism added to his general feeling of misery. He needed a rest, but at the same time he had every intention of plunging into the campaign and working hard to the very end. If Roosevelt were nominated, Norris predicted a relatively easy triumph in Nebraska. But regardless of the nominee, he believed that "the progressive spirit of the age" would require voters to lay aside "the political partisan yoke" and consider measures and men without regard to party politics. Such a condition would mean better legislation, since it would leave officeholders free to vote according to the dictates of their consciences. A free individual, acting in accord with a higher moral law, could only insure greater happiness and progress for a democratic people. Norris believed this end could be achieved in the coming election when voters would have an opportunity to over-

250

throw political bosses and machine rule, and he was determined to play an active role in this effort.[2]

Observers in Nebraska felt that Norris' popularity would have to carry the rest of the ticket if Taft were nominated, and that Norris' name would attract Democratic votes as well. But as Roosevelt won more and more primary elections, Norris was inclined to believe that the former president would be nominated and would lead the ticket to victory in Nebraska. Norris reported that every member of the House from Massachusetts, which Taft had barely won, was absent from Washington for a week or ten days before that primary. They were all Taft supporters. One of them told Norris that if the delegation had not returned to campaign, Roosevelt would have carried practically every district in the state.[3]

With the decisive defeat of Taft in the Ohio primary in mid-May, some politicians and most public opinion began to concede that Roosevelt would win the nomination. After the New Jersey primary, the victorious Roosevelt began to admit that he was "reasonably sure" of becoming his party's standard-bearer. Similar optimism was rampant in Nebraska. On May 22, behind closed doors in Lincoln, the Republican delegates and their alternates to the national convention decided to support Taft and then La Follette only if Roosevelt were unable to obtain the nomination.[4]

In Washington, Norris refused to prepare statements on the issues of the campaign until the platforms were formulated. He did state, however, that in his opinion the most important issue would be an enlargement of the rights of citizens to participate in governmental affairs—the overthrow on the national scene of political machines and boss rule. To achieve this goal he endorsed the widely discussed devices of the initiative, referendum, and recall, the direct election of United States senators, and the direct nomination of presidential candidates. To Norris, the issues of the campaign were projections on the national scene of his experience in the House.[5]

The unwillingness of the Republican machine to yield power became fully evident to Norris and other progressives when they found it impossible to obtain tickets to the national convention. Norris soon concluded that Taft managers intended to steal the nomination by excluding Roosevelt and La Follette supporters from the galleries, by pressuring delegates, and by obtaining control of key convention committees. He believed Taft men would prefer to retain control of the party machinery rather than to win at the polls. He fully expected them to decide arbitrarily against Roosevelt delegates in disputed contests through their control of committees. Concerned as he was

over this situation, Norris could do nothing to prevent it. Since he
had chosen not to be a delegate, he did not plan to go to Chicago, intending instead to stay in Washington.[6]

Two days before the convention convened, Norris told a reporter
he thought the Republican platform should contain a permanent, nonpartisan tariff commission, supplemental antitrust legislation, a work-
men's compensation law applying to interstate railroads, the placing of
the post office on a business basis, a presidential primary law, new
rules determining representation in national conventions on the basis
of voting strength and prohibiting federal officials from the control
and management of political campaigns, the short ballot, and, finally,
the initiative, referendum, and recall. Most of these planks were in accord with the wishes of progressive Republican delegates assembling
in Chicago.[7]

On June 17, the Nebraska delegation at its first caucus in Chicago
censured Victor Rosewater, acting chairman of the National Committee and a devoted Taft supporter. Rosewater found that the delegates
would abide by none of his arrangements. The way they treated him,
however, was only a preview of the bitterness and ill will that was to
characterize relations between progressive and conservative delegates
throughout the convention.[8]

As the convention got under way, Norris anxiously read accounts
of the Republican organization's rejection of the claims of the vast
majority of the Roosevelt delegates for contested seats. When he
learned that Roosevelt men had bolted the Committee on Resolutions
and that a movement was under way for a separate convention, he
made hurried plans to leave for Chicago. He sent the following
nightletter to F. P. Corrick:

> Opposed to organization of new party. The progressive are the
> true Republicans. Fight to purge the roll. If defeated by stolen
> votes . . . organize and nominate candidate without leaving hall.
> We already have control of party and candidates in progressive
> states. We must not give this up. We are the Republicans and en-
> titled to the designation on official ballot.[9]

When Norris arrived in Chicago, Roosevelt already had received
assurances of financial support for a new party. The former president
had prepared a message which was read by Henry J. Allen of Kansas
shortly after the delegates assembled on Saturday, June 22. Roosevelt
chronicled the outrageous frauds of the convention and asked delegates
not to participate any longer in its deliberations. That afternoon it was
announced that a new party would be formed that night at Orchestra

Hall. Hiram Johnson opened the evening meeting with a rousing speech and Roosevelt announced, amid tumultuous roars of approval, that he would accept the nomination of a new party if it were made by a new convention regularly called and honestly elected. Earlier, when Norris was introduced to the audience, another round of cheers went up, and he ascended the platform and probably remained there throughout the remainder of the proceedings.[10]

Returning thereafter to Washington, Norris felt that the exciting events in Chicago insured a Democratic victory in Nebraska. While he was confused about the campaign and his own political future, he was certain that under no circumstances could he be induced to support Taft after "the fraudulent, dishonest and illegal methods by which he received his pretended nomination." Norris had no intention of sanctioning what he considered the unseating of honestly elected delegates by men who had not "a scintilla of an honest or rightful claim to the seats." He drafted a statement, soon released to the press and later expanded into a speech delivered on the House floor, which reviewed the situation in detail. "Democratic Tammany," claimed Norris, "in her worst guise had never more arbitrarily and unlawfully trampled the rights of the individual voter under foot than was done by these political manipulators and bosses, most of whom had already been repudiated in their own states and in their own communities by the rank and file of the Republican party." [11]

To Norris, Roosevelt had been nominated at Orchestra Hall early in the morning of June 23, and a new convention and a third party were unnecessary. Roosevelt had been nominated without opposition in one of the most enthusiastic meetings he had ever attended, and Norris intended to support him as the only lawfully nominated Republican candidate for president.

Full formalities were ignored, Norris explained, because most delegates had been in Chicago for a week and could not remain any longer. The Orchestra Hall delegates, unanimous in their support of Roosevelt, were eager to endorse him and depart as quickly as possible. Thus they passed a resolution, which Norris claimed the newspapers never published, stating that they constituted a majority of the legally elected Republican delegates of the National Republican Convention, and acting on behalf of the Republicans of the nation, had nominated Roosevelt as the Republican candidate for president.[12]

On this basis Norris opposed the creation of a third party, especially in Nebraska where progressives had nominated almost all of the candidates and had complete control of the situation. He feared that if a third party were organized, some progressive candidates might withdraw from the Republican ticket, giving Taft men control of the party in Nebraska. Norris, who had no desire to leave the Republican party, hoped that if a new party were started it would endorse all of the candidates already nominated in progressive Republican states like Nebraska.[13]

Norris' condemnation of machine tactics in securing Taft's nomination "created something of a sensation" in Nebraska. Upon learning the details of the Chicago convention, Nebraskans were more enthusiastic than ever for Roosevelt and looked forward to progressive Republicans dominating the state convention. The Nebraska delegation to the Chicago convention also issued a series of statements challenging the outrage perpetrated on the people by the fraudulently constituted convention. Like Norris' speech, these releases analyzed the contests in disputed states. All concluded that a majority of lawfully elected delegates were for Roosevelt and that enough votes were stolen from him to give Taft the nomination. Norris endorsed these statements and planned to plunge into the fight to capture control of the forthcoming state convention.[14]

Norris had no intention of leaving the party and no desire to conceal and cover the fraud and manipulation that had taken place within it. He thought it his duty to expose it and to repudiate the nominee whose title to the nomination depended upon illegal and fraudulent action. To summarize his feelings in this matter, he used a phrase made memorable by Abraham Lincoln:

> I am not bound to win, but I am bound to be true. I am not
> bound to succeed, but I am bound to live up to what light I have.
> I must stand with anybody who stands right, stand with him
> while he is right and part from him when he goes wrong.[15]

He believed too that Roosevelt had no reason for leaving the party, that he should have accepted without qualification the nomination tendered him, and that he should not attempt to organize a third party. Progressives, Norris contended, should simply recognize the Orchestra Hall meeting and go ahead with the fight. While such a step could no longer be taken on the national level, it could be taken on the state level, and he urged supporters to send progressive delegates to the Republican State Convention in Lincoln to extirpate machine control in Nebraska. He intended to support Roosevelt without joining the new party. If the Taft element in Nebraska claimed he was not a Republican and nominated somebody in his place, Norris admitted his cause would be hopeless. The fate of Norris and of the progressive movement in Nebraska thus depended on which faction gained control of the convention scheduled to meet on July 30 to adopt a party platform.[16]

Norris was displeased about the role of Senator La Follette, who had remained in Washington throughout the national convention. La Follette had refused to let his delegates support Governor Francis E. McGovern of Wisconsin for temporary chairman and, while Norris knew the senator had been treated shabbily, he considered this action a serious mistake.[17] La Follette seemed to prefer the defeat of the progressive cause to victory with Roosevelt as standardbearer. When it became apparent he could not win, La Follette should have given up his individual ambitions for the progressive movement. While he still admired La Follette, Norris nevertheless was critical of his behavior during the primary campaigns and especially during the national convention.[18]

Nebraskans soon supported Norris' repudiation of Taft. Letters, resolutions, editorials all announced that voters agreed with or at least admired his straightforward declaration. His statement, released after his return to Washington from the convention, was the first of its kind. Governor Aldrich followed with one of his own. But McCarl warned Norris that since his position was stronger than the governor's, he should not work too closely with Aldrich in the campaign.[19]

McCarl realized, however, that control of the state convention was more important than the question of Norris' relationship with Aldrich. If the convention were standpat and favored Taft, it would no doubt condemn Norris, Aldrich, and others who had come out against Taft. On the other hand, if the progressive faction could control the convention, the rest of the campaign would be relatively easy. A platform in accord with Norris' views would be adopted and no third party ticket then would appear on the ballot. To bring about this desired result, McCarl proposed to see "the right fellows in person" to make sure that their counties chose progressive delegates to county conventions, thereby insuring a state convention favorable to the progressive cause.[20]

Meanwhile Norris prepared a statement stressing the importance of a progressive platform and the election of progressive delegates to the state convention. Such a platform would show that the rank and file of the party in Nebraska were in favor of progressive principles and were opposed to the methods used "to steal the presidential nomination" for Taft.[21]

It had been rumored that Norris might act as temporary or permanent chairman of the state convention and make a speech, but several friends warned him against such action. Any address would have to endorse other progressive candidates and thus would lose him Democratic and independent votes. While many Democrats might vote for Norris, few would vote for Aldrich or other progressive Republican candidates. Since Norris was the only Republican in the state with a chance of being elected, these friends felt it would be political suicide to aid candidates who had been more or less indifferent to his success in the past. All agreed, however, that the chances that progressives would control the convention were good.[22]

So persistent were rumors that the standpatters, if they controlled the convention, would ask Norris to withdraw from the ticket, that he wrote a letter to the chairman of the State Republican Committee, John L. Kennedy. In it he stated that if his course in refusing to recognize Taft as his party's nominee were unsatisfactory to the Republicans who nominated him, he would withdraw. If his candidacy depended on supporting Taft, given the fraudulent methods used in obtaining his nomination, he would return to private life. But Kennedy claimed that Norris had been properly nominated and that no state committeeman had questioned his right to a place on the ticket. Norris' proposal, however, coming on the eve of the state convention, dramatically presented his views and took the initiative away from the regular Republicans.[23]

The Red Willow County convention meeting in McCook on July 20 chose Norris as a member of its delegation and reiterated his views in a resolution which was unanimously adopted. Other counties also chose progressive delegates, and several conventions denounced Taft and the Chicago convention. A large majority of the counties comprising the Fifth Congressional District endorsed Norris' position. Meanwhile, Norris, who was expected to attend the state convention and perhaps to serve as temporary chairman and keynote speaker, announced at the last moment that pressure of congressional business would prevent his return. By remaining in Washington he would lose few, if any, votes from Democrats who intended to support him, and progressives would support him whether he attended or not. Taft men, unless they voted Democratic or forced him off the ticket, would have no alternative but to vote for him on election day. Thus Norris strengthened his position by staying in Washington during the convention.[24]

Another factor which may have helped him decide not to attend the convention was that he expected a bitter battle to take place there. Previously, behind the scenes, he had indirectly tried to prevent such a battle from developing. In Omaha the county committee, controlled by Rosewater, had met on July 16 and called for the convening of the

Douglas County Convention on July 20. To be sure that they would control this convention, the committee appointed a group of their own members to select delegates to the convention and a committee to select their own successors. Norris, learning of these procedures from Rosewater's Omaha *Bee*, considered them brazen political skulduggery. He wrote to Howell, asking him to take the lead in calling for a genuine county convention. He also requested that Roosevelt write to Howell and urge him to take the lead in challenging Rosewater's manipulation of the Douglas County committee. But Roosevelt was of no help in this matter. While he agreed with Norris' sentiments, his solution was "to come out straight for the third ticket" rather than to submit to such infamy.[25]

Thus at the state convention Taft men controlled the Douglas County delegation, the largest single delegation. Nine or ten counties had contested delegations, and in every instance both sets of delegates were on hand. Indications did not point to a harmonious gathering. The night before the convention was to get under way, leaders of the Taft and Roosevelt groups met together in a futile effort to resolve their differences. Norris sent a telegram which was indicative of the temper of most of the delegates. He insisted, "Any compromise is an unconditional surrender." At the same time he knew, despite bitter feeling between contending factions, that the progressive Republicans were in control.[26]

McCarl played an important role at the convention, helping to organize progressives to combat any unforeseen tactics by Taft men. At a conference, the Taft leaders boldly demanded that Roosevelt electors get off the Republican ticket. Norris was informed, "They wanted the party name and the party machinery." Rebuffed at this informal meeting, the Taft men received a further blow the next day, July 31, when the Executive Committee, headed by Aldrich, decided most of the contested cases in favor of progressive delegates, thereby insuring their control of the convention by a large majority. Once these decisions were announced many of the regular Republican delegates, with the Douglas County delegation in the lead, reversed the procedure of the Chicago convention and walked out, bitterly complaining of what they called Governor Aldrich's "steam roller" tactics.[27]

The real trouble came when Rosewater found himself unable to control John L. Kennedy, a Taft supporter and a member of the Executive Committee hearing the contested cases. Kennedy, deciding the cases on their merits, was compelled in most instances to support delegates favorable to Roosevelt. Rosewater, furious over Kennedy's behavior, decided to "bust the convention," and, largely through Kennedy's courageous stand, the progressive group gained control. This was not the opinion of all observers. None of the newspapers, according to McCarl, reported the facts fairly. But from his vantage point as a prominent delegate, McCarl saw Kennedy as the real hero of the state convention and Rosewater as the villain.[28]

The platform enthusiastically adopted by the convention was short but vague as to the test of Republicanism. It made no mention of Taft, his administration, the Chicago convention, and used no vindictive language reflecting the division of the party. At the same time, the Taft delegates, who had walked out of the state convention, were holding a meeting and claiming that they were the only true Republicans. They intended to obtain a court order validating their contention. Rosewater moved that the state central committee be given the power to fill all vacancies on the Republican ticket with candidates who supported Taft.[29]

Norris was warned not to attend the Progressive convention in Chicago and to stay away from the new party altogether. The third party, if and when it was organized in the state, could endorse his candidacy, but Norris' job was to remain in the Republican party and keep the control which progressive elements had firmly established as a result of the state convention. As McCarl explained it, "We can be Republicans without supporting Taft and that's what we are." Though there was disappointment in Lincoln because Norris was not present at the convention, there was also strong sentiment for him. The preliminaries, as far as Norris was concerned, were over. It was now his responsibility, as soon as Congress adjourned, to take his candidacy to the people of Nebraska.[30]

Chapter 28

Campaigning

THROUGHOUT Nebraska people discussed whether Norris should attend and play a prominent role in the Progressive party convention to be held in Chicago early in August. However, he still saw no reason to leave the Republican party. He would abide by a recall election if voters demanded one and, if recalled, would get off the Republican ticket. He made this announcement to illustrate dramatically his belief in the recall and to make it difficult if not impossible for the regular Republicans to read him out of the party. With progressive Republicans fully in control of the party organization in Nebraska, Norris still tended to his congressional duties in Washington.[1]

The question of selecting a new chairman of the state committee was an important one and threatened to disrupt progressive Republican leaders. F. P. Corrick, who had ably guided the destinies of the Progressive Republican League, thought the job should be his, but he was quickly opposed. On August 13, the Republican State Committee chose Judge Ambrose Epperson as chairman. He regarded Norris' election as one of the most important items of business facing the committee. McCarl, though satisfied with Epperson, felt that Corrick deserved the post and, having been treated unjustly, would now direct the third party campaign in Nebraska. If Corrick remained angry, McCarl feared he might place a Progressive party candidate against Aldrich, who was largely responsible for Epperson's choice, and thus further jeopardize Republican chances.[2]

Norris intended to leave no doubt as to his stand on national issues. He would support Roosevelt and denounce the political robbery that was perpetrated at Chicago. He was disturbed and puzzled by reports that Roosevelt electors in Nebraska would probably withdraw from the Republican ticket. Since they had been chosen at the April primary and their course in supporting Roosevelt had been vindicated by the state convention, he could not understand why they would not continue to support Roosevelt on the Republican ticket. The only reasonable explanation was that the progressive Republicans intended to trade electoral votes for state votes: Roosevelt electors would appear only on the Progressive ticket, state candidates would appear on both tickets, and organization men could then substitute a list of Taft electors to replace the Roosevelt men. Norris announced that he would play no part in such a compromise.[3]

He received several letters indicating that Aldrich favored such an arrangement, but though Norris stood to benefit by it, he refused to be swayed. He firmly believed that some form of harmony could be maintained within Republican ranks, avoiding the need to bring additional Progressive candidates into the field.[4]

McCarl, after attending several meetings in Lincoln, confirmed this impression. The executive committees of both the Republican and Progressive state organizations had met in separate rooms of the same hotel while the Republican candidates or their representatives were meeting with the Republican State Committee. McCarl, who represented Norris, reported that a state convention of the third party would be held in Lincoln on September 3. At this time the matter of endorsement of the state Republican ticket would be officially decided upon, though the Progressive Executive Committee had already approved the arrangement. It was the sentiment of this meeting that if the state-wide candidates would agree not to show any inconsistency to the Progressive party by advocating Taft's election in their speeches, all such candidates would be endorsed in the interest of harmony and victory in November.[5]

Furthermore, the Republican Executive Committee, McCarl informed Norris, had taken "the proper attitude." They intended to support Norris and the entire state ticket, including the presidential electors. If any elector wanted to withdraw to be placed on the third party ticket, this would be considered a personal matter beyond the committee's jurisdiction. Most members of the committee thought the electors would do so, since leaders in the Roosevelt headquarters in Chicago had indicated that they wished them to. McCarl regarded this position as sensible, but thought it should not be publicly discussed. Few voters actually understood that the politicians wished to give the Taft men a chance to vote for Taft electors to prevent many of them from voting for Wilson and possibly Shallenberger as well.

Though Norris disagreed with this scheme, McCarl thought there was wisdom in it. Since the decision for the Roosevelt electors to withdraw had been made in Chicago in the best interests of Roosevelt's candidacy, McCarl felt that Norris should be less concerned with this decision than with the fact that Taft voters and third party voters as well would be able to support his candidacy.[6]

Shortly after Congress adjourned on August 26, Norris announced that he intended to return to Nebraska on or about September 10, stopping first in Chicago for a conference with Senator Joseph Dixon of Montana, Roosevelt's campaign manager, and other Progressive party leaders. His delay in returning to Nebraska was wise politically because it allowed him to be absent when the Progressive state convention opened and gave him time to prepare campaign material.

The Progressive state convention met on September 3 to organize formally the new party by nominating a set of electors who would support Roosevelt and Hiram Johnson. This convention chose Corrick as chairman of its state committee, endorsed six of the eight electors nominated at the April primary on the Republican ticket—the Roosevelt men—and added two new men to complete the list. All other Republican nominees chosen at the April primary were endorsed by the Progressive convention, making it possible for their names to appear on the ballot in November under both the Republican and Progressive labels. Thus Norris was officially endorsed by two parties, and the arrangements between the parties had been worked out without involving him in bitterness and acrimony.[7]

On September 9, before returning to McCook, Norris stopped in Lincoln to speak and to visit with leaders of the state committees. To reporters he repeated that he supported Roosevelt and believed Taft unfairly nominated. Norris made great efforts to clarify his position because the campaign, he maintained, would be a crusade for political and civic righteousness, a national manifestation similar to the fight against Cannonism.[8]

Meanwhile, McCarl's job was to supervise Norris' campaign in cooperation with the Republican and Progressive state committees. He also collected information about the less honorable aspects of Shallenberger's record in order to be prepared in the event Shallenberger's campaign degenerated to the level of that of Fred Ashton's, Norris' opponent in 1908, and to satisfy a request from the Republican State Committee for a file on all Democratic candidates.[9]

Norris launched his campaign with a nonpolitical speech before some three thousand Odd Fellows assembled outside Omaha for their annual picnic. Governor Aldrich and several others delivered welcoming remarks before Norris started his speech on "Fraternity." No sooner did he begin than it started to rain. He continued his speech anyway, although only a few members of the audience stayed to hear him out.[10] Afterwards Norris spent a day or two in Omaha and Lincoln discussing politics with Progressive and Republican party leaders. He was to deliver his first political speech in Lincoln on September

20, and thereafter was scheduled for two speeches almost every day for the rest of the campaign. But at the last minute, Norris changed his plans for the Lincoln meeting because Roosevelt expected him to spend that day on board his campaign train. Roosevelt, coming east from Denver over the Burlington route, spoke at Minden, Hastings, Lincoln, and Omaha, and Norris appeared on the platform with the former president during these addresses. In Omaha, Roosevelt spoke before an audience of 7,500 enthusiasts who waved handkerchiefs and cheered wildly when he appeared. Norris accompanied Roosevelt to the platform and addressed the crowd briefly after the former president had spoken. In this dramatic way Norris began his grueling campaign.[11]

The next day he started a one-week tour of the western part of the state to get "in good working order" before appearing in the eastern counties. Nine formal meetings were scheduled. He returned to Lincoln on September 29 to spend two days in the First Congressional District. Thereafter he was scheduled to spend a few days early in October speaking in the south central part of the state before embarking on a tour of northeastern Nebraska. He agreed to devote most of his time to the more populous eastern end of the state where he was less well known, and to appear before as many people there as possible. Automobile transportation helped him carry out this plan.[12]

By the end of September McCarl thought that Norris might have to speak three or four times a day. He was encouraged by the interest aroused in Norris' first meetings in the eastern end of the state, an interest not matched in the western part of Nebraska where voters already knew their candidate. McCarl wanted Norris to be continually on the move, returning to certain areas, if necessary, to speak again. By going back to a locality he could defend himself against rumors, opposing local politicians who thought there was no danger of a "return engagement." Furthermore, if Norris moved continually, his opponents would be unable to trace or evaluate fully the change of sentiment following his meetings.[13]

Early in their campaigns both Norris and Shallenberger spoke before attentive audiences in Merrick County in east central Nebraska. As was his custom, Norris made no attempt whatever at oratory, preferring to let the facts make their own impression. Favorable comments from listeners suggested that this type of address, though it lasted over an hour, was eminently successful.[14]

Several days later Shallenberger spoke in another community in Merrick County, addressing about two hundred people, primarily businessmen or town loafers. Very few farmers were present, chiefly because this was an afternoon meeting. Shallenberger criticized Norris' record in the Cannon fight because he had not voted to unseat Cannon and had opposed the creation of a tariff commission. He was applauded only when he referred to Bryan and the Baltimore convention. At the conclusion, as apparently was his custom, Shallenberger included a peroration to the flag. The speech was reported to be unimpressive; at least one prominent Democrat in the audience predicted that Norris would win the election, a prediction repeated elsewhere by Democrats after Norris spoke in their communities. Observers felt that if voters deserted their traditional tickets, Roosevelt might win Nebraska's electoral vote; otherwise, Wilson would win. In no case would Taft carry the state. Democratic support for Norris, therefore, would be beneficial to the Progressive party.[15]

McCarl was delighted with these reports of Norris sentiment and by a report that at one place Norris was in such demand that he was forced to make a speech to the crowd outside before they would let him enter the hall. McCarl's optimism grew when he learned that Corrick and Epperson were working harmoniously and effectively together. As a result, he decided to let the combined Speakers' Bureau of both parties arrange Norris' speaking dates for the rest of the campaign—subject, of course, to McCarl's approval.[16]

By early October Norris' itinerary for the remainder of the campaign was completed. At no time was he scheduled for less than two meetings a day, and on a few days five meetings had been arranged; this schedule, of course, did not include the many brief speeches and unscheduled appearances he would make en route. Sundays would provide him with all the rest he would obtain till after the election.

This busy itinerary, however, had one serious flaw. Norris had found that he was unable to give an effective short talk; he could make a point or two, but would be unable to discuss his record or say much of recent developments. Consequently, voters who did not know him sometimes received an unfavorable impression. McCarl suggested that when Norris was scheduled to make a number of brief stops, he have someone accompany him to give a short general talk before introducing him. This arrangement would keep Norris out of petty controversies in which local candidates, who might otherwise introduce him, were involved. Harry Sackett, a young and prominent Progressive from Beatrice, assumed this responsibility and proved eminently satisfactory.[17]

On October 5 and 6, Wilson spoke in Omaha and Lincoln and was the guest of Bryan at his home, Fairview. Bryan introduced Wilson at the auditorium in Lincoln and at the close of his address the enthusiastic audience called for Bryan to speak as well. He refused, however, merely motioning the audience to disperse. The appearance of Wilson in Nebraska was not only a tribute to Bryan but a move seemingly well calculated to throw the Roosevelt supporters into the depths of suspense and anxiety. McCarl, for example, confessed:

> I am a little afraid of the Wilson boom, afraid of too many straight Wilson votes this fall. I am in hopes his visit won't set everybody crazy.[18]

Norris was much too busy to take notice of Wilson's speeches in Nebraska. To avoid possible rancor, he contributed one hundred and fifty dollars to aid the Progressive cause, matching a previous contribution to the Republican campaign chest. Speaking several times a day, shaking hands and talking with people in every community on his route, by and large he enjoyed the campaign.[19]

Years later Norris related an amusing anecdote, supposedly illustrating the evil of partisanship, that occurred during this campaign. A minister, who had come some distance to hear him speak, claimed to have followed his record with pleasure and admiration and to be much in favor of his election. The following conversation took place between the two men:

> "Mr. Norris, I am so anxious to have you succeed that every night before I retire, on my bended knees I ask God to see that you are elected to the Senate. Why, I sometimes get so anxious to see you elected that I almost feel as if I ought to vote for you myself."
>
> "My friend," said Norris, "if you feel that way about it, why don't you vote for me?"
>
> "Oh," he replied, "I could not do that. I am a Democrat." [20]

The opposition, meanwhile, had a difficult time seriously challenging or embarrassing Norris. To aid Shallenberger, the Lincoln *Daily Star*, a Democratic paper, dredged up the story of the 1895 disputed judicial election between Norris and Welty. Another possible threat was that Secretary of State Addison Wait would prepare the ballot in such a way as to create confusion among the voters. The presidential electors' names were arranged with the six Roosevelt Republicans appearing first under the name "Republican-Progressive." After all the other names on the ballot appeared those of the two regularly chosen Republican electors in the primary as Republican. These were followed by six names bearing no party label but only the words "by petition." These names had been filed as Taft electors, but this fact was not clearly established on the ballot. Once news of this arrangement became known, attention quickly turned away from actual campaigning to the perplexing question of which electors favored Taft and which favored Roosevelt. Protests were made, and Democrats hoped that animosity between Taft and Roosevelt supporters would burst forth once more into the open.[21]

On October 16, the Republican State Central Committee brought a petition for a writ of mandamus in the district court of Lancaster County to compel the secretary of state to remove the heading "Republican-Progressive" from the ballot. The names under this heading would appear as Progressives while the Republican ticket would bear the names of the two regularly chosen electors plus the six names filed by petition. On October 19, the judges of the district court granted the writ of mandamus. Thus the eight Taft electors would go on the ballot as Republicans, while the names of the six Roosevelt Republican electors chosen in the primary would appear under the Progressive party designation.[22]

The matter did not rest here. Wait, a Roosevelt supporter, appealed the decision to the Supreme Court on October 22. At noon on October 24, only hours before the deadline for certification of the ballot, the Supreme Court of Nebraska unanimously affirmed the action of the district court, thereby assuring the Taft electors a place on the ballot and finally solving this complex and thorny problem. Now there was a chance that voters favoring Taft would vote the entire Republican ticket, whereas previously it was feared that many would scratch the Democratic ticket on election day.[23]

When the matter of the ballot was settled there remained for McCarl only his concern about Norris' campaign. Though Norris was covering a large portion of the state, he could not speak at even half the places from which requests had been received. Before mid-October nearly two hundred different Nebraska communities had requested his appearance and fourteen states had clamored for a day or two of his time. Norris had no intention of campaigning outside the state, and would be unable to speak to voters in most of these communities.

To offset this factor McCarl had prepared a two-column plate with a cut of Norris and a statement of some of the things he had accomplished and was working for. He sent this plate to editors throughout Nebraska and distributed copies of Norris' speeches and other campaign literature. By mid-October, only one Republican country editor had told McCarl that he would not use the plate. Most

Taft papers had agreed to publish it. This widespread acceptance, plus the fact that the Democrats had to go back to 1895 to find anything to criticize, pleased McCarl.[24]

The outlook was further brightened by a telephone conversation between McCarl and John L. Kennedy. Kennedy said that Norris would receive a fine hearing in Omaha, that an address would climax the good work being done there for the entire Republican ticket and particularly for Norris. Kennedy reassured McCarl regarding a rumor of railroad opposition, claiming that most railroad officials, while personally opposed to Norris, thought he would be easily elected and would not work against him.[25]

Though all reports about Norris' meetings were good, no relaxation was contemplated. Norris was so tired that on Sundays, even when feasible, he did not return home to spend the day with his family, but rested instead in the community where he had last spoken. Until McCarl reported his conversation with Kennedy, Norris had been reluctant to attempt a meeting by himself in Omaha for fear he might not receive a satisfactory hearing; a poor meeting, coming at the end of the campaign, could hurt his chances. But now he began to reconsider. His speeches, however, did not change. While their content varied from town to town, all were crammed full of facts and devoid of oratorical flourishes or partisan criticism. They appealed to the intelligence rather than to the emotions of his hearers, and received a favorable reception.[26]

Besides Kennedy's comments, Norris heard further favorable reports about the situation in Omaha. Travelers told of growing sentiment, and the Omaha *Daily News* in October published two editorials, both well received, endorsing Norris. R. B. Howell, attempting to sense the political situation, secured a number of straw votes at strategic points throughout the city. His conclusion was that Norris could carry Douglas County, though Roosevelt's prospects did not seem "overly bright." With these observations in mind, McCarl prepared twenty-five hundred personal letters to be mailed to Omaha residents on the Wednesday or Thursday before election, while Norris planned to spend November 1, the Friday before the election, speaking in Omaha and South Omaha.[27]

At times, the effects of the tiring campaign showed on Norris. In the privacy of his hotel room and elsewhere, among friends, he sometimes became irritable, cursed, and complained about being driven too hard. But the public and most politicians rarely saw this side of his personality. By the end of October he looked haggard and tired but was well pleased with the course of his campaign and felt assured of success on election day.[28]

Norris concluded his campaign in the eastern end of the state on the first day of November. At noon he spoke before a luncheon meeting of the Omaha Commercial Club and spent the rest of the day in Omaha and South Omaha. Kennedy introduced him to the members of the Commercial Club. "Because we disagree on president," said Kennedy, "is not to me a sufficient reason why I should withhold from him my support." Indeed, Kennedy's help, climaxed at this meeting, had been invaluable throughout the campaign.[29]

McCarl had yet to finish his work. He arranged for Norris to spend the last days of the campaign in the Fifth Congressional District. There were numerous meetings scheduled, including one at Hastings on Saturday evening, November 2, and a final homecoming rally in McCook on election eve. The Chicago *Tribune* summed up the feeling of many voters just before election day by predicting that while the state might enter the Democratic fold, "It is more than likely that Representative George W. Norris will be the next United States Senator from Nebraska." [30]

Though the election of 1912 was infinitely more exciting than that of 1908, seventeen thousand more votes were cast in Nebraska in the earlier campaign. Slightly less than two hundred and fifty thousand Nebraska citizens went to the polls in 1912. Wilson easily carried the state, running more than thirty thousand votes ahead of Roosevelt. But the combined Roosevelt and Taft votes surpassed Wilson's 109,109 votes. For governor, Aldrich was defeated by his Democratic opponent John H. Morehead by almost four thousand votes. This race was so close that Aldrich refused to admit defeat until several days after the election. All other state officers on the Republican and Progressive tickets were elected by pluralities of ten thousand to fifteen thousand, an indication of Aldrich's alienation of many voters. Control of the state legislature was divided. The Democrats would dominate the next session of the lower house, electing fifty-six members to forty-four for the Progressive and Republican parties. In the state senate the Progressive and Republican members won a three-man majority, electing eighteen members to the Democrat's fifteen. In the congressional races there was an even split, Democrats electing candidates in the three eastern districts, while Progressive and Republican candidates, including Silas R. Barton, Norris' successor in the Fifth District, won the remaining three districts. Finally, in the preference race for the United States Senate seat to be vacated by incumbent Norris Brown,

George Norris handily defeated Shallenberger. Norris received 126,022 votes to Shallenberger's 111,946.[31]

Norris was deeply gratified by the outcome. His exuberance, however, was tempered by the knowledge that his triumph was a notable exception to a general pattern of Progressive and Republican defeat throughout the nation. He was pleased that he carried Douglas County which went for Wilson by more than two thousand votes. Friction over prohibition between Shallenberger and James C. Dahlman, Democratic Mayor of Omaha, helped Norris' vote in the state's largest city. Democratic strife, while beneficial to Norris, nevertheless did not harm Wilson, who benefited immeasurably from Republican factionalism. Despite ballot adjudication, Wilson's vote was increased by conservative Taft supporters who resented the liberal group controlling the state party organization and its close cooperation with the Progressive State Committee. Others, fearful of a Roosevelt victory in Nebraska, voted for Wilson. Democratic managers did all in their power to encourage these resentments and fears. Despite Wilson's impressive victory, Shallenberger, though defeated by Norris, polled better than twenty-five hundred more votes than the head of his ticket, and Morehead, with 124,000 votes, polled almost fifteen thousand more votes than Wilson. Norris was the leading vote getter in Nebraska in 1912; his 126,022 votes were surpassed by no other candidate.[32]

Both Republican and Progressive leaders were delighted with Norris' victory. Harry Sackett noted that it had an effect "upon the young men of the State in leading them to follow their honest and conscientious convictions in all matters pertaining to the public welfare as well as in business matters." Thus Norris' work in opposing Cannonism had born fruit by 1912. Nebraska voters accepted and even admired his independence and lack of partisanship. As one of his admirers, possibly summing up the views of the electorate, wrote, "We all expect him to just be honest with himself and square with the people of Nebraska." By 1912 Norris had been able to do just that. He had been able to throw off the yoke of partisanship and yet to obtain improved legislation benefiting his constituents.[33]

Norris quickly regained his physical strength and by mid-November was feeling fine, though still deluged with correspondence and office work. He could not take an extended vacation, however, because the third session of the Sixty-second Congress was scheduled to convene early in December. This forthcoming short session, his last as a member of the House, promised to be an active one. It was also a session which cast Norris in a different role from any he had previously experienced in Congress.

Chapter 29

Senator-Elect

THE THIRD SESSION of the Sixty-second Congress convened on Monday, December 2, 1912 at noon with Senator-elect George Norris on hand to complete his service as a member of the House. He had resumed bachelor quarters at the Y.M.C.A. and plunged into congressional duties. For the first part of the session his time and energies were devoted to the impeachment trial of Judge Robert W. Archbald of the United States Commerce Court.

On July 11, 1912, the House had voted 223 to 1 to impeach the judge.[1] Norris, as a member of the Judiciary Committee, had been appointed one of the House managers to prosecute him before the Senate convened as a court of impeachment. The trial committee usually consisted of five members. This time, however, the chairman had appointed and the House approved a seven-member committee so that Norris and John W. Davis of West Virginia, both of whom were among the ablest lawyers in Congress, but neither of whom had been on the Judiciary Committee long enough to warrant the appointment, could serve. From December 2, 1912, until Archbald's fate was decided on January 13, 1913, Norris appeared in the Senate chamber every day that Congress was in session, an experience which introduced him to a body wherein he would play a significant role for the next thirty years.

This impeachment trial was the ninth in the history of the federal government. In essence, the charges against Archbald were that he had engaged in business deals with litigants before his court and had sought favors from them to an extent that violated the canons of good behavior and constituted high crimes and misdemeanors. He had been appointed by William McKinley in 1901 as a district judge. In 1911 he had been promoted by President Taft and confirmed by the Senate as an additional circuit judge, designated to serve on the United States Commerce Court which had been created under the Mann-Elkins Act of 1910. Thirteen articles of impeachment were prepared with the last serving as a summary article. They called attention to eleven distinct acts of misconduct and misbehavior. Five of the charges had occurred during his district judgeship, the remainder during his circuit judgeship. From the beginning many senators were dubious about convicting a person of charges that had occurred while serving in a previous position, different from the one he held at the time of the trial.[2]

Of the six counts against Archbald as a circuit judge, five had to do with transactions between himself and officers of railroads or their subsidiaries in the Pennsylvania anthracite coal region, and one pertained to correspondence between Archbald and counsel for a railroad company with reference to a pending case. In no instance was he involved in the expenditure or investment of money, but in each instance he and his friends gained or stood a chance of gaining handsome profits. Archbald did not actively seek such activity, but was usually approached by a third party who requested him to take up a matter with a railroad company or one of its subsidiaries. No railroad could afford to incur the displeasure of a judge of the Commerce Court, which concentrated on litigation pertaining to rates and facilities offered by railroads engaged in interstate commerce. Hence it was argued that Judge Archbald by his conduct had undermined public confidence in his honesty and had cast suspicion upon his judicial integrity.

As a House manager in these proceedings Norris played a minor role. He questioned witnesses only occasionally, but at the conclusion of the proceedings he delivered an effective summary argument. Representing Judge Archbald, as his chief counsel, was Colonel A. S. Worthington, a capable lawyer whom Norris would encounter in later years as a lobbyist for public utility corporations. Appearing every day in the Senate Chamber, Norris, as a former prosecuting attorney and judge, keenly followed the trial. But he had further reason, a more personal and individual one, for his great interest in the outcome.

During the Judiciary Committee's investigation of Judge Archbald, Norris met and befriended William P. Boland, owner and president of the Marian Coal Company of Scranton, Pennsylvania. Boland, associated with anthracite mining all his life, was being ruined by railroad rate practices, and was convinced that Archbald was trying to take advantage of his plight for his own benefit. Norris listened with interest to Boland's story. It seemed that in the summer and fall of 1909, the Marian Coal Company was defendant in a case pending before Judge Archbald's court. Archbald, a district judge at this time, had drawn a note for five hundred dollars payable to himself and then agreed to allow the note to be presented to either Boland or his brother for the purpose of having it discounted. At the time Archbald's note was presented to the Bolands, the Marian Coal Company was a litigant in his court. In spite of this inducement to accept the note, William Boland refused. Archbald soon found someone else to accept it but, as of the end of 1912, this person had not yet been paid.

Then just prior to Archbald's service on the Commerce Court, the Marian Coal Company had filed before the Interstate Commerce Commission a complaint against the Delaware, Lackawanna & Western Railroad Company and five other interstate railroad companies, charging discrimination in rates and excessive fees for the transportation of coal. While the case was pending, Boland employed an attorney, George M. Watson, to settle the matter by selling to the Delaware, Lackawanna & Western Railroad Company two-thirds of the stock of the Marian Coal Company. If the case were not settled out of court, any party to the dispute had the option under the Mann-Elkins Act of appealing the decision of the Interstate Commerce Commission to the United States Commerce Court which had just welcomed Judge Archbald as a new member.

Judge Archbald, knowing of the general plight of the Marian Coal Company, and informed of further details by Watson, had agreed for a consideration to assist Watson in the sale of Marian Coal Company stock to the Delaware, Lackawanna & Western Railroad Company. Archbald interfered in this matter without the consent of the Boland brothers; Watson had merely raised the price to include the fee Judge Archbald would receive.

William Boland, distraught over his business situation, became frantic when he learned of Archbald's interference in his affairs. He denounced the judge and began to collect evidence he thought would reveal Archbald's culpability. Most people in Scranton, however, thought his suit before the ICC was affected by his impending financial collapse and dismissed his accusations; others thought him a crank casting aspersions on judicial integrity. Norris, however, took him seriously. He had listened sympathetically in the Judiciary Committee hearings, during long walks, and in other conversations to Boland's tale of personal woe and judicial disgrace. He had even advised Boland how to prepare his case before the ICC. Boland's story eventually became the basis of the second and eighth articles of impeachment, both of which the Senate, sitting as a court of impeachment, rejected.[3]

In his summary argument requesting the conviction and removal of Robert W. Archbald from judicial office, Norris did not discuss the facts as they had been developed in the case. Rather he came to the core of the problem and discussed the constitutional issues involved.

Archbald's lawyers had claimed that while he may have been guilty of misbehavior in office, he was not guilty of any offense which could properly be the subject of prosecution in a criminal court. They forcefully argued that a man may be impeached only for offenses which are criminal in their nature and could legally be the subject of prosecution by indictment.

Norris rejected this position and proceeded to demonstrate, citing the Constitution and several commentaries, that a federal judge could be impeached, convicted, and removed from office "for any act from treason down to conduct that tends to bring the judiciary into disgrace, disrespect or disrepute." Furthermore, holding that an official with a fixed tenure of office should not be impeached and removed for misdemeanors that were not indictable offenses was entirely different from holding that a judge, who usually enjoyed a lifetime tenure, should not be impeached and removed. Norris claimed that the framers of the Constitution had this distinction in mind when they wrote the section which applies exclusively to the judiciary and which provides that judges shall hold their offices during good behavior. If this were not so, he stated, Congress and the country could not get relief from a judge who had dragged "the judicial ermine down into disgrace" but who at the same time had been careful not to commit any criminal offense. Judge Archbald, Norris admitted, had not committed any criminal offense. But by secretly engaging in private agreements with attorneys on one side of a case, and by continually and carefully asking favors of litigants in his court, he was guilty of misbehavior and was perverting the ends of justice. Unless his interpretation of the Constitution were accepted, such conduct could continue unabated and the whole judicial system would be undermined. The government, he concluded, could not perform its function unless courts were above reproach and judges above suspicion.[4]

On January 13, 1913, the Senate voted on the articles of impeachment against Judge Archbald. While he was adjudged not guilty of eight charges, he was found guilty on five counts, including article thirteen, the summary article. It was the judgment of the Senate that Archbald be removed from office and "forever disqualified to hold and enjoy any office of honor, trust or profit under the United States." [5]

This trial was the most important piece of congressional business in which Norris engaged during this short session. Once the verdict was announced, he returned to the House and resumed an active interest in legislative matters pending before that chamber. At the time, evidence was being collected in cases involving violations of the Sherman Antitrust Act. The method of acquiring this information, however, was being challenged and highly publicized.

The evidence was being taken by referees or masters traveling to many localities throughout the country. In 1912, in the case of the *United States v. The United Shoe Machinery Company of New Jersey et al.*, pending in a district court, the defendants objected to the taking of testimony by the master in public, and the question was submitted to the court. After an exhaustive hearing and the filing of briefs, the court issued an order excluding the public from such proceedings. According to Norris, who consulted Attorney General Wickersham on the matter, this was the first time that the question had been raised. If the decision of the court stood and Congress did not take immediate action, Norris believed that in all suits arising under the Sherman Antitrust Act the government would be asked to take evidence in private. He was convinced that such secrecy was not only contrary "to the fundamental idea of our jurisprudence," but would often result in a denial of justice. Throughout his career he opposed secrecy in public affairs, whether in party caucuses or conferences of diplomats. In this particular instance, he thought secret hearings would surround the courts with "a mystery of doubt" and bring them into disrepute. He realized that there would have to be exceptions to this general proscription, but, he argued, "If our courts are to retain the confidence and respect of the country generally their official conduct must be entirely free from any suspicion of star-chamber proceedings." [6]

On March 2, just before the end of the session, he had the satisfaction of voting with the majority for a bill prohibiting testimony from being taken in secret in suits arising under the Sherman Antitrust Act. Norris himself had introduced this measure at the request of the attorney general. It had previously passed the Senate and was signed into law by President Taft on March 3, his last full day in office. Thus Norris, as he ended his service in the House, was cooperating closely with the Taft administration, an administration which had fought him and which he in turn had attacked throughout most of its stormy course.

Other bills to improve the effectiveness of the antitrust law or to deal more directly with the problem of monopoly were also under consideration, but Norris' measure was the only one upon which Congress acted. Norris desired further legislation along these lines, favoring, for example, certain patent-law changes that would lessen the power of patent monopolies. He wanted to amend the law so that a person would lose his patent if he did not begin manufacturing his article within a reasonable time. Thus, improvements on patented items could not be kept off the market and out of public reach. Norris believed that the patentee should have the exclusive right to manufacture an article, but that the public should have the benefit of the patent on reasonable terms. Under existing law, as construed by the Supreme Court, the owner of a patent could attach conditions to the use of items produced under it. Norris, bearing in mind the recent Supreme Court decision wherein the United Shoe Machinery Company was allowed to control the leasing and use of their patented machinery while requiring manufacturers to use other items entirely independent of these patented machines, thought the law was giving too much power to monopoly.[7]

The Panama Canal, which interested Norris early in his Senate career, briefly caught his attention during the last days of this session. His remarks revealed his pacifism as well as his maturity as a legislator. Though he had opposed fortification of the canal when the matter was originally before the House, after Congress had decided to fortify it Norris deemed it foolish and even unpatriotic to prevent proper implementation of a decision that had been made. He explained:

> As long as we have decided to fortify, as long as we have decided to take any particular port and fortify it, we ought not to do it in any slipshod or half-way manner. The minute we begin to fortify the Panama Canal we invite the attack of any nation that is at war with us, and it would be silly, it seems to me, to build any fortification that is not ample, that is not absolutely the best that modern ingenuity can devise.[8]

This pattern of initial, strenuous opposition followed by final support of the majority view was one that would be repeated by Norris on a more dramatic scale at the time of World War I.

As the short session drew to a close, its time was given to the consideration of necessary appropriation bills. Other items were cast aside in the rush to provide the functioning agencies of government with necessary funds. Norris, though interested in some of the other items, realized that nothing would come of them at this time and that he would have another chance to consider most of them in the Senate. He looked forward to service in the other branch of the federal legislature, and it was with some anticipation early in January that he awaited his formal election as a United States senator by the Nebraska legislature.

Shortly after the election, defeated Democratic candidates for seats in both houses of the state legislature from Douglas County announced they would contest their rivals' victory. Rumor had it, however, that their real objective was to prevent Norris from becoming senator. If the Democrats could control the legislature, they could choose someone other than Norris for the post, despite their pledge to vote for the people's choice. This potential threat, however, did not materialize. Early in December the Democrats dropped their contest.[9]

Norris was too busy to pay much attention to these charges. Returning to McCook during the Christmas recess, he devoted most of his time to congressional matters, particularly the Archbald impeachment. He did not discuss politics, though McCarl assured him that he had nothing but good reports about members of the state legislature who would be meeting to choose a United States senator on January 22.[10]

By the end of the second week in January, things seemed "to be in mighty good shape"; the legislature would probably elect him without a hitch. Nevertheless, rumors were rampant. According to law and the personal pledge of many members, the legislature would have to vote for Norris, but for the first time since Nebraska adopted the "Oregon" pledge system in 1909, one house of the legislature was not of the same political persuasion as the people's choice for senator. The legislature would vote in joint session, and the fact that the Democrats outnumbered the Republicans seventy-one to sixty-two made observers anxious about Norris' selection. McCarl insisted that Norris be in Lincoln on January 22 to forestall by his presence any untoward action and, if none occurred, to address the legislature and promote political goodwill.[11]

At this time it was rumored that Norris might be appointed to Wilson's cabinet. This report may have helped to insure Norris' unanimous selection by the Nebraska legislature. In January, the New York *Times* announced that Wilson was considering placing a political opponent in his cabinet and that Norris was the opponent in question. Liberals in the Democratic party, especially those from New Jersey, argued that the progressives were largely responsible for recent changes in public sentiment on economic issues; placing a prominent exponent of their point of view in the cabinet might lead many such individuals into the Democratic party.[12] Norris was not appointed and never mentioned the suggestion, but the episode helped his election by the legislature to go smoothly even in his absence.

On January 21, the Nebraska legislative bodies, meeting separately, unanimously elected George Norris as United States senator from Nebraska. The next day in joint session they repeated the formality in an election which was significant in several ways. Norris was the first and only senator from Nebraska to receive the unanimous vote of the entire legislature. He was the first and only Republican to be elected by a Democratic legislature and the only senator in the history of the state to receive his election while absent from the state. His election, furthermore, was the last in which the Nebraska legislature elected a senator. Several months later the Seventeenth Amendment to the Constitution went into effect and direct election of senators became the established procedure.[13]

Members of the legislature who had not signed a pledge during the campaign, emphatically voted for Norris; others, who had supported him, spoke his full name "in sonorous tones that respectfully but emphatically expressed their joy at the happy culmination of his campaign." One Lincoln newspaper commented, "Never in the history of this state has a man gone to the United States Senate more closely identified with the people and possessing a larger degree of confidence on the part of the public, than Senator Norris." [14]

McCarl, who was present at these proceedings, summarized by saying "it was splendid." He reported that Democrats and Republicans vied with one another in lauding Norris, while visitors in the galleries and members on the floor applauded. A large group from the Fifth District, including old friends from Beaver City, were on hand for the ceremony and were prepared to give him a royal reception. But legislators and visitors were not totally disappointed by Norris' absence; the secretary of the senate read a letter he had written to the joint session expressing his gratitude for the confidence placed in him and apologizing for his absence.[15]

Norris was delighted with the reports he received of the proceedings in Lincoln. A number of things about his election seemed remarkable to him, especially when compared to the situation that had existed before the insurgency revolt and the broader progressive movement. He would enter the Senate with a clear conscience, beholden to no man. It gave him much pleasure to think that during the recent campaign, one of the most hotly contested in the history of the state, he had never been asked even indirectly to make any promise or pledge. No member of the legislature had approached him after the election with a suggestion that could in any way be construed as an effort to control his vote. Recalling the political bartering that had occurred in the past, Norris thought that all Nebraska citizens were to be congratulated. He was convinced that his efforts in Congress against boss rule and blind partisanship, in favor of progressive legislation and the restoration of governmental control to the people, had not been in vain. He appreciated the efforts that were made in his behalf because they represented a vindication of the democratic process and of popular government. Thus, having received support for his past efforts, he intended to continue to pursue the same path even though progressive-minded citizens were confused about their future course.[16]

Norris was keenly aware of the dispute raging among progressives concerning organization. As long as they remained divided, he felt they could accomplish little and hoped that all progressive-minded citizens would eventually unite in a separate party. But so great were the prevailing divisions and so bitter the feeling among numerous leaders that he did little to ally himself with the debilitated third party, though Roosevelt considered him a leading Progressive.[17]

Norris himself was confused about his political status. Preparing a biographical sketch for the forthcoming *Congressional Directory*, McCarl retained the word "Republican," though he was not sure of Norris' wishes on this matter. He told Norris he could change it, and suggested "Progressive-Republican" as a more satisfactory delineation. However, in the *Congressional Directory* for the first session of the Sixty-third Congress, Norris listed himself as a Republican.[18]

On February 17, 1913, Senator Norris Brown, recognizing the action of the Nebraska legislature, presented to the president pro tempore of the Senate, Jacob H. Gallinger of New Hampshire, the credentials of his successor and asked to have them read. The secretary of the Senate read the credentials of George Norris, chosen by the legislature of Nebraska as senator for the term beginning March 4, 1913, and they were ordered to be filed.[19] Two weeks later Norris' notable career as a member of Congress from the Fifth Congressional District of the state of Nebraska came to an end, and a more distinguished one—one that would span the following thirty years—began. As a congressman, Norris had proven himself one of the most forceful and intelligent fighters in the House, alert to every parliamentary opportunity to advance the progressive cause. Strong in debate, knowing neither fear nor favor, he had been a most valuable member. While his apprenticeship as a legislator had come to an end, the character, ideas, and approach to national problems of the senator-elect were already defined. The future years in the Senate of the United States would write in large letters on the national scene what was already evident in smaller print to the citizens of Nebraska. Thus Norris had gradually moved from a conservative Republican politician to a prominent progressive leader who, already entitled to historical notice for his role in the insurgency revolt, was destined to become one of the outstanding legislators in American history.

Notes to Chapters

NOTES TO CHAPTER 1 (pages 1–10)

1. Eugene Holloway Roseboom and Francis Phelps Weisenburger, *A History of Ohio* (New York, 1934), p. 171.

2. Eugene Holloway Roseboom, *The Civil War Era (1850–1873)*, Vol. IV of *The History of the State of Ohio* (Columbus, 1944). See map, p. 80.

3. Sherwood Anderson, *A Story Teller's Story* (New York, 1924), pp. 48–49.

4. Since both parents were unable to receive even a rudimentary education (they could scarcely write, though both could read), dates and facts as to their families and background are very vague. See for example, Alfred Lief, *Democracy's Norris* (New York, 1939), p. 11, where Chauncey Norris is born both in New York and in Connecticut. Norris, however, believed that his father was born in Connecticut and moved to Cayuga County after the death of his parents where Chauncey and his sisters were cared for by a German family named Martin. George W. Norris, *Fighting Liberal* (New York, 1946), p. 3. A pension claim filed by Mary Norris in 1893, as the mother of a deceased soldier under the terms of the Dependent Pension Act of 1890, stated that Chauncey Norris was born on May 21, 1809, in Cayuga County, New York. I have followed this statement. See John Henry Norris, Pension Claim, War Department Records, National Archives.

5. Norris, *op. cit.*, pp. 4, 14–15.

6. W. Dean Burnham, *Presidential Ballots 1836–1892* (Baltimore, 1955), pp. 692–93, 210.

7. Norris, *op. cit.*, p. 32.

8. Basil Meek (ed.), *Twentieth Century History of Sandusky County, Ohio* (Chicago, 1909), p. 270; John Henry Norris, *loc. cit.* John Henry had been engaged to a local girl, Lizzie Tuck, who apparently never married. Years later Norris wrote her, "I remember well the last time I saw you. It was at the old school house at Mt. Carmel, when I was quite a small boy, and I remember yet that I wondered then why you seemed to take such an interest in me, but learned in later years that it was the love you bore for my soldier brother whom I can scarcely remember." George Norris to Miss Tuck, January 15, 1900. George W. Norris Papers, Manuscripts Division, Library of Congress. Hereafter, unless otherwise noted, all manuscript citations are from this collection. See also Norris, *op. cit.*, pp. 27–28.

After his mother's death in 1900, Norris received and treasured his brother's watch. See Melissa Lowe to Norris, October 4, 1900.

9. Norris, *op. cit.*, pp. 7–8.

10. *Ibid.*, p. 11.

11. Marquis W. Childs, *I Write from Washington* (New York, 1942), pp. 38–39; Norris, *op. cit.*, pp. 18–19.

12. Norris, *op. cit.*, pp. 12–14.

13. *Ibid.*, p. 15. Jeanne Williamson, Chief Deputy Clerk of Courts, Sandusky County, Fremont, Ohio, to author, July 13, 1957.

14. Childs, *op. cit.*, p. 38.

15. Norris, *op. cit.*, p. 32; Lief, *op. cit.*, p. 18. Norris came from an area where some neighbors believed that Democrats could not go to heaven.

16. David Lindsey, "George W. Norris As A Student at Baldwin University," *Nebraska History*, Vol XXXIV, No. 2, June, 1953, p. 117. Most of my information about this phase of Norris' education comes from this article.

17. *Ibid.*, p. 118.

18. *Ibid.*, p. 120.

19. Norris to Mrs. W. H. (Cora Hall) Billing, July 29, 1942; Mrs. Billing to Norris, September 5, 1942.

20. Writers' Program of the Works Projects Administration in the State of Indiana, *Indiana: A Guide to the Hoosier State* (New York, 1941), p. 310.

21. Norris, *op. cit.*, p. 36.

22. Richard L. Neuberger and Stephen B. Kahn, *Integrity: The Life of George W. Norris* (New York, 1937), p. 17.

23. Norris, *op. cit.*, p. 144.

24. See Norris, *op. cit.*, pp. 39–40 for one account and Lief, *op. cit.*, pp. 29–30 for another. Lief in his account quotes Norris. Norris in these two volumes was dredging his memory, which on the whole was good, to recall these events. Few manuscripts exist for the period of his life prior to his residence in Beaver City, Nebraska. For Norris' eloquent tribute to the L.U.N. see the chapter devoted to it in his autobiography.

25. Lief, *op. cit.*, p. 34.

26. Norris, *op. cit.*, p. 52.

NOTES TO CHAPTER 2 (pages 11–19)

1. George W. Norris, *Fighting Liberal* (New York, 1946), p. 54.

2. Norris to A. M. Webster, August 10, 1889, Letterpress book; Webster to Norris, August 13, 1889, August 30, 1889. George W. Norris Papers, Manuscripts Division, Library of Congress. Unless otherwise noted, all manuscript citations are from this collection.

3. George Evert Condra, *Geography, Agriculture, Industries of Nebraska* (Lincoln, 1946). See map, p. 73.

4. Norris to H. J. Taylor, April 20, 1895.

5. So stated on the stationery of the Beaver City Board of Trade, G. W. Norris, Secretary.

6. Norris to Fletcher W. Merwin, March 26, 1914; Norris to Jesse Hadley, April 29, 1933; Norris to M. E. Cadwallader, January 17, 1939.

7. Norris to Melissa Lowe, February 12, 1889, Letter-press book.

8. Norris, *op. cit.*, p. 57.

9. Betty Jones to Alfred Lief, October 5, 1937; Norris, *op. cit.*, pp. 79–80. Norris refused, even in his autobiography, written when he was over eighty years of age, to name the friend who accidentally shot him.

10. Norris, *op. cit.*, p. 56.

11. W. F. Mappin, "Farm Mortgages and the Small Farmer," *Political Science Quarterly*, Vol. IV, No. 3, September, 1889, p. 435; Hallie Farmer, "The Economic Background of Frontier Populism," *Mississippi Valley Historical Review*, Vol. X, No. 4, March, 1924, p. 419. Mortgage companies served as middlemen in the making of loans. They sold their mortgages to other investors, such as insurance companies, savings banks, and individuals.

12. Mappin, *op. cit.*

13. J. P. Dunn, Jr., "The Mortgage Evil," *Political Science Quarterly*, Vol. V, No. 1, March, 1890, p. 78.

14. Fred S. James to Norris, April 11, 1889; George H. Smith to Norris, August 26, 1889; Albert Ottaway to Norris, December 16, 1889.

15. Norris to F. L. Wiseman, September 26, 1887, Letterpress book; Norris to Charles M. Sawyer, October 18, 1887, Letter-press book.

16. Norris to J. H. Dibben, October 29, 1887, Letter-press book; Vigilant Wholesale Creditors' Agency, J. A. Cavanagh, Attorney, to Norris, November 20, 1886. A contemporary writer noted that in western areas it was often difficult to obtain a loan at the high rate of 7½ per cent, and that 20 per cent of the entire amount of interest paid during the life of the mortgage would approximate the agent's commission. D. M. Frederiksen, "Mortgage Banking in America," *The Journal of Political Economy*, Vol. II, March, 1894, pp. 222, 228.

17. H. M. Marquis to Norris, June 8, 1889; Charles J. Bell (Omaha branch manager) to Norris, March 2, 1891; Thurber, Whyland & Company to Norris, March 21, 1889; Credit Guarantee Company to Norris, March 20, 1890; William Deering & Company to Norris, June 6, 1888.

18. Frank B. Stephens to Norris, July 2, 1890; Lamb, Ricketts & Wilson to Norris, April 12, 1890; Marquis to Norris, June 8, 1889.

19. According to the National Banking Act of 1863, national banks were not permitted to make mortgage loans on real estate, therefore this part of the business was handled by Miles separately from the authorized banking aspects.

20. Norris to J. H. Miles, May 29, 1889, Letter-press book; Norris to First National Bank (Rulo, Nebraska), December 5, 1889, Letter-press book.

21. Norris to First National Bank (Rulo), December 22, 1888, Letter-

press book; Norris to Mrs. Lowe, January 9, 1889, Letter-press book; Norris to Miles, January 12, 1889, Letter-press book.

22. Norris to Miles, March 19, 1889, May 29, 1889, Letter-press book; Norris to Mrs. Lowe, January 9, 1889, Letter-press book; Norris to Miles, April 5, 1889.

23. Norris to Miles, December 6, 1889, Letter-press book.

24. Norris to B. F. Cunningham, April 14, 1890, Letter-press book; Cunningham to Norris, April 12, 1890, April 16, 1890, April 18, 1890, July 2, 1890.

25. Miles to Norris, July 1, 1890.

26. Norris, *op. cit.*, pp. 81–82 and Lief, *op. cit.*, p. 38. Though both these volumes cite 1890 as the year of the marriage, Norris' correspondence indicates that it occurred in 1889. See, for example, C. H. Martin to Norris, June 8, 1889, in which Martin congratulates Norris and offers him advice in the form of trite poetry.

NOTES TO CHAPTER 3 (pages 20–26)

1. Hallie Farmer, "The Economic Background of Frontier Populism," *Mississippi Valley Historical Review*, Vol. X, No. 4, March, 1924, pp. 416, 418. Also see the charts in James C. Olson, *History of Nebraska* (Lincoln, 1955), pp. 216, 242.

2. G. W. Norris to Mrs. L. S. (Melissa N.) Lowe, September 28, 1894. George W. Norris Papers, Manuscripts Division, Library of Congress. Hereafter all manuscript citations, unless otherwise noted, are from this collection.

3. Farmer, *op. cit.*, p. 420.

4. *Nebraska Blue Book: 1948* (Lincoln, 1948), pp. 341, 342. The 1890 census stated that the average debt per Nebraska farm was $1,517.32. "Now it would not be safe to estimate the average value of these farms, even when well improved, was above, say, $25, an acre, so we can see what a large proportion on the average the debt on the mortgaged farm bears to their total value, being in fact considerably over one-third. With interest to pay on such a sum, and with the final payment to provide for, it is no wonder that the years of partial failure, always liable to occur in agriculture, become doubly discouraging to any but the most energetic farmer." Quote from Arthur F. Bentley, *The Economic History of a Nebraska Township* (Baltimore, 1893), pp. 61, 62. This volume provides an excellent study of Harrison township in Hall County in 1892 where conditions were very similar to those Norris encountered in nearby Furnas County.

5. B. F. Cunningham to Norris, September 5, 1890, October 15, 1890. The Bank of Rulo by mid-December, 1890, did over fifty-five thousand dollars worth of business ($34,251 in loans) while its deposits were more than forty-three thousand dollars. Cunningham to Norris, December 18, 1890.

6. Norris to Cunningham, July 16, 1891, April 30, 1892, Letter-press book. Cunningham to Norris, January 13, 1891, May 2, 1892; *Nebraska Blue Book: 1948*, p. 392 for statistics on annual and seasonal rainfall.

7. J. H. Miles to Norris, August 26, 1891, November 25, 1892, January 21, 1893, June 22, 1893.

8. In 1893 the average rainfall for western Nebraska was 9.87 inches, the lowest recorded figure for the years 1867–1947. In 1894 it was 11.15 inches. *Nebraska Blue Book: 1948*, p. 392.

9. Miles to Norris, October 11, 1894. Norris to Miles, July 20, 1894, December 29, 1894, July 18, 185, Letter-press books. It is interesting to note that their lengthy correspondence throughout these difficult years contains no comments about free silver agitation among the people with whom Norris comes in contact, though political comments are interspersed throughout their letters.

10. Norris to C. C. Chapman, December 23, 1890, Letter-press book; Norris to Peter Foland, February 6, 1891, Letter-press book; Norris to Mrs. E. G. Armstrong, September 11, 1894, Letter-press book; Norris to Mrs. Lowe, September 28, 1894, Letter-press book; Norris to Messrs. Estey & Camp, June 14, 1894, Letter-press book; Norris to R. G. Dun & Co., November 17, 1894, Letter-press book; Norris to O. C. Sands, May 31, 1895, Letter-press book; L. D. Hollingsworth to Norris, February 27, 1891; Milo I. Whitman to Norris, September, 1891.

11. Wright & Stout to Norris, December 30, 1891; George W. Moore & Co. to Norris, November 8, 1892; Norris to Rock Island Stove Company, April 16, 1894, Letter-press book.

12. Burnham, Trevett & Mattis to Norris, October 17, 1891, March 17, 1892, November 8, 1892, July 26, 1894, March 9, 1895, June 4, 1895.

13. Norris to Stanley E. Filkins, November 30, 1890, March 13, 1894, Letter-press book; Filkins to Norris, May 8, 1894, July 27, 1894, October 6, 1894, December 12, 1894, February 11, 1895.

14. J. A. Cavanagh (President, Snow, Church & Company, Omaha office) to Norris, March 22, 1893, April 5, 1893, May 26, 1893; Norris to Snow, Church & Company (Omaha), May 24, 1893; Letter-press book.

15. Norris to Cunningham, February 4, 1891, Letter-press book; G. W. Clawson to Norris, November 10, 1890; A. Q. Miller to Norris, May 28, 1891; Will H. McShane to Norris, April 9, 1894; Norris to J. W. Brown, May 26, 1894; Norris to Alexander Robinson, April 2, 1894; Letter-press book; Norris to M. S. Stoner, April 2, 1894, Letter-press book; Norris to L. H. Lashley, April 18, 1892, Letter-press book; Norris to Treasurer, Decatur County, Oberlin, Kansas, February 28, 1893; Norris to Treasurer, Norton County, Norton, Kansas; Norris to Newton C. Johnson, November 12, 1894, Letter-press book.

16. Foland to Norris, July 27, 1894; E. Sanford to Norris, May 29, 1891, September 23, 1891; P. W. Price to Norris, July 8, 1895; L. P. Miller to Norris, January 27, 1893; Price to Norris, July 22, 1895; Norris to Mrs. Lowe, October 24, 1894, Letter-press book.

17. Norris to Arieadne (Lashley) Andrus, January 24, 1895, February 2, 1895, February 15, 1895, Letter-press book; W. M. Davies to Norris, April 17, 1895; A. A. Meeker to Norris, December 16, 1895; Norris to H. J. Taylor, April 20, 1895, Letter-press book.

18. Norris to W. B. Colvin, January 19, 1893, January 24, 1893, February 22, 1893, Letter-press books; Norris to Miles, June 20, 1893, Letter-press book.

19. Norris to Paxton & Vireling, April 1, 1893, Letter-press book; E. E. Jones to Norris, May 30, 1893; Miles to Norris, June 17, 1893; Norris to Miles, June 20, 1893, July 1, 1893, Letter-press books; Miles to Norris, June 22, 1893.

20. Norris to Schneider & Scheurer, August 23, 1893, Letter-press book; Norris to Frank H. Jones (First Assistant Postmaster General), October 9, 1893, Letter-press book; Muscatine Sash and Door Company to Norris, October 28, 1893; Norris to Filkins, February 22, 1894, Letter-press book.

21. Miles to Norris, October 31, 1893; Walter H. Green (Massachusetts Mutual Life Insurance Company) to Norris, March 29, 1895; H. S. Ford (New York Life Insurance Company) to Norris, April 18, 1895; Norris to Miles, April 23, 1895, Letter-press book; Norris to A. T. Lardin, June 26, 1895, Letter-press book.

22. Norris to Lardin, June 26, 1895, Letter-press book; Norris to Miles, July 18, 1895, Letter-press book; Lardin to Norris, June 28, 1895, July 5, 1895; H. H. Harrington to Norris, November 25, 1895.

NOTES TO CHAPTER 4 (pages 27–37)

1. A similar analysis, in accord with my findings, is succinctly presented in James C. Olson, *History of Nebraska* (Lincoln, 1955), p. 244.

2. George W. Norris, *Fighting Liberal* (New York, 1946), p. 61.

3. B. F. Cunningham to Norris, October 18, 1890; J. L. Lashbrook to Norris, December 19, 1890; George W. Norris Papers, Division of Manuscripts, Library of Congress. Unless otherwise noted all manuscript citations are from this collection.

Alfred Lief in his biography, written while Norris was still alive and available for consultation, states that with the large number of desertions to the Populist party in 1890 there were only two Republican lawyers left in Furnas County, hence his nomination and influence in Republican affairs. See Alfred Lief, *Democracy's Norris* (New York, 1939), pp. 39–40.

4. J. E. Cochran to Norris, September 25, 1891; D. T. Welty to Norris, September 6, 1891; Norris, *op. cit.*, pp. 62–63.

5. W. S. Morlan to Norris, December 12, 1892, January 1, 1893; Norris to George H. Crosby, May 26, 1894, Letter-press book. Norris wrote to Crosby, "I am the local attorney for the B & M and, of course, can not take a case against the Company." However, as a member of the Beaver City Board of Trade, Norris was prepared on behalf of commissioners to commence proceedings against the Burlington and Missouri in order to compel

the company to put in a crossing on the main line west of Oxford so that wagons and other traffic could cross the tracks on a more direct route to Beaver City. See Norris to B. V. Haley, July 6, 1894.

6. Norris to J. H. Sherwood, September 28, 1892, Letter-press book.

7. By comparing the number of voters in this and the previous two presidential elections, the reader can obtain an idea of how the drought and financial stringency affected the county. In 1884, the year before Norris arrived, 1,229 votes were cast; in 1888, when Norris voted for Harrison and the boom period had not fully collapsed, 2,100 votes were cast. In 1892 the figure was 2,125, an increase of twenty-five voters in four years. See W. Dean Burnham, *Presidential Ballots: 1836–1892* (Baltimore, 1955), p. 609.

8. Mrs. Anna George to Norris, July 14, 1891; William M. Arnold to Norris, November 9, 1892; W. M. Ward to Norris, November 10, 1892; J. E. Cochran to Norris, November 10, 1892; Frank H. Selby to Norris, November 11, 1892; Norris to Geneva National Bank, December 3, 1892; S. B. Moore to Norris, May 17, 1893, June 3, 1893; Sherwood to Norris, July 16, 1899; Edward Alstat to Norris, November 15, 1894; Norris to M. Z. Taylor, March 16, 1899.

9. E. N. Allen to Norris, July 2, 1894; T. A. Boyd to Norris, July 9, 1894; Morlan to Norris, August 9, 1894, August 17, 1894; Perry L. Hole to Norris, August 16, 1894.

10. Addison Erwin Sheldon, *Nebraska: The Land and the People* (Chicoga, 1931), pp. 738–40, for a discussion of the year in Nebraska.

11. A. M. Robbins to Norris, August 4, 1894; Sheldon, *op. cit.*, pp. 744–46.

12. Norris to First National Bank of Buchanan County (St. Joseph, Missouri), May 10, 1895, Letter-press book; Norris to Noyes, Norman & Co., March, 1895, Letter-press book.

13. Norris to C. D. Fuller, January 26, 1895, Letter-press book; Norris to F. M. Rathbun, February 6, 1895, Letter-press book; Norris to R. C. Orr, February 11, 1895, Letter-press book.

14. Norris to Boyd, February 27, 1895, Letter-press book; Rathbun to Norris, August 31, 1895; J. A. Green to Norris, August 31, 1895; Hole to Norris, September 7, 1895.

15. A. V. Perry to Norris, September 15, 1895; Norris to J. H. Miles, September 16, 1895, Letter-press book.

16. D. T. Welty to Norris, September 19, 1895.

17. James A. Cline to Norris, October 23, 1895.

18. J. W. Tomblin to Norris, September (no date), 1895; S. R. Smith to Norris, November 8, 1895. Several days later Smith explained his activities in detail: "I may possibly have gone farther than I should in the expense matter, without consulting you, but I did not know just where to reach you at any time, and men would come to me at the last moment and say, now for $5 or $10 or so & so we can do so & so, and I simply placed myself in your position and did what I would have liked that you would

do under the same circumstance. In order to show you that my work was quite effectual let me cite to you certain precincts in this county where my influence went out. Mo. Ridge is the strongest pop precinct in the County save one, the balance of the State Republican ticket ran 5 to 6 votes. You received 16. My German friends were at home that day. In Fritsch precinct the usual Republican vote is 10 to 12. Your vote this year was 20. In Indianola precinct a hard fight for both yourself and Judge Noval was made you ran 4 ahead of Noval, 11 ahead of the highest vote on the balance of the state ticket and 23 ahead of the highest vote on the county ticket."

19. Charles W. Meeker to Norris, October 12, 1895; W. R. Starr to Norris, October 18, 1895.

20. S. R. Smith to Norris, October 26, 1895. Typewritten memo, p. 7, George W. Norris Papers, Nebraska State Historical Society, Lincoln, Nebraska.

21. Lief, *op. cit.*, pp. 45–47, for press comment on the campaign.

22. A. T. Lardin to Norris, November 7, 1895; Henry Rice to Norris, November 7, 1895; George C. Eisenhart to Norris, November 7, 1895; Charles W. Meeker to Norris, November 8, 1895; J. A. Williams to C. E. Hopping, November 8, 1895; Hole to Norris, November 14, 1895.

23. Norris to S. R. Smith, November 11, 1895, Letter-press book; Eisenhart to Norris, November 16, 1895, December 3, 1895, December 5, 1895.

24. Hole to Norris, November 13, 1895; Charles W. Meeker to Norris, December 6, 1895; J. A. Williams to Norris, December 12, 1895; J. A. Lynch (Sheriff) to Norris, December 16, 1895; Norris, *op. cit.*, pp. 65–67.

25. S. R. Smith to Norris, November 15, 1895; Norris to Miles, November 12, 1895, Letter-press book.

26. Lief, *op. cit.*, p. 37. See also affidavits of Norris and two members of the Furnas County canvassing board in 1895 which were printed before election day in 1899, when Norris sought a second term as judge in Beaver Valley *Tribune*, November, 3, 1899, as well as in other papers throughout the eight-county judicial district.

27. Lincoln *State Journal*, November 30, 1895.

28. The Secretary of State of Nebraska did not file the oath of office left by Welty as judge of the Fourteenth Judicial District. He returned it to him claiming that he had already issued a certificate of election to Norris as judge-elect of that judicial district. See J. A. Piper to Norris, January 8, 1896.

29. Welty dismissed the action primarily because it was bankrupting him and his supporters would not or could not come to his aid. Norris had some knowledge of Welty's financial predicament, which was similar to his own, before he went to Lincoln. See M. C. Reynolds to Norris, February 23, 1896; Eisenhart to Norris, February 22, 1896; Henry Lehman to Norris, March 31, 1896.

30. Norris, *op. cit.*, pp. 64–65. Charles W. Meeker to Norris, January 22, 1896; L. H. Cheney to Norris, January 22, 1896; Norris to A. P. Van

Burgh, January 25, 1896; Eisenhart to Norris, December 3, 1895, December 5, 1895, January 16, 1896, February (no date), 1896, February 22, 1896, for evidence that Eisenhart and others were tracking down further evidence of fraud until literally the very moment Welty gave up the fight.

31. Norris to S. O. Simonds, January 31, 1896, Letter-press book.

32. Norris to W. E. Andrews, January 11, 1896, Letter-press book; Norris to George W. Post, September 4, 1896; Lardin to Norris, December 31, 1895.

NOTES TO CHAPTER 5 (pages 38-45)

1. G. W. Norris to D. M. Ure, September 4, 1896; Norris to Mrs. Melissa N. Lowe, September 6, 1897; Norris to A. Campbell, October 9, 1897; George W. Norris Papers, Manuscripts Division, Library of Congress. Unless otherwise noted all manuscript citations are from this collection.

2. Jeanne Williamson, Chief Deputy, Clerk of Courts, Sandusky County, Fremont, Ohio, to author, July 13, 1957.

3. See John Henry Norris, Pension Claim, War Department Records, National Archives. Claim was filed by Mary Norris in 1893.

4. Solomon Mook to Norris, March 1, 1896; Norris to Mrs. Lowe, January 7, 1897.

5. Mrs. Lowe to Norris, June 30, 1897, September 26, 1897, November 26, 1897; Norris to Mrs. Lowe, May 4, 1898, June 21, 1898; Norris to D. R. Limbocker, October 8, 1898.

6. Norris to John M. Smuth Company, June 11, 1897; Norris to The Harvey & Watts Company, November 21, 1897; Norris to Baker Boyles Shoe Company, January 6, 1899.

7. Norris to Clara Wheeler, March 30, 1891, Letter-press book; Norris to Colfax Mineral Water Company, August 28, 1892, Letter-press book; Norris to Brunswick-Balke-Callender Company, December 26, 1891, Letter-press book.

8. West Publishing Company to Norris, January 8, 1896 and January 15, 1896.

9. Norris to *North American Review*, June 5, 1888, Letter-press book; Norris to Toledo *Blade*, November 16, 1893, Letter-press book; Norris to *State Journal* Company, July 30, 1898; Norris to Honolulu *Advertiser*, July 18, 1898.

10. Norris to Perry L. Hole, September 24, 1896; Norris to Brother (a fellow member of the IOOF), September 25, 1896.

11. Norris to Hole, March 17, 1897; Norris to Charles Bailey, March 24, 1897; Norris to L. H. Blackledge, February 2, 1899; Norris to George Williams, February 20, 1899; Norris to E. N. Rakestraw, April 15, 1899; Norris to Dr. Lucas, April 29, 1899; Norris to W. S. Morlan, April 29, 1899.

12. Hole to Norris, July 1, 1899; Norris to A. H. Andrus, August 21, 1897; Norris to Rakestraw, April 15, 1899.

13. Mrs. Lowe to Norris, May 29, 1893; Norris to F. C. Schroeder, June 6, 1898; Grant D. Harrington to Norris, November 20, 1897; Norris to Morland, November 16, 1897; Norris to C. L. Kinney, February 17, 1898; Norris to Mrs. Lowe, May 4, 1898; William A. Poynter (Governor) to Norris, November 13, 1899; Norris to Poynter, November 24, 1899.

14. E. A. Armstrong Company to Norris, July 22, 1892; J. E. Coapar to Norris, December 8, 1892; J. A. Miller to Norris, March 18, 1896; Norris to George C. Eisenhart, January 8, 1897; Norris to Hole, September 16, 1897, September 10, 1899; Norris to C. K. Wilbur, July 21, 1898; Norris to I. P. Gage, October 7, 1898.

15. Norris to Mrs. Lowe, January 7, 1897, Letter-press book.

16. Norris to Mrs. Lowe, January 7, 1897, Letter-press book. By July, 1898, he had paid back most of the money he had borrowed from her. See Norris to Mrs. Lowe, July 25, 1898.

17. Norris to W. S. Colvin, July 15, 1896; Stull Brothers to Norris, October 31, 1896; R. E. Moore to Norris, October 31, 1896; Norris to J. W. Tomblin, November 12, 1896, Letter-press book.

18. Norris to H. C. Fletcher, March 27, 1897; Norris to J. E. Axtell, April 14, 1898; Norris to E. A. Wyatt, July 27, 1897; Norris to A. Lofgreen, February 23, 1898; Norris to Secretary of Agriculture, December 26, 1897.

19. Norris to J. W. Thayer, January 6, 1898, March 9, 1899; Norris to Daniel Bisbee, December 12, 1899; Norris to J. W. Holt, February 2, 1898; Norris to Arie Andrus, February 3, 1898; Norris to J. H. Miles, February 17, 1898, April 8, 1898, May 4, 1898.

20. Norris to M. J. Evans, August 11, 1897; Norris to Mrs. Eva Kenestrick, September 28, 1897; Hole to Norris, March 1, 1898; Norris to Holt, July 28, 1899.

21. Norris to Albert Andrus, January 18, 1897.

22. Norris to Miles, March 15, 1898; Norris to W. B. Whitney, March 28, 1898.

23. Norris to Frank Neubauer, December 12, 1898; Norris to George Zulauf, December 12, 1898; Norris to C. P. Lashley, February 14, 1899; Norris to Creamery Package Company, February 2, 1899; Norris to Rakestraw, April 15, 1899; Norris to Miles, March 30, 1899; Norris to Nordyke & Marmon Company, June 5, 1899.

24. G. W. Shafer to T. J. Cress, June 24, 1899; Norris to W. P. Slocum, June 24, 1899; Norris to Cress, June 30, 1899; Norris to Miles, July 24, 1899.

25. Norris to W. W. Tallman, September 11, 1899, December 18, 1899, December 28, 1899.

26. H. H. Harrington to Norris, January 26, 1896; A. T. Lardin to Norris, March 30, 1896, May 23, 1896; Norris to Lardin, October 8, 1896; Norris to E. E. Smith, January 12, 1897; Norris to A. J. Cole, November 9, 1899; Fleming Brothers (Western managers of Mutual Life Insurance Company of New York) to Norris, November 24, 1899.

NOTES TO CHAPTER 6 (pages 46–54)

1. George W. Norris, *Fighting Liberal* (New York, 1946), p. 69.
2. *Ibid.*, p. 69.
3. Mark De Wolfe Howe, *Justice Oliver Wendell Holmes: The Shaping Years 1841–1870* (Cambridge, Massachusetts, 1957), Vol. I, p. 278. Holmes' review appeared in *The American Law Review*, Vol. III, January, 1869, p. 357.
4. I have relied heavily for the material in this paragraph upon the insights contained in William Dudley Foulke, *A Hoosier Autobiography* (New York, 1922), p. 42. For the quote by Oliver Wendell Holmes, see Howe, *op. cit.*, p. 250.
5. Norris to F. C. Krotter, July 23, 1896, Letter-press book; George W. Norris Papers, Manuscripts Division, Library of Congress. Unless otherwise noted all manuscript citations are from this collection.
6. E. J. Dudley to Norris, May 17, 1896; Norris to A. E. Baller, December 31, 1897; Norris to J. D. Shahan, March 9, 1899.
7. Norris, *op. cit.*, p. 70.
8. *Ibid.*, pp. 70–71.
9. W. F. Button to Norris, January 13, 1896; W. S. Morlan to Norris, February 2, 1896; F. M. Flausburg to Norris, February 3, 1896; F. B. Sheldon and E. E. Harden to Norris, February 6, 1896; N. S. Harwood to Norris, February 7, 1896; Norris to H. W. Sipe, November 27, 1896, Letter-press book.
10. L. H. Cheney to Norris, January 22, 1896; T. L. Warrington to Norris, January 23, 1896; J. W. Hann to Norris, March 10, 1896; Norris to J. E. Cochran, August 5, 1896.
11. Harlow W. Keyes to Norris, October 2, 1896; Norris, *op. cit.*, pp. 72–77; Alfred Lief, *Democracy's Norris* (New York, 1939), pp. 48–51.
12. Morlan to Norris, July 29, 1896, December 15, 1896.
13. Norris to W. E. Andrews, January 11, 1896, Letter-press book.
14. Norris to Andrews, July 15, 1896.
15. G. W. Meiklejohn to Norris, January 21, 1896; D. F. Smith to Norris, February 6, 1896; A. C. Wright to Norris, March 24, 1896; Lon Cone to Norris, April 6, 1896; Norris to Charles F. Manderson, September 21, 1896; Norris to G. W. Post, September 4, 1896; Post to Norris, September 8, 1896.
16. Norris to A. T. Lardin, November 27, 1896; Norris to John M. Thurston, November 27, 1896.
17. John H. Christner to Norris, October 18, 1897; Norris to Andrews, September 16, 1897; A. E. Sheldon, *Nebraska: The Land and the People* (Chicago, 1931), p. 767.
18. H. H. Taylor to Norris, November 5, 1897; H. A. Rowe to Norris, November 8, 1897.

19. Norris to H. H. Taylor, November 11, 1897; for the Bartley and Moore matter see A. E. Sheldon, *op. cit.*, pp. 767, 772–73, 788, 810.

20. Norris to M. L. Hayward, July 2, 1898; Norris to W. V. Van Patten, February 15, 1899. Hayward, elected in 1899, died before he could be sworn in as a senator and the governor chose the defeated candidate, Populist W. V. Allen, to serve until a special election could be held; Norris to G. H. Thummel, October 22, 1898.

21. I. P. Gage to Norris, September 3, 1898; Perry L. Hole to Norris, February 10, 1899.

NOTES TO CHAPTER 7 (pages 55–62)

1. G. W. Norris to Perry L. Hole, February 15, 1899; George Williams to Norris, February 22, 1899, George W. Norris Papers, Manuscripts Division, Library of Congress. Unless otherwise noted all manuscript citations are from this collection.

2. Norris to P. W. Scott, July 7, 1899.

3. George Eisenhart to Norris, August 1, 1899; Norris to Eisenhart, August 16, 1899.

4. Eisenhart to Norris, August 20, 1899; Norris to A. A. White, September 7, 1899; Norris to Scott, September 8, 1899.

5. Scott to Norris, September 10, 1899.

6. L. H. Cheney to Norris, September 19, 1899; Norris to G. W. Dow, September 11, 1899; Norris to J. L. McPheeley, September 11, 1899.

7. O. L. Burson to Norris, October 12, 1899; Charles W. Meeker to Norris, October 7, 1899; C. C. Vennum to Norris, October 27, 1899.

8. Vennum to Norris, October 27, 1899, October 28, 1899.

9. Vennum to Norris, October 31, 1899; Williams to Norris, October 28, 1899.

10. C. W. Meeker to Norris, October 31, 1899; Vennum to Norris, October 31, 1899.

11. Vennum to Norris, October 31, 1899.

12. Williams to Norris, November 8, 1899; D. T. Welty to Norris, November 10, 1899.

13. Norris to F. I. Foss, November 13, 1899; Norris to Stanley E. Filkins, November 24, 1899; Norris to Hole, December 12, 1899.

14. Norris to Welty, November 13, 1899; Statement and Affidavit of Election Expenses, Notarized November 13, 1899.

15. Cyrus E. Watson, *Nebraska's Industries and Resources* (Lincoln, 1902), pp. 138, 230–31; See Norris to Lizzie Tuck, March 10, 1900, where Norris gives his reason for moving to McCook.

16. Norris to C. H. Wilson, February 13, 1900, May 5, 1900; Norris to J. F. Fults, April 7, 1900; Norris to O. E. Champe, April 19, 1900; Norris to W. L. Leonard, May 3, 1900.

17. Norris to M. F. Doud, April 19, 1900.

18. Norris to J. W. Gull, July 25, 1900.

19. Norris to Williams, July 7, 1900; Norris to J. W. Holt, June 23, 1900.

20. Norris to Judge of Probate Court, Fremont, Ohio, June 11, 1900; Mrs. Melissa N. Lowe to Norris, October 4, 1900.

21. Roscoe Lashley to Norris, August 14, 1900; Norris to A. A. McCoy, August 16, 1900. The dry weather and the failure of the wheat crop bankrupted W. W. Tallman who had rented the Beaver City mill owned by Norris and Shafer. In mid-October it was leased to another tenant. See Norris to Western Mutual Millers Insurance Company, October 12, 1900.

22. Norris to R. C. Orr, September 9, 1900; Norris to T. A. Boyd, September 9, 1900.

23. Norris to Charles M. Riggs, September 11, 1900; Norris to J. O. Hane, September 10, 1900.

24. Norris to Riggs, September 11, 1900; Norris to H. C. Lindsay, October 25, 1900; Norris to C. H. Dietrich, January 11, 1901; Norris to C. A. Ferrand, November 3, 1900.

25. Norris to C. E. Hopping, November 21, 1900; Norris to John M. Thurston, December 27, 1900; Wilson to Norris, November 10, 1900; Norris to J. H. Miles, November 24, 1900, December 21, 1900.

NOTES TO CHAPTER 8 (pages 63–70)

1. G. W. Norris to F. I. Foss, January 18, 1901; E. N. Allen to Norris, January 17, 1901; Norris to Allen, January 31, 1901. George W. Norris papers, Manuscripts Division, Library of Congress. Unless otherwise noted, all manuscript citations are from this collection.

2. Norris to H. M. Sullivan, February 2, 1901; Norris to J. W. Holt, March 11, 1901; Norris to W. F. Wood, March 6, 1901.

3. A. J. Green to Norris, March 29, 1901, March 31, 1901.

4. Emma McKean to Norris, April 8, 1901; Norris to G. W. Holdrege, April 14, 1901; Mrs. A. J. Green to Norris, May 5, 1901.

5. Arie Andrus to Norris, May 22, 1901, July 15, 1901.

6. A. J. Green to Norris, July 1, 1901; Perry L. Hole to Norris, June 5, 1901; Norris to Thomas Kirtley, July 9, 1901; Sara S. Harrington to Norris, July 22, 1901; Norris to W. A. McCarl, August 23, 1901; Norris to Arie Andrus, May 29, 1901.

7. Norris to J. C. Gammill, April 25, 1901; Norris to J. H. Miles, April 13, 1901.

8. Norris to C. H. Dietrich, September 30, 1901.

9. Norris to Dietrich, September 30, 1901; Norris to Fletcher W. Merwin, September 30, 1901; Norris to A. Bonham, October 3, 1901; Norris to C. C. Green, November 6, 1901.

10. Norris to Hole, December 9, 1901.

11. Norris to Miles, November 19, 1901, June 5, 1902; Norris to Fred D. Webster, April 1, 1902; Norris to Mrs. Knowles, February 5, 1902.

12. Norris to T. Sumney, November 25, 1901; Norris to G. W. Shafer,

November 25, 1901; Norris to A. P. Hyatt, June 3, 1902; Norris to Stanley E. Filkins, January 30, 1902.

13. Ella Leonard to Norris, January 28, 1902; Norris to H. J. Thorpe, April 29, 1902.

14. Fletcher W. Merwin to Norris, February 6, 1902.

15. Merwin to Norris, February 6, 1902; Norris to Merwin, February 10, 1902.

16. Norris to Walker Smith, February 11, 1902; Norris to George Judkins, February 14, 1902.

17. Norris to H. M. Grimes, February 11, 1902, February 15, 1902.

18. Norris to C. H. Tanner, March 10, 1902; Norris to E. C. Shobell, March 25, 1902.

19. Norris to A. J. Green, April 1, 1902; Norris to Merwin, April 1, 1902; Norris to Mrs. Watie Van Patten, April 8, 1902.

20. Norris to Walker Smith, May 3, 1902; Norris to Merwin, May 13, 1902.

21. Merwin to Norris, May 12, 1902; Norris to Hole, May 13, 1902.

22. Nebraska *State Journal*, May 21, 1902; Norris to Walker Smith, May 20, 1902; Norris to Hole, May 21, 1902.

23. Norris to John Sanders, June 3, 1902; Norris to W. A. McCool, June 4, 1902; H. M. Crane to Norris, June 12, 1902; Nebraska *State Journal*, June 11, 1902.

24. *Nebraska Blue Book: 1948* (Lincoln, 1945), p. 392.

25. Norris to Crane, June 18, 1902. Norris at first thought the chairman of the congressional committee should be a resident of Hastings which seemed to him "by common consent to be the capital of the district," but on account of the many factional differences there he soon concluded that he could not select anyone there who would prove satisfactory to all of the Republicans even of Hastings. He offered the position to E. G. Titus of Holdrege before finally choosing Merwin. See G. W. Norris to E. G. Titus, June 21, 1902.

26. Norris to F. J. Coates, June 19, 1902.

27. Norris to S. C. Brady, June 25, 1902; Norris to J. D. Stine, June 26, 1902.

NOTES TO CHAPTER 9 (pages 71–78)

1. George W. Norris to C. W. Lindsay, July 28, 1902; George W. Norris Papers, Manuscripts Division, Library of Congress. Unless otherwise noted, all manuscript citations are from this collection.

2. Norris to Elliott Lowe, July 1, 1902.

3. Norris to C. P. Schwer, July 22, 1902; Norris to W. B. Ireland, August 19, 1902; Norris to M. B. Carman, September 16, 1902; Norris to J. S. Hoagland, September 20, 1902.

4. J. M. Hollingsworth to Norris, September 24, 1902; E. V. Overman

to Norris, September 29, 1902, October 17, 1902; A. Galusha to Norris, October 17, 1902.

5. Norris to G. W. Holdrege, July 10, 1902.

6. The Swanson Reservoir near Trenton in Hitchcock County was completed after World War II.

7. Norris to E. A. Hitchcock, August 15, 1902; Norris to H. C. Lindsay, August 15, 1902; Norris to C. H. Dietrich, August 15, 1902.

8. Dietrich to Norris, September 29, 1902.

9. Dietrich to Norris, August 2, 1902.

10. Dietrich to Norris, August 8, 1902, August 10, 1902, August 14, 1902; A. H. Clarke to Dietrich, August 9, 1902 (copy in Norris papers).

11. Norris to Dietrich, August 30, 1902; W. S. Shallenberger to Dietrich, September 4, 1902.

12. Dietrich to Norris, September 23, 1902, September 28, 1902, September 29, 1902, October 17, 1902, October 21, 1902; Norris to C. W. McConaughy, September 20, 1902; J. L. Lashbrook to Norris, September 29, 1902.

13. Norris to J. W. Babcock, September 8, 1902; Norris, *Fighting Liberal* (New York, 1946), p. 93.

14. Typewritten résumé of the early career of Norris, p. 8, for information about Champ Clark. George W. Norris Papers, Nebraska Historical Society, Lincoln, Nebraska; David H. Mercer to Norris, October 17, 1902; Harlow W. Keyes to Norris, October 18, 1902; Norris, *op. cit.*, pp. 90–91. The Republican press in the district unmercifully attacked Shallenberger's banking connections. For example, the Superior *Journal*, in its issue of July 10, 1902, asked, "Will Congressman Shallenberger take his name out of the list of officers in his bank advertisement in his home paper this year? He resorted to this cheap trick two years ago." This same paper also argued on its editorial page on August 7, 1902, "The result of the elections in November can not change the complexion of either branch of Congress; both will remain Republican. The Fifth Nebraska District consequently should make sure to send up a representative belonging to the dominant party, who can accomplish something for the district after he is elected." See also editorial on September 4, 1902.

15. Norris to F. B. Johnson, August 30, 1902; Norris to J. W. Hamm, September 27, 1902; Norris to J. R. Mercer, September 27, 1902; George Eisenhart to A. T. McCoy, September 27, 1902. Norris received the support of many small town Republican newspapers of which the following are a partial listing: the Superior *Journal*, the Hildreth *Telescope*, the Holdrege *Citizen*, the Edgar *Post*, the Oxford *Standard*, the Franklin *Free Press*, the Benkelman *News*, the Alma *Journal* in Shallenberger's home town, the Cambridge *Clarion*, the Hastings *Tribune*, the McCook *Republican*, and the McCook *Tribune*.

16. Norris, *op. cit.*, p. 90.

17. George A. Allen to Norris, September 26, 1902, October 3, 1902.

Typewritten résumé of the early career of Norris, p. 8. Copy in Nebraska Historical Society. For Welty's statement see the Benkelman *News,* October 17, 1902.

18. Will Brookley to Fletcher W. Merwin, September 30, 1902, October 9, 1902; A. B. Allen to Norris, October 8, 1902, October 9, 1902, October 13, 1902; Galusha to Norris, October 17, 1902; J. B. Dinsmore to Norris, October 8, 1902; Keyes to Norris, October 18, 1902.

19. W. W. Campbell to Norris, October 23, 1902.

20. George A. Allen to Norris, October 23, 1902. See also the Franklin *Free Press,* October 24, 1902, for an account of Norris' position on national issues. In addition to following the administration on pertinent national issues, Norris in a speech before a veterans' reunion favored the direct election of United States senators and complained about American millionaires and heiresses spending so much time and money in Europe. The Franklin *Free Press,* August 22, 1902.

21. Allen to Norris, October 24, 1902, October 25, 1902; Norris, *op. cit.,* pp. 90–91. Two of Shallenberger's brothers owned banks in the district: one at Elwood and the other at Imperial, while another of his brothers was an official of the International Harvester Company in Chicago. This third brother, a writer for the Lincoln *Daily Star* assured Norris, was not interested in the re-election of his brother to Congress. A charge of this kind to be effective had to be backed by evidence, and the writer urged Norris to secure such evidence "by persuasion, if possible, but beg, steal or borrow it, and use dynamite if necessary." See G. W. Bemis to Norris, December 10, 1902.

22. Allen to Norris, November 1, 1902, November 5, 1902; W. W. Campbell to G. W. Norris, November 11, 1902.

23. A. E. Sheldon, *Nebraska: The Land and the People* (Chicago, 1931), p. 796; Norris to A. R. Cruzen, December 5, 1902; Norris to A. J. Halford, December 10, 1902.

24. James A. Cline to Norris, November 6, 1902; George R. Chaney to Norris, November 5, 1902; Dietrich and J. H. Millard to Norris, November 5, 1902; J. S. and W. V. Hoagland to Norris, November 7, 1902.

25. Merwin to Norris, November 10, 1902, December 6, 1902.

26. Allen to Norris, November 10, 1902; W. W. Campbell to Norris, November 11, 1902.

27. Most Republican newspapers in the district believed along with the Oxford *Standard* (clipping, n.d.) that "old General Prosperity and a big crop have this year emblazoned a way to Republican success."

NOTES TO CHAPTER 10 (pages 79–87)

1. G. W. Norris to D. S. Hasty, July 14, 1902; Norris to G. W. Shafer, September 16, 1902; Norris to C. S. Graham, November 24, 1902; Norris to C. O. Morse, January 24, 1903, January 30, 1903; Norris to Mill Own-

ers' Mutual Insurance Company (Des Moines, Iowa), April 4, 1903; Norris to C. H. Pierce, June 6, 1903. George W. Norris Papers, Manuscripts Division, Library of Congress. All manuscript citations, unless otherwise noted, are from this collection.

2. Norris to J. F. Fults, December 28, 1902; Norris to C. E. Hopping, June 8, 1903, September 6, 1903.

3. Norris to May & Feiberger, April 17, 1903; Norris to I. P. Gage, September 20, 1902; Norris to Fleming Brothers, October 27, 1902; Norris to E. T. McGuire, December 6, 1902; Norris to M. T. Phelps, August 30, 1902.

4. Norris to Andrew Carnegie, June 12, 1903.

5. Norris to H. C. Miller, December 29, 1902; Miller to Norris, January 12, 1903.

6. Miller to Norris, May 3, 1903; Norris to Miller, May 2, 1903; Fletcher W. Merwin to A. T. Lardin, May 18, 1903.

7. Merwin to J. W. Eby, May 9, 1903; Merwin to Lardin, May 18, 1903; Merwin to W. D. Pruitt, May 5, 1903.

8. W. E. Horton to Norris, May 29, 1903; C. C. Green to Norris, May 30, 1903.

9. Norris, *Fighting Liberal* (New York, 1946), pp. 83–85. Norris wrote this account in which he stresses his loss of will to live after his heartbreaking defeat in 1942 by Kenneth Wherry. Repudiation at the polls induced a feeling of depression which probably lasted until his death in 1944 and colored his writing of this incident. That Norris was originally very ill is attested by both of the letters cited in note 8. While Norris claimed in his autobiography that this illness occurred in the fall of 1903, it actually happened in the spring. And Norris, as soon as he regained his strength, married Ellie Leonard, a McCook school teacher, whom he must have courted, however briefly, before his illness.

Norris, in his autobiography (pp. 85–86), mentions his second marriage and the marvelous change that occurred in his life and that of his children. He correctly states the date of the marriage as July 8, 1903, while on the previous two pages when discussing this illness which occurred "after my election [November, 1902] to the House of Representatives, but before I was sworn in [November, 1903]" and "in the fall of the year" which would place it from these statements in either September or October, 1903. He is, in his autobiography, still a lonely bachelor obviously mourning the loss of his first wife. In other words, Norris, in writing of these events, had his chronology confused and was probably projecting his current condition back to a serious illness suffered forty years previously.

Furthermore, during his illness the doctor had to convince Norris that it would be imprudent for him to travel and deliver the commencement address at the Wilsonville High School. Norris also wanted to get up and about before he had fully recovered his strength, an action not usually associated with a person who had no desire to get well or to live. See

Merwin to The Class of '03, May 18, 1903; C. C. Green to Norris, May 30, 1903, where Dr. Green writes, "I am glad that you have improved to such an extent that you feel able to go to Fairfield."

10. John H. Mickey to Merwin, May 21, 1903; Norris to William Peterson, June 4, 1903; Norris to F. Kuenneth, June 4, 1903.

11. "Jeanette" to Norris, January 6, 1903, May 23, 1903.

12. A. J. Green to Norris, March 14, 1903.

13. Norris to C. J. Miller, March 28, 1903; Clyde Castle to Norris, March 25, 1903.

14. Grant Harrington to Norris, September 2, 1903; Norris to Grant Harrington, September 10, 1903; Norris to H. H. Harrington, September 10, 1903; Norris to G. H. Merriam, September 10, 1903.

15. Merwin to J. R. Balding, July 21, 1903; C. E. Stine to Norris, July 10, 1903; Norris, op. cit., p. 86.

16. Norris to G. W. Shafer, September 22, 1903; R. H. Allard to Norris, December 28, 1903.

17. Norris to J. W. Edwards, December 6, 1902; Norris to Mickey, December 28, 1902.

18. Joseph G. Cannon to Norris, November 16, 1902.

19. C. H. Dietrich to Norris, December 4, 1902.

20. Norris to E. J. Burkett, December 9, 1902.

21. Norris to Cannon, September 15, 1903.

22. Norris to Charles F. Manderson, December 9, 1902.

23. E. W. Eckerman to Norris, November 22, 1902; Norris to Merwin, December 29, 1902; Merwin to Norris, January 11, 1903.

24. Norris to E. F. Ware, December 8, 1902. Norris, as befitted a Republican politician, was ready to do anything he could "to contribute to the welfare and comfort of the gallant boys in blue who preserved this glorious nation." In the matter of pensions or in private bills for the relief of veterans, he intended to make "a direct contribution." See Norris to Pruitt, April 20, 1903.

25. Norris to J. M. Jones, February 20, 1903; Norris to James McNally, December 30, 1902; Norris to A. W. Machen, March 14, 1903.

26. Norris to J. A. Andrews, March 25, 1903; the Stockville *Republican,* October 2, 1903.

27. The Stockville *Republican,* October 9, 1903. Incidentally, Judge Orr was elected in the November, 1903, judicial election.

NOTES TO CHAPTER 11 (pages 88–96)

1. G. W. Norris, *Fighting Liberal* (New York, 1946), p. 93–94.

2. *Ibid.*, pp. 95–96.

3. *Congressional Record,* Fifty-eighth Congress, Second Session, January 13, 1904, p. 728.

4. William Dudley Foulke, *Fighting the Spoilsmen* (New York, 1919), footnote 1, p. 174.

5. *Congressional Record, loc. cit.*

6. *Congressional Record,* Fifty-eighth Congress, Second Session, March 14, 1904, pp. 3256–57.

7. Fletcher W. Merwin to George Allen, March 12, 1904. George W. Norris Papers, Library of Congress. All manuscript citations, unless otherwise noted, are from this source.

8. Norris in his later years related an anecdote which all previous biographers have accepted about an incident that occurred during his first term in Congress. The incident, involving his growing awareness of the evils of partisanship, supposedly took place on February 20, 1904, in the House, when John Sharp Williams, the minority leader, moved that the House adjourn on February 22 after the reading of George Washington's Farewell Address. Congressman Sereno Payne, who had the floor, objected and claimed that it would be "a far more patriotic observance of duty for this Congress to be in session on Monday, and to provide for the building of a proper navy, than to take a holiday on account of the birthday of George Washington." Since Payne had moved for immediate adjournment before Williams made his motion to adjourn after the Farewell Address was read on Washington's birthday, the speaker ruled that Payne's motion to adjourn had precedence and this motion was agreed to by the House which thereupon adjourned. Williams' motion was not voted upon.

On February 22, Williams again presented a motion to adjourn after the reading of the Farewell Address. When the yeas and nays were called for, 93 Democratic members voted to adjourn, 104 Republican members voted to remain in session, 10 members answered present, and 175, including Norris, were listed as not voting.

Norris' biographers claim that on February 20, 1904, on a standing vote on Williams' motion, Norris was the lone Republican to stand, and that this incident started his questioning the validity of partisanship—especially when two days later he found the Republican-controlled Senate chamber empty out of respect for the memory of George Washington.

The *Congressional Record* (Fifty-eighth Congress, Second Session) reveals no vote on a motion by John Sharp Williams on February 20 to adjourn on Washington's birthday (p. 2178), while the vote on February 22 (pp. 2208–09) is recorded above. Moreover, the Senate, on February 22, 1904, adjourned at 5:15 P.M. (p. 2207) after conducting a full day's business.

One of Norris' biographers relates this Washington's birthday incident and then cites in his footnote the relevant pages of the *Congressional Record.* My examination of the *Record* has yielded no such verification and has convinced me that this incident must be regarded as a fictional anecdote which, like Patrick Henry's famous oration (though never delivered), should have occurred. In 1912, on Washington's birthday, Norris offered a motion to adjourn which was defeated when the question was taken. At this time the Democrats controlled the House and Champ Clark of Missouri was speaker. The Senate on this day met at twelve noon and adjourned after the reading of the Farewell Address. See *Congressional Record,* Sixty-second Congress, Second Session, February 22, 1912, pp. 2317, 2325.

9. Norris Typescript, p. 8. George W. Norris Papers, Nebraska State Historical Society, Lincoln, Nebraska.

10. Norris to James R. Mann, June 7, 1904; Norris to Perry L. Hole, June 15, 1904.

11. George Allen to Norris, July 23, 1904. Allen wrote, "We can win as the feeling is so strong in this state against the Parker deal that the kicking would be so vigorous that it would carry everything and we would win all lines in the state."

12. Quoted in Addison E. Sheldon, *Nebraska: The Land and the People,* (Chicago, 1932), Vol. I, p. 805.

13. James C. Olson, *History of Nebraska* (Lincoln, 1955), p. 251.

14. George Allen to Norris, July 23, 1904; Norris to E. H. Hinshaw, August 5, 1904.

15. Allen to Norris, July 29, 1904.

16. W. E. Andrews to Norris, August 27, 1904.

17. Allen to Norris, September 17, 1904. In another letter on this same date Allen noted that in Hall County a fight had broken out between the Democrats and Populists because some Populist leader proclaimed that they could not support the Democratic nominee.

18. Cannon delivered his main speech for Norris at Hastings on September 26; Norris appeared with the Speaker when Cannon campaigned for him throughout his three day visit.

19. Norris to J. J. McCarthy, October 16, 1904; Allen to Merwin, October 18, 1904; Norris to B. K. Schaeffer, October 24, 1904.

20. Allen to Merwin, November 3, 1904; Merwin to Allen, November 5, 1904; Allen to Norris, November 5, 1904; C. E. Stine to Norris, November 4, 1904.

21. Merwin to A. T. Lardin, November 14, 1904; Addison E. Sheldon, *op. cit.,* pp. 808–09; Edgar Eugene Robinson, *The Presidential Vote: 1896–1932* (Stanford University, California, 1934), p. 66.

22. Norris to Joseph G. Cannon, November 14, 1902.

23. Norris to Mrs. Emma Scott, August 5, 1904, September 12, 1904; Norris to Mrs. Julia G. Yager, November 14, 1904.

24. Merwin to J. F. Cordeal, January 31, 1905; Norris to Allen, January 30, 1905.

25. Norris to J. F. Crocker, January 14, 1905; Allen to Norris, February 18, 1905.

26. Norris to Editor of the *Outlook,* January 16, 1905; *Congressional Record,* Fifty-eighth Congress, Third Session, December 8, 1904, p. 92.

27. Norris to W. H. Moore, February 14, 1905.

28. Norris to E. A. Hitchcock, September 12, 1904; Cordeal to Merwin, December 18, 1904.

29. Cordeal to Merwin, December 18, 1904.

30. Norris to Cordeal, December 23, 1904; Norris to F. M. Rathbun, December 23, 1904.

31. Norris to Allen, March 27, 1905.

NOTES TO CHAPTER 12 (pages 97–108)

1. G. W. Norris to George Allen, April 15, 1905; Norris to C. A. Brandt, October 4, 1905. George W. Norris Papers, Manuscripts Division, Library of Congress. All manuscript citations, unless otherwise noted, are from this collection.

2. Norris to Patrick Heogney, May 18, 1905.

3. Norris to James Wilson, February 24, 1906.

4. *Congressional Record,* Fifty-ninth Congress, First Session, May 1, 1906, pp. 6218–19.

5. For good brief discussions of the Kinkaid Act and its significance see A. E. Sheldon, *Land Systems and Land Policies in Nebraska* (Lincoln, 1936), pp. 159–65, and James C. Olson, *History of Nebraska* (Lincoln, 1955), pp. 268–70.

Several years later Norris claimed that he was the originator of the 640-acre homestead concept. On March 20, 1908, he wrote the following letter to H. E. Langerin explaining his role: "I supposed at one time that I was the originator of the idea of the 640-acre homestead in Nebraska. When I first came to Washington I told a newspaper correspondent that I intended to introduce this kind of a bill in Congress. A day or so afterwards Mr. Kinkaid came to me and said that he had read my interview in the paper and that he also had been thinking of introducing this kind of a bill. He asked me to withhold my bill and to consult with him over the matter with a view of agreeing upon a bill and thus securing united and harmonious action. I most cheerfully agreed to this and after waiting some time, saw Mr. Kinkaid in regard to it and suggested we get together and commence work upon the bill. I did this several times and on each occasion he agreed with me that we should get together with a view of agreeing upon the terms of the bill, but each time he postponed the meeting for one reason or another. It seems that during this time he was working on the bill, which he finally introduced. I have always thought that he made studied effort to prevent me from introducing any bill on the subject. His conduct and representations certainly did deceive me, because if it had not been for his requests for delay I would have introduced that kind of a bill long before he introduced his. In fact I had the matter practically mapped out when he came to me and requested the delay. It rather looks to me that he did this with a studied effort to get whatever credit there might be in the introduction of such a measure. I do not know much foundation there was in his claim that he had been thinking about introducing the same kind of bill. He may have given it much thought, but I never knew of it until he told me at the time he requested me to practically make a joint matter out of it. . . . I have never given any publicity to this matter, because I did not want to get into a controversy with the members of the delegation and I have suffered in silence what to me seems an injustice from Mr. Kinkaid, rather than to have the matter aired in public. I have no desire now to have the matter made public and prefer that nothing be said about it."

6. Norris to Franklin E. Brooks, June (?), 1905.

7. Fremont *Herald,* February 24, 1906; Norris in the Fifty-ninth Congress actually introduced a bill (H.R. 16132) incorporating these suggestions. See Norris to S. N. Wolback, March 12, 1906.

Norris changed his mind chiefly because of several cases where defendants were charged with unlawfully fencing thousands of acres of the public domain and with intimidating homesteaders. Theodore Roosevelt endeared himself to many more Nebraska citizens when he obtained the resignations of several federal officials in Nebraska who were lax in their duties and responsibilities. For a discussion of these cases, see A. E. Sheldon, *Land Systems and Land Policies in Nebraska,* pp. 194–203.

8. Merle Curti, *Peace or War* (New York, 1936), pp. 218–19. Curti (p. 219) states, "Within a few years more than two hundred senators and representatives were enrolled as members of the Interparliamentary Union." Norris to Richard Bartholdt, April (?), 1905.

The Interparliamentary Union helped indirectly to bring about the meeting of the first peace conference at the Hague, while the second was due directly to its initiative. See William I. Hull, *The Two Hague Conferences* (Boston, 1908), pp. 4–5.

9. Norris to Bartholdt, June 10, 1905; incidentally, Norris did not bother to acquire a passport from the Department of State, and later claimed that he had found no use for one. See Norris to Cora A. Garber, March 16, 1906.

10. Bartholdt, *From Steerage to Congress* (Philadelphia, 1930), pp. 260–75, *passim.*

11. *Congressional Record,* Sixty-fourth Congress, First Session, July 13, 1916, p. 10932.

12. Norris to Bartholdt, October 13, 1905, October 16, 1905.

13. George Allen to J. R. McCarl, November 3, 1905; Norris to W. A. McCool, October 13, 1905; Norris to M. B. Carman, June 8, 1906. An article by Norris on the Interparliamentary Union appeared in the December 1, 1905 issue of the Beaver City *Times-Tribune.*

14. For example, see Norris to L. T. Brooking, October 26, 1905.

15. Joseph Cannon to Norris, September 17, 1905.

16. Norris to Eugene Allen, June 5, 1906; Cannon to Norris, October 20, 1905.

17. William W. Phillips, "The Growth of a Progressive: Asle J. Gronna" (Master's thesis, University of North Dakota, 1951), p. 47.

18. Norris, *Fighting Liberal* (New York, 1946), p. 86; Adams County *Democrat,* March 9, 1906, which quotes an Omaha *World Herald* news item from Washington.

19. Norris to David Diamond, December 18, 1905; Norris to William

Loeb, Jr., January 8, 1906; Norris to E. Benjamin Andrews, May 24, 1906.

20. *Congressional Record*, Fifty-ninth Congress, First Session, January 13, 1906, pp. 1044–48, for the entire speech. The tariff measure, while easily passing the House, was never acted upon in the Senate.

21. Norris to W. L. Hilyard, January 24, 1906; Norris to W. F. Buck, January 26, 1906. For another view of the Philippine tariff bill see John M. Blum's essay, "Theodore Roosevelt and the Legislative Process: Tariff Revision and Railroad Regulation, 1904–1906," printed as Appendix 1 in Elting E. Morison (ed.), *The Letters of Theodore Roosevelt* (Cambridge, 1951), Vol. IV, pp. 1333–42. Blum argues that Roosevelt used the threat of tariff legislation as a lever to obtain an effective railroad bill from Congress and that he never vigorously supported the Philippine tariff bill. Blum further develops his views in *The Republican Roosevelt* (Cambridge, 1954), Chapter VI. Norris insisted that while the interests of his "beet sugar" constituents were considered, his position on the bill was a matter of principle and he would always do what he believed "to be right on principle" even though he felt sure "that the effect would prove injurious" to the personal interests of some of his constituents. Concern about unduly benefiting the sugar refiners and not hostility to American policy in the Philippine Islands was central to his position. See Norris to A. F. Buechler, March 30, 1906.

22. George Allen to Norris, January 25, 1906; Norris to Buechler, January 26, 1906; Norris to George Lyon, Jr., January 26, 1906.

23. Norris to C. E. V. Smith, April 30, 1906, for a full analysis of the tariff situation.

24. C. A. Patton to Norris, November 1, 1905; McCarl to Patton, November 4, 1905.

25. Norris to Daniel Cook, December 12, 1905.

26. Norris to Charles F. Manderson, December 28, 1905. This letter has been edited and published. See Richard Lowitt (ed.), "George W. Norris, James J. Hill, and the Railroad Rate Bill," *Nebraska History*, Vol. 40, No. 2, June, 1959, pp. 137–45.

27. A. E. Sheldon, *Nebraska: The Land and the People* (Chicago, 1931), Vol. I, p. 815.

28. Norris to Manderson, January 20, 1906.

29. Norris to Fletcher W. Merwin, May 18, 1906; Norris to McCool, May 19, 1906, May 26, 1906; Norris to A. H. Thomas, May 19, 1906, May 26, 1906.

30. Norris to First National Bank of Holdrege, Nebraska, June 8, 1906; Norris to C. E. V. Smith, June 11, 1906; Norris to T. L. Jones, June 18, 1906.

31. Washington, D.C. *Times*, January 20, 1906; *Congressional Record*, Fifty-ninth Congress, First Session, June 20, 1906, pp. 8827–29.

32. *Congressional Record*, Fifty-ninth Congress, First Session, December 16, 1905, p. 509 in particular, for entire speech see pp. 509–11. In his initial message to the Fifty-ninth Congress, Roosevelt requested such regulation, though it made no effective headway in Congress. In the Senate,

Morgan G. Bulkeley of Connecticut, since 1879 the president of the Aetna Life Insurance Company, led the fight against national regulation of the life insurance industry.

33. George Allen to Norris, December 4, 1905.

NOTES TO CHAPTER 13 (pages 109–116)

1. G. W. Norris to C. M. Brown, January 13, 1906; Norris to Charles W. Meeker, January 19, 1906; George Allen to Norris, June 21, 1906; Norris to T. C. Hacker, June 14, 1906, June 18, 1906. George W. Norris Papers, Manuscripts Division, Library of Congress. All other manuscript citations, unless otherwise noted, are from this collection.

2. Norris to A. F. Buechler, August 2, 1906.

3. Norris to Buechler, August 2, 1906.

4. Norris to A. C. Wright, August 20, 1906; Adams County *Republican*, August 17, 1906.

5. Norris to Alexander DcDowell, August 20, 1906, September 18, 1906.

6. Wright to Norris, August 14, 1906; Norris to Wright, August 20, 1906; Norris to W. L. Hilyard, September 1, 1906; Norris to the American Protective Tariff League, July 23, 1906; for other and later statements of Norris' optimism about the outcome of his campaign, see Norris to W. E. Andrews, September 24, 1906; and J. R. McCarl to W. L. Crounse, October 23, 1906. Crounse, a former congressman and governor of Nebraska, now a lobbyist for the National Cigar Leaf Tobacco Association offered on behalf of the association to support Norris' campaign because of his vote against the Philippine tariff measure. See Crounse to Norris, October 13, 1906.

7. George Allen to McCarl, September 7, 1906; Allen to Norris, September 8, 1906.

8. Allen to McCarl, September 8, 1906, September 12, 1906; Allen to Norris, September 18, 1906.

9. Norris to Harry Hallenbeck, September 17, 1906; Norris to Charles Montgomery, September 19, 1906.

10. Allen to Norris, October 6, 1906.

11. McCarl to H. M. Crane, October 8, 1906; McCarl to H. C. Miller, October 15, 1906; Allen to McCarl, October 18, 1906. Allen, of course, handled all of the arrangements when Norris spoke in Clay County; McCarl to S. A. Dravo, October 22, 1906; McCarl to John S. Wise, October 8, 1906.

12. Allen to McCarl, October 25, 1906.

13. Allen to McCarl, October 28, 1906, October 30, 1906.

14. Allen to McCarl, November 4, 1906.

15. McCarl to Buechler, October 15, 1906.

16. Allen to McCarl, November 4, 1906, November 10, 1906.

17. Allen to McCarl, November 4, 1906, November 5, 1906.

18. McCarl to W. A. McCool, October 30, 1906; McCarl to Samuel Premer, November 1, 1906; McCarl to Allen, November 1, 1906, November 13, 1906.

19. Norris to Joint Committee on Printing, February 1, 1907; A. E. Sheldon, *Nebraska: The Land and the People* (Chicago, 1931), Vol. I, pp. 820–21; James C. Olson, *History of Nebraska* (Lincoln, 1955), pp. 251–52.

20. Norris to James McNally, November 26, 1906; Allen to Norris, November 8, 1906; Allen to McCarl, November 7, 1906, November 10, 1906.

21. Norris to Joseph G. Cannon, November 12, 1906; Cannon to Norris, November 14, 1906.

22. Norris to George Williams, December 14, 1906; Norris to Buechler, February 19, 1907.

23. *Congressional Record,* Fifty-ninth Congress, Second Session, January 24, 1907, pp. 1594, 1596; Norris to D. M. Francis, February 2, 1907; Roosevelt, in February, 1907, signed the McCumber Act which provided graduated pensions to veterans of the Mexican or Civil War. On reaching the age of sixty-two the veteran was eligible to receive twelve dollars a month, at sixty-five, fifteen dollars a month, and after seventy-five, twenty dollars a month. The great advantage of this law was that it obviated the necessity for most special pension bills.

24. *Congressional Record,* Fifty-ninth Congress, Second Session, February 23, 1907, pp. 3785, 3803–04; McCarl to McNally, October 2, 1906; Norris to E, J. Overing, November 10, 1906.

25. *Congressional Record,* Fifty-ninth Congress, Second Session, February 18, 1907, pp. 3209–10; Allen to Norris, February 19, 1907; Alfred Lief, *Democracy's Norris* (New York, 1939), p. 78.

26. Norris to Fred Brown, January 4, 1907 (1908); see A. E. Sheldon, *Land Systems and Land Policies in Nebraska* (Lincoln, 1936), pp. 196–98, for a 1905 Nebraska example of Roosevelt's insistence upon the honesty of government employees.

27. At least one congressman, disgruntled with Speaker Cannon and his authority, thought that Norris was sympathetic with his critical views during the Fifty-ninth Congress. However, he was not sure where Norris stood on this issue, and Norris never committed himself, on paper at least, to any criticism of Cannon at this time. See E. A. Hayes to Norris, September 30, 1907; see also the discussion in Chapter 14, pp. 126–28.

NOTES TO CHAPTER 14 (pages 117–128)

1. G. W. Norris to George D. McGill, March 27, 1907; George W. Norris Papers, Manuscripts Division, Library of Congress. Unless otherwise noted, all manuscript citations are from this collection.

2. J. R. McCarl to George Allen, April 9, 1907; McCarl to Fletcher W. Merwin, July 26, 1907; McCarl to Norris, July 8, 1907.

3. Norris to J. K. Kalanianaole, April 13, 1907; McCarl to Burt E. Brown, Epril 29, 1907.

4. McCarl to Louis A. Arthur, May 6, 1907; Norris to L. A. Thurston, September 21, 1907.

5. A. E. Sheldon, *Nebraska: The Land and the People* (Chicago, 1931), Vol. I, pp. 824–26; the editorial (April 7, 1907) is quoted on p. 826.

6. McCarl to Norris, September 2, 1907; McCarl to Allen, July 11, 1907; Norris to William Loeb, November 8, 1907; Norris to McCarl, March 30, 1908.

7. McCarl to Norris, September 2, 1907; McCarl to H. M. Grimes, September 18, 1907; McCarl to M. B. Reese, September 19, 1907.

8. A. E. Sheldon, *op. cit.,* p. 827; A. I. Vorys to Norris, September 19, 1907; Norris to Fred Brown, January 4, 1908.

9. McCarl to Reese, September 19, 1907; Norris to F. P. Corrick, October 9, 1907, October 23, 1907; Corrick to Norris, November 6, 1907.

10. Norris to McCarl, December 13, 1907, December 20, 1907; Norris to Percy M. Bell, December 23, 1907; McCarl to Norris, December 17, 1907, January 23, 1908; De Alva Stanwood Alexander, *History and Procedure of the House of Representatives* (Boston, 1916), p. 40.

11. Norris to Edward W. Hoch, November 18, 1907; Norris to George L. Sheldon, November 18, 1907.

12. Norris to Sheldon, November 18, 1907; Norris to Charles Bunce, November 18, 1907; Norris to I. D. Evans, December 20, 1907; *Congressional Record,* Sixtieth Congress, First Session, January 7, 1908, p. 520.

13. Norris to Sheldon, November 18, 1907; *Congressional Record,* Sixtieth Congress, First Session, January 17, 1908, p. 520; Norris to S. M. Davis, December 14, 1907.

14. Norris to Davis, December 14, 1907; Norris to D. J. Wood, December 23, 1907; *Congressional Record,* Sixtieth Congress, First Session, January 7, 1908, pp. 519–22, for the entire speech.

15. This was the chief criticism Norris had for the bill introduced by Charles N. Fowler, chairman of the House Banking and Currency Committee; Norris to S. C. Smith, December 17, 1907.

16. Norris to S. C. Smith, December 17, 1907; *Congressional Record,* Sixtieth Congress, First Session, January 7, 1908, p. 522.

17. Norris to S. H. Burnham, March 27, 1908; Norris to W. E. Stephenson, April 13, 1908; Norris to Charles K. Hart, May 13, 1908. The provision in the Aldrich-Vreeland Act calling for a national monetary commission to investigate the currency problem and suggest permanent reform assured those members of Congress, including Norris, who wanted a stronger bill, that banking and currency reform would again be a subject of legislation in the near future. This provision pleased many members of Congress who thought it might not be wise for Congress to enact a comprehensive banking and currency law at this time, that more study and thought were needed on the subject and the situation.

18. Norris to C. F. Bentley, December 20, 1907; Norris to Hart, May 13, 1908; Norris to B. Travis, May 18, 1908.

19. *Congressional Record,* Sixtieth Congress, First Session, February 3, 1908, Appendix: pp. 22–23; Norris to A. A. Burdick, November 16, 1907; Norris to F. N. Richardson, November 19, 1907; McCarl to H. C. Miller, March 24, 1908; McCarl to George Allen, March 24, 1908. In 1912 there were 2,348 veterans in Nebraska receiving federal pensions. See William H. Glasson, *Federal Military Pensions in the United States* (New York, 1918), p. 257, footnote 2.

20. *Congressional Record,* Sixtieth Congress, First Session, January 15, 1908, p. 760; Norris to Merwin, February 10, 1908.

21. Norris to Adam Breede, February 4, 1908; Norris to Merwin, February 10, 1908; Norris to A. F. Buechler, February 24, 1908.

22. *Congressional Record,* Sixtieth Congress, First Session, January 21, 1908, p. 936; incidentally, Norris was aware that Champ Clark derived part of his livelihood by appearing on the lecture platform.

23. Norris to J. E. Costello, May 20, 1908; Norris to O. T. Kountze, May 23, 1908; Norris to Chester M. Culver, May 25, 1908.

24. Norris to Isaac Le Droyt, November 9, 1907.

25. The Philippine tariff measure was probably the only instance where Norris did not support Theodore Roosevelt, though he did not agree with Roosevelt's requests for appropriations for more battleships. For a list of measures he did support see McCarl to Allan Elliott, October 22, 1908, and Norris to Corrick, May 1, 1908.

26. Norris to McCarl, March 30, 1908; McCarl to C. W. Meeker, April 2, 1908; Norris to McCarl, February 21, 1908, April 14, 1908.

27. E. A. Hayes to Norris, September 30, 1907; Norris to Hayes, October 9, 1907.

28. Norris to E. F. Baldwin, May 28, 1908; Norris to W. E. Andrews, September 21, 1908; *Congressional Record,* First Session, May 16, 1908, p. 6440.

29. Norris to Baldwin, May 28, 1908; Norris to Allen, June 22, 1908.

30. Norris to W. E. Andrews, September 21, 1908; Norris to W. L. Hilyard, September 26, 1908.

31. Norris to Hayne Davis, August 21, 1908; McCarl to J. F. Boyd, July 15, 1908; G. W. Norris to Hayne Davis, August 21, 1908; Norris to Jacob Fisher, September 3, 1908.

NOTES TO CHAPTER 15 (pages 129–138)

1. A. E. Sheldon, *Nebraska: The Land and the People* (Chicago, 1931), Vol. I, pp. 827, 831; *Nebraska State Journal,* November 29, 1907; William H. Taft to G. W. Norris, January 1, 1908; Norris to Fred Brown, January 4, 1907 (8); George W. Norris Papers, Manuscripts Division, Library of Congress. All other manuscript citations in this chapter, unless otherwised noted, are from this collection.

2. Norris to J. R. McCarl, January 2, 1908.

3. McCarl to George Allen, January 11, 1907 (8); McCarl to Norris, January 12, 1907 (8), April 14, 1908; Norris to M. T. Garlow, March 4, 1908.

4. McCarl to J. F. Boyd, July 15, 1908, September 25, 1908; Norris to George C. Junkin, July 20, 1908; H. C. Lindsay to Charles W. Meeker, July 22, 1908; Norris to Meeker, July 28, 1908.

5. Norris to E. B. Perry, August 11, 1908; Norris to John C. Gammill, August 19, 1908.

6. F. P. Corrick to Norris, December 16, 1907; Fletcher W. Merwin to Norris, February 10, 1908; Jacob Fisher to Norris, September 2, 1908.

7. McCarl to Corrick, September 10, 1908; Norris to Henry Casson, September 10, 1908; McCarl to L. Morse, September 23, 1908.

8. Norris to Corrick, September 16, 1908; Norris to Boyd, September 21, 1908; Norris in his letter to Corrick confused ex-Governor Myron T. Herrick of Ohio (1903–06) with Governor Charles Evans Hughes of New York. Herrick did not campaign for Taft in Nebraska, while Hughes spoke at Hastings in a hall provided by the Democrats early in October, 1908. See Merlo J. Pusey, *Charles Evans Hughes* (New York, 1952), Vol. I, p. 247.

9. Norris to W. E. Andrews, September 21, 1908; *Nebraska State Journal*, September 21, 1908.

10. *Nebraska State Journal*, September 21, 1908; the complete statement made by Norris on September 19 appears on p. 5.

11. Norris to Merwin, September 24, 1908; there were only two daily newspapers in the district at this time, *The Daily Independent* of Grand Island and *The Hastings Daily Tribune,* and they were both Republican in their point of view. The other local papers were usually weeklies and most of them were in continual financial difficulties. Selling their support to the highest bidder in an election year was one way of avoiding bankruptcy. All newspapers in the district had to meet the competition of the large Omaha and Lincoln dailies which circulated throughout the state.

12. Norris to Merwin, September 24, 1908; Norris to H. C. Lindsay, October 4, 1908.

13. Norris to Lindsay, October 4, 1908; McCarl to J. Warren Keifer, Jr., September 26, 1908; McCarl in this letter noted that 50 per cent of the funds contributed by the postmasters of the Fifth Congressional District were to be segregated and kept intact for the use of the congressional committee.

14. McCarl to George C. Eisenhart, September 26, 1908; F. Kuenneth to McCarl, September 30, 1908; McCarl to A. H. Thomas, October 3, 1908; Norris to A. B. Allen, September 28, 1908; McCarl to S. A. Dravo, October 10, 1908; McCarl to Dan Garber, October 10, 1908.

15. McCarl to H. M. Crane, September 28, 1908; McCarl to J. W. Hammond, October 1, 1908; McCarl to A. V. Shaffer, October 2, 1908; Shaffer to McCarl, October 4, 1908; George Allen to McCarl, October 3, 1908.

16. McCarl to John McCallum, October 13, 1908; Merwin to Norris, February 10, 1908.

17. George Allen to McCarl, October 14, 1908, October 15, 1908; McCarl to Allen, October 14, 1908; Shaffer to McCarl, October 16, 1908; *Nebraska State Journal,* October 16, 1908, editorial entitled "Butting Into the Fifth District" delineates Ashton's record.

18. McCarl to Allen, October 14, 1908.

19. Allen to McCarl, October 15, 1908, October 16, 1908; McCarl to Merwin, October 16, 1908.

20. Shaffer to McCarl, October 16, 1908; McCarl to S. W. Clark, October 17, 1908; McCarl to Norris, October 20, 1908.

21. William Lammers to McCarl, October 21, 1908; J. Frank Lantz to McCarl, October 23, 1908; McCarl to Thomas, October 22, 1908; McCarl to Norris, October 23, 1908; Albert Peek to McCarl, October 24, 1908.

22. McCarl to Norris, October 23, 1908; George Allen to McCarl, October 23, 1908; McCarl to Allen Elliott, October 29, 1908; Davis to Kuenneth, November 10, 1908; Norris to A. C. Rankin, November 10, 1908; Norris to J. H. Christner, November 17, 1908.

23. McCarl to C. A. Ready, October 23, 1908; McCarl to H. C. Miller, October 24, 1908; McCarl to E. B. Perry, October 25, 1908; McCarl to J. W. James, October 25, 1908; McCarl to J. A. Martin, October 25, 1908; *Hastings Democrat,* October 30, 1908, caustically discusses the rally.

24. McCarl to H. C. Lindsay, October 29, 1908; Lindsay to J. F. Cordeal, October 28, 1908; M. S. Storer to McCarl, October 30, 1908; McCarl to Dravo, October 31, 1908; A. C. Felt to McCarl, October 31, 1908.

25. McCarl to H. C. Miller, November 1, 1908; McCarl to Merwin, November 2, 1908; McCarl to H. G. Thomas, November 2, 1908.

26. Edgar Eugene Robinson, *The Presidential Vote: 1896–1932* (Stanford, 1934), p. 14.

27. Robinson, *op. cit.,* pp. 99–101, 264; A. E. Sheldon, *op. cit.,* pp. 834–35; James C. Olson, *History of Nebraska* (Lincoln, 1955), pp. 253–54; Norris to J. H. Jones, November 23, 1908; McCarl to Ready, November 4, 1908; Lincoln *Star,* November 9, 1908. This paper, six days after the election, thought that Ashton had probably defeated Norris with a plurality of five hundred votes.

28. H. C. Miller to McCarl, November 5, 1908; George H. Thomas to McCarl, November 6, 1908; Norris to C. P. Auderbury, November 10, 1908.

29. Norris to George C. Junkin, November 10, 1908.

30. Norris to J. F. Boyd, November 10, 1908; Jacob Fisher to Norris, November 21, 1908; Norris to Perry L. Hole, November 21, 1908; Norris to N. M. Ayers, November 23, 1908; Norris to J. H. Jones, November 23, 1908; the congressional committee came out $100.39 behind their expenses and Norris made up this amount out of his own pocket. See McCarl to Garber, November 20, 1908.

31. Junkin to Norris, November 13, 1908; Charles W. Meeker to McCarl, November 24, 1908; Norris to S. M. Erickson, November 24, 1908; McCarl to Garber, November 24, 1908; Norris to H. C. Miller, November 24, 1908; McCarl to Harry Bartenbach, November 25, 1908; McCarl to A. F. Buechler, November 30, 1908.

NOTES TO CHAPTER 16 (pages 139–152)

1. Kenneth W. Hechler, *Insurgency* (New York, 1940), p. 43.

2. J. R. McCarl to A. F. Buechler, November 30, 1908; McCarl to George Allen, December 5, 1908; McCarl to G. W. Norris, December 7, 1908; Norris to James K. Polk, November 19, 1908; Norris to D. C. Turner, November 19, 1908; George W. Norris Papers, Manuscripts Division, Library of Congress. All other manuscript citations in this chapter, unless otherwise noted, are from this collection.

3. McCarl to Norris, December 6, 1908, December 7, 1908; *Congressional Record*, Sixtieth Congress, Second Session, December 9, 1908, p. 74.

4. McCarl to Norris, December 8, 1908; McCarl to Alice Anderson, December 14, 1908; Norris to Turner, December 21, 1908.

5. John Ely Briggs, *William Peters Hepburn* (Iowa City, 1919), p. 320.

6. *Ibid.*, pp. 320–21.

7. Briggs, *op. cit.*, p. 322; Norris to Norman Hapgood, November 17, 1908; *Congressional Record*, Sixtieth Congress, Second Session, January 12, 1909, p. 817.

8. The "Reed rules" refers to the arbitrary method, later accepted by the Democrats, by which Speaker Thomas B. Reed in the Fifty-first Congress in 1890, with a Republican majority of less than a dozen votes, proceeded to count silent members as present to achieve a quorum necessary for the House of Representatives to conduct its business.

9. House Resolution 417 stated in part: "The States of the Union shall be divided into nine groups, each group containing, as near as may be, an equal number of Members belonging to the majority party, and such Members in each of said groups shall meet and select one of their number as a member of said Committee on Rules. The States of the Union shall likewise be divided into six groups, each containing, as near as may be, an equal number of Members belonging to the minority party, and such Members in each of said groups shall meet and select one of their number as a member of said Committee on Rules." This resolution, Norris hoped, would limit the use of the caucus, since the most important committee in the Congress, chosen according to a geographic basis, would then choose chairmen of all standing committees.

10. *Congressional Record*, Sixtieth Congress, Second Session, January 18, 1909, pp. 1056–58; Representative Mann's questions occur on p. 1057.

11. The House Calendar consists of all bills of a public character that do not have as a purpose the raising or appropriating of money, while the Calendar of the Committee of the Whole House on the State of the Union,

George William Norris between three and four years old.
(Courtesy Mr. and Mrs. John P. Robertson)

Norris, age eight, with his mother.
(Courtesy Nebraska State Historical Society)

The Norris home in McCook, Nebraska, as it looked when the family moved in. Remodeled in the late 1920's, it is Mrs. Norris' home today.

(Courtesy Omaha *World-Herald*)

As a young schoolteacher in Whitehouse, Ohio, Norris took part in a play.
(Courtesy Mr. and Mrs. John P. Robertson)

Norris as a young attorney just arrived in Beaver City, Nebraska.
(Wide World Photos)

Left to right:
H. H. Harrington,
George W. Norris, and
Charles A. Murray,
practicing attorneys,
1885, Beatrice,
Nebraska.
(Courtesy Mr. and
Mrs. John P. Robertson)

Norris as he appeared on campaign posters when he first ran for Congress in 1902. (Courtesy Nebraska State Historical Society)

The L.U.N. Club about 1908: Norris, Harrington, Lardin, Smith. (The Archives of Valparaiso University)

Norris in 1908.
(Library of Congress)

A rare picture of Norris
with full beard, taken in
Omaha in 1895 after his
election as district judge.
(Wide World Photos)

Cartoon from Omaha
Daily News, March 20, 1910.
(Courtesy Nebraska State
Historical Society)

1913 — Norris enters
the Senate.
(Courtesy Mr. and
Mrs. John P. Robertson)

or the Union Calendar, consists of all bills, previously considered and reported by committees, that involve the raising or spending of money. Normally when these measures are taken from the calendar they are considered by the entire House of Representatives acting as if it were a committee.

12. Briggs, *op. cit.,* pp. 322–23.

13. *Congressional Record,* Sixtieth Congress, Second Session, February 9, 1909, p. 2116.

14. Congressman A. P. Gardner, while one of the twenty-nine sponsors of this resolution, had previously on January 6, 1909, sponsored a "Calendar Tuesday" resolution. For a discussion of this point see Briggs, *op. cit.,* footnotes 463 and 495 on pp. 429, 430–31.

15. Briggs, *op. cit.,* pp. 324–27.

16. *Congressional Record,* Sixtieth Congress, Second Session, March 1, 1909, p. 3570.

17. *Ibid.*

18. In order to placate the few people in Furnas County who did not take kindly to Norris' part in the rules fight, Fletcher W. Merwin suggested that he send them a government document and an explanatory letter. Merwin's list of critics contained ten names. See Merwin to Norris, January 17, 1909.

19. See Charles R. Atkinson, *The Committee on Rules and the Overthrow of Speaker Cannon* (New York, 1911). Chapter VI, pp. 71–93, entitled "The Development of Public Sentiment Against the Speaker," presents an excellent survey of growing press and periodical hostility. The author has surveyed all the major magazines at this time on the question. *La Follette's Magazine* between February and the end of April, 1909, contained six articles attacking the power of the Speaker. The magazine, a weekly, started publication in January, 1909. Blair Bolles, *Tyrant from Illinois* (New York, 1951), is a study of Cannon as Speaker. This book, while not carefully researched, is well written; the author, unlike Norris, is more concerned with the Speaker than with the rules.

20. See Elting E. Morison (ed.), *The Letters of Theodore Roosevelt* (Cambridge, 1951, 1952), volumes III-VI, for the large correspondence the president conducted with the Speaker. And see especially the Chronology in Volume VI for an indication of how frequently Cannon visited the White House when Congress was in session.

21. Norris to O. E. Reynolds, November 21, 1908.

22. Norris to O. E. Reynolds, November 21, 1908.

23. Norris to W. A. Reynolds, December 21, 1908; Norris to Lon Cone, January 19, 1909.

24. Norris to Adam Breede, November 12, 1908; Norris to J. C. Hedge, January 25, 1909.

25. Norris to William Howard Taft, February 15, 1909.

26. Norris to Mrs. N. L. Cronkhite, February 12, 1909. Norris was one of the few House members to return home. Most of the insurgents and

Cannon men remained in Washington trying to obtain support for their position from the administration and Democratic members of the House of Representatives. See Hechler, *op. cit.*, pp. 49–55.

27. Norris to James G. King, March 13, 1909.

28. *Congressional Record*, Sixty-first Congress, First Session, March 15, 1909, p. 32. For a discussion of administrative pressure against the insurgents which Norris comments upon see Hechler, *op. cit.*, pp. 52–53. Taft apparently was confused as to how to handle this situation. While he had some sympathy for the insurgents and was very critical of Cannon, he knew that he needed the Speaker's support if tariff revision were to be accomplished.

29. *Congressional Record*, Sixty-first Congress, First Session, March 15, 1909, p. 32.

30. *Ibid.*

31. Hechler, *op. cit.*, pp. 54–59. Hechler's evidence of this arrangement is understandably rather skimpy, coming entirely from insurgent sources such as a 1910 newspaper article by Victor Murdock and a 1939 interview with John M. Nelson. For another version of this arrangement see Bolles, *op. cit.*, p. 181. Norris, too, believed that a deal had been made between Cannon and the Tammany Democrats. Commenting upon the charges by his New York Republican colleague, Herbert Parsons, that a tie-up existed, Norris said, "I can not prove absolutely what I think; but I could come pretty near it if forced, though some of this proof is confidential." See *Nebraska State Journal*, October 10, 1910.

32. Norris to E. A. Van Valkenburg, March 19, 1909; incidentally, the insurgents at this time aroused the admiration of Champ Clark, the Democratic leader, who on the floor of the House on March 15, 1909, said that the Republican insurgents were entitled to more credit than the Democrats who supported them.

33. *Congressional Record*, Sixty-first Congress, First Session, March 15, 1909, p. 18.

34. Norris to Breede, June 4, 1909. Norris in this letter denied that he had promised during the campaign of 1908 to vote against Cannon. His correspondence and his statement to the press during the campaign reveal the opposite to be true. The first words of a press statement, which he commended to his correspondents, reads, "I am opposed to the re-election of Mr. Cannon as Speaker." (See *Nebraska State Journal*, September 21, 1908, and the discussion in Chapter 15.) In his defense Norris noted, somewhat ingenuously, in this 1909 letter, that he did not state in the campaign interview that he would *vote* against Cannon. He also correctly argued that in his campaign speeches he said he would vote for Cannon, notwithstanding his opposition, before he would vote for a Democrat as Speaker. In a February, 1910, article in *Current Literature* (pp. 127–31) Norris, reminiscing about the contest that occurred at the opening of this session, wrote, "It is doubtful if there was a single insurgent who did not most devoutly hope that the Speaker might be defeated for re-election."

See Norris to W. G. Partridge, December 20, 1909, where he tries to explain his position.

35. Atkinson, *op. cit.*, p. 97, suggests that a number of the insurgents were in favor of continuing their agitation against the rules even at the risk of postponing tariff legislation. But at one of their conferences a member (possibly Gardner of Massachusetts) reported that the manufacturers in his district were becoming demoralized over the uncertainty of business conditions and feared a panic on Wall Street. After discussion the insurgents then decided to cease their tactics, deeming it the patriotic thing to put nothing in the way of the earliest possible revision of the tariff.

36. Norris to J. H. Rushton, March 16, 1909.

37. Norris, *Fighting Liberal* (New York, 1946), pp. 101–02. Though Norris was not a member of the subcommittee, his old friend Edgar D. Crumpacker of Indiana was a Republican member. Crumpacker had been practicing law in Valparaiso when Norris was attending law school there. Incidentally, this account in Norris' autobiography adds further indirect evidence to Hechler's thesis of a deal between Cannon and some Democratic members to raise the rates on petroleum in return for their votes against a major curtailment of his powers. See *supra*, footnote 31.

38. Norris, *op. cit.*, p. 102; Hechler, *op. cit.*, pp. 60–63; *Congressional Record*, Sixty-first Congress, First Session, April 7, 1909, pp. 1164–65, 1168, 1170, and April 9, 1909, p. 1266.

39. McCarl to Norris, April 8, 1909.

40. Norris to C. E. V. Smith, April 13, 1909.

41. *Congressional Record*, Sixty-first Congress, First Session, April 12, 1909, p. 1344.

42. Norris to Tom Cook, May 3, 1909; Norris to James E. Buck, May 30, 1909. Norris in this letter comments on conditions in the Canal Zone.

43. Norris to McCarl, May 14, 1909; Norris to L. Morse, June 1, 1909; Norris to E. M. Pollard, July 7, 1909. In 1896 while traveling in an official capacity for the IOOF he was overcome with heat prostration and found it necessary for the rest of his life to be very careful of his health in the hot weather, although for a period of about ten years after 1896 he thought he had completely recovered.

44. *Congressional Record*, Sixty-first Congress, First Session, July 9, 1909, p. 4374.

45. *Ibid.*, pp. 4374–75.

46. Hechler, *op. cit.*, p. 136.

47. Norris to W. A. Lindley, July 19, 1909; Norris to A. H. Burnham, July 26, 1909; Norris to Thomas R. Kimball, July 19, 1909; for a discussion of Taft's role in the corporation tax proposal, see Henry F. Pringle, *The Life and Times of William Howard Taft* (New York, 1939), Vol. I, pp. 433–36.

48. Norris to Clayton C. Rhoades, August 3, 1909; Hechler, *op. cit.*, p. 141; *Congressional Record*, Sixty-first Congress, First Session, July 31, 1909, pp. 4754–55.

49. *Nebraska State Journal,* October 10, 1909. For a devastating analysis of the cost of production tariff theory, which was included in the Republican platforms of 1904 and 1908, see F. W. Taussig, *The Tariff History of the United States* (New York, 1931), pp. 363–67.

50. *Congressional Record,* Sixty-first Congress, First Session, August 4, 1909, p. 4909, and August 5, 1909, pp. 5091–92; Norris to Breede, September 4, 1900.

NOTES TO CHAPTER 17 (pages 153–165)

1. An open primary allowed a voter to cast his primary vote for any candidate of any party running for nomination, regardless of what party ticket he had previously voted. Wisconsin already had such a system in operation.

2. Addison E. Sheldon, *Nebraska: The Land and the People* (Chicago, 1931), Vol. I, pp. 838–39; James C. Olson, *History of Nebraska* (Lincoln, 1955), p. 254; *Nebraska State Journal,* July 7, 1909. Incidentally, both Norris and Burkett had criticized the tariff during the debate and then voted for it in its final version.

3. G. W. Norris to J. R. McCarl, July 16, 1909; Norris to T. A. Boyd, July 15, 1909; Norris to A. C. Christensen, December 6, 1909; George W. Norris Papers, Manuscripts Division, Library of Congress. All letters, unless otherwise noted, are from this collection.

4. Norris to J. T. McBrien, July 26, 1909; McCarl to George Allen, October 4, 1909.

5. Norris to A. J. Watson, December 24, 1908.

6. Orleans *Chronicle,* September 10, 1909; Nebraska *State Journal,* October 11, 1909, November 2, 1909; Norris to F. Milton Willis, April 20, 1910.

7. In the next session of Congress he introduced an amendment which, if it carried, would have reduced naval appropriations by five million dollars, because it struck out one battleship and called for six merchant vessels in place of it. These vessels, he claimed, would develop our trade with Central and South America, provide for a merchant marine, expedite the services of the Panama Railroad Company which had the responsibility for carrying freight, mail, and passengers from American ports to those of Panama, and at the same time reduce naval expenses. See *Congressional Record,* Sixty-first Congress, Second Session, April 8, 1910, p. 4433.

8. Nebraska *State Journal,* October 11, 1909; Norris to William S. Mattley, February 18, 1910.

9. Norris to McBrien, August 3, 1909; Norris to J. C. Murtland, January 5, 1910; Nebraska *State Journal,* January 2, 1910, quoting an article by Judson C. Welliver in *Success Magazine.*

10. Another criticism, besides expense, was that it gave an incentive "to dishonorable and disreputable men" to enter the primary for the purpose of "holding up" candidates, securing money from special interests or individuals

desiring particular legislation, or defeating another candidate. It gave moneyed men another undue political advantage. See Norris to Samuel Merwin, December 17, 1909.

11. McCarl to George Allen, October 4, 1909; Nebraska *State Journal*, October 10, 1909, January 2, 1910; Norris to Welliver, September 14, 1909.

12. Norris to Mrs. J. A. Andrews, September 22, 1909; McCarl to Norris, November 14, 1909.

13. Norris to F. M. Richard, December 18, 1909. In a letter to Richard on December 23, 1909, Norris noted that the Republican National Congressional Committee had recently launched a systematic campaign to defeat insurgent congressmen through the country press. This committee, "under the absolute control of Speaker Cannon," had just issued the first of a series of weekly newsletters purporting to present congressional news. By presenting in these letters critical items and malicious statements about the insurgents, the committee, Norris thought, hoped to reach the constituents of these men through the rural newspapers.

14. Norris to W. T. K. Thompson, December 22, 1909; Norris to C. A. Bride, June 10, 1909.

15. Norris to Mrs. Mary H. Williams, January 11, 1910.

16. Norris to David Cole, February 8, 1910; Norris to R. M. Joyce, February 25, 1910; Norris to C. P. Grandfield, January 15, 1910, January 28, 1910; Norris to L. A. Sheldon, January 28, 1910; Norris to H. A. Talcott, January 3, 1910; Norris to A. E. Yorkel, January 21, 1910.

17. Norris to L. A. Sheldon, January 28, 1910; Norris to Ben Patterson, January 31, 1910; Norris to S. R. McKelvie, February 5, 1910, February 18, 1910; Norris to W. B. Hargleroad, April 20, 1910.

18. S. L. Perkins to Norris, February, n.d., 1910; Norris to F. C. Robb, January 31, 1910.

19. Norris to William T. Evans, February 2, 1910; Norris to B. J. Seger, April 16, 1910. The settlers in the North Platte project requested that the term of payment be extended from ten to fifteen or twenty years, with the first two payments not to exceed a dollar per year per acre, construction charges. See Perkins to Norris, February, n.d., 1910.

20. *Congressional Record*, Sixty-first Congress, Second Session, June 21, 1910, p. 8696.

21. *Congressional Record*, Sixty-first Congress, Second Session, January 31, 1910, p. 1305.

22. *Congressional Record*, Sixty-first Congress, Second Session, February 3, 1910, p. 1456.

23. Rose M. Stahl, *The Ballinger-Pinchot Controversy* (Northampton, Massachusetts, 1926), p. 123; Norris to C. L. Abbott, December 31, 1909.

24. Stahl, *op. cit.*, pp. 123–24; *Congressional Record*, Sixty-first Congress, Second Session, January 7, 1910, p. 390.

25. *Congressional Record*, Sixty-first Congress, Second Session, January 7, 1910, pp. 390, 404. The vote was 149 to 146 with five members answering "present" and eighty-seven not voting. Over forty pairs were announced.

Norris in later years became confused as to the details of what occurred. He thought that Walter Smith of Iowa, an amiable supporter of Cannon and a "warm personal friend," granted him the two minutes while Dalzell was out to lunch. But the *Congressional Record* for January 7, 1910 (p. 390) reveals that it was Dalzell who yielded him the two minutes in which he presented the amendment. After Norris spoke, Dalzell then yielded time to Smith who held the floor and allotted time to other members. For Norris' later version of what occurred see his speech of June 25, 1932, at a Cosmos Club dinner honoring Harry Slattery and printed in the *Congressional Record,* Seventy-second Congress, First Session, July 15, 1932, pp. 15456–57 and Norris to Harold Ickes, May 26, 1933.

26. Norris to Alfred Lief, May 4, 1934; Norris erred in his recollection when he thought a ten-man committee was to be chosen and that consequently the insurgent member would prevent a standpat Republican majority from dominating it. Kenneth W. Hechler, *Insurgency* (New York, 1940), p. 64.

27. Norris to Walter J. Locke, January 22, 1910; Norris to Lief, May 4, 1934; Norris to Ickes, May 26, 1933; Norris, *Fighting Liberal* (New York, 1946), p. 110; Senator Knute Nelson of Minnesota, the chairman of the committee, was personally sympathetic to Ballinger's position and intensely disliked Pinchot. Eventually the seven Republican members prepared a report exonerating Ballinger, while the Democratic members and Madison held that Ballinger should not be retained in office since he had violated the trust reposed in him as secretary of the interior. Congressman Edwin Denby of Michigan, who later as secretary of the navy was involved in the Teapot Dome scandal, signed the majority report. In the light of the strict party vote on these reports, Norris' claim about a "real investigation" can be singularly applied to Madison, who was probably the only member willing to reach a conclusion on the basis of the evidence. Madison filed a separate report, agreeing in less partisan terms with the Democratic members that Ballinger should resign. For a thorough monographic study of the Ballinger-Pinchot affair see Alpheus T. Mason, *Bureaucracy Convicts Itself* (New York, 1941); Stahl, *op. cit.,* is a careful study based on easily accessible published materials. Mason had access to manuscript collections, notably the papers of Louis D. Brandeis. More recent studies by Samuel P. Hays, *Conservation and the Gospel of Efficiency* (Cambridge, 1959), and Elmo R. Richardson, *The Politics of Conservation* (Berkeley and Los Angeles, 1962), present well balanced scholarly accounts which are more critical of Pinchot and more favorable to Ballinger than is Mason's study.

28. Henry F. Pringle, *The Life and Times of William Howard Taft* (New York, c. 1939), Vol. I, p. 480. The quote is from a letter of June, 1909, from the president to his brother Horace.

29. Norris to William Howard Taft, January 6, 1910.

30. Norris was here referring to the pressure supposedly exerted by Taft and other administration members to prevent the insurgents from making a fight against the rules on March 15, 1909. See Norris to Taft,

January 10, 1909; Hechler, *op. cit.*, pp. 50–53, reveals that Taft, though secretly sympathetic, made no commitment to insurgent members in March, 1909. Of course Taft, by taking no part in the fight against the House rules, became to many insurgents an avowed supporter of Cannonism.

31. Norris to Taft, January 6, 1910.

32. Hechler, *op. cit.*, p. 216.

33. Taft to Norris, January 7, 1910.

34. Norris to Taft, January 10, 1910.

35. *Ibid.* The measures cited by Norris as indicative of his support of the administration were the following: increase in the power of the Interstate Commerce Commission, further regulation of corporations, physical valuation of railroads, publication of campaign expenses, a postal savings bank law, conservation of natural resources, regulation of injunctions, reform of federal court procedures, and a permanent nonpartisan tariff commission. Norris opposed the administration on the ship subsidy question, but so did many of the regular Republicans who continued to benefit from patronage. Incidentally, for the rest of his congressional career, Norris never again received executive patronage.

36. Taft to Norris, January 11, 1910; Constance Gardner, (ed.), *Some Letters of Augustus Peabody Gardner* (Boston, 1920), p. 59. Gardner attended an insurgent meeting on the evening of January 10, 1910, at which a show of hands was requested to find out which insurgents had had trouble with their patronage.

37. Archie Butt, *Taft and Roosevelt: The Intimate Letters of Archie Butt* (Garden City, New York, 1930), Vol. I, p. 41; Pringle, *op. cit.*, Vol. II, pp. 612–13 discusses Taft's handling of the patronage at this time; Hechler, *op. cit.*, pp. 216–19.

38. Congressman Gardner, for example, had previously informed Norris that he could depend on his vote in matters pertaining to the rules at any time he notified him. See Constance Gardner, *op. cit.*, p. 57.

39. G. L. Keith to Norris, January 7, 1910.

40. McCarl to Norris, January 7, 1910.

41. Norris to C. L. Fahnestock, January 11, 1910.

NOTES TO CHAPTER 18 (pages 166–179)

1. George W. Norris, "Cannonism: What It Is," Part II, *La Follette's Magazine*, Vol. II, No. 14, April 9, 1910, p. 8.

2. William Kittle, "The Progressive Movement," *Twentieth Century Magazine*, Vol. I, No. 4, January, 1910, p. 315. With the economic analysis presented in this statement, Norris was in full accord. At the time this article appeared, Norris wrote to a critical constituent, "The facts are, that behind this power given by the rules to the Speaker, are intrenched all the special interests and combines that are seeking special favors at the hands of Congress."

3. Kittle, *loc. cit.*, p. 315.

4. Lillian Tuttle, "The Congressional Career of Victor Murdock: 1909–1911" (master's thesis, University of Kansas, 1948), p. 63. Quoting from

the "Mail and Breeze" column of the Topeka *Daily Capital,* January 16, 1910.

5. Kittle, *loc. cit.,* p. 315.

6. The articles were entitled "The Secret of His Power," January 8, 1910, and "Cannonism: What It Is," which appeared in two parts on April 2, 1910 and April 9, 1910. The articles on Cannonism, though appearing after the Speaker's defeat in March, 1910, were undoubtedly written before that time. Norris inserted all three articles in the *Congressional Record,* Sixty-first Congress, Second Session, May 14, 1910, pp. 6274–78.

7. Norris to George A. Mosshart, January 15, 1910; Norris to Walter J. Locke, January 22, 1910; Norris to Ross L. Hammond, February 4, 1910; George W. Norris Papers, Manuscripts Division, Library of Congress. Unless otherwise noted, all letters are from this collection.

8. Norris to G. E. Hager, February 15, 1910. In a letter to a former judicial colleague, for example, Norris revealed that the insurgents were divided over what position to take on membership of the committee to investigate the Ballinger-Pinchot controversy once his amendment had been accepted. See Norris to H. M. Grimes, January 14, 1910.

9. Norris to T. L. Porter, January 15, 1910; Norris to H. C. Miller, January 18, 1910; Norris to Hammond, February 4, 1910; Norris to A. F. Buechler, February 7, 1910.

10. *Congressional Record,* Sixty-first Congress, Second Session, March 15, 1910, pp. 3221–22.

11. *Congressional Record,* Sixty-first Congress, Second Session, March 16, 1910, pp. 3250–51.

12. Detroit *News,* March 20, 1910.

13. *Congressional Record,* Sixty-first Congress, Second Session, March 17, 1910, p. 3290.

14. *Ibid.,* p. 3285.

15. Detroit *News,* March 20, 1910; Washington *Times,* March 21, 1910; *Congressional Record,* Sixty-first Congress, Second Session, March 17, 1910, p. 3292; Norris to D. J. Cowden, May 19, 1910.

16. *Congressional Record,* Sixty-first Congress, Second Session, March 17, 1910, pp. 3292, 3294.

17. *Ibid.,* p. 3294.

18. *Ibid.,* p. 3307.

19. Chicago *Daily Tribune,* March 19, 1910; Brooklyn *Eagle,* March 19, 1910.

20. Chicago *Daily Tribune,* March 19, 1910; *Congressional Record,* Sixty-first Congress, Second Session, March 17, 1910, pp. 3320–21.

21. Detroit *News,* March 20, 1910.

22. After the House had been in session thirteen and one-half hours, James Tawney of Minnesota, one of the Speaker's lieutenants, tried for the last time to secure a recess. The House remained in continuous session for another twelve and one-half hours.

23. *Congressional Record,* Sixty-first Congress, Second Session, March 18, 1910, p. 3405.

24. *Ibid.,* pp. 3396–97.

25. Brooklyn *Eagle,* March 19, 1910.

26. Chicago *Daily Tribune,* March 19, 1910; Brooklyn *Eagle,* March 19, 1910.

27. New York *Evening Telegram,* March 18, 1910; Washington *Herald,* March 20, 1910.

28. New York *Evening Telegram,* March 18, 1910.

29. *Ibid.*

30. New York *Evening Telegram,* March 18, 1910; Brooklyn *Eagle,* March 19, 1910.

31. New York *Evening Telegram,* March 18, 1910; Washington *Herald,* March 20, 1910; *Congressional Record,* Sixty-first Congress, Second Session, March 18, 1910, pp. 3415–16.

32. New York *Evening Telegram,* March 18, 1910.

33. Detroit *News,* March 19, 1910; Washington *Herald,* March 20, 1910; Kenneth W. Hechler, *Insurgency* (New York, 1940), p. 70.

34. *Congressional Record,* Sixty-first Congress, Second Session, March 18, 1910, pp. 3416–17.

35. Chicago *Sunday Tribune,* March 20, 1910. Since the House did not adjourn until late in the afternoon of March 18, these proceedings were included in the Journal of March 17, 1910.

36. Chicago *Sunday Tribune,* March 20, 1910. Taft, on a speaking tour, first heard of the events in the House in Erie, Pennsylvania, on March 18. Though urged to return to Washington to save the regular organization from defeat, the president, unmoved by these requests and apparently convinced that he could do nothing if he returned, continued his speaking trip. See, Archie Butt, *Taft and Roosevelt: The Intimate Letters of Archie Butt* (Garden City, New York, 1930), Vol. I, pp. 306–08.

37. *Congressional Record,* Sixty-first Congress, Second Session, March 19, 1910, pp. 3426–28; Chicago *Sunday Tribune,* March 20, 1910.

38. Chicago *Sunday Tribune,* March 20, 1910.

39. *Congressional Record,* Sixty-first Congress, Second Session, March 19, 1910, p. 3429.

40. Chicago *Sunday Tribune,* March 20, 1910; *Congressional Record,* Sixty-first Congress, Second Session, March 19, 1910, pp. 3434-35.

41. *Ibid.,* pp. 3435–36.

NOTES TO CHAPTER 19 (pages 180–188)

1. *Congressional Record,* Sixty-first Congress, Second Session, March 19, 1910, pp. 3436–37.

2. Chicago *Sunday Tribune,* March 20, 1910; *Congressional Record,* Sixty-first Congress, Second Session, March 19, 1910, p. 3437. The Chicago *Sunday Tribune,* March 20, 1910, claimed that A. S. Burleson had planned

his resolution beforehand and that news of it had reached the Speaker probably before the House convened at noon on March 19, 1910.

3. Chicago *Sunday Tribune,* March 20, 1910; *Congressional Record,* Sixty-first Congress, Second Session, March 19, 1910, p. 3438.

4. *Congressional Record,* Sixty-first Congress, Second Session, March 19, 1910, p. 3438. Asle Gronna, one of the nine who voted to remove Cannon, was very unsure of himself. He first voted against the Burleson resolution and then requested that his vote be changed to favor it.

5. Chicago *Sunday Tribune,* March 20, 1910; Washington *Times,* March 20, 1910.

6. Washington *Times,* March 18, 1910.

7. Lincoln *Star,* March 20, 1910; Washington *Times,* March 20, 1910; Washington *Herald,* March 20, 1910.

8. George W. Norris, *Fighting Liberal* (New York, 1946), p. 119. In the Sixty-second Congress, controlled by the Democrats, the Speaker was shorn of his power to appoint standing committees, though he could still appoint members of conference and other select committees, as well as the chairman of the Committee of the Whole. His power of recognition and deciding points of order is still virtually intact.

9. Washington *Times,* March 20, 1910; Washington *Herald,* March 20, 1910.

10. *Congressional Record,* Sixty-first Congress, Second Session, March 25, 1910, p. 3759. It would be well to acknowledge at this point that the splendid study by Charles R. Atkinson, *The Committee on Rules and the Overthrow of Speaker Cannon* (New York, 1911), served as my guide through the parliamentary maze of the rules fight.

11. Norris to William Owen Jones, May 8, 1910. George W. Norris Papers, Manuscripts Division, Library of Congress. Unless otherwise noted, all manuscript citations are from this collection.

12. Norris to William Owen Jones, May 8, 1910; Norris to C. H. Aldrich, May 8, 1910.

13. Norris to C. A. Murray, June 29, 1910.

14. *Congressional Record,* Sixty-first Congress, Second Session, March 24, 1910, p. 3725. When almost two months later Dalzell, Payne, and Joseph Fordney of Michigan, all prominent regular Republicans, announced their opposition to the section of the Payne-Aldrich Tariff that called in effect for a board of experts to assist the president in securing information about maximum and minimum rates, Norris similarly chided them for their insurgency. He warned them that in a recent speech in New York Cannon was reported to have said that all insurgents ought to be hanged, and that a terrible fate was awaiting them. Norris, of course, favored this provision, believing it would remedy some of the inequity of the tariff, while regretting that the law did not provide for "a permanent, genuine, full-fledged tariff commission." See *Congressional Record,* Sixty-first Congress, May 24, 1910, p. 6808.

15. Norris to David D. Leahy, March 15, 1910; Norris, "Cannonism:

What It Is," Part I, *La Follette's Magazine*, Vol. II, No. 13, April 2, 1910, pp. 8–9; William Bayard Hale, "The Speaker or the People?" *World's Work*, Vol. XIX, April, 1910, pp. 12809–810.

16. Norris to Leahy, March 15, 1910; *Congressional Record*, Sixty-first Congress, Second Session, April 18, 1910, p. 4931.

17. *Congressional Record*, Sixty-first Congress, Second Session, June 25, 1910, pp. 9083, 9087, 9118.

18. For a brief but comprehensive discussion of the Mann-Elkins Act of 1910 see William Z. Ripley, *Railroads: Rates and Regulation* (New York, 1927), pp. 557–79; for the legislative side, particularly the role of the Senate, see Kenneth W. Hechler, *Insurgency* (New York, 1940), pp. 163–77; Norris to Arthur C. Smith, April 26, 1910; Norris to John W. Towle, April 29, 1910; Norris to Z. T. Lindsey, April 30, 1910; Norris to Wright and Wilhelm, April 30, 1910.

19. Norris to Aldrich, May 8, 1910; Norris to William Owen Jones, May 8, 1910.

20. Norris to H. M. Bushnell, May 13, 1910; Norris to William Owen Jones, September 13, 1910.

21. *Congressional Record*, Sixty-first Congress, Second Session, June 17, 1910, p. 8444.

22. H. B. Walker to Norris, May 20, 1910; Norris to A. R. Sauer, May 31, 1910; Norris to Samuel Gompers, May 31, 1910; Perry Arnold to Norris, June 4, 1910.

NOTES TO CHAPTER 20 (pages 189–196)

1. G. W. Norris to J. J. McCarthy, December 18, 1909, December 30, 1909; McCarthy to Norris, December 25, 1909; J. R. McCarl to Norris, January 2, 1910; McCarl to Jacob Fisher, January 25, 1910. Norris agreed with the harsh evaluation of Senator Burkett that was gaining ground throughout Nebraska. On February 18, 1910, Norris, writing to McCarthy, claimed that Burkett was really against the insurgents, that he was unfair as well as unscrupulous. George W. Norris Papers, Manuscripts Division, Library of Congress. Unless otherwise noted, all manuscript citations are from this collection.

2. Norris to J. M. Campbell, January 27, 1910; Norris to Ross Hammond, February 10, 1910; Omaha *Daily Bee*, February 2, 1910.

3. Norris to Frank Harrison, April 26, 1910; Norris to George F. Milbourne, May 8, 1910; Norris to J. M. Campbell, May 23, 1910; McCarl to Norris, May 15, 1910.

4. Norris to W. A. McCool, June 10, 1910; McCarl to Norris, June 13, 1910; Norris to G. R. Woods, June 14, 1910; Norris to J. M. Fuller, June 15, 1910.

5. Norris to McCarl, June 15, 1910, June 17, 1910, June 23, 1910; Norris to Perry L. Hole, June 30, 1910.

6. Norris to J. P. Hurley, April 27, 1910; McCarl to L. G. Sherman,

July 8, 1910; McCarl to Hamilton Fish, July 8, 1910; McCarl to Edward R. Sizer, July 9, 1910; Norris to M. B. Carman, July 19, 1910.

7. McCarl to I. H. Dempsey, July 12, 1910; McCarl to George Allen, July 12, 1910; McCarl to A. F. Buechler, July 14, 1910.

8. McCarl to W. W. Hawley, July 18, 1910; McCarl to Emma L. Talbot, July 19, 1910; Norris to Carman, July 19, 1910; McCarl to J. M. Campbell, July 19, 1910; McCarl to Buechler, July 19, 1910; McCarl to J. L. McBrien, July 21, 1910.

9. McCarl to J. W. Turner, July 23, 1910; McCarl to S. A. Dravo, July 23, 1910; McCarl to O. K. Olmstead, July 25, 1910; McCarl to P. W. Scott, July 25, 1910.

10. McCarl to J. C. Welliver, July 28, 1910; McCarl to Victor Murdock, July 28, 1910; A. E. Sheldon, *Nebraska: The Land and the People* (Chicago, 1931), Vol. I, p. 847.

11. McCarl to E. E. Smith, August 6, 1910; McCarl to Carman, August 8, 1910; McCarl to Charles W. Meeker, August 12, 1910.

12. Roosevelt delivered his "New Nationalism" speech at the dedication of the John Brown battlefield at Osawatomie, Kansas, on August 31, 1910.

13. Robert M. La Follette to Norris, August 19, 1910, August 22, 1910; Norris to La Follette, August 26, 1910; McCarl to H. M. Crane, August 27, 1910; McCarl to W. H. Banwell, Jr., August 30, 1910; McCarl to Joseph Polcar, August 31, 1910.

14. Norris to Roosevelt, July 21, 1910; McCarl to B. F. Hastings, August 31, 1910; Belle Case La Follette and Fola La Follette, *Robert M. La Follette* (New York, 1953), Vol. I, pp. 305–06; Robert La Follette to Norris, September 24, 1910.

15. McCarl to Hastings, August 31, 1910; McCarl to Albert R. Peck, September 1, 1910; McCarl to George C. Humphrey, September 6, 1910; Norris to William Owen Jones, September 13, 1910; Meyer Lissner to Norris, September 20, 1910; Norris to Lissner, September 21, 1910, October 17, 1910.

16. McCarl to Arthur V. Shaffer, September 20, 1910; McCarl to A. G. Williams, September 29, 1910; H. C. Miller to McCarl, September 20, 1910; McCarl to Allen Elliott, September 22, 1910; E. E. Wolfe to Norris, October 1, 1910.

17. James C. Olson, *History of Nebraska* (Lincoln, 1955), pp. 254–55; A. E. Sheldon, *op. cit.*, pp. 848–49; George Allen to McCarl, October 6, 1910; Norris to C. H. Aldrich, September 24, 1910.

18. McCarl to Gus Abrahamson, October 8, 1910; Hawley to McCarl, October 11, 1910; McCarl to Buechler, October 8, 1910; McCarl to William Husenetter, October 11, 1910.

19. McCarl to Polcar, October 19, 1910; Omaha *Daily News,* October 26, 1910; McCarl to C. R. Judkins, October 28, 1910.

20. James A. Tawney to Norris, October 20, 1910.

21. McCarthy to McCarl, October 25, 1910; McCarl to McCarthy,

NOTES TO CHAPTERS

October 27, 1910, November 2, 1910; McCarl to Charles Galloway, October 28, 1910.

22. H. E. Bowman to Hawley, November 1, 1910; Lincoln *Star*, November 3, 1910; George Allen to McCarl, November 3, 1910; Murdock to Norris, November 6, 1910.

23. McCarl to W. P. Burns, November 7, 1910; Nebraska *State Journal*, November 22, 1910.

24. A. E. Sheldon, *op. cit.*, pp. 850–51; Norris to R. J. Clancy, November 22, 1910. Norris lost Adams County by 104 votes, Gosper County by 24 votes, and Nuckolls County, where Sutherland resided, by 13 votes.

25. Nebraska *State Journal*, November 22, 1910; McCarl to George S. Scott, November 10, 1910; McCarl to Frank A. Harrison, November 18, 1910.

26. Norris to G. W. Kline, November 16, 1910; Norris to Charles W. Meeker, November 24, 1910.

NOTES TO CHAPTER 21 (pages 197–206)

1. G. W. Norris to Charles D. Norton, November 22, 1910; Norris to Fred W. Rice, May 30, 1911; J. R. McCarl to Norris, January 18, 1911, February 3, 1911. George W. Norris Papers, Manuscripts Division, Library of Congress. All manuscript citations, unless otherwise noted, are from this collection.

2. *Congressional Record*, Sixty-first Congress, Third Session, December 12, 1910, pp. 209, 218, 220.

3. Norris to William Howard Taft, December 9, 1910; Norris to E. Bowker, December 23, 1910.

4. *Congressional Record*, Sixty-first Congress, Third Session, January 25, 1911, pp. 1433–34; Norris to E. F. Baldwin, January 21, 1911, January 31, 1911.

5. San Francisco *Examiner*, January 26, 1911; Topeka *Daily Journal*, January 9, 1911, cited in Alberta Doyle, "The Progressive Movement in the Republican Party in Kansas: 1902–1917" (master's thesis, University of Kansas, 1939), p. 101.

6. McCarl to George Allen, January 5, 1911, January 8, 1911; McCarl to H. M. Grimes, January 7, 1911, January 12, 1911; McCarl to Harrie G. Thomas, January 7, 1911.

7. Norris to George F. Work, January 14, 1911; Cummins statement is quoted by McCarl in his January 7, 1911, letter to Grimes.

8. McCarl to Norris, January 18, 1911; Norris to Baldwin, January 21, 1911; Omaha *World Herald*, January 18, 1911; Topeka *Capitol*, January 19, 1911.

9. *Congressional Record*, Sixty-first Congress, Third Session, January 5, 1911, p. 586; Minneapolis *News*, January 6, 1911.

10. Charles R. Atkinson, *The Committee on Rules and the Overthrow*

322 GEORGE W. NORRIS

of Speaker Cannon (New York, 1911), pp. 121–23; *Congressional Record,* Sixty-first Congress, Third Session, January 9, 1911, pp. 679–86.

11. Dayton (Ohio) *Herald,* January 10, 1911. Since the Democrats had committed themselves to further revision of the House rules when they took over its administration in the next Congress, this vote was of no serious consequence, except as it allowed the Speaker and his supporters an opportunity to vent their spleen against the insurgents, and as it gave the Democrats an opportunity to aid in encouraging further dissension in the Republican party. Democratic members voted in this instance as they saw fit; no caucus was held to determine a party position. Meeting in caucus on January 19, 1911, the Democrats agreed in the next Congress to grant the Ways and Means Committee the power to name the standing committees of the House, subject to caucus ratification. See Atkinson, *op. cit.,* p. 129, footnote 1.

12. *Congressional Record,* Sixty-first Congress, Third Session, January 16, 1911, pp. 964–65, 975–76; Washington *Post,* January 17, 1911.

13. Norris to Joseph Polcar, March 16, 1911.

14. Robert M. La Follette, *La Follette's Autobiography* (Madison, Wisconsin, 1913), pp. 495–96.

15. McCarl to Norris, February 2, 1911; Norris to Henry Fox, Jr., February 11, 1911; Norris to E. E. Correll, February 11, 1911; *Congressional Record,* Sixty-first Congress, Third Session, February 26, 1911, pp. 3488–89.

16. The quote was the initial sentence on numerous printed petitions that Norris received in opposition to parcel post legislation. The other points were also included in these petitions.

17. Norris to W. S. Delano, April 29, 1911; Norris to George Bartenback, June 14, 1911; Norris to I. W. Crary, June 15, 1911, July 5, 1911; George E. Mowry, *Theodore Roosevelt and the Progressive Movement* (Madison, 1947), p. 171, footnote 57.

18. Norris to E. Clippiner, February 18, 1911.

19. Norris to J. R. Cameron, April 10, 1911.

20. Norris to M. Danielson, March 23, 1911.

21. A comprehensive study of this reciprocity proposition can be found in L. Ethan Ellis, *Reciprocity: 1911* (New Haven, 1939).

22. Norris to Baldwin, February 11, 1911; Norris to Wilbur W. Anness, July 3, 1911; Norris to A. J. Cornish, February 12, 1911.

23. *Congressional Record,* Sixty-first Congress, Third Session, February 14, 1911, p. 2559; Kenneth W. Hechler, *Insurgency* (New York, 1940), p. 180; Ellis, *op. cit.,* pp. 99–100.

24. *Congressional Record,* Sixty-first Congress, Third Session, Appendix, February 14, 1911, p. 136.

25. *Ibid.* The entire speech will be found on pp. 136–39.

26. Norris to W. A. Smith, March 10, 1911; McCarl to Norris, February 16, 1911, February 26, 1911; for early examples of Nebraska sentiment

against reciprocity see letters in Nebraska *State Journal* on March 8, 1911 and the editorial in the Oshkosh *Herald,* February 24, 1911.

27. This line is the first couplet of a poem Norris had written and first delivered at an early L.U.N. banquet. The text may be found in the *Congressional Record,* Sixty-second Congress, First Session, July 12, 1911, p. 2876. On this day Norris regaled his colleagues with an account of the Y.M.C.A. speech and its aftermath.

28. Washington *Post,* February 6, 1911; *Congressional Record,* Sixty-second Congress, First Session, July 12, 1911, p. 2876.

29. Washington *Post,* January 7, 1911; *Congressional Record,* Sixty-second Congress, First Session, July 12, 1911, p. 2877.

NOTES TO CHAPTER 22 (pages 207–215)

1. J. R. McCarl to John Cordeal, March 11, 1911. George W. Norris Papers, Manuscripts Division, Library of Congress. All other manuscript citations, unless otherwise noted, are from this collection.

2. Norris to Herman H. Schultz, June 3, 1911.

3. McCarl to Cordeal, March 11, 1911; Norris to John L. Kennedy, March 17, 1911; Norris to Frederic C. Howe, March 21, 1911.

4. McCarl to Mary G. Welles, March 31, 1911; John M. Nelson to Norris, March 21, 1911.

5. Kenneth W. Hechler, *Insurgency* (New York, 1940), p. 202; Norris, *Fighting Liberal* (New York, 1946), p. 131.

6. For example, the Sixty-second Congress enacted legislation establishing a Children's Bureau and an Industrial Bureau. An eight-hour day for workers on government projects and a federal corrupt practices bill were enacted. A parcel post act was passed and existing legislation, such as the Food and Drug Act, was improved by amendments.

7. De Alva Stanwood Alexander, *History and Procedure of the House of Representatives* (Boston, 1916), pp. 81–83; Norris, *op. cit.,* p. 131.

8. Norris, *op. cit.,* pp. 131–32; *Congressional Record,* Sixty-second Congress, First Session, April 11, 1911, p. 161.

9. *Congressional Record,* Sixty-second Congress, First Session, April 5, 1911, p. 64. Later in the session John J. Fitzgerald of New York chided Norris and other progressive Republicans who attacked caucus rule for supporting "every single measure indorsed by a Democratic caucus." See *ibid.,* August 3, 1911, p. 3571.

10. *Ibid.,* April 5, 1911, p. 64.

11. Norris to Woodrow Wilson, April 15, 1911; Wilson to Norris, April 18, 1911. It is perhaps of interest to observe here that while Wilson was criticizing committee secrecy, Bryan, in the pages of *The Commoner,* also was attacking the secret caucus. See for example editorials on July 28, 1911, August 11, 1911, August 18, 1911.

12. *Congressional Record,* Sixty-second Congress, First Session, April 5, 1911, pp. 63–65; Norris to M. J. Turner, April 10, 1911.

13. *Congressional Record,* Sixty-second Congress, First Session, April 27, 1911, p. 691.

14. *Congressional Record,* Sixty-second Congress, First Session, April 13, 1911, pp. 231–32. For a brief discussion of the disputed election of William Lorimer, see George E. Mowry, *Theodore Roosevelt and the Progressive Movement* (Madison, 1947), pp. 168–71. In 1912 Lorimer was unseated and the proposed constitutional amendment for direct election of senators passed.

15. *Ibid.,* April 13, 1911, pp. 230–31, June 21, 1911, pp. 2411–12.

16. *Congressional Record,* Sixty-second Congress, First Session, May 22, 1911, pp. 1472–73. Chances for these two territories entering the union during this session were destroyed when the president in August vetoed the enabling act creating the states of Arizona and New Mexico. Taft was violently opposed to the provision in the Arizona constitution permitting the recall of judicial officials. See Mowry, *op. cit.,* p. 171.

17. *Congressional Record,* Sixty-second Congress, First Session, April 21, 1911, pp. 538, 559; Hechler, *op. cit.,* p. 182.

18. Hechler, *op. cit.,* p. 188; Norris to James Pratt, May 18, 1911. In the last weeks of the session both houses finally accepted the farmers' free list bill and two other "Pop-Gun" tariff bills which the president promptly vetoed. See Hechler, *op. cit.,* pp. 189–93.

19. Norris to Oscar W. Underwood, May 25, 1911; Springfield *Republican,* May 12, 1911; Norris to George Watkins, August 15, 1911. The House on June 20 and August 14 approved the Underwood wool bill; the second time it merely approved the conference report. The bill was designed as a counterweight for the unjust treatment accorded to farmers by Canadian reciprocity. See Hechler, *op. cit.,* pp. 188–90.

20. *Congressional Record,* Sixty-second Congress, First Session, August 19, 1911, pp. 4424–25.

21. *Ibid.,* pp. 4425–26.

22. Cambridge University Press to Norris, March 7, 1911; Norris to J. C. Welliver, March 22, 1911; Norris to chief of Bureau of Statistics, March 24, 1911.

23. *Congressional Record,* Sixty-second Congress, First Session, April 26, 1911, p. 635.

24. *Ibid.,* p. 636.

25. *Ibid.*

26. *Ibid.,* p. 637. The wholesale price of No. 7 Rio coffee in New York in December, 1908, was 6½ cents a pound. In January, 1911, the same coffee in the same market was selling at 13½ cents a pound.

27. *Ibid.,* pp. 639–41.

28. *Ibid.,* p. 642.

29. Norris to William H. Okers, May 24, 1911, October 14, 1911; Norris to Erving Winslow, May 20, 1911; Norris to Welliver, March 23,

1911. It should be noted here that Norris probably did not deliver this speech from a manuscript. Using notes, charts, and other material, he was able to deliver the speech extemporaneously. His dictated drafts were probably not consulted once he started to speak.

NOTES TO CHAPTER 23 (pages 216–222)

1. G. W. Norris to Ross L. Hammond, May 1, 1911; Norris to J. R. McCarl, May 4, 1911, May 11, 1911; McCarl to Norris, May 10, 1911. George W. Norris Papers, Manuscripts Division, Library of Congress. All manuscript citations, unless otherwise noted, are from this collection.

2. McCarl to Norris, May 10, 1911; Norris to F. M. Richard, May 10, 1911; Norris to E. W. Rankin, July 22, 1911; Norris to Grant D. Harrington, May 29, 1911.

3. Norris to William B. Ely, May 23, 1911; Robert M. La Follette, *Autobiography* (Madison, 1913), pp. 516–29; Belle Case La Follette and Fola La Follette, *Robert M. La Follette* (New York, 1953), Vol. I, pp. 329–31.

4. Norris to F. A. Shotwell, May 26, 1911; Norris to W. P. Pierce, May 30, 1911; Lincoln *Star*, May 27, 1911.

5. Norris to Frank A. Harrison, June 14, 1911, June 26, 1911; Norris to W. P. Pierce, June 15, 1911; Norris to I. D. Evans, June 23, 1911; Norris to Gilson Gardner, June 27, 1911; Norris to G. L. Keith, July 3, 1911. The Norris endorsement of La Follette was released to the press on August 5, 1911.

6. McCarl to Harrie (Thomas), July 11, 1911; Norris to T. A. Boyd, July 15, 1911; Norris to Lon Cone, July 15, 1911.

7. Norris to J. L. McBrien, March 31, 1911, July 15, 1911; R. J. Whiteford to Norris, May 30, 1911; Norris to J. F. Duncan, August 14, 1911; Norris to J. R. Ellison, March 15, 1911.

8. Norris to Harrison, July 12, 1911; Norris to McCarl, July 17, 1911.

9. McCarl to Harrie (Thomas), July 17, 1911; Norris to McCarl, July 17, 1911.

10. Actually the Red Willow County convention merely endorsed La Follette. No office was mentioned. This was the result of a fight among the delegates. Norris was endorsed without any opposition.

11. John E. Arnold to Norris, July 20, 1911; George Allen to McCarl, July 21, 1911; McCarl to Norris, July 20, 1911, July 27, 1911. The quote is from the July 27, 1911 letter.

12. Norris to John L. Kennedy, July 21, 1911; Harrison to Robert M. La Follette, July 29, 1911 (copy in Norris Papers); Norris to McCarl, July 10, 1911.

13. George Allen to Norris, August 8, 1911; *Nebraska State Journal,* September 6, 1911.

14. Norris to McBrien, August 15, 1911; Norris to C. R. Draper, August

5, 1911; *Nebraska State Capitol,* August 25, 1911; Norris to W. R. Mellor, August 15, 1911, August 24, 1911.

15. *Nebraska State Journal,* September 7, 1911; Norris to McBrien, September 1, 1911; Norris to J. E. Jones, September 24, 1911.

16. Norris to J. E. Jones, September 24, 1911; Norris to J. S. Ewart, September 24, 1911; Norris to C. E. Neir, September 24, 1911. In his speeches illustrating that a protective tariff meant higher prices for farm produce, Norris often cited the case of Portal, North Dakota, located on the boundary line with grain elevators on both sides. Wheat always was fifteen cents higher on the American side. The town was served by one railroad and freight rates on the other side of the line were the same to any point.

17. Norris to E. F. Denison, September 27, 1911; Norris to E. J. Burkett, September 27, 1911, October 2, 1911; *Nebraska State Journal,* September 29, 1911.

18. Norris to William Owen Jones, October 9, 1911; Norris to Walter L. Houser, October 4, 1911.

19. Hattie Schmidt to H. N. Jewett, September 28, 1911; McCarl to W. H. Harrison, October 7, 1911; Norris to Kennedy, October 7, 1911; Norris to W. H. Harrison, October 12, 1911.

20. Moses E. Clapp to Norris, October 23, 1911. For an account of the Chicago meeting see Robert M. La Follette, *op. cit.,* pp. 532–34.

21. Norris to Hannah A. Foster, September 24, 1911; Norris to Houser, September 24, 1911, October 4, 1911; Norris to John S. Phillips, September 26, 1911.

22. McBrien to Norris, October 12, 1911; Norris to Fletcher W. Merwin, October 11, 1911; Norris to A. B. Allen, October 12, 1911; George Allen to Norris, November 4, 1911; F. P. Corrick to McCarl, November 9, 1911.

23. Norris to Messrs. Ellison & White, October 3, 1911, October 30, 1911.

NOTES TO CHAPTER 24 (pages 223–234)

1. Merrill G. Carman to J. Q. A. Fleharty, April 13, 1912. George W. Norris Papers, Manuscripts Division, Library of Congress. All manuscript citations, unless otherwise noted, are from this collection.

2. Norris to T. E. Jamison, November 3, 1911; Norris to A. B. Cummins, June 20, 1912; Norris to August E. Gans, June 20, 1912; Norris to Samuel Berger, August 2, 1912.

3. Washington *Post,* January 12, 1912; Omaha *Daily Bee,* January 12, 1912.

4. The minority leader would select committee members, obtain caucus approval, and submit his list privately to the chairman of the Ways and Means Committee, which would then pass on them. Norris claimed there was nothing in the House rules that sanctioned this procedure.

5. *Congressional Record,* Sixty-second Congress, Second Session, January 11, 1912, pp. 855–56, 862.

6. Lynn Haines, *The Story of the Democratic House of Representatives: A Condensed Chapter from Law Making in America.* Introduction by Norris (Bethesda, Maryland, 1912), pp. 3–4.

7. Detroit *News,* February 3, 1912; Omaha *Daily Bee,* February 4, 1912.

8. *Congressional Record,* Sixty-second Congress, Second Session, February 3, 1912, p. 1688. For a perceptive analysis of this controversy see the letter of A. P. Gardner to E. H. Abbott, February 6, 1912, in which Congressman Gardner concluded, "In the debate . . . Mr. Norris' statement of the situation is in my opinion absolutely correct." The letter is found in Constance Gardner, (ed.), *Some Letters of Augustus Peabody Gardner* (Boston, 1920), pp. 66–71.

9. Norris to W. A. Stacy, March 16, 1912.

10. *Congressional Record,* Sixty-second Congress, Second Session, February 24, 1912, pp. 2412–13, May 18, 1912, pp. 6744–45.

11. *Congressional Record,* Sixty-second Congress, Second Session, July 8, 1912, p. 8718, July 13, 1912, p. 9000. For a good general discussion of the rules situation in the House at this time, see Haines, *Law Making in America: The Story of the 1911–1912 Session of the Sixty-Second Congress* (Bethesda, Maryland, 1912), *passim.*

12. Norris to J. G. Lower, February 7, 1912; Norris to Niles E. Olsen, February 10, 1912; Norris to Charles C. Ryan, February 10, 1912. For an earlier statement of Norris' views about the necessity of revising the sugar schedule see the interview reported in the Springfield *Republican,* May 12, 1911.

13. Norris to Linn S. Andrews, March 9, 1912; Norris to Nathan Merriam, June 11, 1912.

14. Norris to A. M. Lane, December 22, 1911.

15. *Congressional Record,* Sixty-second Congress, Second Session, March 15, 1912, pp. 3409–10.

16. *Ibid.,* p. 3410; Norris to F. J. Sharp, April 1, 1912.

17. *Congressional Record,* Sixty-second Congress, Second Session, March 15, 1912, p. 3410.

18. Omaha *Daily Bee,* March 18, 1912; Norris to Jamison, April 19, 1912.

19. Norris to F. P. Corrick, January 4, 1912; Omaha *Daily Bee,* January 5, 1912.

20. Norris to D. F. Gruver, January 20, 1912; Norris to E. F. Baldwin, February 7, 1912; Norris to I. H. Rickel, April 1, 1912.

21. Norris to Frank H. Hitchcock, January 20, 1912; Frank H. Hitchcock to Norris, February 55, 1912.

22. Norris to J. R. McCarl, February 10, 1912; Norris to Theodore Roosevelt, March 25, 1912; Roosevelt to Norris, March 26, 1912, Theodore

Roosevelt Papers (Vol. 457), Manuscripts Division, Library of Congress. Norris' article in the *Editorial Review* of March, 1912 can be conveniently located in the *Congressional Record,* Sixty-second Congress, Second Session, April 13, 1912, pp. 4743–45.

23. Norris to S. R. McKelvie, March 1, 1912.

24. Norris to A. F. Buechler, April 27, 1912; Norris to J. G. Ludlam, May 14, 1912; *Congressional Record,* Sixty-second Congress, Second Session, April 16, 1912, p. 4878, July 10, 1912, p. 8872.

25. *Congressional Record,* Sixty-second Congress, Second Session, August 23, 1912, p. 11757; Norris to A. W. Sinclair, February 22, 1912; Norris to M. E. McClellan, March 18, 1912; Norris to Penn P. Fodrea, April 15, 1912; Norris to J. D. Ream, May 4, 1912; Norris to William Stull, May 4, 1912.

26. Norris to A. D. Boehm, February 24, 1912; Norris to Jerry Kosmowski, May 16, 1912; Norris to David Diamond, May 20, 1912.

27. *Nebraska State Journal,* March 2, 1912; Omaha *Daily Bee,* April 3, 1912; Norris to McCarl, June 6, 1912.

28. Norris to T. J. Mahoney, April 6, 1912, June 6, 1912; Norris to McCarl, June 6, 1912; Norris to A. J. Bowle, June 7, 1912; Norris to Lyman Cary, June 10, 1912.

29. Norris to Cary, June 25, 1912; Norris to Bowle, July 3, 1912; A. C. Epperson to "Dear Sir," November 1, 1912.

30. *Congressional Record,* Sixty-second Congress, Second Session, March 12, 1912, p. 3237; Norris to McCarl, March 21, 1912; Omaha *Daily Bee,* July 6, 1912; Norris statement: Bill for Presidential Primaries, n.d. (typewritten draft).

31. Roosevelt to Norris, July 10, 1912. Roosevelt Papers (Vol. 468), Manuscripts Division, Library of Congress. Incidentally, not only did Roosevelt endorse this bill, he invited Norris to discuss it and other matters with him over the luncheon table at Oyster Bay; Norris to Woodrow Wilson, July 10, 1912, Woodrow Wilson Papers (File II, Box 24), Manuscripts Division, Library of Congress.

32. *Congressional Record,* Sixty-second Congress, Second Session, July 5, 1912, Appendix, pp. 299–302. Norris' testimony is reprinted on these pages. Norris to O. J. Mayborn, March 20, 1912; Norris to Ream, March 25, 1912; Norris to George E. Richtmyer, March 16, 1912.

33. *Congressional Record,* Sixty-second Congress, Second Session, July 5, 1912, Appendix, p. 302.

34. *Congressional Record,* Sixty-second Congress, Second Session, May 26, 1912, p. 7198, April 14, 1912, p. 4767.

NOTES TO CHAPTER 25 (pages 235–242)

1. G. W. Norris to Dan Cook, January 20, 1912. George W. Norris Papers, Manuscripts Division, Library of Congress. Unless otherwise noted, all manuscript citations are from this collection.

2. Norris to W. L. Minor, December 23, 1911; Norris to W. A. McCool, December 15, 1911; Norris to J. J. McCarthy, December 30, 1911.

3. Confidential source. Nebraska was entitled in 1912 to sixteen delegates at the Republican National Convention, two from each of the six congressional districts and four at large.

4. Norris to F. P. Corrick, December 19, 1911.

5. J. R. McCarl to Arthur V. Shaffer, December 22, 1911.

6. Norris to Theodore Roosevelt, December 27, 1911, Theodore Roosevelt Papers (Box 306), Manuscripts Division, Library of Congress.

7. Elting E. Morrison, et al., *The Letters of Theodore Roosevelt* (Cambridge, 1954), Vol. VII, pp. 470–71, 445.

8. Norris to Roosevelt, January 5, 1912, Roosevelt Papers (Box 306), Manuscripts Division, Library of Congress.

9. Corrick to Norris, January 8, 1912; Corrick to Joseph Dixon, March 4, 1912 (copy in the Norris Papers). Though Corrick was denounced as a traitor by La Follette men, Norris was impressed with his devotion to the cause of a progressive Republican victory in Nebraska.

10. Norris to Corrick, January 4, 1912; Norris to D. McLeod, January 5, 1912.

11. Omaha *Daily Bee*, January 19, 1912, January 28, 1912; McCarl to Norris, January 18, 1912.

12. Norris to Corrick, January 24, 1912; Norris to McCarl, January 24, 1912. Norris in his correspondence at this time stressed the fact that while he had no grievance against Roosevelt, he was honor-bound to support Senator La Follette. Despite his efforts Aldrich was rebuffed by the Taft men and had to face a primary campaign.

13. Norris to McCarl, January 24, 1912; Norris to H. E. Larimer, January 25, 1912.

14. Norris to John O. Yeiser, January 27, 1912; Omaha *Daily Bee*, January 31, 1912; Norris to Corrick, February 1, 1912.

15. Omaha *Daily Bee*, January 31, 1912; Corrick to Norris, January 30, 1912; Norris to Corrick, February 2, 1912.

16. R. A. Simpson to Norris, February 1, 1912; McCarl to Fletcher W. Merwin, January 28, 1912; Omaha *Daily Bee*, January 29, 1912.

17. Norris to Yeiser, February 2, 1912.

18. McCarl to Norris, January 28, 1912; *Nebraska State Journal*, February 2, 1912; McCarl to Corrick, February 5, 1912.

19. Norris to D. C. Van Deusen, February 6, 1912; Corrick to Norris, February 5, 1912; Norris to Chester H. Aldrich, February 6, 1912; Omaha *Daily Bee*, February 7, 1912, February 8, 1912.

20. Omaha *Daily Bee*, February 8, 1912, February 9, 1912.

21. Norris to Corrick, February 8, 1912; Norris to Simpson, February 9, 1912; Norris to McCarl, February 10, 1912.

22. Corrick to Norris, February 13, 1912.

23. McCarl to A. V. Pease, February 19, 1912; McCarl to H. M. Grimes,

February 21, 1912; McCarl to J. Frank Lantz, February 21, 1912; McCarl to Norris, February 15, 1912.

24. Norris to McCarl, February 16, 1912; McCarl to Norris, February 19, 1912; Norris to Corrick, February 19, 1912.

25. McCarl to Norris, February 19, 1912.

26. Norris to W. B. Ely, February 20, 1912; McCarl to Norris, February 20, 1912; Norris to M. E. Wells, February 29, 1912; Norris to R. W. Devoe, February 26, 1912; Norris to Norm Parks, February 29, 1912.

27. Confidential source.

NOTES TO CHAPTER 26 (pages 243–249)

1. J. R. McCarl to E. O. Lewis, March 2, 1912; McCarl to R. W. Devoe, March 5, 1912; McCarl to G. W. Norris, March 2, 1912; McCarl to J. J. McCarthy, March 2, 1912; George W. Norris Papers, Manuscripts Division, Library of Congress. All manuscript citations, unless otherwise noted, are from this collection.

2. Norris to Joseph Polcar, March 2, 1912; Norris to McCarl, March 8, 1912; R. B. Howell to McCarl, March 6, 1912.

3. F. P. Corrick to Norris, March 4, 1912; Corrick to Joseph Dixon, March 13, 1912 (copy in Norris Papers).

4. Norris to Corrick, March 9, 1912.

5. Corrick to Norris, March 13, 1912; Corrick to Robert M. La Follette, March 13, 1912 (copy in Norris Papers).

6. Norris to Corrick, March 18, 1912.

7. McCarl to Norris, March 16, 1912; McCarl to McCarthy, March 18, 1912; McCarl to Norris, March 18, 1912, March 19, 1912.

8. Norris to McCarl, March 22, 1912; Norris to McCarthy, March 25, 1912; Belle Case La Follette and Fola La Follette, *Robert M. La Follette* (New York, 1953), Vol. I, pp. 428–29.

9. Corrick to McCarl, March 29, 1912; Norris to McCarl, March 29, 1912; Norris to Corrick, April 1, 1912.

10. Belle Case La Follette and Fola La Follette, *op. cit.*, p. 428; McCarl to Norris, April 2, 1912.

11. C. E. Stine to McCarl, April 3, 1912; McCarl to B. K. Schaeffer, April 4, 1912.

12. Belle Case La Follette and Fola La Follette, *op. cit.*, pp. 429–30; Omaha *Daily Bee*, April 6, 1912, April 8, 1912; Corrick to Norris, April 6, 1912; Norris to Corrick, April 8, 1912.

13. George Allen to Norris, April 9, 1912.

14. McCarl to J. H. Christner, April 9, 1912; McCarl to H. C. Miller, April 9, 1912; McCarl to Dan Garber, April 9, 1912.

15. Norris to Corrick, April 13, 1912; Lewis to McCarl, April 13, 1912; C. H. Aldrich to Norris, April 16, 1912; Norris to Aldrich, April 16, 1912.

16. Norris to Editor, *State Journal*, April 17, 1912; Norris to Howell, April 17, 1912.

17. Norris to McCarl, April 16, 1912.

18. A. E. Sheldon, *Nebraska: The Land and the People* (Chicago, 1931), pp. 873–74; Omaha *Daily Bee*, April 21, 1912.

19. G. O. Van Meter to Norris, April 23, 1912; Lon Cone to Norris, April 23, 1912; W. P. Pierce to Norris, April 23, 1912.

20. McCarl to Lewis, April 24, 1912; Norris to J. F. Sharp, April 27, 1912.

21. Confidential source.

22. For an interesting discussion of "How the Farmers Used the Primary," see the interview conducted under this title in the *Nebraska State Journal*, April 28, 1912. When asked if Taft could carry Nebraska in the November election, Frank G. Odell, secretary of the Nebraska Rural Life Commission, replied: "Not unless the farmers are chained up so they can not get to the polls. Look at the primary vote: The Roosevelt-La Follette vote four to one as compared with that for Taft; there is no conceivable combination of circumstances which will induce the farmers to condone what they believe to be a direct attack by the president on their prosperity."

NOTES TO CHAPTER 27 (pages 250–258)

1. F. P. Corrick to G. W. Norris, May 1, 1912, May 10, 1912; J. R. McCarl to E. R. Sadler, May 2, 1912. George W. Norris Papers, Manuscripts Division, Library of Congress. All citations, unless otherwise noted, are from this collection.

2. Norris to H. W. McFadden, May 4, 1912; Norris to Charles S. Scranton, May 4, 1912; Norris to W. H. Harrison, May 4, 1912.

3. William B. Ely to Norris, May 4, 1912; Norris to Ely, May 9, 1912; Norris to R. B. Howell, May 4, 1912.

4. McCarl to Norris, May 22, 1912; George E. Mowry, *Theodore Roosevelt and the Progressive Movement* (Madison, 1947), pp. 234–35; Patricia Claire Mulvey, "The Republican Party in Nebraska" (master's thesis, University of Nebraska, 1934), p. 138.

5. Norris to J. G. Lundlam, May 30, 1912; Norris to H. A. Bereman, May 30, 1912.

6. Norris to J. J. McCarthy, June 3, 1912; McCarl to Thomas Nelson, June 11, 1912; Norris to J. F. Lawrence, June 17, 1912.

7. *Nebraska State Journal*, June 16, 1912.

8. Victor Rosewater, *Backstage in 1912* (Philadelphia, 1932), p. 132.

9. Norris to Corrick, June 20, 1912.

10. Mowry, *op. cit.*, pp. 249, 253–54; *Nebraska State Journal*, June 23, 1912; Norris to Ely, June 26, 1912.

11. Norris to Ely, June 26, 1912; Norris to H. W. Short, June 27, 1912; *Nebraska State Journal*, June 28, 1912; *Congressional Record*, Sixty-second

Congress, Second Session, July 24, 1912, pp. 9575–77, 9581–82, July 25, 1912, pp. 9639, 9641–43, July 27, 1912, p. 9723; Philadelphia *North American*, July 25, 1912; Omaha *Daily Bee*, July 26, 1912, July 27, 1912.

12. Norris to Ely, June 26, 1912; Norris to Short, June 27, 1912.

13. Norris to Ely, June 26, 1912; Norris to Short, June 27, 1912; Norris to William Colton, June 27, 1912.

14. Corrick to Norris, June 28, 1912; Norris to Corrick, July 1, 1912; "Nebraska's Attitude Made Plain: Authorized Statement by Republican Delegates to Chicago Convention," n.d. (typewritten copy); Norris to H. E. Sackett, July 5, 1912.

15. Norris to Aaron Chadwick, July 5, 1912; *Congressional Record*, Sixty-second Congress, Second Session, July 25, 1912, p. 9643.

16. Norris to Ely, July 11, 1912.

17. Elihu Root defeated McGovern by a vote of 558 to 502. Since La Follette at best had control over only thirty-six delegates at Chicago, Root possibly could have been defeated if these delegates had voted for McGovern. For an interesting discussion of this point see Belle Case La Follette and Fola La Follette, *Robert M. La Follette* (New York, 1953), Vol. I, pp. 437–39.

18. Norris to Lawrence, June 29, 1912.

19. Omaha *Evening News*, June 29, 1912; Bloomington *Advocate*, July 5, 1912; E. J. Overing to McCarl, June 29, 1912; McCarl to Norris, June 30, 1912; A. J. Bowle to Norris, July 1, 1912.

20. McCarl to Norris, June 30, 1912, July 9, 1912.

21. *Nebraska State Journal*, July 10, 1912; Norris to McCarl, July 2, 1912.

22. Norris to Norman T. Johnston, July 2, 1912; Norris to William S. Mattley, July 5, 1912; McCarl to Richard May, July 13, 1912; F. W. Merwin to McCarl, July 5, 1912; Corrick to Norris, July 5, 1912; McCarl to Norris, July 9, 1912.

23. Baltimore *News*, July 19, 1912; Omaha *Daily Bee*, July 19, 1912, July 24, 1912.

24. McCarl to Norris, July 20, 1912; McCarl to Karl L. Spence, July 24, 1912; McCarl to H. M. Grimes, July 28, 1912; Omaha *Daily Bee*, July 23, 1912; *Nebraska State Journal*, July 27, 1912.

25. Norris to Theodore Roosevelt, July 19, 1912, Theodore Roosevelt Papers (Box 309), Manuscripts Division, Library of Congress; Roosevelt to Norris, July 22, 1912, Roosevelt Papers (Box 468).

26. Omaha *Daily Bee*, July 30, 1912; McCarl to Norris, August 1, 1912.

27. McCarl to Norris, August 1, 1912; McCarl to Lawrence, August 2, 1912; Omaha *Daily Bee*, July 31, 1912.

28. McCarl to Norris, August 1, 1912; McCarl to Lawrence, August 2, 1912.

29. McCarl to Norris, August 1, 1912, August 4, 1912; Omaha *Daily Bee*, August 1, 1912.

30. McCarl to Norris, August 1, 1912.

NOTES TO CHAPTER 28 (pages 259–268)

1. J. R. McCarl to William B. Ely, August 3, 1912; McCarl to G. W. Norris, August 4, 1912; George W. Norris Papers, Manuscripts Division, Library of Congress. All manuscript citations, unless otherwise noted, are from this collection.

2. McCarl to Norris, August 10, 1912, August 14, 1912; Omaha *Daily Bee*, August 4, 1912, August 19, 1912.

3. Norris to G. O. Van Meter, August 21, 1912.

4. Norris to F. P. Corrick, August 31, 1912.

5. McCarl to Norris, August 22, 1912.

6. McCarl to Norris, August 22, 1912.

7. Norris to Corrick, August 31, 1912; Omaha *Daily Bee*, September 2, 1912; A. E. Sheldon, *Nebraska: The Land and the People* (Chicago, 1931), Vol. I, p. 877.

8. *Nebraska State Journal*, September 10, 1912.

9. McCarl to A. C. Epperson, September 4, 1912, September 6, 1912, September 17, 1912; McCarl to H. E. Sackett, September 6, 1912; McCarl to Norris, September 8, 1912.

10. Omaha *Daily Bee*, September 16, 1912.

11. Norris to Corrick, September 18, 1912; Omaha *Daily Bee*, September 20, 1912, September 21, 1912; Corrick to McCarl, September 16, 1912.

12. McCarl to James Schoonover, September 18, 1912; McCarl to M. F. Harrington, September 19, 1912; Epperson to McCarl, September 19, 1912; Corrick to McCarl, September 20, 1912; McCarl to Epperson, September 23, 1912.

13. McCarl to J. M. Cottrell, September 22, 1912; McCarl to Epperson, September 23, 1912.

14. H. G. Taylor to McCarl, September 24, 1912.

15. H. G. Taylor to McCarl, September 25, 1912; W. V. Hoagland to McCarl, September 25, 1912.

16. McCarl to H. G. Taylor, September 26, 1912; McCarl to Meyer Brandvig, September 24, 1912; McCarl to E. J. Mitchell, September 24, 1912; McCarl to Corrick, September 25, 1912; McCarl to Epperson, October 3, 1912.

17. McCarl to George Thomas, October 3, 1912, October 6, 1912; George Thomas to McCarl, October 5, 1912.

18. A. E. Sheldon, *op. cit.*, pp. 877–78; McCarl to George Thomas, October 6, 1912.

19. Don L. Love to Norris, October 4, 1912; Norris to Secretary of the United States Senate, October 7, 1912; Norris to H. D. Duncan, May 14, 1912.

20. Norris, "Bryan as a Political Leader," *Current History* (September, 1925), Vol. XXII, p. 866. See also Alfred Lief, *Democracy's Norris* (New York, 1939), p. 133, for a slightly different version.

21. Lincoln *Daily Star,* October 10, 1912; Omaha *Bee,* October 10, 1912, October 13, 1912, October 14, 1912.

22. Omaha *Bee,* October 17, 1912, October 20, 1912.

23. Omaha *Bee,* October 22, 1912, October 24, 1912; McCarl to Ferdinand Proebaska, October 25, 1912.

24. McCarl to F. C. Marshall, October 10, 1912; McCarl to T. W. Barton, October 10, 1912; McCarl to Arthur V. Shaffer, October 12, 1912; McCarl to G. A. Dudley, October 22, 1912; McCarl to Norris, October 13, 1912.

25. McCarl to Norris, October 13, 1912; McCarl to John L. Kennedy, October 14, 1912.

26. McCarl to Kennedy, October 14, 1912.

27. George H. Thomas to McCarl, October 14, 1912; McCarl to Joseph Polcar, October 14, 1912; R. B. Howell to Norris, October 14, 1912; McCarl to Howell, October 23, 1912. While Norris carried Douglas County, Roosevelt lost it to Wilson by less than three thousand votes. For the presidential vote see Edgar Eugene Robinson, *The Presidential Vote: 1896–1932* (Stanford, 1934), p. 263.

28. H. G. Thomas to McCarl, October 15, 1912; McCarl to Will Rice, October 22, 1912. Norris spent $585.30 on his campaign. This sum included a $150 contribution to the Republican State Committee and a similar amount to the Progressive State Committee. See *Nebraska State Journal,* November 15, 1912.

29. McCarl to Corrick, October 14, 1912; Omaha *Bee,* November 2, 1912; *Nebraska State Journal,* November 3, 1912.

30. Chicago *Tribune,* November 3, 1912.

31. Edgar Eugene Robinson, *op. cit.* (Stanford, 1934), p. 49; A. E. Sheldon, *op. cit.,* p. 878–79; Omaha *Bee,* November 7, 1912, November 8, 1912, November 10, 1912; Norris to Chester H. Aldrich, November 8, 1912.

32. Edgar Eugene Robinson, *op. cit.,* p. 263; Norris to Gifford Pinchot, November 22, 1912, Gifford Pinchot Papers (Box 155) Manuscripts Division, Library of Congress; Norris to Theodore Roosevelt, November 22, 1912, Theodore Roosevelt Papers (Box 309), Manuscripts Division, Library of Congress; J. W. Hoagland to McCarl, September 28, 1912; A. E. Sheldon, *op. cit.,* pp. 877–79.

33. Epperson to McCarl, November 8, 1912; Sackett to McCarl, November 9, 1912; A. V. Pease to McCarl, November 9, 1912.

NOTES TO CHAPTER 29 (pages 269–277)

1. *Congressional Record,* Sixty-second Congress, Second Session, July 11, 1912, p. 8933. John R. Farr of Scranton, Pennsylvania, Archbald's home town, was the only congressman to vote against impeachment. The House Judiciary Committee unanimously agreed to all the charges and indictments it presented to the House for approval.

2. Archbald was voted not guilty under articles Seven through Twelve

which pertained to his tenure as a district judge. See *Congressional Record,* Sixty-second Congress, Third Session, January 13, 1913, pp. 1442–45.

3. George W. Norris, *Fighting Liberal* (New York, 1946), pp. 120–28 for Norris' reminiscences on the Archbald impeachment. The information used here has been gleaned from the impeachment trial proceedings in the Senate chamber which are printed in the *Congressional Record,* Sixty-second Congress, Third Session, from December 3, 1912 through January 13, 1913. See pp. 1440–43 for the vote on articles Two and Eight involving the Marian Coal Company.

4. *Congressional Record,* Sixty-second Congress, Third Session, January 9, 1913, pp. 1263–66.

5. *Ibid.,* January 13, 1913, pp. 1438–48.

6. *Congressional Record,* Sixty-second Congress, Third Session, February 3, 1913, pp. 2511, 2513, March 2, 1913, pp. 4621, 4626–27.

7. Norris to D. L. Davies, May 13, 1912; Norris to W. R. McKean, May 18, 1912; Norris to L. T. Pedley, May 20, 1912. George W. Norris Papers, Manuscripts Division, Library of Congress. All other manuscript citations, unless otherwise noted, are from this collection.

8. *Congressional Record,* Sixty-second Congress, Third Session, February 21, 1913, p. 3610.

9. Omaha *Daily Bee,* November 24, 1912, December 5, 1912.

10. J. R. McCarl to Harrie Thomas, December 29, 1912; McCarl to Norris, December 11, 1912.

11. McCarl to Norris, January 10, 1913, January 16, 1913; F. P. Corrick to McCarl, January 11, 1913. There was nothing in the 1909 law to compel a legislator to vote for the winner of the November senatorial popularity contest. No legal penalty was provided to force members to keep their pledges.

12. New York *Times,* January 10, 1913.

13. McCarl to Norris, January 23, 1913; Omaha *World Herald,* January 22, 1913.

14. New York *Times,* January 22, 1913; Omaha *World Herald,* January 22, 1913; Lincoln *Trade Review,* January 25, 1913.

15. McCarl to Norris, January 23, 1913.

16. Norris to R. M. Gillan, January 25, 1913.

17. Norris to William P. Culp, January 22, 1912; Theodore Roosevelt to Joseph M. Dixon, January 31, 1913, Theodore Roosevelt Papers (Box 390), Manuscripts Division, Library of Congress.

18. *Congressional Directory,* Sixty-third Congress, First Session, April, 1913, p. 62.

19. *Congressional Record,* Sixty-second Congress, Third Session, February 17, 1913, p. 3243.

Index